The Resilience of the Latin

The Resilience of the Latin American Right

EDITED BY

Juan Pablo Luna

AND

Cristóbal Rovira Kaltwasser

Johns Hopkins University Press

Baltimore

© 2014 Johns Hopkins University Press
All rights reserved. Published 2014
Printed in the United States of America on acid-free paper
2   4   6   8   9   7   5   3   1

Johns Hopkins University Press
2715 North Charles Street
Baltimore, Maryland 21218-4363
www.press.jhu.edu

Library of Congress Cataloging-in-Publication Data

The resilience of the Latin American right / edited by Juan Pablo Luna and Cristóbal
Rovira Kaltwasser.
    pages cm
Includes bibliographical references and index.
ISBN-13: 978-1-4214-1389-1 (hardcover : alk. paper)
ISBN-13: 978-1-4214-1390-7 (pbk. : alk. paper)
ISBN-13: 978-1-4214-1391-4 (electronic)
ISBN-10: 1-4214-1389-2 (hardcover : alk. paper)
ISBN-10: 1-4214-1390-6 (pbk. : alk. paper)
ISBN-10: 1-4214-1391-4 (electronic)
    1. Latin America—Politics and government—21st century.   2. Right and left (Political
science)—Latin America.   3. Conservatism—Latin America.   4. Political parties—Latin
America.   5. Political culture—Latin America.   I. Luna, Juan Pablo, author, editor of
compilation.   II. Rovira Kaltwasser, Cristóbal, author, editor of compilation.
JL966.R3878 2014
320.52098—dc23   2013043617

A catalog record for this book is available from the British Library.

*Special discounts are available for bulk purchases of this book. For more information, please
contact Special Sales at 410-516-6936 or specialsales@press.jhu.edu.*

Johns Hopkins University Press uses environmentally friendly book materials,
including recycled text paper that is composed of at least 30 percent post-consumer
waste, whenever possible.

CONTENTS

The origins of this volume can be traced to August 2010, when the coeditors had an informal meeting in Washington, DC, at the annual meeting of the American Political Science Association. We discussed the lack of research on the right in Latin America and decided to try to obtain funding to organize an academic workshop on this underexplored topic. Our ambition became a reality thanks to the support of the Fritz Thyssen Foundation, whose generous contribution enabled us to finance a two-day workshop, "Bringing the Right Back in: Exploring the Right and Democracy in Contemporary Latin America," held at the Social Science Research Center Berlin in July 2011. We thank all of those who participated in this event by presenting papers: Sonia Alonso, James D. Bowen, Barry Canon, David Doyle, Heiko Giebler, Riitta-Ilona Koivumaeki, Carlos Meléndez, Alfred P. Montero, Detlef Nolte, Peter M. Siavelis, Nina Wiesehomeier, Laura Wills-Otero, and Steven T. Wuhs. We express our sincere gratitude to three scholars who gave the keynote addresses: Wolfgang Merkel, Kenneth M. Roberts, and Andreas Schedler.

The academic workshop in Berlin was an excellent opportunity to discuss our ideas with a great team of colleagues and to receive valuable feedback, not only to rethink the framework that we originally developed—which, in a substantially improved version, constitutes the introduction to this volume—but also to consider the importance of commissioning special contributions by other scholars. Accordingly, we thank all of those we contacted after the workshop and who accepted our invitation to write a chapter for this book: Kent Eaton, James Loxton, Sergio Morresi, and Gabriel Vommaro. We are also pleased that Kenneth M. Roberts agreed to reformulate his inspiring workshop notes into what now constitutes chapter 1.

After compiling a book manuscript comprising the contributions by the aforementioned authors, we submitted the volume to Johns Hopkins University Press for review. To our fortune, the manuscript was sent to one of the foremost scholars of the right in Latin America—Edward Gibson from Northwestern University. His thorough reading, detailed comments, and insightful remarks helped us to significantly enrich the manuscript. Moreover, he generously agreed to reveal his identity. We thank him for his invaluable feedback and efforts to help us improve the volume. We also thank Suzanne Flinchbaugh at Johns Hopkins University Press, who has been an enthusiastic supporter of our book project and has assisted us with professionalism through all the stages of publication. Ashleigh McKown, Catherine Goldstead, and Dania Straughan have also been of great help throughout the production process.

Last but not least, each of us has counted on the support of friends and colleagues who gave us invaluable comments and ideas. We are particularly grateful to

Alan Angell, Fernando Filgueira, Steven Levitsky, Cas Mudde, Timothy Power, Kenneth M. Roberts, Paul Taggart, and Kurt Weyland. In terms of institutional and financial support, Juan Pablo Luna acknowledges support from FONDECYT Project 1110565, from the Millennium Nucleus for the Study of Stateness and Democracy in Latin America (NS 100014), and from the Instituto de Ciencia Política of the Pontificia Universidad Católica de Chile. Cristóbal Rovira Kaltwasser would like to thank the Alexander von Humboldt Foundation, the Social Science Research Center Berlin, the European Commission (grant agreement PIEF-GA-2010-273525), the Department of Politics of the University of Sussex, FONDECYT Project 1140101, and the Escuela de Ciencia Política of the Diego Portales University.

AD-M-19	Alianza Democrática Movimiento 19
ADN	Acción Democrática Nacionalista
ANEP	Asociación Nacional de Empresa Privada
AR	Acción por la República
ARENA	Aliança Renovadora Nacional (Brazil)
ARENA	Alianza Republicana Nacionalista (El Salvador)
CBA	City of Buenos Aires
CD	Cambio Democrático (El Salvador)
CEDLAS	Centro de Estudios Distributivos, Laborales y Sociales
CEP	Centro de Estudios Políticos Dr. José Antonio Rodriguez Porth
CIDE	Centro de Investigación y Docencia Económicas
CMP	Comparative Manifesto Project
CONFILAR	Confederación Internacional por la Libertad y Autonomía Regional
CPC	Compromiso para el Cambio
CREO	Movimiento Creando Oportunidades
ELN	Ejército de Liberación Nacional
EPL	Ejército Popular de Liberación
FA	Frente Amplio
FAN	Frente Amplio Nacional
FARC	Fuerzas Armadas Revolucionarias de Colombia
FEDECAMARAS	Federación de Cámaras y Asociaciones de Comercio y Producción de Venezuela
FMLN	Frente Farabundo Martí para la Liberación Nacional
FPL	Fuerzas Populares de Liberación Farabundo Martí
FPV	Frente para la Victoria
FREDEMO	Frente Democrático
FREPASO	Frente por un País Solidario
FRG	Frente Republicano Guatemalteco
FSLN	Frente Sandinista de Liberación Nacional
FUNDE	Fundación Nacional para el Desarrollo
FUSADES	Fundación Salvadoreña para el Desarrollo Económico y Social
GBA	greater Buenos Aires
GDP	gross domestic product
ISI	import substitution industrialization

LAPOP	Latin American Public Opinion Project
MAPU	Movimiento de Acción Popular Unitario
MAS	Movimiento al Socialismo
MDB	Movimento Democrático Brasileiro
MIR	Movimiento de Izquierda Revolucionaria
ML	Movimiento de Libertad
MNR	Movimiento Nacionalista Revolucionario
MOLIRENA	Movimiento Liberal Republicano Nacionalista
MPN	Movimiento Popular Neuquino
MRTA	Movimiento Revolucionario Túpac Amaru
MUD	Mesa de la Unidad Democrática
NFR	Nueva Fuerza Republicana
NGO	nongovernmental organization
NPC	Nuevo Poder Ciudadano
ORDEN	Organización Democrática Nacionalista
PAN	Partido Acción Nacional (Mexico)
PAN	Partido Autonomista Nacional (Argentina)
PAN	Partido Avanzada Nacional (Guatemala)
PC	Partido Colorado (Uruguay)
PCC	Partido Comunista Colombiano
PCC	Partido Conservador de Colombia
PCN	Partido de Conciliación Nacional
PCS	Partido Comunista Salvadoreño
PDA	Polo Democrático Alternativo
PDC	Partido Demócrata Cristiano (Chile)
PDC	Partido Demócrata Cristiano (El Salvador)
PDS	Partido Democrático Social
PELA	Proyecto de Élites Parlamentarias de América Latina
PFL	Partido da Frente Liberal
PJ	Partido Justicialista
PL	Partido Liberal (Brazil)
PL	Partido Liberal (Colombia)
PMDB	Partido do Movimento Democrático Brasileiro
PN	Partido Nacional
PNP	Partido Nacionalista Peruano
PNUD	Programa de las Naciones Unidas para el Desarrollo
PODEMOS	Poder Democrático y Social
PP	Partido Progresista
PPB	Partido Progressista Brasileiro

PPC	Partido Popular Cristiano
PPR	Partido Progresista Reformador
PR	Radical Party
PRD	Partido de la Revolución Democrática
PRI	Partido Revolucionario Institucional
PRIAN	Partido Renovador Institucional Acción Nacional
PRM	Partido Revolucionario Mexicano
PRO	Propuesta Republicana
PRSC	Partido Reformista Social Cristiano
PS	Partido Socialista
PSC	Partido Social Cristiano
PSDB	Partido da Social Democracia Brasileira
PSUN	Partido Social de Unidad Nacional
PSUV	Partido Socialista Unido de Venezuela
PT	Partido dos Trabalhadores
PTB	Partido Trabalhista Brasileiro
PU	Partido Social de Unidad Nacional
RECREAR	Recrear para el Crecimiento
RN	Renovación Nacional
SNTE	Sindicato Nacional de Trabajadores de la Educación
UCD	Unificación Cristiana Democrática
UCEDE	Unión del Centro Democrático
UCR	Unión Civíca Radical
UCS	Unidad Civíca Solidaridad
UDI	Unión Demócrata Independiente
UJC	Unión Juvenil Cruceñista
UP	Unión Patriótica
VERDES	Verdad y Democracia Social
WVS	World Values Survey

The Resilience of the Latin American Right

The Right in Contemporary Latin America

A Framework for Analysis

JUAN PABLO LUNA AND CRISTÓBAL ROVIRA KALTWASSER

The 2000s have been difficult years for the right in Latin America. Since the end of the 1990s, left-of-center leaders and parties gained increasing electoral support in the region in what came to be known as "the turn to the left." While this resurgence of the left is related to contingent factors such as the weakening of the US hegemony in the region and rising political discontent in the late 1990s,[1] it is also true that structural factors have played an important role. Latin America's turn to the left can be conceived, at least partially, as a popular reaction against the policies implemented by the right in the 1980s and 1990s. Not by coincidence, scholars have argued that the current turn to the left should be considered as the result of a second crisis of incorporation.[2] Such a crisis resulted from the exhaustion of the conservative modernization project that right-of-center leaders, parties, and technocrats have championed after Latin America's return to democracy.

The conservative modernization project entailed the defense of electoral democracy and of the market economy, in a context in which the range of acceptable policies was limited in such a way that inequality and the uneven distribution of opportunities remained a dominant feature of the region.[3] Although the recent rise of different types of left-of-center forces across Latin America demonstrates that the times are ripe for experimentation with policies that go beyond the so-called Washington Consensus, it would be naive to assume that the right has become irrelevant in the region. Yet the growing academic and public interest in the left has had as a counterpart a lack of scholarly production on the strategies pursued by the right.[4] In our opinion, the exclusive focus on the "turn to the left" is shortsighted for at least two reasons. First, some countries that were governed by the right in the 1990s continued to be ruled by rightist political leaders in the 2000s (e.g., Colombia and El Salvador until 2009). In addition, some countries have "turned right" in recent years (e.g., Mexico in 2000 or Chile in 2009). Second, the exclusive focus on "electoral politics," in particular on the "winners" of the electoral game, tends to produce selection biases. Even if not in the presidential office (as in much of contemporary Latin

America), and even if electorally devastated (as, for instance, in Bolivia or Ecuador), rightist forces can still shape policy outcomes in important ways.

This volume fills the void of comparative analysis of the right in contemporary Latin America. The aim of the book is less to speculate about the chances of an electoral comeback of the right than to shed light on the mechanisms of political action of right-of-center forces in the region. We believe that this perspective is crucial to improve our understanding of contemporary Latin America. That the left is in power in most countries of the region does not preclude the right from having considerable maneuvering room to influence governments, for instance, by building political parties that are well represented in congress, using the mass media to shape the public agenda, mobilizing experts and technocrats to shape the policy-making process, funding electoral campaigns, or lobbying elected officials. By way of illustration, it might be that moderate leftist administrations, such as that of "Lula" da Silva in Brazil (2003–10) or Michelle Bachelet in Chile (2006–10), not only "overlearned" lessons from the 1970s and 1980s but also faced severe constraints from rightwing actors, thereby failing to take advantage of a historic opportunity to bring about far-reaching social change.[5]

Given that there is almost no research on the right in contemporary Latin America,[6] our main task in this introduction is to advance a framework for analysis. We hope this framework turns useful for future and much-needed research of rightwing politics across the region. The remainder of this introduction is organized in five sections. First, we provide a working definition of "the right" and compare it to available alternatives on how to conceive it. Second, on the basis of the conceptualization of the right proposed, we argue that the electoral difficulties of rightist forces in contemporary Latin America are directly related to the levels of economic inequality prevalent in the region. Otherwise stated, the very institutionalization of electoral competition since the 1990s allowed leftist forces to win office by articulating social grievances, calling for economic change, and promoting electoral programs that seek to overcome the conservative modernization project defended by the right. As long as Latin American societies continue to be characterized by high levels of socioeconomic inequality, the right faces structural constraints when seeking to compete electorally.

Third, we turn our attention to the ways in which rightwing forces are trying to defend their ideas and interests in the face of this difficult political environment. We sketch three strategies for rightist political action in the region: engaging in interest representation through nonelectoral means, engaging in electoral politics via the development of nonpartisan or antiestablishment electoral vehicles, and engaging in party building. Although variant across time and space, these three different "vehicles" for rightist political action contribute to shape public policy and yield significant (and also variant) political and distributional implications. Fourth, we present a brief account of how the ambivalent relationship between the Latin American right and democratic politics has been studied so far. We claim that researchers should shift attention from the impact of the right on democratic survival to the right's possible impacts on different dimensions related to democratic quality. Finally, we outline the structure of this volume and anticipate the main topics discussed by its contributors.

Defining the Right

The contemporary division between left and right is rooted in an ideological controversy about social equality that traces back to the French Revolution.[7] Even though the cleavage between left and right emerged in eighteenth-century France, this spatial notion of politics spread globally with great success. According to Alain Noël and Jean-Phillipe Thérien, the rise of socialism in the 1890s was pivotal.[8] Socialist ideas paved the way for the formation of a new left, which sought to mobilize the working classes and to organize an international movement. This approach not only pushed the nonsocialist left to the right, but also led to the consolidation of a laissez-faire stance in terms of social and economic development in the "new" right. It was as a result of this particular juncture that "the left-right metaphor took on its contemporary meaning, as a permanent cleavage about *equality*, which is sufficiently open to be redefined with time and allow shifting alliances, without losing its relevance as a collective representation of the enduring conflict that divides democracies."[9]

Norberto Bobbio has provided perhaps the best analysis of the modern conceptualization of the left-right divide. It is worth stressing three central contributions of his work.[10] First, left and right must be conceived as antithetical terms. In other words, the terms are mutually exclusive, and thus one camp exists because of the very existence of the other. The strength of each camp is not constant; it varies in both time and place. Accordingly, the study of the left-right divide is contingent on the national and historical context.

Second, according to Bobbio, the left and right distinction is based on the conception and ideal of equality. Whereas the right conceives most inequalities as natural and difficult (or even inconvenient) to eradicate, the left conceives most inequalities as socially constructed and as a target for progressive social change. Third, by analyzing the left-right axis as an ideological conflict between different attitudes toward equality, Bobbio assumes explicitly that there can be other conflicts orthogonal to the left and right distinction. In this respect, he takes authoritarianism as an example because the latter can be defended by leftwing (e.g., Castro in Cuba) and rightwing (e.g., Pinochet in Chile) dictators. In a similar vein, Pierre Ostiguy maintains that issues related to social order and authority, as well as moral conservatism and liberalism, constitute a related (yet distinct and sometimes orthogonal) dimension to the left-right divide.[11]

In line with Bobbio's work, and its interpretation by Cas Mudde, we define the right as a political position distinguished by the belief that the main inequalities between people are natural and outside the purview of the state.[12] By contrast, we define the left as a political position characterized by the idea that the main inequalities between people are artificial and should therefore be counteracted by active state involvement.[13] It is worthwhile noting that this definition does not imply that the left is egalitarian and the right is not. The key difference between both camps lies in a dissimilar standard of equality.[14] This conceptualization of the left-right axis follows a deductive approach, by which it is possible to identify an ideological core that represents the substantive meaning of left and right in abstract terms. As Detlef Jahn has recently indicated, this conceptualization has the advantage of providing a definition of left and right that is valid and stable over time and context but at the same time has to be complemented with other elements in order to explain the particularities of the left-right axis in specific countries and periods.[15]

While agreeing with Scott Mainwaring, Rachel Meneguello, and Timothy Power's view that programmatic standings are continuously evolving and relational, we believe that anchoring ideological demarcations on the relative status of inequality provides a useful way to efficiently map programmatic platforms along the left-right spectrum and across time.[16] The proposed *ideological* definition of the right—understood as a political stance rooted in the belief that the main inequalities between the people are natural and outside the purview of the state—offers a substantive starting point. Because the definition in question is a minimal one, it can "travel" across different national and historical contexts while avoiding conceptual stretching.[17] But this does not preclude the need to complement our proposed definition when applying to particular cases (or at lower steps in the *ladder of abstraction*).

Our definition of the right (and the left) differs from others'. Alternative definitions of the right could be organized in three groups. The first pursues ideological definitions, such as the one we proposed above. The second assumes that the (empirical) distinction between left and right refers to (contingent) policy positions on issues such as economic preferences and moral values. The third and last approach defines the right in sociological terms; that is, on the basis of parties' core constituencies and electoral bases. To what extent is our definition compatible with, or different from, these approaches? We explore this below.

Ideological Definitions

A long-standing intellectual tradition defines the Latin American right as a conservative ideology that is in favor of the status quo and defended by the traditional sectors of society. For instance, José Luis Romero maintains that the roots of the Latin American right lie in the rural elites of the colony.[18] Given that the latter were opposed to the process of modernization, they defended traditional institutions and an essentialist point of view regarding the nation.[19]

Ideological definitions of the right have been developed to study not only the past, but also contemporary Latin America. Power's study on the right in postauthoritarian Brazil proposes to classify political actors along a "democratic-authoritarian" cleavage, by which parties of the right usually align and carry the heritage of an authoritarian alternative.[20] From this viewpoint, the right alludes to those politicians who are veterans of an authoritarian power structure and remain active after the (re)establishment of democracy. Given that this definition is based on the identification of a cohort of politicians who shared a common ideological position in the past (i.e., defense of the authoritarian system in Brazil), we are dealing with an approach that is more retrospective than prospective and that, as such, was set to expire.[21] Power's definition would not apply to cases lacking a recent authoritarian experience or where the (semi)authoritarian system was commanded by a nonrightist party, like that of the Institutional Revolutionary Party (Partido Revolucionario Institucional, or PRI) in Mexico.

Michael Coppedge, in his expert survey characterization of political parties in Latin America, also resorted to ideology to refer to the left-right axis.[22] Assuming that the right varies along time, he proposes to differentiate between four types of rightwing parties, which have emerged in Latin America in the twentieth century. First, some rightwing parties have their roots in the oligarchic parties of the nineteenth century. Those parties did not moderate their political platform at the same time as they appealed to mass support from the lower classes after the expansion of suffrage (e.g., Chilean Conservative Party). A second type of rightwing party is characterized by the adherence to the fascist ideology (e.g., Chilean Nazi Party). Those who support a current or a former authoritarian regime and have origins in such an authoritarian past (e.g., the National Renovating Alliance in Brazil) comprise a third group. Finally, center-right parties are those that seek to incorporate middle- and lower-class support to their traditional base by promoting ideas related to private-public strategic cooperation, public security, morality, or the prioritizing of economic growth over distribution (e.g., the Argentine Union of the Democratic Center).

Undoubtedly, Coppedge's distinction between these four types of right parties can be useful for undertaking a historical overview of the Latin American right. But the approach is problematic for at least two reasons. First, it is not clear which ideological features the above-mentioned parties have in common, and thus on what ground they can be labeled as "right." Second, this definition is excessively broad, and, by following the Wittgensteinian principle of "family resemblance," it runs the risk of stretching the concept we want to define.[23] By contrast, the minimal concept we proposed has the advantage of setting a benchmark that not only can be used as a starting point to differentiate left and right, but also can be complemented in order to identify the configuration of different types of right across time and space.

Identifying the Right through Policy Positions

A second approach for identifying left and right is based on the analysis of the policy positions that different political parties and leaders promote. This approach has been developed on the basis of two methodological strategies: the comparison of party manifestos and the analysis of survey instruments applied to different types of relevant respondents (e.g., party elites, political experts, or partisan electorates and voters).

The first strategy has rarely been used in Latin America because the so-called Comparative Manifesto Project (CMP) has mostly focused in other world regions so far. Even so, Kathleen Bruhn maintains that CMP data compiled for the case of Mexico match qualitative assessments of policy positions in the Mexican party system, placing the National Action Party (Partido Acción Nacional, or PAN), PRI, and the Party of the Democratic Revolution (Partido de la Revolución Democrática, or PRD) regularly as right, center, and left, respectively.[24] Meanwhile, on the basis of a new manifesto database for Chile, López Varas and Baeza Freer argue that since the return to democracy the Chilean right has increasingly shifted its political positions toward the center.[25]

The second method has been applied more frequently in Latin America on the basis of data collected through regional public opinion barometers such as the Latinobarómetro and the Latin American Public Opinion Project. On this basis, for instance, Morales argues that although Latin Americans tended to identify more with the right in the 1990s and seemed to shift to the left during the 2000s, the majority of the population has stuck to centrist ideological identities.[26] Furthermore, the database of the Latin American Congressional Elites Project developed by the Universidad de Salamanca has provided valuable information on legislators' ideological positioning and issue preferences across Latin America and over time. According to available results, the state-market divide is the substantive dimension that displays the greater correlation to the left-right axis in Latin America.[27] Nina Wiesehomeier reaches a similar conclusion while replicating such analysis, but on the basis of an original expert survey data set.[28]

In general, available works in this line suggest that the state-market dimension is crucial to distinguish left and right party positions in Latin America, while other dimensions—such as moral values or positions on the issue of globalization—are not equally important. While we agree on stressing the centrality of state-market issues for identifying leftist and rightist forces, we instead proceed deductively than inductively. Both of the methodological approaches described here are either applied inductively (i.e., identifying rightist parties as those that are empirically placed to the right) or on the basis of preexisting (and oftentimes implicit) criteria regarding the relative ideological position of parties for which issue positions are then empirically analyzed.

Sociological Definitions

The third approach to defining the right follows a sociological approach, and it is most notably represented by Edward Gibson's monograph on Argentine conservatism.[29] This type of definition, which Gibson proposes to apply in comparative works on the subject, was then adopted in Kevin J. Middlebrook's edited volume on the right in Latin America.[30] Gibson anticipated this definition in his chapter in Chalmers et al. (1992), thus also influencing the theoretical framework of the earlier edited volume on the right and democracy.[31] Gibson's definition is based on the identification of each party's core constituency and on the assumption that to become electorally viable, the right needs to engage in multiclass electoral coalition making. In his words:

> as a minimal definition, conservative parties are parties that draw their core constituencies from the upper strata of society . . . A party's core constituencies are those sectors of society that are most important to its political agenda and resources. Their importance lies not necessarily in the number of votes they represent, but in their *influence* on the party's agenda and capacities for political action. A party's core constituencies shape its identity; they are necessary to its existence. However, given the competitive imperatives of mass politics, they are usually not enough. A party's political leadership must usually forges alliances between its core constituencies and other social sectors if it is to succeed at the polls. This is especially so when, as is the case with conservative parties, their core constituencies constitute a small share of the population. The study of conservative party politics is, therefore, the study of the construction of polyclassist coalitions.[32]

Gibson proposes to define Latin American rightist parties as those that draw their core constituencies from the upper strata of society, and that consequently face a particular challenge when seeking to appeal to the masses. Such challenge can only be successfully addressed by combining alternative sources of electoral mobilization targeted at different social segments.[33] A clear example are traditional conservative parties in the region that achieved electoral success by combining the programmatic representation of wealthy elites with the clientelistic mobilization of peasants and the rural poor.[34]

Gibson's study represents an important reference for our own framework, particularly when it comes to thinking about the strategic dilemmas that rightist forces face in the context of unequal societies. Yet we think an ideological definition of the right serves our identification purposes better than a sociological one. As Gibson's own research reveals, *ideological* conflicts between core constituencies can well obstruct the configuration of rightwing parties, explaining why in many Latin American countries these parties have not been able to prosper. At the same time, rightwing parties can sometimes draw their core constituencies from the middle class, turning problematic the assumption that the upper strata inevitably form the core constituency of the right. For instance, the realignment of Western European party systems in the postindustrial era reveals that left-of-center parties can develop a core constituency among high-income voters, while rightwing parties can mobilize segments of the working class facing downward mobility.[35]

Similar examples can be found in Latin America, where leftwing parties have sometimes drawn their core constituencies from intellectuals coming from the middle and upper classes (e.g., the Frente Amplio in Uruguay and the Partido dos Trabalhadores in Brazil, especially in their origins). More importantly, in other cases, political leaders were able to replace their "core" constituency. For example, the Peronist party under Menem substituted its historical labor-based constituency through its electoral penetration of the popular sectors.[36] At the same time, by implementing market reforms, which went against the interests of its historical constituency, the Partido Justicialista was able to make electoral inroads in the upper sectors of Argentinean society, which were historically anti-Peronist.

We believe that the social bases of rightist parties should be seen as variable properties of specific parties (as opposed to constant characteristics of a given ideological current). While analytically useful, we believe that a sociological definition of the right might not be able to pinpoint, for identification purposes, the distinction between left and right, namely, ideology. As other variable properties, the analysis of parties' different social bases could nonetheless contribute to identifying relevant variance regarding rightist politics across time and space. From this perspective,

Gibson's work suggests a series of criteria for *complementing* our ideological definition of the right, descending one step in the *ladder of abstraction*.

Complementing the Minimal Definition

The abstract distinction advocated above between left and right, anchored around
ideological preferences tight to equality, is worth pursuing. One of its main advantages lies in its proposal for a positive definition of the right, which is stable over
time and space. In addition, this definition is directly related to the economic policy
dimension (i.e., state versus market) that many scholars rely upon to conceptualize
and operationalize the left-right divide in contemporary Latin America.[37]

Our minimal definition is likely too abstract for guiding empirical research, however. We believe that such a definition should be complemented for the analysis of
particular cases. Available cross-national evidence at both the elite and citizen levels
suggests that left-right self-placements map reasonably well on distinct views on equality (e.g., through different predispositions regarding inequality or through preferences on state intervention in distinct sociopolitical arenas).

Yet the strength of the state-market divide varies across cases and materializes in
distinct empirical realities. The relationship between left-right positions and other conflict lines (e.g., authoritarian-democratic, secular-confessional, liberal-conservative,
national-local) also varies. While in some cases these dividing lines can be either
irrelevant or highly correlated to the left-right divide, in others they might be orthogonal. If multidimensional cleavage structures are present, the right has an opportunity
to compete on nondistributive issues. In such cases it could eventually carve out a
minimum winning coalition on programmatic (but not *only* distributive) grounds.
Alternatively, in weakly structured party systems currently (or recently) governed
by leaders identified as being left of center, opposition leaders could try to "draw"
a rightist platform or identity as a contingent strategy to differentiate their platform from the governing coalition or leader. Finally, the right might also deploy
nonprogrammatic strategies or try to defend valence issues such as economic growth
or public security.

Structural Constraints for Rightist Politics

Latin America is the most unequal region in the world.[38] If we assume for a moment
that parties compete on a one-dimensional distributive divide and that voters select
parties according to their "true" economic interest, the median Latin American voter
would not vote for the right. In other words, the existing levels of inequality in Latin

America represent a fertile breeding ground for left-of-center parties and leaders because the latter are prone to put forward redistributive appeals that should benefit the great majority of the electorate.

The standard prediction of a median-voter model functioning in the context of high inequality is to observe democratic redistribution from the rich to the poor.[39] Drawing on such a model, Boix maintains that "transitions to democracy occur only in countries with low Gini indexes," because in countries with high levels of inequality, elites support and promote nondemocratic outcomes in fear of redistributive pressures from the poor.[40] Boix also argues that in social structures in which the elite draws its income from fixed assets (e.g., natural resources such as minerals, oil, or gas) a cyclical pattern of political rule is observed: the government is overthrown by elite sectors or by a popular rebellion demanding economic redistribution and then a new plan of exploitation of the natural resources is laid down, but corrupt practices and mismanagement set in motion a new wave of popular anger, paving the way for the formation of an authoritarian regime that will be defeated sooner or later. In the same vein, Acemoglu and Robinson extend the median voter model to argue that democratization might be fostered by economic globalization, which enhances capital mobility and thus diminishes local threats to elites.[41] In other words, economic globalization reduces the redistributive pressure over privileged sectors, which as a result are keen on accepting the democratic rules of the game.

But these predictions are not borne out by the recent Latin American experience, where high economic inequality and democratic politics have coexisted without significant shifts toward redistribution or regime backlashes for the last twenty-five years. On the one hand, as Nancy Bermeo has recently indicated, persistent economic inequality does not in itself constitute an insurmountable barrier to democratic durability.[42] On the other hand, democratic contestation, when practiced in the context of high inequality, does not translate (as expected) into significant redistribution.[43] At least partially, the absence of significant redistribution is tied to the political organization of economic elites, which even in a context of globalization can effectively mobilize to protect its local interests.

Let us briefly illustrate the point with data and simulations from Latin America. Figure I.1 presents comparative data on the levels of income concentration in the top 1% of the population, estimated on the basis of tax returns.[44] The data include capital gains and represent pretax and transfer estimates. As shown in the figure, income concentration in the top 1%, top 0.1%, and top 0.01% is the highest in Chile (the first Latin American country for which this type of estimate is available). In this case, the top 1% of the population has more than 30% of the total income, and 0.01% of the population has more than 10%. The same numbers for the United States, which has the highest inequality figures of all countries in the Organisation for Economic

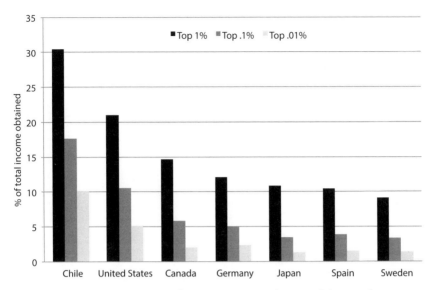

Figure I.1. Income concentration in the top 1%, 0.1%, and 0.01% of the population.
Source: Adapted from López et al. (2013)

Co-operation and Development, are significantly lower than those observed in Chile.

In contexts similar to the Chilean one, a moderate redistributive initiative could produce significant yields in terms of reducing inequality. Among the cases included in figure I.1, Chile has (along with the United States) the lowest tax burden on top personal incomes (40%). Simulations presented by Huber and Stephens (2012) and Huber et al. (2009) clearly convey the possible effects of moderate distributive reforms in such a context.[45] Figure I.2 displays the income distribution (by quintiles) observed in Brazil (1997) and Chile (2000), along with the simulated income distribution that would be obtained under two theoretical scenarios. The first scenario, identified as "flat rate universalism," assumes that a flat tax rate of 20% is imposed on the income of every quintile, and that such tax earnings are then distributed equally to all of them. Although this scenario could be considered as one of only "moderate redistribution," it would produce tangible reductions of income differentials among quintiles. The second scenario, identified as "basic universalism," is more progressive. In this case, the same tax earnings are redistributed only to the poorest 60% (the bottom three quintiles). Once again, as shown in figure I.2, this would further contribute to a significant decline of inequality.

Median voter–based models of political distribution under democratic rule would predict that in the context of a high concentration of income like the one observed in Latin America, redistribution would ensue. This is not the case, however.

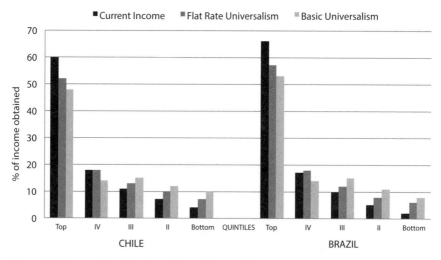

Figure I.2. Income distribution and simulation of income earning by quintile under flat rate universalism and basic universalism in Chile (2000) and Brazil (1997). *Source:* Adapted from Huber and Stephens (2012, chap. 3) for Brazil and Huber et al. (2009, appendix) for Chile

Although inequality has recently declined in Latin America, the extent to which it has declined owing to the enactment of explicitly redistributive schemes is still unclear and subject to cross-case variations. The latter could well relate to the differential impact of rightist political forces across cases.[46]

Furthermore, political coalitions proposing such types of redistributive programs have not consistently crystallized in the region, even in a case such as Chile's, where between 2000 and 2010 socialist presidents headed the government in a context of sustained economic growth, stable democratic rule, and rampant inequality. Instead, either measured through household surveys or tax information, between 2005 and 2010 the Gini coefficient has declined by 0.02 in the most optimistic estimate.[47] In the meantime, left-of-center governments did not enact significant tax reforms,[48] while the right-of-center government elected in 2010 was able to pass a tax reform in 2012 that actually lowered the personal tax burden on top incomes.[49]

The causal mechanisms that connect inequality and redistributive outcomes in a democratic context are complex, distorting and usually contradicting the overly simplistic expectations of median-voter models of redistribution.[50] The capacity of the political right to shape policy outcomes—either through electoral coalition making or through alternative ways—is one crucial factor that mediates the relationship between social inequality, political representation, and distributive outcomes. And yet it is a factor that has been often overlooked by recent academic research on the region.

Vehicles for Rightist Political Action

We assume that the electoral mobilization of distributive grievances is not a promising tool for the right to build a large-enough electoral coalition. This conclusion follows directly from our definition of the right (as a political position that takes inequalities as natural and outside the purview of the state) and from the structural situation in which political parties compete in Latin America: high inequality. Therefore we need to identify a series of strategies that have allowed rightist political forces to gain significant leverage in achieving electoral competitiveness and in shaping policy making in spite of the structural constraints they face in the region.

The capacity of the political right to protect its economic interests from the vast majority of the population, in the context of high inequality and democratic contestation, is in itself puzzling. If the "natural constituency" of the right comprises at most 20–30% of Latin American citizens, how can the right be so influential in shaping policy outcomes and, at least in some cases, in crafting electorally successful parties? This volume illuminates this question by analyzing cases in which the right has been able to gain political leverage through three strategies: first, by engaging in interest representation through nonelectoral strategies; second, by crafting innovative "electoral movements" with a nonpartisan outlook; and third, through party building. These three strategies might be complementary and can be used not only by the right but also by the left. More importantly, these three vehicles for rightist action are key to understanding distributive and regime outcomes in cases where the right is *not* in a government position. In this section we briefly refer to these three vehicles that the right might successfully employ to shape politics and policies in contemporary Latin America. The chapters that follow subsequently analyze instances in which each of these three main vehicles had been used.

First, we claim that rightist political organizations and interest groups should usually decide whether to compete for elective office. When they choose not to directly contest elections, they draw on nonelectoral vehicles. Staging a coup d'état is one such vehicle, one that had been used extensively in the history of Latin America. Yet, with specific exceptions, such a vehicle is no longer available to the right. In the new regional and global context, rightist forces may seek to influence public policy outcomes by engaging in political action by other means. Cases in this nonelectoral category range from paramilitary and *auto-defensa* (self-defense) groups to business and morally conservative groups that seek influence through congressional lobbying, from business and media conglomerates to relatively autonomous armed forces, and from technocratic networks and rightist think tanks to individuals and groups that invest massive economic resources in seeking to influence policy making. Disproportionate access to economic resources is an important precondition for developing this type of vehicle.

The second and third vehicles we identify are electoral ones. Both entail engaging in electoral politics to shape public policy by gaining access to elective office. Yet we distinguish between two fundamental ways in which rightwing actors and parties seek to win elections. The nonpartisan one entails the buildup of an electoral coalition outside institutionalized party politics. In these cases, rightist leaders are able to contest (and sometimes win) elections by running independent campaigns, which are usually run against the political establishment or against an incumbent leftist leader. The cases of Alberto Fujimori in Peru, Fernando Collor de Mello in Brazil, and Álvaro Uribe in Colombia exemplify this type of electoral, nonpartisan right. Although some of these leaders attempted to institutionalize their electoral coalition through the creation of new parties after being elected, they first ran as nonpartisan candidates.

Finally, the third vehicle we identify in the book is the partisan right, which engages in party building. Brazil's traditional conservative parties—PAN in Mexico, Alianza Republicana Nacionalista (ARENA) in El Salvador, and National Renewal (Renovación Nacional, or RN) and the Independent Democratic Union (Unión Demócrata Independiente, or UDI) in Chile—represent the most salient examples of this type of rightist political vehicle in contemporary Latin America. These parties have a rightist core constituency and in some cases have made impressive electoral gains by expanding their electoral appeal to new electoral segments. In this way, they have gained increasing leverage in shaping public policy in each country. These cases reveal that, in spite of structural constraints, right-of-center political parties can form and consolidate in the region. They do so by engaging in either nonprogrammatic electoral mobilization (clientelism, personalism, etc.) or programmatic mobilization of nondistributive divides (e.g., moral conservatism, order and security, economic growth and efficiency, etc.).

The chapters in this volume represent different instances of each type of vehicle. In the conclusion, we come back to this typology, take stock of recent trends in the region regarding each of these three vehicles, and speculate on pending tasks regarding future analyses of rightist politics in Latin America.

The Right and Democracy in Contemporary Latin America

Despite the existence of a few studies on the Latin American right, a series of arguments have been put forward and are part of the research agenda on contemporary democracy. In their work on transitions from authoritarian rule, Guillermo O'Donnell and Philippe C. Schmitter assumed that the establishment of new democratic regimes represents a major challenge for the right because the latter not only has little democratic credibility but is also divided between soft-liners and hard-liners.[51] It was therefore theorized that the right would win elections only if it (at least partially) sacrificed its ideas and interests and was capable of adapting its political agenda to the new rules of the game. If this was not the case, then the right would not achieve a significant electoral power and would probably threaten the stability of the new regime by calling for military intervention.

Other authors—in particular Dietrich Rueschemeyer, Evelyne Huber Stephens, and John D. Stephen—have complemented this thesis.[52] In their work on capitalist development and democracy, they claim that the emergence and survival of democracy are determined not so much by economic development in isolation, but rather by democracy's impact on society. Their argument is that capitalist expansion transforms the class structure, weakening the landed upper class and strengthening not only the lower and middle classes but also the labor unions. Under these circumstances, new class alliances are possible, paving the way for both the emergence of democracy and its further development.[53] While it is true that the authors in question pay special attention to the positive effect of labor unions on democratization, they also stress another aspect, namely, the existence of a party system affording protection to the ideas and interests of the right. This means that rightwing political parties and leaders play a crucial role in the durability of democracy because they represent powerful social groups that, if excluded from the political system, could seek to promote political or regime instability.

Similarly, Gibson's study suggests that the absence of strong right-of-center parties fosters the desertion of certain social groups from the electoral arena in favor of dubious channels for exercising influence.[54] From this angle, the stability of democracy goes hand in hand with the existence of rightwing parties because they serve as vehicles for defending political demands that are rooted in society and thus should be part of the partisan competition. Gibson maintains, however, that the formation of rightwing parties does not occur automatically but rather depends on the relationship between business elites and the state. When the former have a direct access to the latter through firm state contacts or corporatist institutions, there are few incentives for the involvement of the right in party politics.[55]

As this brief overview reveals, past research has focused, for valid reasons, on the right's possible effects on democratic survival. Latin American democracies have nonetheless survived, although strong rightwing parties are the exception rather than the rule in the region today. Not by coincidence, some scholars speak of the unexpected resilience of democracy in the region.[56] Contrary to the predictions of many who in the 1980s and 1990s discussed the prospects of Latin American democracies, the third wave of democratization has turned out to be durable.[57]

How can we explain the right's growing acceptance of the democratic rules of the game? The answer lies not only in the influence of foreign democratizing pressure because of the links Latin American countries have with the Western world and the fact that knocking at barracks' doors is a risky strategy. It lies also in the very transformation of the left. Given that the democratic failures of the past have led to a process of political learning within leftist forces, and that the fall of communism has deprived the Latin American left of a viable political model other than democracy, the right has fewer reasons than before to be scared about the rise of left-of-center administrations. At the same time, the implementation of market-oriented reforms has seriously limited the capacity of governments—regardless of their political ideology—to develop policies at odds with economic globalization. In other words, the opening of the economy reduces the pressure over privileged sectors, which as a result are keen on accepting the democratic rules of the game.[58]

Against this backdrop, we have to differentiate two research agendas that sometimes remain undistinguished in the academic literature on the impact of the right on Latin American democracy: on the one hand, the stabilization of democratic *access* to political power, and on the other hand, the development of institutions that seek to democratize the *exercise* of political power.[59] Most studies of the Latin American right have primarily dealt with the first research agenda. As we argued above, however, rightist forces have adapted to the democratic scenario, and they are much less inclined than before in promoting the intervention of the military. Scholars interested in exploring the impact of the right on Latin American democracy should pay more attention to the second research agenda. Several chapters in this volume take this approach, showing that rightist forces hold a significant amount responsibility for many symptoms of low institutional quality, such as lobbying elected officials, unequal access to party financing, and the influence of technocratic networks.

Outline of the Book

This book is organized in four parts. The first complements this introduction, providing a general overview of the challenges that rightist actors must confront while pursuing their policy agenda in the region. In chapter 1, Kenneth Roberts examines the problems that the right has encountered in succeeding in the electoral arena since the return to democracy. In chapter 2, Nina Wiesehomeier and David Doyle characterize the ideological and issue positions of rightist electorates across the region.

The remainder of the book subsequently analyzes the three main vehicles for rightist political action in contemporary Latin American introduced above. Part II is focused on the nonelectoral vehicle. The contributions by Kent Eaton (chap. 3) and James Bowen (chap. 4) describe different nonelectoral strategies that rightist actors have recently used when seeking policy influence in Latin America. Whereas Eaton's contribution provides a comprehensive overview of different types of nonelectoral vehicles that the right is employing (particularly in the Andean region), Bowen's chapter provides an in-depth comparative study of how nonelectoral forms of political organization are being promoted by the right in Bolivia and Ecuador as ways to counteract the actions of governing leftist forces. In addition, James Loxton (chap. 5) examines the nondemocratic roots of several rightwing parties, showing how the organizational efforts pursued under previous authoritarian regimes have paid off electorally for these parties after democratization.

The chapters by Cristóbal Rovira Kaltwasser (chap. 6), Carlos Meléndez (chap. 7), and Laura Wills-Otero (chap. 8) consider different instances of nonpartisan mobilization by rightist leaders. Whereas Rovira Kaltwasser explains why rightwing populist leaders were elected in countries such as Argentina, Brazil, and Peru at the beginning of the 1990s and draws lessons for the contemporary period, Meléndez explores the factors that shape the capacity of nonelectoral rightist vehicles to succeed electorally in the Andean region. In turn, Wills-Otero presents a case study of the strategy deployed in Colombia by Álvaro Uribe, who managed to win two subsequent presidential elections by combining nonpartisan and partisan strategies.

Finally, the third vehicle we analyze in the book is the partisan right, which organizes around relatively stable and successful political parties. The chapters by Steve Wuhs (chap. 9), Peter Siavelis (chap. 10), and Riitta-Ilona Koivumaeki (chap. 11) deal with instances of successful rightist party building in contemporary Latin America, subsequently focusing on the Mexican PAN (Wuhs), the Chilean RN and UDI (Siavelis), and the Salvadoran ARENA (Koivumaeki). Turning to less successful instances of rightist party building, in chapter 12 Alfred Montero explains the decline of a historically strong partisan right in the case of Brazil. In turn, in chapter 13, Sergio Morresi and Gabriel Vommaro examine the incipient attempts of the Propuesta Republicana in Argentina at making electoral inroads in a country where the partisan right has been historically weak. The volume closes with a brief conclusion by Juan Pablo Luna and Cristóbal Rovira Kaltwasser summarizing the main arguments developed in the book and identifying possible lines of inquiry for future works on the Latin American right.

ACKNOWLEDGMENTS

Previous versions of this chapter were presented at the conference organized by the editors at the Social Science Research Center Berlin in July 2011 and at the Latin American Center of the University of Oxford in November 2011. For helpful suggestions, the authors would like to thank Alan Angell, Edward Gibson, Wolfgang Merkel, Cas Mudde, Timothy Power, Kenneth Roberts, and Andreas Schedler as well as the participants of both events mentioned above. All remaining errors are the authors' own. The research leading to these results has received funding from the European Community's Seventh Framework Program (FP7/2007-2013) under grant agreement PIEF-GA-2010-273525.

NOTES

1. Eric Hershberg, "Latin America's Left: The Impact of the External Environment," in *Latin America's Left Turns: Politics, Policies, and Trajectories of Change*, ed. Maxwell A. Cameron and Eric Hershberg (Boulder, CO: Lynne Rienner, 2010), 233–49; Francisco Panizza, *Contemporary Latin America: Development and Democracy beyond the Washington Consensus* (London: Zed Books 2009).

2. Juan Pablo Luna and Fernando Filgueira, "The Left Turns as Multiple Paradigmatic Crises," *Third World Quarterly* 30, no. 2 (2009): 371–95; Kenneth M. Roberts, "The Mobilization of Opposition to Economic Liberalization," *Annual Review of Political Science* 11 (2008): 327–49; Eduardo Silva, *Challenging Neoliberalism in Latin America* (New York: Cambridge University Press, 2009).

3. Fernando Filgueira, Luis Reygadas, Juan Pablo Luna, and Pablo Alegre, "Shallow States, Deep Inequalities, and the Limits of Conservative Modernization: The Politics and Policies of Incorporation in Latin America," in *The Great Gap: Inequality and the Politics of Redistribution in Latin America,* ed. Merike Blofield (University Park: Pennsylvania State University Press, 2011), 245–77.

4. Cristóbal Rovira Kaltwasser, "Toward Post-Neoliberalism in Latin America?," *Latin American Research Review* 46, no. 2 (2011): 233–34.

5. Steven Levitsky and Kenneth Roberts, "Conclusion: Democracy, Development, and the Left," in *The Resurgence of the Left Latin American Left*, ed. Steven Levitsky and Kenneth Roberts (Baltimore: Johns Hopkins University Press, 2011), 425.

6. To the best of our knowledge, since the emergence of the third wave of democratization only four books in English have been dedicated to analyzing the Latin American right. See Douglas A. Chalmers, Maria do Carmo Campello de Souza, and Atilio Borón, eds., *The Right and Democracy in Latin America* (New York: Praeger, 1992); Edward Gibson, *Class and Conservative Parties: Argentina in Comparative Perspective* (Baltimore: Johns Hopkins University Press, 1996); Kevin J. Middlebrook, ed., *Conservative Parties, the Right, and Democracy in Latin America* (Baltimore: Johns Hopkins University Press, 2000); Timothy Power, *The Political Right in Postauthoritarian Brazil: Elites, Institutions, and Democratization* (University Park: Pennsylvania University Press, 2000). Another interesting book that goes beyond party politics is Leigh A. Payne's study on armed rightwing groups in Latin America, and the rise of what she refers to as "uncivil movements." *Uncivil Movements: The Armed Right Wing and Democracy in Latin America* (Baltimore: Johns Hopkins University Press, 2000).

7. As is well known, the French Revolution gave birth to a new understanding of politics because it changed the notion of three estates ordered vertically (i.e., the clergy, the nobility,

and the common people) to the conception of two camps confronting each other in a horizontal space. In fact, the three estates discussed in a national assembly how to rule the country, and in this process of debate two poles emerged: on the one hand, the supporters of the king and of gradual change positioned themselves on the right, and on the other hand, the promoters of liberty, equality, and radical change went to the left side. See Jean A. Laponce, *Left and Right: The Topography of Political Perceptions* (Toronto: University of Toronto Press, 1981), 47.

8. Alain Noël and Jean-Phillipe Thérien, *Left and Right in Global Politics* (New York: Cambridge University Press, 2008), 15.

9. Ibid., 16. Our italics.

10. Norberto Bobbio, *Left and Right: The Significance of a Political Distinction* (Polity: Chicago University Press, 1996).

11. Pierre Ostiguy, "The High-Low Political Divide: Rethinking Populism and Anti-Populism" (working paper 35, Committee on Concepts and Methods, Distrito Federal, Mexico, 2009); see also Cas Mudde and Cristóbal Rovira Kaltwasser, eds., *Populism in Europe and the Americas: Threat or Corrective for Democracy?* (Cambridge: Cambridge University Press, 2012).

12. Cas Mudde, *Populist Radical Right Parties in Europe* (New York: Cambridge University Press, 2007), 26.

13. While it is true that in the contemporary world rightwing leaders usually avoid saying that inequalities are natural and do not base their electoral campaigns on this idea, we do believe that the propensity toward egalitarianism is a key feature for illuminating the difference and conflict between left and right politics. Moreover, there are rightwing leaders and parties that explicitly claim that inequalities are natural. There is no better example than the so-called populist radical parties in present-day Europe (see Mudde 2007). For a Latin American example, see the recent book by Jovino Novoa, Chilean senator and member of the rightist party UDI, in which he explicitly claims that inequalities are natural and outside of the purview of the state. *Con la fuerza de la libertad, La batalla por las ideas de la centro-derecha en el Chile de hoy* (Santiago: Editorial Planeta, 2013).

14. Noël and Thérien (2008, 21).

15. Detlef Jahn, "Conceptualizing Left and Right in Comparative Politics: Towards a Deductive Approach," *Party Politics* 17, no. 6 (2011): 745–65.

16. Scott Mainwaring, Rachel Meneguello, and Timothy Power, *Partidos Conservadores no Brasil Contemporâneo: Quais são, o que de fendem, quais são suas bases* (São Paulo: Paz e Terra, 2000).

17. Giovanni Sartori, "Concept Misformation in Comparative Politics," *American Political Science Review* 64, no. 4 (1970): 1033–53.

18. José Luis Romero, *El pensamiento político de la derecha latinoamericana* (Buenos Aires: Paidos, 1970).

19. Jorge Larraín, *Modernidad, razón e identidad en América Latina* (Santiago: Editorial Andres Bello, 2000), 144.

20. Power (2000).

21. Ibid., 39. Power is of course aware of the fact that his "experiential" concept of the right was temporally restricted because the old authoritarian cohort would vanish.

22. Michael Coppedge, "A Classification of Latin American Parties" (working paper 244, Kellogg Institute, Notre Dame, Indiana, 1997).

23. David Collier and James Mahon, "Conceptual 'Stretching' Revisited: Adapting Categories in Comparative Analysis," *American Political Science Review* 87, no. 4 (1993): 845–55.

24. See Kathleen Bruhn, "The Making of the Mexican President, 2000: Parties, Candidates, and Campaign Strategy," in *Mexico's Pivotal Democratic Election: Candidates, Voters, and the Presidential Campaign of 2000,* ed. Jorge I. Domínguez and Chappell Lawson (Stanford, CA: Stanford University Press, 2004), 138.

25. Miguel Ángel López Varas and Jaime Baeza Freer, "The Chilean Right Party's Appeal to the Electorate: A Party Manifesto Analysis, 1989–2009" (paper presented at the 29th meeting of the Latin American Studies Association, Toronto, Canada, 2010).

26. Marco Morales, "Have Latin Americans Turned Left?," in *Leftovers: Tales of the Latin American Left,* ed. Jorge Castañeda and Marco Morales (New York: Routledge, 2008), 19–41.

27. Manuel Alcántara, "La escala de la izquierda: La ubicación ideológica de los presidentes y partidos en América Latina," *Nueva Sociedad* 217 (2008): 72–85. See also Herbert Kitschelt, Kirk Hawkins, Juan Pablo Luna, Guillermo Rosas, and Elizabeth Zechmeister, *Latin American Party Systems* (New York: Cambridge University Press, 2010).

28. Nina Wiesehomeier, "The Meaning of Left and Right in Latin America: A Comparative Overview" (working paper 373, Kellogg Institute, Notre Dame, Indiana, 2010). See also David Altman and Juan Pablo Luna, "Cristalización Programática de los Sistemas de Partidos Latinoamericanos: Congruencias, Desafecciones y Calidad de la Democracia" (Proyecto FONDECYT 1060749, Fondo Nacional de Desarrollo Científico y Tecnológico, Santiago, 2009). http://dspace.conicyt.cl/ri20/handle/10533/16917.

29. Gibson (1996).

30. Middlebrook (2000).

31. Edward Gibson, "Conservative Electoral Movements and Democratic Politics: Core Constituencies, Coalition Building, and the Latin American Electoral Right," in *The Right and Democracy in Latin America,* ed. Douglas A. Chalmers, Maria do Carmo Campello de Souza, and Atilio Borón (New York: Praeger, 1992), 13–42.

32. Gibson (1996, 7–8); italics in original.

33. Gibson (1992, 19).

34. See, for instance, Sofia Correa, *Con las riendas del poder: La derecha chilena en el siglo XX* (Santiago: Sudamericana, 2004), 73–82.

35. Herbert Kitschelt, *The Logics of Party Formation: Ecological Politics in Belgium and West Germany* (New York: Cornell University Press, 1989); Hanspeter Kriesi, Edgard Grande, Romain Lachat, Martin Dolezal, Simon Bornschier, and Timotheos Frey, *West European Politics in the Age of Globalization* (New York: Cambridge University Press, 2008).

36. Steven Levitsky, *Transforming Labor-Based Parties in Latin America: Argentine Peronism in Comparative Perspective* (New York: Cambridge University Press, 2003).

37. Alcántara (2008); Kitschelt et al. (2010); Wiesehomeier (2010).

38. See Merike Blofield, "Introduction: Inequality and Politics in Latin America," in *The Great Gap: Inequality and the Politics of Redistribution in Latin America,* ed. Merike Blofield (University Park: Pennsylvania State University Press, 2011), 5.

39. Allan Meltzer and Scott Richard, "A Rational Theory of the Size of Government," *Journal of Political Economy* 89, no. 5 (1981): 914–27.

40. Charles Boix, *Democracy and Redistribution* (Cambridge: Cambridge University Press, 2003), 139.

41. Daron Acemoglu and James A. Robinson, *Economic Origins of Dictatorship and Democracy* (New York: Cambridge University Press, 2006).

42. Nancy Bermeo, "Does Electoral Democracy Boost Economic Equality?," *Journal of Democracy* 20, no. 4 (2009): 21–35.

43. Robert R. Kaufman, "The Political Effects of Inequality in Latin America: Some Inconvenient Facts," *Comparative Politics* 41, no. 3 (2009): 359–79.

44. Ramón López, Eugenio Figueroa, and Pablo Gutiérrez, "La 'Parte del León': Nuevas estimaciones de la participación de los super ricos en el ingreso de Chile" (SDT 379, Serie de Documentos de Trabajo, Facultad de Economía y Negocios de la Universidad de Chile, Santiago, 2013).

45. Evelyne Huber, Jennifer Pribble, and John D. Stephens, "The Politics of Effective and Sustainable Redistribution," in *Stuck in the Middle: Is Fiscal Policy Failing the Middle Classes?,* ed. Antonio Estache and Danny Leipziger (Washington, DC: Brookings Institution Press, 2009), 155–88; E. Huber and J. D. Stephens, *Democracy and the Left: Social Policy and Inequality in Latin America* (Chicago: University of Chicago Press, 2012), chap. 3.

46. According to Luis F. López-Calva and Nora Lustig, the reduction of income inequality observed in Latin America in the 2000s was most likely driven by contingent factors, making such a trend likely to reverse under different contextual conditions. *Declining Inequality in Latin America: A Decade of Progress?* (Washington, DC: Brookings Institution Press).

47. López et al. (2013).

48. Tasha Fairfield, "Business Power and Tax Reform: Taxing Income and Profits in Chile and Argentina," *Latin American Politics and Society* 52, no. 2 (2010): 37–71.

49. The rate remained at a maximum of 40% but was reduced de facto by a declining tax burden on lower tax brackets. See http://diario.latercera.com/2012/09/05/01/contenido/pais /31-117647-9-reforma-recaudara-us-1257-millones-el-proximo-ano.shtml.

50. Pablo Beramendi and Christopher J. Anderson, "Income Inequality and Democratic Representation," in *Democracy, Inequality, and Representation,* ed. Pablo Beramendi and Christopher J. Anderson (New York: Russell Sage Foundation, 2008), 1–24.

51. Guillermo O'Donnell and Philippe C. Schmitter, *Transitions from Authoritarian Rule: Tentative Conclusions about Uncertain Democracies* (Baltimore: Johns Hopkins University Press, 1986).

52. Dietrich Rueschemeyer, Evelyne Huber Stephens, and John D. Stephens, *Capitalist Development and Democracy* (Chicago: University of Chicago Press, 1992).

53. For questions as to the validity of Rueschemeyer's thesis in Latin America, see Scott Mainwaring and Steven Levitsky, "Organized Labor and Democracy in Latin America," *Comparative Politics* 39, no. 1 (2006): 21–42.

54. Gibson (1996).

55. See also Ben Ross Schneider, *Business Politics and the State in 20th Century Latin America* (New York: Cambridge University Press, 2004).

56. See, among others, Kathleen Bruhn, "The Unexpected Resilience of Latin American Democracy," in *The Dynamics of Democratization: Dictatorship, Development, and Diffusion,* ed. Nathan J. Brown (Baltimore: Johns Hopkins University Press, 2011), 64–92; Omar Encarnación, "The Strange Persistence of Latin American Democracy," *World Policy Journal* 20, no. 4 (2003/4): 30–40.

57. There is certainly increasing debate about presidential breakdowns in Latin America that have been promoted by both left- and rightwing forces. While the latter have employed "old tactics" by involving the military forces in some cases (e.g., Fujimori's self-coup in 1992 or the coup d'état against Chávez in 2002 and Zelaya in 2009), the former have tended to mobilize the people and create pressure on the streets (e.g., the Argentine crisis of 2001–2 and the "water war" in Bolivia).

58. Daniela Campello, "The Politics of Redistribution in Less Developed Democracies: Evidence from Brazil, Ecuador, and Venezuela," in *The Great Gap: Inequality and the Politics of Redistribution in Latin America*, ed. Merike Blofield (University Park: Penn State University State, 2011), 185.

59. Sebastián L. Mazzuca, "Access to Power versus Exercise of Power: Reconceptualizing the Quality of Democracy in Latin America," *Studies in Comparative and International Development* 45, no. 3 (2010): 334–57.

PART ONE

THE CONTEMPORARY CONTEXT

CHAPTER ONE

Democracy, Free Markets, and the Rightist Dilemma in Latin America

KENNETH M. ROBERTS

During the first decade of the twenty-first century, the political right was on the defensive in much of Latin America. It was an unexpected turn of events, given the alignment of political forces in the region at the end of the Cold War. Conservative predominance in Latin America appeared unassailable in the early 1990s: the Cold War had ended with the collapse of communism in the Soviet bloc and the virtual extinction of socialism as a model of economic development; revolutionary movements had been defeated or contained, and outside Colombia their remnants were transformed into party organizations that competed for influence in electoral arenas;[1] and the class-based labor and peasant movements that challenged Latin American elites for most of the twentieth century had been gravely weakened by political repression, the debt crisis, and market-based economic restructuring. Even the right's most formidable historical rivals—the labor-based populist parties that were synonymous with state-led development—had embraced (and often led) the crisis-induced process of market liberalization in the 1980s and early 1990s. The technocratic convergence around free market or "neoliberal" policies that resulted—the so-called Washington Consensus[2]—seemingly attested to the resiliency of US political and economic hegemony in post–Cold War Latin America. This hegemony provided international reinforcement and democratic legitimation for a project of "conservative modernization" that had begun, under authoritarian auspices, in Pinochet's Chile and then rapidly diffused across the region.[3]

By the start of the new millennium, however, the tables had clearly turned. A range of different social and political actors increasingly called into question the economic effectiveness and political viability of the neoliberal model. Popular movements were on the ascendance, with a succession of pro-market governments being toppled by mass protests in Argentina, Ecuador, and Bolivia. An unprecedented series of electoral victories by leftist parties or movements placed eleven different countries with some two-thirds of the regional population under left-leaning national governments by 2011. Although this political shift to the left became a focal point of scholarly attention,[4] its flip side—the weakness of the right in democratic

competition—has too often been neglected. This weakness is hardly a novel development in Latin American politics,[5] but its accentuation during the first decade of
the twenty-first century is still puzzling, given the predominance of conservative
forces at the beginning of the 1990s.

To understand this paradox, it is necessary to explore the political challenges
encountered by the Latin American right during the unique historical juncture of
the 1990s and early 2000s. This period had three distinctive political markers that
shaped the strategic opportunities and constraints faced by conservative forces: post–
Cold War, postdemocratic transition and posteconomic adjustment. The confluence
of these three factors buttressed the political position of the right in the short term
while undercutting its historic populist and leftist competitors. Over the longer term,
however, they weakened the institutionalized (i.e., partisan) political representation
of conservative forces in much of the region while creating new opportunities for a
variety of leftist contenders. The seemingly impregnable position of the right during
the heyday of the Washington Consensus—a position derived largely from the collapse of historic rivals and the presumed structural imperatives of global market
integration—may well have undermined conservative parties by making them appear dispensable to the central task of protecting elite interests in the democratic
arena.

Ironically, rightist parties in many countries entered into decline precisely when
their economic project was most hegemonic in policy-making circles. Traditional
rightist parties rarely led or capitalized politically on the dramatic shift in public
policy toward their positions in the 1980s and 1990s, and with few exceptions—
most notably the National Action Party (Partido Acción Nacional, or PAN) in
Mexico—their electoral support declined as social and political resistance to market
liberalization intensified in the postadjustment era. These shifting political winds
have forced the right to reassess its strategies for competing in democratic contexts
under unfavorable structural conditions—that is, where deep structural inequalities
create popular majorities with objective material interests in redistributive policies
that the right opposes.

Contextualizing Competition between the Left and Right

As Juan Pablo Luna and Cristóbal Rovira Kaltwasser explain in their introduction
to this volume, the left-right cleavage is in essence an ideological conflict centered
on the politics of inequality and redistribution. So conceived, rightist actors defend
elite interests against redistributive pressures mobilized from below. How they do so
can vary considerably across time and space, however; the political and organizational resources they employ, the ideological framing of class and national interests,

and the prospects for forging middle- and lower-class support on the basis of non-redistributive appeals are all heavily context dependent. This can clearly be seen in Latin America, where the left-right cleavage and the conflict it sows have shifted dramatically over the course of the last generation. Three key dimensions of this shift are discussed below: the end of the Cold War, the region-wide transition to democratic governance, and the process of "structural adjustment" associated with neoliberal reform.

The End of the Cold War

From the 1940s through the 1980s, the left-right cleavage in Latin America was embedded in the larger global Cold War struggle between capitalism and communism. In this ideological struggle, the right—staunchly supported by the regional hegemon, the United States—defended capitalism and private property (as well as religious identities), while the left advocated redistributive policies and statist or socialist development models. Neither pole of the ideological continuum was consistently democratic. Especially in the aftermath of the Cuban Revolution, many on the left viewed liberal democracy as a façade for class domination and renounced the pursuit of social and economic reforms within established democratic regimes. Part of the left thus opted for strategies of armed revolution or, in a number of Andean countries, supported left-leaning military regimes that adopted redistributive social reforms.

The specter of revolution, however—whether real or imagined—provided a rationalization for conservatives to abandon democracy and "knock on the barracks door." This pattern was especially prevalent in the 1960s and 1970s, when the right in much of the region supported military intervention and authoritarian coercion to repress leftist rivals, demobilize working- and lower-class movements, and defend the status quo.[6] Given the intensity of ideological polarization, the right could often exploit the politics of fear, portraying even moderate and democratic leftists as communist allies and revolutionary threats to the social order. For the right, then, anti-communism and the fear of disorder created a powerful "negative referent" against which to mobilize support, not only among privileged and propertied sectors but also among middle classes who feared insurgent threats from below, and anyone else threatened by social upheaval.

The collapse of communism in the Soviet bloc and the gradual demise of revolutionary movements in Latin America allowed the right to celebrate an ideological victory and breathe a sigh of relief, given the virtual extinction of its most dangerous adversaries. The early 1990s found leftist movements of all types in Latin America on the political defensive and beset by fractious internal debates, a clear sign of their strategic and ideological uncertainty.[7] In a context of diminished threat, elites had less to fear from democratic competition, and the right was able to distance itself from patterns of military intervention and authoritarian rule that had long tainted its democratic credentials. If elite interests could be defended within democratic institutions, then authoritarianism was an increasingly dispensable tool of rightist politics in the region.

The flip side of this victory, however—as Castañeda recognized[8]—was that the demise of revolutionary projects also opened new political space for leftist democratic alternatives that were not easily discredited by an association with communism. The democratic left after the Cold War was less threatening to middle-class groups and more capable of building broad-based coalitions for redistributive social and economic reform. And without the specter of communism looming in the background, rightist actors in the post–Cold War era could not easily play the "military card" or cultivate US support for authoritarian alternatives to block the mobilization of democratic majorities for redistributive policies;[9] they would have to compete in the democratic arena to uphold the status quo.

That democratic arena was furthermore occupied by citizens with a newfound sense of individual civil and political rights—a legacy, in part, of the human rights and women's movements that contested military regimes,[10] as well as the broader struggles to restore democratic citizenship. And by the 1990s, political mobilization by indigenous groups was pressuring democratic regimes to recognize new forms of collective and communal rights rooted in ethnic identities.[11] If the right could no longer fall back on authoritarian solutions, neither could it assume that traditional methods of social control under democracy—such as patriarchy, vote buying, and patron-clientelism—would suffice to contain popular demands. New forms of civic associationism had created a more complex, heterogeneous, and autonomous civil society that articulated claims for an expanded set of citizenship rights and enhanced democratic accountability. The post–Cold War era thus dovetailed with a second major shift in the political context, one that was fraught with both opportunities and challenges for the political right: a region-wide process of democratic transition that began in the late 1970s and then gathered steam and consolidated in the 1980s and 1990s.

Democratic Transition and Consolidation

As the previous section suggests, rightist political actors—from civilian parties to military institutions and landowning and business elites—have historically been ambivalent and contingent supporters of democratic regimes in Latin America. This is hardly surprising, given the challenges of democratically reproducing highly inequitable social and economic orders such as those found in Latin America. As the formal models proposed by Meltzer and Richard[12] and Acemoglu and Robinson[13] suggest, median voters have an objective material interest in redistributive policies where high levels of inequality exist. The greater the degree of inequality, the larger the popular majorities who stand to benefit from redistribution; Huber and Stephens estimate those majorities at two-thirds of the regional population, a level that, if fully mobilized, would clearly make democracy a significant threat to elite interests.[14]

As Huber and Stephens are quick to note, however, partisan alignments do not map directly onto structural divides, and neither partisan nor policy preferences can simply be derived from objective material conditions. Until recently—when leftist parties in Venezuela, Bolivia, and Nicaragua surpassed the 60% electoral threshold and Ecuador was approaching it—the mobilization of democratic supermajorities behind redistributive projects has been exceedingly rare in Latin America. The structuralist logic of formal models like those of Acemoglu and Robinson do not take into account how concentrated economic power or institutional arrangements can shape and constrain democratic competition. The threats posed by democracy to conservative elites are diminished when they are confident of their ability to compete for popular support on nonredistributive grounds—for example, by developing patron-client linkages to lower-class constituencies, articulating religious identities, or nominating prominent personalities for public office. Conservative parties may thus be able to cultivate nonprogrammatic linkages to popular constituencies that do not require commitments to redistributive policies.[15] Conservative parties can also compete by cultivating a reputation for competence on "valence" issues that enjoy an overarching societal consensus—at least in terms of ultimate goals, if not necessarily policy means—such as economic growth, modernization, clean government, or public order and security. Following Gramsci, they may aspire to forms of ideological hegemony under which low-income voters are convinced that they do best when elite interests are served—something that any US Republican who advocates tax breaks for "job creators" implicitly understands.

Nevertheless, the effectiveness of such nonredistributive appeals to lower-class constituencies is historically contingent, and Latin American history provides ample evidence of the democratic dilemma encountered by the right when they falter.[16] Conservative oligarchic rule predominated in the region for a century after independence, sometimes through competitive (though highly exclusive) civilian regimes that strictly limited mass democratic participation, but often through military or patrimonial forms of authoritarian rule. The onset of mass politics did not begin in earnest until the early decades of the twentieth century, when urbanization and industrialization spawned new working- and middle-class groups that clamored for democratic citizenship rights.[17] As popular mobilization eclipsed oligarchic rule, the political right struggled to defend elite interests under more inclusive democratic regimes and to ward off the rise of labor-based populist and leftist competitors who invariably politicized socioeconomic inequalities. Where the left threatened to mobilize democratic majorities for redistributive policies that threatened core elite interests, the right often responded by abandoning the democratic arena and seeking shelter behind the protective shield of military rule.

This dynamic was especially prevalent in the 1960s and 1970s, when a series of military takeovers led to violent repression of the political parties and popular movements that had been activated during the populist era of the mid-twentieth century.[18] When militaries began to retreat to the barracks in the late 1970s and 1980s, considerable uncertainty surrounded the fate of the new democratic regimes that took their place. In particular, scholarly accounts questioned the commitment of conservative business and political elites to the new democratic regimes; wary of a return to polarizing patterns of social mobilization, O'Donnell and Schmitter, for example, warned that political and economic pacts would be necessary to restrain popular mobilization and safeguard elite interests under democracy.[19]

Ultimately, however, Latin America's new democratic regimes proved to be far more durable and resilient that anyone imagined at the onset of the wave of regime transitions. With military institutions widely discredited as political actors by economic mismanagement and egregious human rights violations, and with the United States shifting to a more consistent (if hardly unconditional) pro-democratic stance as the Cold War wound down, the political right progressively lost the option of resorting to authoritarian rule to protect elite interests. Instead, the right would have to compete within the parameters of democratic institutions that became increasingly consolidated, despite the political traumas associated with the debt and inflationary crises of the 1980s and early 1990s.

Paradoxically, the region-wide economic crisis may have enhanced the prospects for democratic consolidation in two crucial ways, both of which helped to alleviate the potential threats posed by democratization to elite interests. First, the debt crisis and its ensuing hyperinflationary spirals thoroughly undermined the statist development models that had been in vogue in the region since the Great Depression of the 1930s, ushering in a period of austerity, state retrenchment, and market-based structural adjustment that largely conformed to the policy preferences of leading business and financial interests.[20] With staunch support from the United States and international financial institutions, market reforms deepened the insertion of Latin American economies in global circuits of investment, production, finance, and exchange, thus tightening global market constraints on the macroeconomic and redistributive social policies of democratic governments in the region. If austerity and market liberalization did not fully tie the hands of democratic rulers, they surely narrowed their range of options and thus their ability to challenge elite interests. Second, the combination of economic crisis and market liberalization wreaked havoc on the class-based labor and peasant movements that historically mobilized redistributive pressures through democratic institutions.[21] With labor unionization in steep decline and populist and leftist parties hamstrung by the collapse of statist development models, democratic competition seemingly posed little threat to the political right and its core elite constituencies—at least in the short term, as explained below.

Structural Adjustment and Market Liberalization

During the era of state-led import substitution industrialization (ISI) in the middle of the twentieth century, conservative parties in Latin America were not necessarily supporters of free markets, much less the Chicago School neoliberal orthodoxy that was subsequently imported by Chilean technocrats and a legion of imitators after the mid-1970s. Agrarian export elites with close ties to conservative parties generally supported open trade regimes, as they were threatened by the protectionism and price distortions of ISI policies that forced them to subsidize industrial development. But ISI policies appealed broadly to urban workers and sectors of industrial capital that depended on protected domestic markets or state contracts and subsidies. Consequently, business and elite groups were often divided by sectoral interests that forced conservative parties to water down ideological commitments to market liberalism, even if they were clearly more market oriented than their labor-based populist and leftist rivals.

Over time, however, severe market distortions and related economic inefficiencies combined with the ascendance of more diversified and internationalized business-financial groups to create powerful business lobbies with vested interests in free market reform.[22] Business groups that operated in competitive niches or had mobile capital and international ties were positioned to capitalize on trade liberalization, the privatization of public enterprises and services, and the deregulation of capital and foreign exchange markets. As Schamis argues,[23] these business groups provided a crucial domestic support base for market liberalization, in alliance with technocratic elites who directed the process of policy reform. Labor unions, however, invariably opposed these reforms as threats to the organizational, political, and material interests of workers.[24]

One of the great puzzles of the neoliberal reform period is that elite groups often did not channel their demands for market liberalization through conservative parties. Furthermore, these parties often failed to assume political responsibility for structural adjustment policies. This was especially the case in countries that developed strong labor-based populist or leftist parties during the ISI era. Since conservative parties were sure to encounter well-organized opposition to neoliberal reforms in these countries, parties with historic ties to organized labor had a comparative advantage in the reform process: they could offer inducements for cooperation, co-opt union leaders, and draw upon reservoirs of political capital and trust to contain popular mobilization, at least in the short term.[25] Consequently, historic populist or labor-based parties (such as the Peronists in Argentina, the Partido Revolucionario Institucional in Mexico, the Acción Democrática in Venezuela, and the Movimiento Nacionalista Revolucionario in Bolivia) assumed political responsibility for initiating structural adjustment policies in the midst of economic crises, even though these policies clashed dramatically with their historic programmatic commitments and societal linkages. In other countries with weaker labor movements—such as Costa Rica and Ecuador—center-left parties sometimes led or collaborated in the reform process (i.e., the Partido Liberación Nacional in Costa Rica and the Izquierda Democrática in Ecuador). Elsewhere, military dictatorships (Chile and Uruguay) or independent figures with a popular touch but no significant party organization (Fernando Collor in Brazil and Alberto Fujimori in Peru) launched market liberalization. Conservative parties played major roles in the reform process primarily in countries where labor-based parties were historically weak or where recent experiences with authoritarian rule and military repression had constrained the political mobilization of popular sectors—Colombia, Honduras, Paraguay, the Dominican Republic, El Salvador, and Uruguay.

The fact that such a diverse range of political parties and independent leaders played major roles in the process of market liberalization attests to the economic constraints faced by governments in the region, as well as the breadth of the technocratic consensus for neoliberal policies in the late 1980s and early 1990s. This technocratic consensus—while it lasted—surely diminished ideological conflict in Latin America[26] and lowered the stakes of democratic competition, but it also made it difficult for parties to construct collective identities or societal linkages on the basis of meaningful programmatic distinctions. Where even historic statist and populist parties could be counted on to adhere to the Washington Consensus, rightist parties were largely dispensable to the process of market liberalization, and economic elites had little need to invest in party organizations as institutional vehicles for interest representation. Such interests, after all, were seemingly safeguarded by the structural imperatives of global markets that disciplined national governments. Not surprisingly, then, established conservative parties entered into decline in most of the countries (with the exception of Mexico) where market reforms were adopted in a "bait-and-switch" fashion by traditional populist or center-left parties or independent populist figures, including Argentina, Bolivia, Costa Rica, Ecuador, Peru, and Venezuela. The erosion of traditional clientelist linkages to popular constituencies could also weaken conservative parties as economic austerity and market liberalization eliminated rent-seeking opportunities.[27]

In short, conservative political actors did not necessarily lead the dramatic shift in public policies toward the right, which often undermined rather than enhanced their institutionalized political representation. Although neoliberal reforms clearly strengthened the economic and political influence of business and financial elites, such elites were often loathe to engage in partisan politics, as many preferred to cultivate direct access to policymakers rather than work through partisan intermediaries. As Middlebrook states, "Economic and social elites rarely depend upon political parties as the exclusive means for advancing their policy goals."[28] Indeed, rather than invest in party-building activities that would bind their interests to the fate of a particular political organization, business elites could hedge their bets and cultivate fluid relationships with a number of parties to ensure that they retained policy-making access no matter the outcome of electoral contests. This pattern was only reinforced by the technocratic consensus around the neoliberal model, or at least the dearth of perceived alternatives, which lowered the stakes of electoral competition and diminished the centrality of parties "as direct vehicles for elite interest articulation."[29]

The technocrats who played such a vital role in the design and implementation of neoliberal reforms often shared elite disdain for partisan representation.[30] The hallmark of technocratic policy making is the application of social scientific principles to problem-solving tasks, and its legitimacy rests on its alleged expertise and efficiency rather than popular democratic mandates. The basic ingredients of democratic politics—the need to cultivate popular support; to articulate, represent, and reconcile a plurality of interests and ideological perspectives; to secure citizen input regarding the content of public policies; and to hold public officials accountable to their constituents—are fundamentally at odds with technocratic claims to the professional possession and application of authoritative knowledge. Technocrats thus perceive themselves to be providers of public goods who rise above the narrow self-interests of parties and interest groups that inevitably place restrictions on policy-making autonomy and skew public policies toward the pursuit of particularistic ends.[31] In short, parties and other representative bodies interfere with technocratic policy making, which thrives where society is disorganized, demobilized, and politically inert or detached. It is for this reason that neoliberal technocrats seek "to withdraw the economy from all processes of democratic decision," making economic efficiency the ultimate goal and subordinating politics to "the alleged technical imperatives of the economy."[32]

In many respects, technocratic market reforms were a classic expression of the "politics of anti-politics" in Latin America; that is, an attempt to insulate macroeconomic policy making from societal pressures and democratic contestation. This began with the military dictatorships of the Southern Cone in the mid-1970s, then spread across the region under more democratic auspices in the 1980s as labor movements entered into decline, the debt crisis narrowed the range of policy alternatives, and market constraints shielded technocratic policymakers from popular democratic pressures. Although conservative parties were relatively modest players in the market reform process, the right was able to draw upon less institutionalized, de facto power resources—what Latin Americans call *poderes fácticos*—to shape public policy. As debt-saddled states liberalized markets and retreated from a broad range of developmental and social welfare responsibilities, the structural power of internationalized business and financial elites was accentuated, and economic well-being became increasingly dependent on their market incentives and behavior. The ability of markets and capital flight to "discipline" governments that failed to toe the line was amply driven home by the 1980s hyperinflationary spirals in Bolivia, Argentina, Brazil, Nicaragua, and Peru. International lenders—both public and private—reinforced the message by making financial relief conditional on the adoption of structural adjustment policies.

Highly concentrated and commercialized broadcast media that were closely intertwined with local business establishments further buttressed market pressures and financial leverage. As Hughes and Prado assert, "Mass media in Latin American societies, especially broadcast media, are controlled by a small elite that uses the media's definitional power to further, consciously or unconsciously, a set of class- and family-based interests and ideologies," thus influencing "the political and policy-making process" as well as "societal norms of cultural appropriateness."[33] Consequently, even where rightist parties did not win elections and directly control national governments, conservative forces wielded powerful economic and political resources to shape and constrain national policy-making agendas.

This dependence on *poderes fácticos* did not appear especially threatening to the right during the period of economic adjustment. With the left plagued by ideological uncertainty, labor movements in decline, and populist parties abandoning their historic commitments to failed statist and heterodox policies, every country in Latin America responded to inflationary pressures and balance of payments constraints by liberalizing markets in the late 1980s and early 1990s.[34] The Washington Consensus proved to be fleeting, however,[35] a temporary and often tactical convergence around a set of policy prescriptions that had been artificially narrowed by financial distress and the political disarticulation of its natural adversaries. The convergence corresponded to a period of crisis-induced austerity and economic adjustment, but it quickly unraveled when political and economic conditions changed in the post-adjustment era after the mid-1990s—an era when the right would pay a steep political price for the organizational fragilities of its partisan representatives.

Repoliticization in the Postadjustment Era

The signature political achievement of the adjustment era was economic stabilization; that is, the defeat of inflationary pressures driven by acute fiscal and balance of payments deficits. Once the scourge of hyperinflation had been extinguished from the region, however—Brazil in 1994 was the last country to escape its grasp—the political winds began to shift, and a new postadjustment era began to take shape. The urgency for stabilizing austerity measures diminished, while the long-promised payoffs of painful adjustment policies proved elusive to obtain. Stabilization yielded only anemic growth in the 1990s, while the Mexican peso crisis of 1994–95 and the regional stagnation that followed in the wake of the 1997–98 Asian financial crisis demonstrated that Latin America's liberalized financial markets remained highly vulnerable to global shocks. When international conditions turned more favorable and a commodity export boom finally produced steady growth after 2003, Latin America had already started its political shift to the left, and the Washington Consensus had been broken.

In reality, the Washington Consensus had never extended far beyond the technocratic circles that implemented it, and the neoliberal model certainly did not achieve ideological hegemony within Latin American societies at large. Although prominent market reformers like Menem in Argentina, Fujimori in Peru, and Cardoso in Brazil—none of them representatives of established conservative parties—were reelected after successively stabilizing economies plagued by hyperinflation, neoliberalism had advanced in much of the region without an electoral mandate. Neoliberalism was often adopted "by surprise,"[36] in a "bait-and-switch" fashion by presidents who ran for office on radically different platforms, demonstrating that many political leaders did not believe they could win elections by advocating structural adjustment policies; that is, by truthfully divulging what they would do after taking public office.

Once stabilization had been achieved, the longer-term social deficits of the neoliberal model—in particular, low wages, underemployment, and acute inequalities[37]—became increasingly salient politically. Unemployment consistently ranked as the most important problem facing Latin American countries in Latinobarómetro surveys taken from 1995 through 2008, when it was overtaken by crime.[38] More striking, perhaps, an overwhelming 75–85% of citizens said that the distribution of income in their society was unjust, with half of them claiming that it was "very unjust"

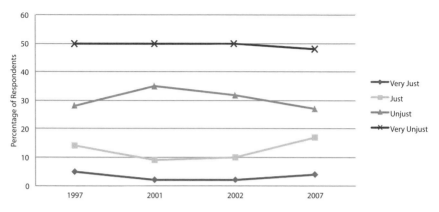

Figure 1.1. Public opinion toward income distribution in Latin America, 1997–2007 (rational average). *Source:* Latinobarómetro

(fig. 1.1). Given the tensions between universal democratic citizenship and widespread social exclusion, these sentiments encouraged a repoliticization of macroeconomic and social policy making as the Washington Consensus unraveled in the postadjustment era. This repoliticization could be seen in three principal arenas, all of which put the right on the political defensive.

First, although organized labor remained a greatly diminished political actor, other social groups demonstrated a newfound capacity for collective action and social mobilization in the postadjustment era. Most prominently, a series of mass protests led to the collapse of multiple pro-market governments in Argentina, Bolivia, and Ecuador in the late 1990s and early 2000s, with indigenous movements, unemployed workers, and community associations often taking the lead in social mobilization.[39] Second, following a series of experiments with leftist governments at the municipal level,[40] an unprecedented electoral shift to the left began at the national level, starting with Hugo Chávez's landslide victory in the 1998 presidential elections in Venezuela. The "left turn" ushered into power presidents from a diverse range of established populist (Argentina) or leftist parties (Brazil, Chile, El Salvador, Nicaragua, and Uruguay), as well as independent populist figures (Ecuador, Paraguay, Peru, and Venezuela) and leaders of mass movements (Bolivia) who outflanked traditional party systems on the left.

Third, public opinion surveys manifested widespread ambivalence or opposition to central pillars of the neoliberal model, especially after the late 1990s. Surveys demonstrated that most Latin American citizens supported a market economy, although the percentage dropped from two-thirds to a little over half of survey respondents between 1998 and 2007 (fig. 1.2).[41] Given the absence of viable alternatives to a market economy in the post–Cold War era, this growing ambivalence was

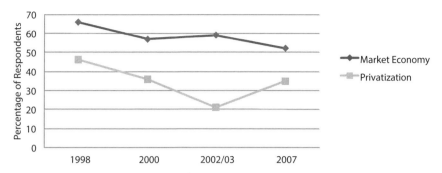

Figure 1.2. Support for privatizations and a market economy, 1998–2007 (rational average). *Source:* Latinobarómetro

notable. Moreover, satisfaction with the *performance* of the market economy was much lower, bottoming out at 16% of survey respondents in 2003 before recovering slightly as the commodity boom ushered in a new era of relative prosperity.[42]

Perhaps more telling were public attitudes toward specific features of the neo-liberal model, as citizens demonstrated a capacity to differentiate among its varied components. Free trade policies that provided consumers with access to a wide range of imported goods were the most popular, receiving support from over 70% of survey respondents.[43] Support for privatization policies was much lower, however, and it tended to decline over time, in part because of concerns over higher prices for basic utilities like water, electricity, and telecommunications. The percentage of survey respondents who said that privatizations had benefited their country fell from a regional average of 46% in 1998 to 21% in 2002–3 before partially recovering as macroeconomic conditions improved (fig. 1.2).[44] Despite generalized support for private enterprise in the process of development, 71% of citizens expressed dissatisfaction with the privatization of basic utilities.[45]

Most citizens looked to the state to provide social welfare and promote economic development. This created a public opinion profile that was strikingly "statist" in Latin America's postadjustment era, certainly in comparison to that of the United States, where economic liberalism is more deeply entrenched. Surveys conducted throughout the Americas in 2008 by Vanderbilt University's Latin American Public Opinion Project found that Latin American citizens were far more likely than US citizens to believe that the state should own major industries and assume primary responsibility for job creation, health care, and social welfare (fig. 1.3). A majority of survey respondents favored state ownership of key enterprises in every Latin American country except Costa Rica and Venezuela (where only 37.3% of respondents favored state over private ownership, compared to 20.8% in the United States). A majority in every Latin American country favored state responsibility for job creation,

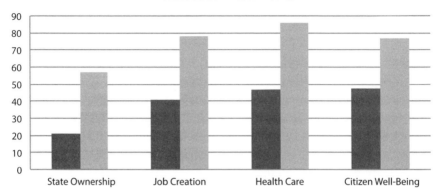

Figure 1.3. Average support for state economic responsibilities in Latin America and the United States, 2008. *Source:* Calculated from the Latin American Public Opinion Project

ranging from 66.3% in Honduras to 90.4% in Paraguay. Similar majorities in every country assigned primary responsibilities to the state for health care (ranging from a low of 76.3% in Honduras to a high of 94.0% in Paraguay) and social well-being (ranging from 62.6% in Honduras to 85.8% in Paraguay). In none of these policy spheres did a majority of US citizens—even prior to the rise of the Tea Party movement—assign primary responsibilities to the state. The statist preferences of Latin American citizens grew more pronounced after the mid-1990s; by 2008, over 80% of citizens supported state control of major social services like primary and university education, health care, and pensions, as well as major extractive industries (oil and gas) and some public utilities (i.e., electricity; see fig. 1.4).[46]

This strong and growing support for vigorous state developmental and social welfare roles helps to explain why the right lost political ground to a variety of leftist alternatives in Latin America's postadjustment era. Paradoxically, as Arnold and Samuels demonstrate,[47] the political turn to the left did *not* signify that more Latin American citizens necessarily identified themselves as leftist; ideological self-placements across the region changed little during this period and in fact remained slightly right of center. What is clear, however, is that statist policy preferences were strong and growing, and they were not restricted to citizens who identified ideologically with the left. As such, leftist parties and leaders could solicit electoral support on policy or programmatic grounds from citizens who did not self-identify with the left but nevertheless preferred a more active economic role for the state.

The organizational weaknesses of conservative parties, and the tendency to rely on *poderes fácticos* to defend elite interests, put the right at a significant competitive

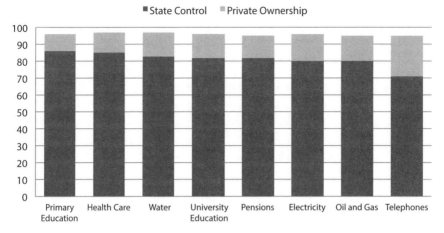

Figure 1.4. Preferences for state and private control over social and economic activities, 2008 (regional averages). *Source:* Latinobarómetro

disadvantage in the electoral arena. The decline of conservative parties in the post-adjustment era was strikingly consistent, as it spanned across a range of different types of party organizations. Through the end of the 1990s, for example, conservative nineteenth-century oligarchic parties that predated the rise of mass politics remained electorally dominant in four countries: Colombia, Honduras, Paraguay, and Uruguay. During the first decade of the twenty-first century, however, these parties weakened and lost control of national executive offices for the first time, being displaced by a new conservative party in Colombia (the Partido de la U) and by new leftist rivals in Paraguay and Uruguay. Only in Honduras did traditional oligarchic parties retain state power—with the assistance of a military coup—and even there an emerging leftist contender increasingly challenged their rule.

In a second group of countries, one or more major conservative parties emerged in the middle of the twentieth century in response to the rise of mass politics and the demise of nineteenth-century oligarchic parties. Many of these parties also entered into a steep decline in the 1990s and early 2000s, including COPEI in Venezuela, Acción Popular in Peru, the Partido Social Cristiano in Ecuador, and the Partido Reformista Social Cristiano in the Dominican Republic. The main outlier was the Mexican PAN, which strengthened and came into power for the first time in 2000 and represented the only case of a conservative party that was positioned to play a leadership role in a process of democratization as Mexico transitioned from single-party rule to multiparty competition.

In a third group of countries, major efforts at conservative party building occurred in the 1980s during the period of democratization and market liberalization.

Parties like Acción Democrática Nacionalista in Bolivia, the Partido de Unidad Socialcristiana in Costa Rica, and the Partido Liberal Constitucionalista in Nicaragua achieved short-term success and captured national executive offices, but they also entered into steep decline in the first decade of the twenty-first century. The Partido da Frente Liberal and other small conservative parties were significant alliance partners in Brazil, but they clearly played a secondary role to more powerful centrist and leftist rivals in the postadjustment era. Conservative forces were more electorally powerful in Guatemala and Panama, but personalistic and organizational rivalries blocked the construction of cohesive national party organizations. Meanwhile, conservative party-building efforts in Argentina remained an abysmal failure.

The handful of cases where strong new conservative parties did arise in recent decades—namely, Chile, El Salvador, and Colombia (after the demise of traditional conservative parties in 2002)—are highly instructive, as they possessed a number of distinctive features that marked their institutional development. All three countries were major battlegrounds of the Cold War, during which radical socialist or revolutionary projects directly threatened economic elites. As such, elites had strong incentives to invest in conservative party organizations to defend their interests in the electoral arena, if and when they were forced to compete. More telling, perhaps, is that the major new parties of the right were not organized exclusively in the electoral arena; in their formative periods, all were able to draw from extraelectoral organizational networks embedded within authoritarian states or coercive state (or parastatal) institutions.[48] The Unión Demócrata Independiente in Chile, for example, was forged out of the municipal apparatus of the Pinochet military dictatorship; the Alianza Republicana Nacionalista in El Salvador grew out of the paramilitary death squads formed during the country's descent into civil war; and the Partido de la U in Colombia drew cadres from demobilized paramilitary networks as well as the remnants of traditional conservative parties. Paradoxically, some of Latin America's most electorally successful rightist parties are those with the least democratic formative experiences; as Panebianco would suggest,[49] those formative experiences or "genetic models" created organizational bonds that proved to be more resilient than those spawned strictly for electoral purposes.

These anomalies aside, most conservative parties have performed poorly in the electoral arena in Latin America's postadjustment era. This is not necessarily a crisis for elite interests; after all, a number of the new leftist governments in the region have been strikingly moderate, especially in countries where centrist or conservative parties remain viable contenders in the democratic arena (i.e., Brazil, Chile, El Salvador, and Uruguay).[50] Leftist governments in these countries have experimented cautiously with redistributive social policies—including higher wages and more expansive public health, social security, and poverty relief programs—while adhering to relatively orthodox macroeconomic policies and avoiding open confrontations with business interests. Weyland suggests provocatively that this moderate left may actually enhance the political sustainability of market economies in Latin America by helping them address their accumulated social deficits.[51]

Where the partisan right has collapsed or deinstitutionalized, however—Argentina, Bolivia, Ecuador, and Venezuela—leftist governments have been more inclined to break with neoliberal orthodoxy in both macroeconomic and social policy spheres. These countries have experimented with a broader range of statist and nationalist development policies, even if they fall short of the "twenty-first-century socialism" trumpeted by Hugo Chávez. The differences between these two sets of cases can be seen in figure 1.5, which charts for each country the change between 2000 and 2010 in the "Index of Economic Freedom" from the Heritage Foundation and *Wall Street Journal*, a multivariate indicator of aggregate economic liberalism.[52] Despite political shifts to the left, Chile and Uruguay actually increased their score on the liberalism index between 2000 and 2010, while Brazil under "Lula" experienced a moderate decline of 5.5 points. Much steeper declines were registered in the remaining cases, with Venezuela declining by 19.8 points, Argentina by 18.8, Bolivia by 15.6, and Ecuador by 10.5. The latter four countries accounted for much of the decline in the region-wide average index score (from 64.8 to 60.6) between 2000 and 2010. In short, strong conservative parties—and institutionalized partisan competition in general—exerted a moderating effect on heterodox policy experimentation where the left was in power. By contrast, leftist governments that were unchecked by a major conservative party were more likely to veer sharply away from market orthodoxy.

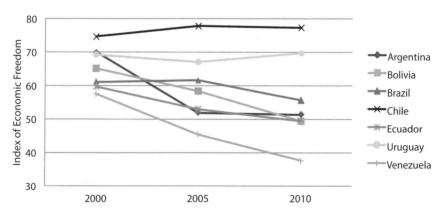

Figure 1.5. Left governments and change in the index of economic freedom, 2000–2010.
Source: Heritage Foundation / *Wall Street Journal* "Index of Economic Freedom," http://www.heritage.org/Index

Even if these more heterodox experiments prove to be economically unviable or uncompetitive in long term, as Weyland and others assert,[53] the right would be remiss to underestimate the significance of its electoral slide—now well into its second decade—and assume that its return to power is just around the corner. Latin America's "left turn" was not a mere cycle of conventional anti-incumbent vote shifts that produced multiple alternations in office. In a region with notorious anti-incumbent voting patterns,[54] thirteen of the first fourteen leftist administrations to complete their term in office since the beginning of the "left turn" in 1998 achieved reelection. This record of incumbent electoral success was not a mere function of the commodity boom and improving economic conditions; by comparison, between 2000 and 2011, incumbent centrist and conservative parties in Latin America achieved a reelection rate of only 30%. The lone outlier to the left's record of incumbent reelection—Chile in 2010—was clearly attributable to institutional restrictions on vote choice, as Chilean electoral laws prohibited the incumbent socialist president, Michelle Bachelet, from standing for reelection after she completed her term with approval ratings hovering near 80%.[55] Within a year, the government, led by Bachelet's successor, Sebastian Piñera—the first conservative to replace a leftist president since the onset of the "left turn"—was all but paralyzed by mass student protests against a highly unequal and heavily privatized educational system.

With the exception of Colombia, where the demise of traditional conservative parties coincided with the rise of a major new rightist alternative, conservative forces have been remarkably slow to reorganize in the aftermath of partial or complete party system collapse. Even where more polarizing populist or leftist alternatives have emerged, creating relatively well-defined left-right sociopolitical cleavages—namely, in Argentina, Bolivia, Ecuador, and Venezuela—conservative forces have been forced to rely on fluid electoral fronts and personalistic electoral vehicles in the absence of cohesive national party organizations. To date, the electoral weaknesses of these conservative party "substitutes"—that is, the asymmetrical partisan organization of profound social and political cleavages—have left elite interests on the margins of national representative institutions.

In short, the partisan right encountered serious electoral challenges and social pressures in Latin America's postadjustment era. Given the failure of neoliberalism as an ideological project, programmatic linkages to voters based on pro-market policies rarely produced electoral majorities for conservative parties, and even patron-clientelism appeared to have diminishing utility as an instrument of elite social and political control over lower-class constituencies. As popular majorities mobilized increasingly behind redistributive political projects, partisan cleavages between rival elite-based, ideologically undifferentiated patronage machines gave way to more programmatically structured and socially differentiated forms of competition between leftist and rightist alternatives. Not surprisingly, since rightist parties that defended the neoliberal model were disadvantaged in this competition, many began to steer programmatically toward the center. This could be done, for example, by prioritizing "valence" issues that had broad public support, such as anticrime and corruption campaigns, or economic growth and modernization. It could also be done by trumpeting the right's own commitment to social welfare policies, a phenomenon that produced the irony of conservative presidential candidates who campaigned for office on promises to "be like Lula," the epitome of an "acceptable"—non-Chavista— left. Although the region remained far from a new consensus on macroeconomic and social policies, it had clearly shifted considerably away from the post–Cold War, Washington-sanctioned technocratic consensus of the 1990s.

Conclusion

Although electoral competition will undoubtedly produce new conservative leaders in countries now governed by the left, this should not disguise the basic political realignment that has occurred in Latin America's postadjustment era. Simply put, political competition in the region more thoroughly revolves around programmatic distinctions between leftist and rightist alternatives that are ultimately grounded in redistributive conflicts. As the defender of minority elite interests opposed to redistributive policies, the right is at an inherent disadvantage where democratic competition politicizes inequality and social exclusion. Their depoliticization during the period of economic adjustment was grounded in a unique confluence of political and economic conditions that ultimately proved to be transitory; these conditions were subject to erosion by the very forces of economic stabilization and institutionalized democratic competition. With the right overly dependent on its *poderes fácticos* and lacking strong institutional intermediaries, this competition gradually empowered its rivals on the left in the postadjustment era. Consequently, even where the left has not come to power in recent years—in countries like Colombia, Costa Rica, Honduras, and Mexico—democratic alternatives of the left have emerged or strengthened.

Nevertheless, the right is hardly lacking in political resources, and it may well discover new or invigorated means of appealing electorally to popular constituencies that diffuse or crosscut distributive conflicts. It has, after all, often been done so historically in Latin America. The right otherwise has little choice but to relax its attachment to a doctrinaire form of market liberalism and to encourage experimentation with more socially inclusive variants of market economies. Such experimentation may even foster a policy convergence with elements of the moderate left that is strikingly different from the market fundamentalism and technocratic antipolitics of the Washington consensus—not to mention the polarized class and ideological battles of the Cold War era.

NOTES

1. Jorge Castañeda, *Utopia Unarmed: The Latin American Left after the Cold War* (New York: Vintage Books, 1993).

2. John Williamson, "What Washington Means by Policy Reform," in *Latin American Adjustment: How Much Has Happened?*, ed. John Williamson (Washington, DC: Institute for International Economics, 1990), 7–20.

3. See the introduction to this volume; Alejandro Foxley, *Latin American Experiments in Neoconservative Economics* (Berkeley: University of California Press, 1982); Hector Schamis, "Reconceptualizing Latin American Authoritarianism in the 1970s: From Bureaucratic-Authoritarianism to Neoconservatism," *Comparative Politics* 23, no. 2 (1991): 201–20.

4. See, for example, Steven Levitsky and Kenneth M. Roberts, eds., *The Resurgence of the Latin American Left* (Baltimore: Johns Hopkins University Press, 2011); Kurt Weyland, Raúl L. Madrid, and Wendy Hunter, eds., *Leftist Governments in Latin America: Successes and Shortcomings* (New York: Cambridge University Press, 2010).

5. See Edward Gibson, *Class and Conservative Parties: Argentina in Comparative Perspective* (Baltimore: Johns Hopkins University Press, 1996).

6. Guillermo O'Donnell, *Modernization and Bureaucratic-Authoritarianism: Studies in South American Politics* (Berkeley, CA: Institute of International Studies, 1973).

7. Kenneth M. Roberts, *Deepening Democracy: The Modern Left and Social Movements in Chile and Peru* (Stanford, CA: Stanford University Press, 1998).

8. Castañeda (1993).

9. This did not mean that they could not try, as seen in the ill-disguised US enthusiasm for the military coup against Hugo Chávez in 2002 and the rather ambivalent US response (including staunch Republican congressional support) for the military coup against populist figure Manuel Zelaya in Honduras in 2009.

10. Sonia Alvarez, *Engendering Democracy in Brazil: Women's Movements in Transition Politics* (Princeton, NJ: Princeton University Press, 1990); Alison Brysk, *The Politics of Human Rights in Argentina: Protest, Change and Democratization* (Stanford, CA: Stanford University Press, 1994).

11. Deborah Yashar, *Contesting Citizenship in Latin America: The Rise of Indigenous Movements and the Postliberal Challenge* (New York: Cambridge University Press, 2005).

12. Allan H. Meltzer and Scott F. Richard, "A Rational Theory of the Size of Government," *Journal of Political Economy* 89, no. 5 (1981): 914–27.

13. Daron Acemoglu and James A. Robinson, *Economic Origins of Dictatorship and Democracy* (New York: Cambridge University Press, 2006).

14. Evelyn Huber and John D. Stephens, *Democracy and the Left: Social Policy and Redistribution in Latin America* (Chicago: University of Chicago Press, 2012), 60.

15. Herbert Kitschelt, "Linkages between Citizens and Politicians in Democratic Politics," *Comparative Political Studies* 33, no. 6/7 (2000): 845–79.

16. Gibson (1996); Kevin J. Middlebrook, ed., *Conservative Parties, the Right, and Democracy in Latin America* (Baltimore: Johns Hopkins University Press, 2000); Timothy Power, *The Political Right in Postauthoritarian Brazil: Elites, Institutions, and Democratization* (University Park: Pennsylvania State University Press, 2000).

17. Ruth Berins Collier and David Collier, *Shaping the Political Arena: Critical Junctures, the Labor Movement, and Regime Dynamics in Latin America* (Princeton, NJ: Princeton University Press, 1991); Dietrich Rueschemeyer, Evelyne Huber Stephens, and John D. Stephens, *Capitalist Development and Democracy* (Chicago: University of Chicago Press, 1992).

18. O'Donnell (1973).

19. Guillermo O'Donnell and Philippe C. Schmitter, *Transitions from Authoritarian Rule: Tentative Conclusions about Uncertain Democracy* (Baltimore: Johns Hopkins University Press, 1986).

20. Hector Schamis, "Distributional Coalitions and the Politics of Economic Reform in Latin America," *World Politics* 51, no. 2 (1999): 236–68.

21. Marcus Kurtz, *Free Market Democracy and the Chilean and Mexican Countryside* (Cambridge: Cambridge University Press, 2004); Kenneth M. Roberts, "Social Inequalities without Class Cleavages in Latin America's Neoliberal Era," *Studies in Comparative International Development* 36, no. 4 (2002): 3–34.

22. Jeffry Frieden, *Debt, Development, and Democracy: Modern Political Economy and Latin America* (Princeton, NJ: Princeton University Press, 1991); Eduardo Silva, *The State and Capital in Chile: Business Elites, Technocrats, and Market Economics* (Boulder, CO: Westview Press, 1996).

23. Schamis (1999).

24. Katrina Burgess, *Parties and Unions in the New Global Economy* (Pittsburgh, PA: University of Pittsburgh Press, 2004); María Victoria Murillo, *Labor Unions, Partisan Coalitions, and Market Reforms in Latin America* (Cambridge: Cambridge University Press, 2001).

25. See Burgess (2004); Steven Levitsky, *Transforming Labor-Based Parties in Latin America: Argentine Peronism in Comparative Perspective* (Cambridge: Cambridge University Press, 2003); Murillo (2001).

26. Forrest D. Colburn, *Latin America at the End of Politics* (Princeton, NJ: Princeton University Press, 2002).

27. Juan Pablo Luna Fariña, "Programmatic and Non-Programmatic Party-Voter Linkages in Two Institutionalized Party Systems: Chile and Uruguay in Comparative Perspectives" (PhD diss., University of North Carolina, Chapel Hill, 2006).

28. Middlebrook (2000, 5–6).

29. Kevin J. Middlebrook, "Introduction: Conservative Parties, Elite Representation, and Democracy in Latin America," in Middlebrook (2000, 6).

30. Jorge I. Domínguez, *Technopols, Freeing Politics and Markets in Latin America in the 1990s* (University Park: Pennsylvania State University Press, 1997); Judith A. Teichman, *The Politics of Freeing Markets in Latin America: Chile, Argentina, and Mexico* (Chapel Hill: University of North Carolina Press, 2001).

31. It goes without saying that this self-image denies that technocracy may itself be an expression of particularistic interests, much as it denies that technocrats' "scientific" claims

to authoritative knowledge may be grounded in contested and ideological conceptions of the common good.

32. Norbert Lechner, "The Transformation of Politics," in *Fault Lines of Democracy in Latin America*, ed. Felipe Agüero and Jeffrey Starke (Miami, FL: North-South Center Press, 1998), 29.

33. Sallie Hughes and Paola Prado, "Media Diversity and Social Inequality in Latin America," in *The Great Gap: Inequality and the Politics of Redistribution in Latin America*, ed. Merike Blofield (University Park: Pennsylvania State University Press, 2011), 109.

34. Eduardo Lora, "Structural Reforms in Latin America: What Has Been Reformed and How to Measure It" (working paper 466, Inter-American Development Bank, Washington, DC, 2001).

35. James E. Mahon, "Good-Bye to the Washington Consensus?," *Current History* 102, no. 651 (2003): 58–64.

36. Susan C. Stokes, *Mandates and Democracy: Neoliberalism by Surprise in Latin America* (Cambridge: Cambridge University Press, 2001).

37. Evelyne Huber and Fred Holt, "Successes and Failures of Neoliberalism," *Latin American Research Review* 39, no. 3 (2004): 150–64.

38. Latinobarómetro, *Informe* (Santiago: Corporación Latinobarómetro, 2010), 7.

39. Eduardo Silva, *Challenging Neoliberalism in Latin America* (New York: Cambridge University Press, 2009); Yashar (2005).

40. Daniel Chávez and Benjamin Goldfrank, eds., *The Left in the City: Progressive and Participatory Local Governments in Latin America* (London: Latin America Bureau, 2004).

41. Figure 1.2 shows the combined average of survey respondents who either agree or strongly agree with the statement "A market economy is best for the country."

42. Latinobarómetro, *Informe* (Santiago: Corporación Latinobarómetro, 2005), 63.

43. Andy Baker, "Why Is Trade Reform So Popular in Latin America? A Consumption-Based Theory of Trade Policy Preferences," *World Politics* 55, no. 3 (2003): 425.

44. Figure 1.2 shows the combined average of survey respondents who either agree or strongly agree with the statement "Privatizations of state enterprises have been beneficial for the country."

45. Latinobarómetro, *Informe* (Santiago: Corporación Latinobarómetro, 2003), 57.

46. The questions asked respondents to identify which economic activities "should be primarily in the hands of the state, and which should be primarily in the hands of the private sector."

47. Jason Ross Arnold and David J. Samuels, "Evidence from Public Opinion," in Levitsky and Roberts (2011, 33–35).

48. James Loxton, "Life after Dictatorship: Post-Third Wave Conservative Parties in Latin America" (unpublished manuscript, Department of Government, Harvard University, 2011).

49. Angelo Panebianco, *Political Parties: Organization and Power* (Cambridge: Cambridge University Press, 1988).

50. See Gustavo Flores-Macías, *After Neoliberalism? The Left and Economic Reforms in Latin America* (Oxford: Oxford University Press, 2012); Levitsky and Roberts (2011); Weyland et al. (2010).

51. Kurt Weyland, "The Left: Destroyer or Savior of the Market Model?," in Levitsky and Roberts (2011, 71–92).

52. The index ranges from zero to one hundred, with higher scores corresponding to more liberalized economies and lower scores indicating greater state interventionism.

53. Weyland (2011).

54. Karen L. Remmer, "The Political Impact of Economic Crisis in Latin America in the 1980s," *American Political Science Review* 85, no. 3 (1991): 777–800.

55. The left was also turned out of power in Paraguay in 2012, but not by electoral means; President Fernando Lugo was abruptly impeached by conservative opponents in the legislature in what was in essence a legislative coup against a leftist president who had no partisan base of his own.

CHAPTER TWO

Profiling the Electorate

Ideology and Attitudes of Rightwing Voters

NINA WIESEHOMEIER AND DAVID DOYLE

The electoral successes of the left that we have been witnessing across the region can be partly explained by the high levels of inequality prevalent in Latin America and the associated demands for redistribution. But this (re)emergence of the left rooted in an egalitarian agenda raises the question of the capacity of the right to formulate electoral appeals and to subsequently influence policy making, if we consider the inequality divide as distinguishing both camps from each other. In other words, if we define the right "as a political position distinguished by the belief that the main inequalities between people are natural and outside the purview of the state," and the left as "a political position characterized by the idea that the main inequalities between people are artificial and should therefore be counteracted by active state involvement,"[1] what are the implications at the level of public support?

In a context where the political right is facing difficulties of competing on egalitarian or distributive issues, it may become crucial for the right to exploit nondistributive issues and to activate electoral mobilization through valence competition. Using public opinion data from the most recent 2010 Latin American Public Opinion Project (LAPOP) wave, we shed light on the feasibility of such a strategy. What are the attitudes of the ideological bases of support for the right regarding distributive preferences? And can we identify issues beyond redistribution that mark distinctive dynamics that may help the right to mobilize the electorate and garner support?

In this chapter we first explore and contrast the ideological profiles and related attitudes and value judgments of the general public according to their ideological self-placement. Second, we tap into the partisan component of the left-right divide and explore not only the ideological and socioeconomic profiles of twenty political parties, of which nine are left-leaning and eleven right-leaning, but also the attitudes and value judgments of supporters of these selected paradigmatic cases. The examination of the ideological profiles of voters and party supporters, as well as their attitudes and values toward issues that may affect electoral competition and the policy agenda of the right, take stock of the contemporary political right in Latin America.

The insights gained from this dual approach advance our understanding of empirical realities in an important way. Whereas the focus on the general public assumes that the ideological scale is meaningful to respondents and that individuals are able to place themselves accordingly, the latter perspective is concerned with whether voters organize and structure their opinions according to the core distinction of the left-right dimension.

But we also take into account as a separate group citizens who did not place themselves on the ideological scale. We believe that this group, which we label as "undeclared," has to be considered, especially having in mind the high volatility of contemporary electoral alliances and their ample heterogeneity.[2] Although these respondents do not declare any ideological preference, it is nevertheless possible that they think in ideological terms, since they do express opinions and in some cases even support for specific political parties. These citizens may then represent an attractive group in terms of electoral strategies and appeals for political parties, especially if it is possible to identify crosscutting cleavages. Because the appeal of an electoral campaign based on orthogonal issues need not to be confined to this group of undeclared citizens, however, we are consequently interested in assessing their attitudes and party preferences in conjunction with ideologically located respondents.

While our focus lies with the right, we understand the left and the right as a dyad whose underlying tenets are mutually exclusive but nevertheless have to be considered jointly. Consequently, we identify survey questions that reflect the distinction of the left and the right as understood in the minimal definition presented above. These are questions of attitudes toward welfare provision and income inequality. We complement this core conceptualization with other dimensions that are relevant either because their relationship with the political right has been considered as potentially problematic or because they are tied to characteristics of the Latin American right rooted in their formation process and thus constitute a contrast to the left. To explore the alleged ambiguous relationship of the right with democracy, we include questions that uncover attitudes toward electoral representation, democratic participation, and leadership capacities. Although, strictly speaking, there was no uniform development of the right across the region, it is nevertheless possible to identify recurring themes and philosophical theories within the right's development that inform our selection of issues related to traditional values.[3]

Most importantly, however, we identify questions that reflect issues with the potential of representing other crosscutting societal divisions enabling competition on nonredistributive issues, such as crime prevention. Given that citizens consider crime to be one of the most pressing issues facing the region today, the political right might be able to garner support to the extent that such topics can be absorbed in electoral campaigns compatible with the attitudinal orientations of the electorate even if new ideological alignments do not take place.

Our evidence indicates that issues of crime and security may become central for the electoral fortunes of the right. The data suggest that parties of the right could profitably capitalize on voters' concern with crime and public security and garner electoral support beyond its core constituency. Increasing public fear about rising crime presents parties of the right with the opportunity to mobilize heterogeneous electoral coalitions centered on issues of public security and increasing delinquency within society that have the potential to overcome the general left-right cleavage and deflate the traditional distributive campaigns of the left.

Ideology and Attitudes of Citizens

We begin our exploration by looking at how the ideological self-placement of citizens across the Latin American region evolved over time to shed light on the potential constituency base of the right vis-à-vis the left. We compare three different sources of survey data for this purpose and use four waves of the World Values Survey (WVS) from 1990 to 2008, data from the annual Latinobarómetro surveys from 1996 to 2009, and the shorter biannual time series of the AmericasBarometer (LAPOP) from 2006 to 2010. Figure 2.1 contrasts three area plots corresponding to our three sources of survey data. We convert the continuous left-right scales into five-point categorical variables and display the percentage of respondents in the different ideological groups of left, center-left, center, center-right, and right by survey period. As highlighted above, we also show the percentage of individuals who did not declare any ideological position as the group of "undeclared." Of the three data sources, the Latinobarómetro uses an eleven-point scale (0 to 10) to measure left-right ideology, whereas WVS and LAPOP employ ten-point scales (1 to 10). In the latter cases, the scale was simply divided into five equally sized groups and summarized accordingly. This means that respondents who scaled themselves as a 1 or 2 were categorized as left; those who scaled themselves as a 3 or 4 as center-left; those who scaled themselves as a 5 or 6 as center; those who scaled themselves as a 7 or 8 as center-right; and those who scaled themselves as a 9 or 10 as right. In the case of the Latinobarómetro, we opted to consider the ideological scores of 4, 5, and 6 as center and to have equally sized groups for the left (scores 0 and 1), center-left (scores 2 and 3), center-right (scores 7 and 8), and right (scores 9 and 10). Finally, for all survey data sources used, we consider those who did not answer the question, or who did not know, as undeclared.

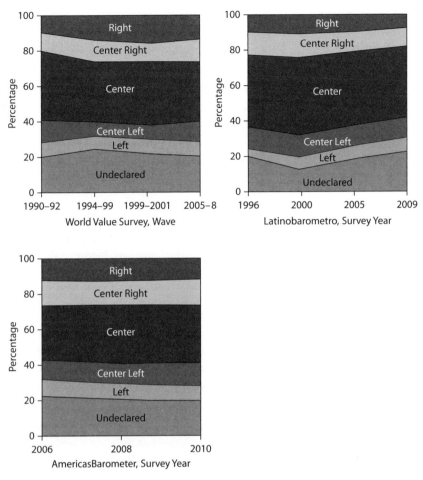

Figure 2.1. The general left-right dimension in Latin America.

Although in the case of the Latinobarómetro data the conversion to the five-point scale slightly inflates the center category, in general, a coherent picture across all sources emerges. Overall, across time and throughout the region, the proportion of respondents identifying with the different ideological groups appears to be rather stable. About 35–40% of Latin Americans place themselves in the ideological center, followed by the second largest group of undeclared citizens of roughly 20%. Whereas the WVS and the LAPOP data designate the right-of-center group as the third in line, confirming the conservative nature of citizens across the region,[4] according to the Latinobarómetro, left-of-center and right-of-center placements are more or less equal.

Looking in more detail at the development over time, the latter surveys also indicate that the most discernible movement among ideological camps was due to a steady decrease from 1996 to 2000 in the group of undeclared to the benefit of the center category and a slight increase of those identifying with extreme right positions. From 2000 onward, the percentage of those claiming no ideology has steadily increased. The ideological camp that mostly diminished during this time is the center. But extreme right positions also suffered a small setback, whereas the extreme left registered a small increment and the center-left and center-right ideological groups largely remained unchanged.

The WVS also displays movements over time. Although some of the movement registered can be traced to different sample sizes across the waves (see Appendix), between the second (1990–92) and the third wave (1994–99) the group of respondents on the extreme right and the group of undeclared expanded, whereas the center and center-left positions lost adherents. Between the fourth wave (1999–2001) and the last (2005–8) that we consider for our analysis, however, the ideological center is actually contracting further, whereas the center-left displays a slightly increased percentage of respondents, as does the center-right. Interestingly, since the second wave of the survey, the group of respondents not declaring any ideology has been diminishing. According to the WVS, in the midnineties, this group comprised more than 20% of respondents, whereas in the late 2000s, in accordance with the Latinobarómetro and the LAPOP data, this group of respondents was at 20%.

By and large, the constituency base in terms of self-placement shows remarkable stability across all ideological camps. This is also the case for the substantial pool of citizens who do not identify with any position on the left-right scale. What is the potential for fostering alliances based on electoral appeals across these groups? For this purpose, in the next stage of our analysis, we turn to individual-level data from the 2010 LAPOP survey in order to ascertain the different attitudes and characteristics that exist among citizens across Latin America as a whole, using the same ideological categories as before plus the category of undeclared respondents.

We start our exploration of citizen's opinions with the question regarding the most serious problems facing the respondent's country today. Figure 2.2 graphs the four issues most frequently identified by LAPOP respondents across Latin America as a percentage of each separate ideological grouping.

What stands out is the congruence in responses across all six groups. Irrespective of ideology, the most serious problem identified by all respondents is crime, and the range of answers across the six ideological categories is rather narrow. While 17% of undeclared, left, and center-left respondents name this issue, 21% of those in the center do so also. The second most serious problem identified by centrist respondents across Latin American countries is unemployment, again with a similar range between 16% and 17%, whereas it comes in third for undeclared, left and right respondents. For the latter group, the state of the national economy comes in third as the

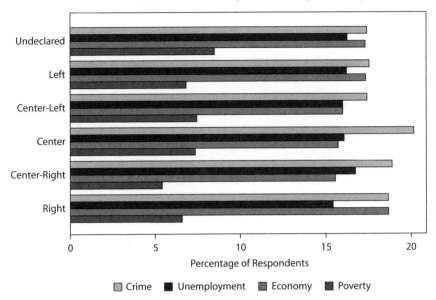

Figure 2.2. Percentage of respondents reporting the most important problem facing their country.

most serious problem, while poverty was the fourth problem mentioned (6–8%) across all ideological groups. Although the difference is not large, the group of undeclared citizens is more concerned about poverty than citizens taking an ideological stance.

We thus see a clear consensus among the electorate regarding the major problems and societal challenges facing Latin American countries today. Interestingly, crime, the most pressing issue identified by respondents regardless of their ideological leanings, is at the same time the only concern without a redistributive policy component. Even so, there may be disagreement regarding the manner in which this and other issues should be addressed, disagreement that may relate to ideological underpinnings and consequently prevent valence competition.

To scrutinize this question, we examine the attitudes of respondents on several issues selected on the basis of our extended ideological definition. Figure 2.3 graphs the total responses across Latin America, by ideological grouping, to two questions from the 2010 LAPOP survey that capture attitudes toward government responsibility of welfare provision and the reduction of income inequality.[5] Each ideological category displays two bars. The darker bar represents the responses to a particular question according to each ideological group as a percentage of all responses to this question. The lighter bar shows again the response to the same question by ideological group, but this time as a percentage of all responses within that specific ideological

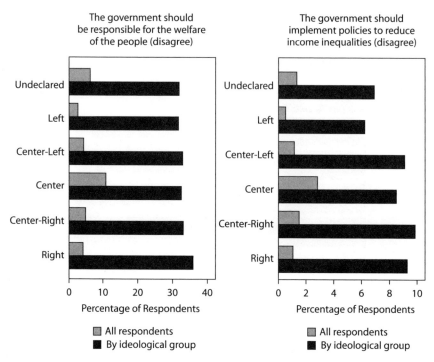

Figure 2.3. Percentage of respondents reporting to what extent government should be responsible for welfare and income inequality.

category. This visual distinction serves as a reminder that Latin American citizens overwhelmingly tend to identify with the ideological center.

The left-hand pane represents all those who disagree with the sentiment that the government, as opposed to individuals, should be responsible for the welfare of the people, while the right-hand pane represents all those who disagree with the assertion that the government should implement policies to reduce income inequality. From both panes, differences among those on the left and right sides of the political spectrum can be ascertained, albeit they seem tenuous. For example, 37% of respondents who identify with the right do not agree that the government should be responsible for the welfare of the people, in comparison to just 31% of those who identify with the left. About 10% of center-right respondents, and 9.7% of right respondents, reject any role for the government in the reduction of income inequality, while 9% of those on the center-left and only 6.1% of those on the left share this attitude. This suggests only a weak divide between those who identify with the left and those who identify with the right with regard to the ideological underpinning of inequality. The attitude of undeclared respondents toward inequality, however, most closely approximates the attitude of those on the left. Similar divisions appear with regard to attitudes toward the extent of state involvement in the economy.[6] While differences between right and left are rather small regarding state ownership of the most important industries, with roughly 30–37% of respondents rejecting it, the distinction is slightly more pronounced regarding government responsibility for job creation; approximately 8.2% of right respondents and 8.4% of center-right respondents reject a role for the state in the creation of employment, in comparison to 6.3% of left respondents.[7]

What is far more illuminating is the contrast between left and right regarding the efficacy of the democratic model and support for democratic norms when faced with rising levels of crime and insecurity. The left-hand pane of figure 2.4 displays respondents who believe that their country needs a government with an iron fist, while the right-hand pane displays those who believe that it would be justified for the military to take power by a coup d'état when there is a lot of crime.

Regarding the necessity of a government with an iron fist, a symmetric shape is apparent, lending some support for the so-called extremism model, suggesting that authoritarian attitudes can be found on either end of the left-right dimension.[8] Beginning with 37% of right respondents, we see a steady decline in support of

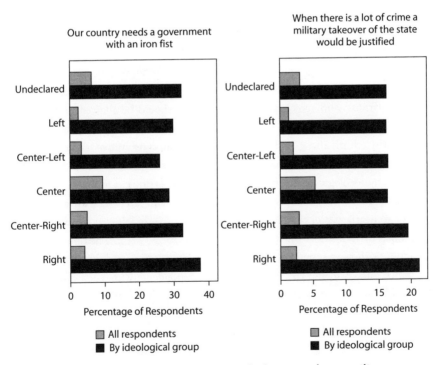

Figure 2.4. Percentage of respondents reporting whether *mano dura* or military takeover is needed.

mano dura politics, to only 26% of respondents on the center-left. Yet 30% of those on the extreme left also favor a government with an iron fist. The left-hand pane of figure 2.4 underscores a dissimilarity between left and right regarding the exercise of political power, with a weaker authoritarian tendency at the far left end. Interestingly, the preference of those with an undeclared ideology for *mano dura* politics most closely resembles the preferences of those on the center-right.

The right-hand pane in turn shows that those on the right are far more authoritarian in their attitudes toward the exercise of power, particularly with respect to valence issues such as crime and public security.[9] Only 16% of respondents identifying with left and center-left ideological positions would support a military coup in the event of increasing public insecurity. This is also true for those who do not declare any ideology. In contrast, nearly 20% of center-right respondents and approximately 25% of right category would support a military takeover of the state to address rising levels of crime. This figure highlights the potential for electoral appeals of the right on nonredistributive issues. Although a drastic step such as military intervention would not be supported of large parts of the electorate, the support for *mano dura* politics of the group of undeclared citizens may open up avenues for electoral strategies for the political right.[10]

Figure 2.5 displays the positive responses to two questions from the LAPOP survey that capture attitudes representing differences that are rooted in the classic liberal-conservative division and may be located in the area of value judgments. Both graphs exhibit discernible disagreement between respondents who identify with the left and those who identify with the right. The left-hand pane of figure 2.5 displays the percentage of those who agree that same-sex couples should be allowed to marry. Although responses reveal that on average Latin Americans still tend to be rather conservative, clearly those on the right have a far more conservative stance than those on the left when it comes to same-sex marriage. Interestingly, at only 16%, respondents without any ideological affiliation are the most conservative. Only 17% of right respondents and 18% of center-right respondents agree with same-sex marriage, in comparison to nearly 25% of center-left respondents and 26% of left respondents.

Similar divisions exist when it comes to democratic activism. The right-hand pane of figure 2.5 shows respondents who reported to have participated in a demonstration or protest march in the last twelve months. Respondents with a left-of-center self-identification have a greater propensity to mobilize on the street in response to political dissatisfaction than those identifying with the right of center. Less than 8% of right respondents and 7% of center-right respondents have participated in some form of protest activity in the last twelve months, compared to over 17% of those on the left and 12% of those on the center-left. The group of undeclared, at only 5%, is the least involved in political protest activities, suggesting that a reason for respondents to not

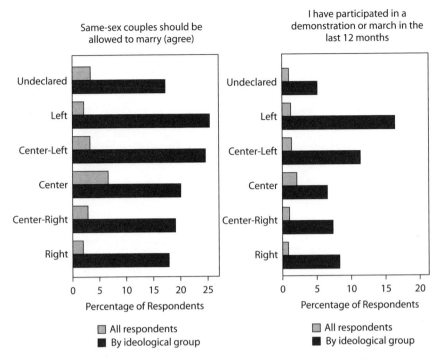

Figure 2.5. Percentage of respondents who support same-sex marriage and have participated in democratic activism.

declare any ideological preference might be a generalized alienation from politics. These results again indicate that although normative attitudes toward democracy are negligible on both the left and right, differences do exist when these attitudes interact.

To get a better understanding of the potential the issues discussed here offer for electoral engineering, it is interesting to examine the relationship among the responses given to the different categories on a country-by-country basis. In other words, can we identify a common conservatism across the Latin American electorate? For example, do pro-market voters favor *mano dura* politics, or do those who take a hard line on security also favor individualistic solutions to inequality?

An examination of Goodman and Kruskal's gamma coefficient for different sets of questions for each Latin American country reveals that there is no uniform relationship between conservative security stances and market preferences or attitudes to inequality across the region, but rather that results are driven by country dynamics.[11] Regarding the association between preferences for a military coup in the event of crime and support for government policies to reduce inequality, the results show a statistically significant association between these issues in only seven countries. Only in Paraguay (0.145; where $p < 0.01$) is this relationship concordant, meaning that in this country respondents who do not support a coup also support government policies to reduce inequality and vice versa. In the remaining six cases the association is inverse. In Mexico, Honduras, Colombia, Ecuador, Chile, and Argentina, respondents in favor of a coup also favor government policies to reduce inequality or, alternatively, respondents who do not support military intervention do not favor government action on inequality.

The relationship between support for a coup in the event of crime and market preferences is just as opaque. This relationship is statistically significant in ten cases, but only in four—Costa Rica, Panama, Paraguay, and Venezuela—is this association concordant, whereby those who would support a coup also proclaim strong market tendencies and vice versa.

When it comes to *mano dura* politics and market preferences, the relationship is clearer, but not necessarily in the direction we might expect. In seven countries, this association is statistically significant at the 10% level or better, but only in the case of Costa Rica is this association concordant. In Costa Rica, those who prefer governance with an iron fist also have a preference for market mechanisms, while those who support citizen participation in government also agree with a large state presence in the national economy. In contrast, in the Dominican Republic, Ecuador, Mexico, Nicaragua, Panama, and Peru, this relationship is opposite. Those with a preference for *mano dura* politics also show strong statist tendencies and vice versa. Similarly, no clear trend is evident from the relationship between *mano dura* politics and attitudes toward inequality across Latin America.

Only when we examine support for military intervention in the event of crime and support for *mano dura* politics can we observe an identifiable pattern. In every country this association is concordant, and in every case (bar Mexico) this relationship is statistically significant. Given our discussion in this section, this is not surprising. It seems that only in conjunction with such valence issues does a uniform pattern across the Latin American electorate emerge, and below we explore whether this is reflected among party supporters.

Ideology and Attitudes of Party Supporters

In the final stage of our exploration we apply the same logic of analysis but consider differences in attitudes among the supporters of prototypical left and prototypical right parties across Latin America. In a first step we explore the ideological and socioeconomic makeup of political parties based on the self-placement responses of individuals claiming to support "prototypical" parties on the left and right and then compare their attitudes toward equality, the economy, democratic norms, crime fighting and public security, and traditional values.

Table 2.1 displays the twenty cases of political parties under consideration. We select these cases in conjunction with recent work on typologies of political parties in Latin America. They are the cases on the left and right that represent more institutionalized parties like the Workers' Party (Partido dos Trabalhadores, or PT) in Brazil, the Socialist Party (Partido Socialista, or PS) in Chile, the Broad Front (Frente Amplio, or FA) in Uruguay, the National Action Party (Partido Acción Nacional, or PAN) in Mexico, and the Conservative Party (Partido Conservador de Colombia, or PCC) in Colombia; parties that represent electoral populist vehicles such as Force 2011 (Fuerza 2011) in Peru and to a certain extent the United Socialist Party of Venezuela (Partido Socialista Unido de Venezuela, or PSUV) in Venezuela and the Republican Proposal (Propuesta Republicana, or PRO) in Argentina; parties with a revolutionary legacy such as the Farabundo Martí National Liberation Front (Frente Farabundo Martí para la Liberación Nacional, or FMLN) in El Salvador; parties with an authoritarian legacy such as the Independent Democratic

TABLE 2.1.
Paradigmatic cases of left and right parties

Country	Left parties	Right parties
Argentina	—	Propuesta Republicana (PRO)
Bolivia	Movimiento al Socialismo (MAS)	Poder Democrático y Social (PODEMOS)
Brazil	Partido dos Trabalhadores (PT)	—
Chile	Partido Socialista (PS)	Renovación Nacional (RN) Unión Demócrata Independiente (UDI)
Colombia	Polo Democrático Alternativo (PDA) Partido Social de Unidad Nacional (PU)	Partido Conservador de Colombia
El Salvador	Frente Farabundo Martí para la Liberación Nacional (FMLN)	Alianza Republicana Nacionalista (ARENA)
Mexico	Partido de la Revolución Democrática (PRD)	Partido Acción Nacional (PAN)
Peru	Partido Nacionalista Peruano (PNP)	Fuerza 2011
Uruguay	Frente Amplio (FA)	Partido Nacional (PN) Partido Colorado
Venezuela	Partido Socialista Unido de Venezuela (PSUV)	—

Union (Unión Demócrata Independiente, or UDI) in Chile or the Nationalist Republican Alliance (Alianza Republicana Nacionalista, or ARENA) in El Salvador; and also more recently emerging parties that are considered new political movements like the Movement for Socialism (Movimiento al Socialismo, or MAS) in Bolivia.[12]

We define party supporters as those who name a party on this list when responding to the 2010 LAPOP survey question, "Which political party do you identify with?" Using the self-placement scores of these respondents allows us to map the ideological profiles of our nine left-leaning and eleven right-leaning political parties identified as paradigmatic cases. Figure 2.6 contrasts two area plots corresponding to left and right parties and displays the percentage of respondents in the different ideological groups of left, center-left, center, center-right, and right by political party. We again show the percentage of respondents that we define as the group of undeclared.

Although we will analytically engage with these ideological profiles throughout the analysis of party supporters' attitudes, there are a number of interesting features we want to highlight at this point. The overall impression is that left parties can rely on an ideologically broader constituency. With the exception of the Alternative Democratic Pole (Polo Democrático Alternativo, or PDA) in Colombia, left-of-center parties are able to draw on supporters from each ideological group and from respondents who do

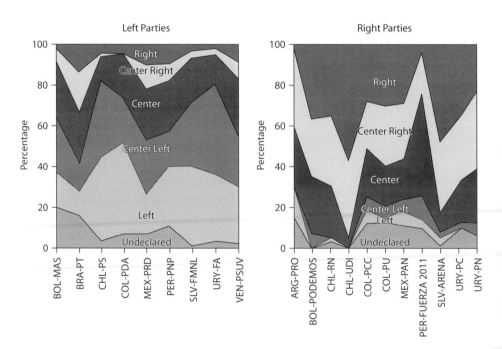

Figure 2.6. Ideological profiles of left and right parties.

not declare any ideological preference. Good examples are MAS in Bolivia and PT in Brazil. Perhaps contrary to what we might expect, the group of supporters of parties identifying with the extreme left is rather small, and certainly smaller than the group of supporters either from the center or drawn from respondents with no ideological affiliation.[13] In particular, PT is also able to engage a significant portion of right-leaning supporters (13%), and even PSUV in Venezuela showcases an important number of conservative voters (7.5%). In contrast, PS (Chile), PDA (Colombia), and FA (Uruguay) rely primarily on supporters emanating from the left and center-left.

For the political right in Latin America, however, the picture is quite different. Seven out of eleven parties show a narrow ideological composition of support that excludes either one or two ideological groups; that is, the left, the center-left, or both. In addition, three parties do not seem to appeal at all, or in a rather limited way, to respondents we defined as the group of undeclared. Given that the results from above show that respondents without any ideological preference predominantly have a closer affinity toward leftist attitudes, this is no surprise. Such parties then have to rely more heavily on the other segments of society. UDI in Chile and ARENA in El Salvador, for example, both draw the vast majority of support from respondents identifying with center-right and extreme right positions on the ideological scale. Of UDI supporters, 56% identify with the extreme right, and ARENA attracts 46% from this ideological group. In the remaining cases with more limited ideological support— that is, both Uruguayan parties (Partido Colorado, or PC, and the Partido Nacional, or PN); the Poder Democrático y Social (PODEMOS) in Bolivia; and National Renewal (Renovación Nacional, or RN), in Chile—a large contingent of party adherents is drawn from the center. A case that stands out within this group of right parties with a rather narrow base is certainly PRO in Argentina since it is the only right-of-center party without any supporters from the extreme right, yet it attracts respondents from the extreme left and a significant number of undeclared (15%).

There are only four parties on the right in our sample of paradigmatic cases that can rely on a broader, mixed ideological base. PCC and the Partido Social de Unidad Nacional (PU; Colombia), PAN (Mexico), and Fuerza 2011 (Peru) attract not only supporters from each of the five ideological groups, but also respondents who do not place themselves on the left-right ideological scale. Of these parties, Fuerza 2011 stands out where 51% of party supporters identify with the political center. As indicated in the following analysis of supporters' attitudes, these parties are all located in countries where the issues of crime and security are high on the political agenda.

The socioeconomic profiles of our selected cases, in turn, are not as clear-cut among the ideological camps. No discernible trends are visible for left parties in relation to right parties regarding education or how party supporters spend their time; that is, whether they are workers, students, or retirees. Regarding occupation, unsurprisingly, parties on the left by and large have more supporters who are public employees, fewer supporters who are self-employed, and a vanishingly low number of supporters who are either owners or partners in a business or unpaid workers. The biggest exceptions are without a doubt MAS in Bolivia, with 69% self-employed supporters, and the Partido Nacionalista Peruano (PNP) in Peru with 60% self-employed supporters. It comes equally as no surprise that parties on the right draw much less support from employees in the public sector, have on average more support from respondents who state that they are self-employed, and feature far more adherents who are owners or partners in business. Owing to space limitations, we refrain from showing the results here.[14]

More interesting, however, are the profiles for income even though it is difficult to uncover an unambiguous trend. Figure 2.7 shows the income profiles of our paradigmatic cases, which are based on respondents' answers regarding their total monthly household income. On average, the political left appears to draw more support among the lower five deciles and unsurprisingly also shows support among respondents with no income. Right parties, however, seem to rely more on support coming from the upper five deciles. Only one party on the right, PAN in Mexico, attracts support from those without any income.

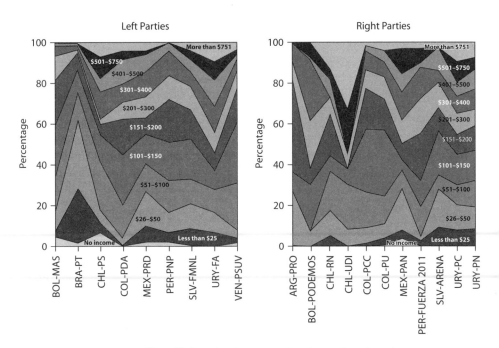

Figure 2.7. Income profiles of left and right parties. Deciles are based on the currency and distribution of the country.

Probably more than anything, figure 2.7 highlights country dynamics. On the left, MAS in Bolivia, despite missing support from the upper two deciles, shows the most equalized presence of income groups. The case most similar to this is PNP in Peru. On the contrary, with more than 90%, PT in Brazil relies heavily on the support of the lower five deciles, whereas the upper five deciles are either negligible or not represented. PS in Chile and FA in Uruguay are the only parties on the left that draw substantive support from the wealthiest deciles. In comparison, PDA in Colombia and PSUV in Venezuela rely much more on the middle-income groups, and in both cases the least wealthy constitute only a small portion of supporters.

The income profiles of the political right are equally diverse. As with the ideological profile, UDI in Chile stands out. About half of UDI's party adherents come from the very wealthy in the upper two deciles, and it relies on negligible support from the middle-income classes and substantive support from low-income earners. Together, the ideological and the income profile of this party echo Luna (2010), who shows that UDI has adapted a dual electoral strategy, engaging on the one hand with the conservative, wealthy upper strata, and with the more popular sectors of Chilean society on the other.[15] The only party that comes close to showing a profile that allows for this type of multiclass coalition, essentially bypassing the middle class, is PAN in Mexico. Comparing RN to UDI shows that the former party relies much more on the lower deciles and middle-income earners than the latter party. Comparing PC and PN in Uruguay, however, shows that although their occupational profiles differed, both parties feature surprisingly similar income profiles and are able to fall back on party adherents from every decile to an almost equal degree. Conversely, PRO (Argentina) and PODEMOS (Bolivia) show a rather narrow constituency in economic terms, as both parties do not attract adherents from the upper strata with some of the high-income deciles not being represented. Finally, in Colombia, both right parties, PCC and PU, show similar income profiles and attract in that sense similar supporters. This contrasts nicely with the left party, PDA, which receives more support from wealthy strata. In this case, parties on the left and on the right clearly cater to different economic segments of society.

With these profiles of parties on the left and the right in mind, similar to our analysis of citizens across Latin America, we turn now to the examination of different attitudes and characteristics that exist among party supporters, and again we highlight questions from the 2010 LAPOP survey that capture our defining dimensions of interest and identify the potential for electoral appeals of the right. For each question that we analyze, we take the average score of all those who stated they identified with a particular political party, thus providing us with a mean score for each party for each issue in question and thereby capturing the composition of the party's electoral base.

Figure 2.8 demonstrates this exercise for our core definition of the left-right divide centered on the role of the state regarding welfare provision and inequality. The solid vertical line represents the mean response of the entire sample of party supporters to the statement that the government should implement policy to reduce income inequality, while the dashed vertical line represents the mean response to the assertion that the government, as opposed to individuals, should be responsible for welfare provision.

Several points stand out. Again, differences seem to be rather weak, although compared to their left-leaning counterparts, supporters of rightwing political parties tend to disagree with government responsibility for welfare provision or inequality reduction. Also, supporters of the three left-leaning political parties—MAS in Bolivia, PNP in Peru, and PT in Brazil—exhibit rather conservative positions on the role of the government with respect to welfare provision. This can be partly explained by the ideological profile of their voters (fig. 2.7). For example, PT draws support from a large number of the center and center-right, as does PNP. As high-lighted above, however, support for MAS is much more diverse and also character-ized by a small group on the center-right, large swathes in the center, and those with an undeclared ideology who tended to identify more with left attitudes on these questions. Equally, the positions of the right-leaning parties can be explained by the ideological composition of their constituency. Note the large number of supporters

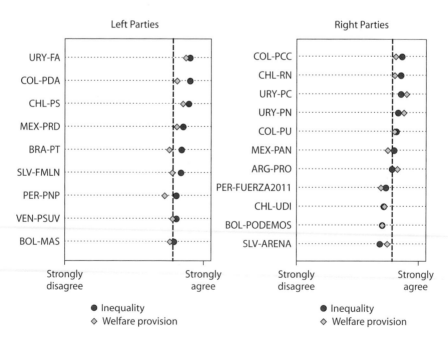

Figure 2.8. Parties reporting to what extent government should be responsible for welfare and income inequality.

on the extreme right in the ideological profile of ARENA (El Salvador), PODEMOS (Bolivia), and UDI (Chile). It is no surprise that supporters of FA in Uruguay strongly favor active state involvement to overcome inequalities, given that the vast majority of its support is drawn from the left and center-left. Finally, we also observe clear country clusters on these dimensions as opposed to a discernible cross-regional distinction between left and right. All party supporters in Colombia, for instance, regardless of their ideological stance, have positions on inequality that lean toward government responsibility. Likewise, supporters of the Uruguayan right- and leftwing parties have moderate positions on inequality, as do their counterparts in Mexico.[16]

Clear distinguishing features for party supporters of both ideological camps emerge when we examine attitudes toward the exercise of power.[17] Figure 2.9 captures the position of the party supporters with respect to two questions from the LAPOP survey that embody attitudes toward the exercise of political power. The first question represents the preference for a strong leader who does not have to be elected. The second question is more specifically related to the implementation of executive power and asks whether the country is in need of a decisive government ruling with an iron fist or whether problems can be resolved with everyone's participation.

Contrasting these two questions reveals interesting results, further strengthening our discussion of results for the general public in the previous section As figure 2.9 shows, the vast majority of the electorate has a preference for democratic elections

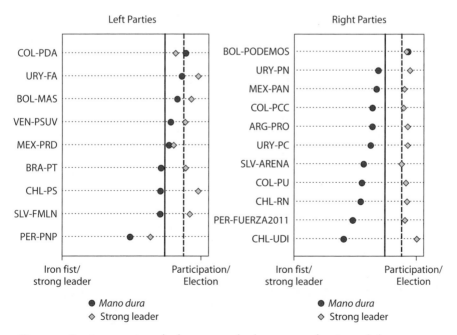

Figure 2.9. Parties reporting whether a strong leader or *mano dura* is needed.

over an unelected strong leader. In fact, three left-leaning political parties—the Party of the Democratic Revolution (Partido de la Revolución Democrática, or PRD; Mexico), PDA (Colombia), and PNP (Peru)—stray across the mean line and trend toward the authoritarian end of the spectrum. When it comes to the exercise of power, however, clear differences emerge between left and right party supporters. All of the right-wing adherents, except for supporters of PODEMOS in Bolivia, have clear preferences for *mano dura*, and although four leftwing parties lean toward the *mano dura* side of the solid line indicating the mean of all respondents to this question, only Humala's nationalistic PNP party displays a significant deviation from the mean. This pattern is in line with results regarding democratic activism of party supporters showing that adherents of our paradigmatic left parties are far more likely to have engaged in protest activity than the supporters of the right parties in our sample.[18] It not only echoes findings for the general public, but also shows major divergences between left and right party supporters regarding the value of participation in democracy.

This manifested distinction between left and right party supporters regarding the exercise of political power is also reflected in attitudes toward issues of crime and public security, albeit to varying degrees. The strongest disagreement between adherents of left and right parties is revealed when it comes to support of a military coup first in the event of an economic crisis and second when crime levels rise. As figure 2.10 shows, overall the Latin American electorate of our paradigmatic cases of left and right parties gives far more support to a coup in the event of crime as opposed to an economic crisis. In the latter case, the means of only two left parties, PRD in Mexico and PNP in Peru, can be found on the coup side of the dotted line indicating the sample mean for this question. In the case of PRD, part of the explanation lies with its ideological profile, attracting support from the center, center-right, and right. Again, both PRD and PNP are the only left-leaning parties whose members believe a military coup would be justified in the event of crime, and when examined in conjunction with their right-leaning counterparts, they reveal clear country dynamics. The vast majority of supporters of our paradigmatic right parties support military intervention when faced with increasing crime. Again, Mexico stands out with the mean of PAN supporters showing the greatest distance from the solid line indicating the sample mean. In general, however, party supporters on the right—with the exception of UDI voters in Chile, PRO voters in Argentina, and PODEMOS voters in Bolivia—are on the coup side of the mean line in the event of crime. These patterns are not surprising given that adherents of rightwing parties have far higher levels of trust in the armed forces of their state than their left-leaning counterparts.[19] Overall, then, and relating to our findings for attitudes of the general public from the previous section, the political right may attract electoral support for *mano dura* politics, provided it abides to the democratic rules of the game.

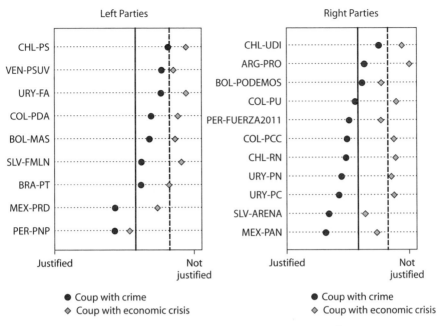

Figure 2.10. Parties reporting whether crime or economic crisis justifies a coup.

The political right in Latin America may be able to foster electoral strategies and appeals that exploit these differences when espousing policy proposals that involve an increased emphasis on the role of the state in handling valence issues such as crime and security.[20]

Conclusion

Throughout the Latin American region, individuals ideologically on the right and supporters of right-leaning political parties tend to conceive of inequality as the manifestation of individual action, prefer less government intervention in the national economy to address this imbalance, favor conservative positions on traditional social issues, and display authoritarian tendencies when it comes to the exercise of political power. Although these are unifying themes in terms of attitudes among the right, our exploration also indicates the existence of different types of right-of-center parties in terms of their ideological and socioeconomic profiles. Some political parties, such as UDI in Chile, have narrow ideological constituencies but can still mobilize cross-class coalitions, while others with broader ideological constituencies, such as PCC or PU in Colombia, draw their support from rather narrow economic groups. These findings seem to highlight, above all, country idiosyncrasies when it comes to forging electoral support along these lines.

Despite this variation among right-leaning parties, however, an increasingly salient issue that unites party supporters appears to be their disposition toward crime and *mano dura* politics. Supporters of right-of-center parties are far more likely to favor *mano dura* politics, particularly in relation to public security, and more repressive measures to deal with crime. It appears that the right is more credible and capable than the left of addressing societal challenges of public security attracting adherents concerned with these issues.

Yet, given that the Latin American electorate, irrespective of their ideology, considers crime as one of the most serious issues facing the region today, the ability of the right to exploit such topics for future electoral campaigns seems crucial. In fact, there does not appear to be any clear relationship between voter attitudes toward crime and preferences for state intervention, suggesting that threats to public security and crime prevention are valence issues that cut across ideological cleavages and are thus orthogonal to the left-right divide. The parties of the right therefore have an opportunity not only to woo supporters of left-leaning parties with visions of public order and strong leadership, but also to appeal to those in the electorate who do not declare any ideological stance.

This opportunity is pertinent for the future electoral health of the right, particularly in light of the stability of ideological trends at the mass level over time. For those with an undeclared ideology, crime and delinquency are the most important problems facing the region today, and although the respondents who comprise this group share similar convictions to those on the left across a number of issues, when it comes to the exercise of power, the position of the undeclared citizen is similar to that of the right. The interaction of public insecurity and the attitude of undeclared voters toward the exercise of power potentially provides parties of the right with a solid foundation upon which to build electoral platforms that could appeal to this group.

In fact, right-leaning parties in the region are already adding issues related to crime to their political platforms. During the recent presidential elections in Peru, for instance, Keiko Fujimori centered her electoral campaign on public insecurity and crime, advocating a return to the *mano dura* politics of her father, Alberto Fujimori. Her electoral vehicle, Fuerza 2011, drew its support not only from all five ideological groups, but also from a large swathe of individuals with an undeclared ideology. Crime and public security are clearly issues that the right can exploit to overcome the general left-right cleavage, and to garner support beyond its core support base.

With regard to inequality, distinctions in attitudes and preferences between voters who self-identify as left and those who self-identify as right are not as clear-cut and prove to be more tenuous than expected. One reason may rest in specific country contexts, such as the absence of programmatically structured party systems, which our exploration is ill equipped to deal with. Of course, it may also be partly a product of the limitations of the survey instrument. Research has shown that the Latin American public comprehends, and can relate to, the labels "left" and "right" in terms of a distinction along an ideal of equality.[21] But an understanding of the left-right distinction is in no way the same as revealing preferences on socially delicate, normative-laden questions, such as whether the government *should* implement policies to eliminate inequality. Therefore the results of our analysis should be interpreted with a modicum of caution, at least with regard to inequality.

APPENDIX

Survey Questions Used, LAPOP 2010*

These data were supplied by the Latin American Public Opinion Project (LAPOP) at Vanderbilt University, which takes no responsibility for any interpretation of the data (see table A2.1).

Most Serious Problem

A4. In your opinion, what is the most serious problem faced by the country?

The theoretical unpinning of inequality and translation into policy.

ROS2. The (country) government, more than individuals, should be the most responsible for ensuring the well-being of the people. To what extent do you agree (7) or disagree (1) with this statement?

ROS4. The (country) government should implement strong policies to reduce income inequality between the rich and poor. To what extent do you agree (7) or disagree (1) with this statement?

Democracy

DEM11. Do you think that our country needs a government with an iron fist, or that problems can be resolved with everyone's participation?

Iron fist (1); participation for all (2); did not know (88); did not answer (98).

AUT1. There are people who say that we need a strong leader who does not have to be elected by the vote of the people. Others say that although things may not work, electoral democracy, or the popular vote, is always best. What do you think?

We need a strong leader who does not have to be elected (1); electoral democracy is the best (2); did not know (88); did not answer (98).

Crime and Public Security

JC10. Some people say that under some circumstances it would justified for the military of this country to take power by a coup d'état. In your opinion would a military coup be justified when there is a lot of crime?

A military takeover of the state would be justified (1); a military takeover of the state would not be justified (2); did not know (88); did not answer (98).

*LAPOP 2010. AmericasBarometer, www.lapopsurveys.org.

TABLE A2.1.
Countries included in the analysis

Survey	Year/wave	Country	N
World Value Survey	Wave 2 (1990–92)	Argentina, Brazil, Chile, Mexico, Peru	5
	Wave 3 (1995–97)	Argentina, Brazil, Chile, Colombia, Dominican Republic, El Salvador, Mexico, Peru, Uruguay, Venezuela	10
	Wave 4 (1999–2001)	Argentina, Chile, Mexico, Peru, Venezuela	5
	Wave 5 (2005–8)	Argentina, Brazil, Chile, Colombia, Guatemala, Mexico, Peru, Uruguay	8
Latinobarómetro	1996–2004	Argentina, Bolivia, Brazil, Chile, Colombia, Costa Rica, Ecuador, El Salvador, Guatemala, Honduras, Mexico, Nicaragua, Panama, Paraguay, Peru, Venezuela	17
	2004–9	All of the above plus the Dominican Republic	18
AmericasBarometer	2006	Bolivia, Brazil, Chile, Colombia, Costa Rica, Dominican Republic, Ecuador, El Salvador, Guatemala, Honduras, Mexico, Nicaragua, Panama, Paraguay, Peru, Venezuela	17
	2008, 2010	All of the above plus Argentina	18

JC1. Some people say that under some circumstances it would justified for the military of this country to take power by a coup d'état. In your opinion would a military coup be justified when there is high unemployment?
A military takeover of the state would be justified (3); a military takeover of the state would not be justified (4); did not know (88); did not answer (98).

Traditional Values

D6. How strongly do you approve (10) or disapprove (1) that same-sex couples have the right to marry?
PROT3. In the last twelve months, have you participated in a demonstration or protest march?
Yes (1); no (2); did not know (88); did not answer (98).

Socioeconomic Questions

Q10. Into which of the following ranges does the total monthly income of this household fit, including remittances from abroad and the income of all the working adults and children?
No income (00); less than $25 (01); $26 to $50 (02); $51 to $100 (03); $101 to $150 (04); $151 to $200 (05); $201 to $300 (06); $301 to $400 (07); $401 to $500 (08); $501 to $750 (09); $751 or more (10); did not know (88); did not answer (98).

NOTES

1. See Luna and Rovira Kaltwasser, introduction, this volume, p. XX; Norberto Bobbio, *Left and Right: The Significance of a Political Distinction* (Polity: Chicago University Press, 1996); Detlef Jahn, "Conceptualizing Left and Right in Comparative Politics: Towards a Deductive Approach," *Party Politics* 17, no. 6 (2011): 745–65.

2. See Luna and Rovira Kaltwasser, introduction, this volume; Francisco Panizza, "Unarmed Utopia Revisited: The Resurgence of Left-of-Centre Politics in Latin America," *Political Studies* 54 (2005): 716–34; Nina Wiesehomeier and David Doyle, "Discontent and the Left Turn," *Political Science and Research Methods* (forthcoming).

3. For an overview, see Chalmers, María do Carmo Campello de Souza, and Atilio Boron, "Introduction: The Right and Latin American Democracies," in *The Right and Democracy in Latin America*, ed. Douglas A. Chalmers, María do Carmo Campello de Souza, and Atilio Boron, (New York: Praeger, 1992), 1–9; Edward Gibson, *Class and Conservative Parties: Argentina in Comparative Perspective* (Baltimore: John Hopkins University Press, 1992); Kevin J. Middlebrook, ed., *Conservative Parties, the Right, and Democracy in Latin America* (Baltimore: John Hopkins University Press, 2000).

4. See Jason Ross Arnold and David J. Samuels, "Evidence from Public Opinion," in *The Resurgence of the Latin American Left*, ed. Steven Levitsky and Kenneth M. Roberts (Baltimore: Johns Hopkins University Press, 2011), 31–52.

5. See Luna and Rovira Kaltwasser, introduction, this volume.

6. Results are not shown but are available upon request.

7. The low level of overall disagreement with this question is indicative of the importance placed upon the state across Latin America to generate employment, while the number of negative responses to the state enterprise question indicates the widespread support and acceptance of privatization across the region. See, for example, Andy Baker, "Why Is Trade Reform So Popular in Latin America? A Consumption-Based Theory of Trade Preferences," *World Politics* 55, no. 3 (2003): 423–55.

8. See William F. Stone and Laurence D. Smith, "Authoritarianism: Left and Right," in *Strength and Weakness: The Authoritarian Personality Today*, ed. William F. Stone, Gerda Lederer, and Richard Christie (New York: Springer-Verlag), 144–56.

9. Sebastián L. Mazzuca, "Access to Power versus Exercise of Power: Reconceptualizing the Quality of Democracy in Latin America," *Studies in Comparative and International Development* 45, no. 3 (2010): 334–57.

10. This is further reflected by the propensity of the electorate to give the government room to maneuver in crime fighting across all ideological camps. More than 40% of respondents in each group agree with the assertion that in order to catch criminals the authorities can occasionally cross the line. Results are available upon request.

11. We use the partial gamma coefficient, which is a weighted summary version of gamma. See Jens Lauritsen and Svend Kreiner, "PARTGAM: Stata Module to Calculate Partial Gamma Coefficient" (Statistical Software Components S377702, Department of Economics, Boston College, revised September 1, 2000).

12. For details, see Steven Levitsky and Kenneth Roberts, eds., *The Resurgence of the Latin American Left* (Baltimore: Johns Hopkins University Press, 2011); Luna and Rovira Kaltwasser, introduction, this volume.

13. See also Marco Morales, "Have Latin Americans Turned Left?," in *Leftovers: Tales of the Latin American Left,* ed. Jorge Castañeda and Marco Morales (New York: Routledge, 2008), 19–41.

14. We find some noteworthy cases, however. Although the percentage of the working population is roughly the same across ideological camps, two parties stand out: PRO in Argentina, with about 64%, and PC in Uruguay, with only 27% of supporters coming from the working population. In the latter case, about 40% of adherents are retired, a substantive amount. According to responses, among all cases, UDI in Chile is the only party without adherents in the student population, whereas PDA in Columbia features the most supporters from this group, with about 30%. Regarding education, the only general trend appreciable is that those without education tend to be drawn to left parties whereas the majority of right parties do not have uneducated adherents. However, PDA in Colombia echoes their high student population, with 55% of its supporters having more than twelve years of education. On the political right, UDI in Chile and Fuerza 2011 in Peru have the largest contingents of highly educated supporters (55% and 50%, respectively).

15. Juan Pablo Luna, "Segmented Party Voter Linkages in Latin America: The Case of the UDI," *Journal of Latin American Studies* 42 (2010): 325–56.

16. Such moderate positions on inequality can be partly explained by the rather centrist composition of the support of the right-leaning parties in these countries.

17. See Luna and Rovira Kaltwasser, introduction, this volume; Mazzuca (2010).

18. Results are not shown but are available upon request.

19. Ibid.

20. See Luna and Rovira Kaltwasser, introduction, this volume; Mazzuca (2010). Repeating our earlier exercise this time for left and right party supporters and again examining the relationship among the responses given to the different categories, we observe that there is no clear relationship between crime and *mano dura* politics and preferences for state intervention across either the left or the right. Again, only when it comes to the association between *mano dura* and crime does a uniform pattern emerge. We observe a clearly concordant and statistically significant relationship among those who support left parties (0.353; where $p < 0.01$) and those who support right parties (0.249; where $p < 0.01$).

21. See Wiesehomeier and Doyle (2012); Elizabeth Zechmeister, "What's Left and Who's Right? A Q-Method Study of Individual and Contextual Influences on the Meaning of Ideological Labels," *Political Behavior* 28, no. 2 (2006):151–73.

PART TWO

THE NONELECTORAL RIGHT

CHAPTER THREE

New Strategies of the Latin American Right

Beyond Parties and Elections

KENT EATON

Dominated by the rise of the left, the opening years of the twenty-first century have been a difficult time for the right in Latin America. Not only have electoral victories propelled the left into power in most countries, but also leftist parties and politicians have sought to use their control of the state to advance significant new attempts at redistribution. According to the definitions established by Juan Pablo Luna and Cristóbal Rovira Kaltwasser in their introduction to this volume, these attempts conflict directly with the right's defining position on socioeconomic inequality. Just as worrisome for the right, the left's margin of victory in many electoral contests since 2000 has been wide, including in the landslide reelections of Presidents Hugo Chávez (2000, 2006, and 2012), Rafael Correa (2009 and 2013), Lula da Silva (2006), Evo Morales (2009), and Cristina Kirchner (2011). The size of these victories underscores the urgency of the party-building efforts that are examined elsewhere in this volume and the significant challenges that these efforts are likely to face going forward. In a further threat to the right, the shift to the left in several countries has also been accompanied—if not produced—by the historic mobilization of indigenous communities with deep socioeconomic grievances. Finally, not only has the left won so many recent elections so handily, but it has also been fortunate to govern during a commodity boom that has given these governments significantly more room to pursue redistribution than was often the case for earlier leftist governments.[1]

All of this comes as a departure from the political climate of the 1990s, when the triumph of neoliberal economics made it seem that democracy was safe for the right and that the right might not even need strong conservative parties to continue supporting the democratic game.[2] A major study of the right in the late 1990s identified the right's successful participation in "neoliberal policy coalitions" as a phenomenon that reduced the importance of its general inability to establish strong parties.[3] If the last decade of the twentieth century was reassuring to socioeconomic elites, then the first decade of the twenty-first century has been anything but.[4] How is the right responding when it now has good reason to conclude that pursuing its preferred policies will be difficult in national political systems that are dominated by the left?

To make matters worse for the right, many of the strategies other than party building on which it traditionally relied to promote its interests (considered in greater detail below) are no longer quite so reliable. For example, the collapse of domestic and international support for military rule means that the armed forces are unlikely to intervene in ways that formerly protected the interests of the right. Whereas the Catholic Church historically operated as a pillar of support for rule by socioeconomic elites, it is now a much more heterogeneous organization, even despite the setbacks faced by progressive Catholics within its hierarchy during and after the papacy of John Paul II. Turning to interest mediation, the erosion of corporatism in Latin America signifies the decaying of institutional arrangements that foreclosed more radical demands from labor while simultaneously guaranteeing the regularized participation of business groups in decision making. Clientelism is alive and well in Latin America, but the recent adoption of conditional cash transfers and other social safety nets has reduced the vulnerability of the marginalized populations that were historically targeted by clientelistic politicians on the right.[5]

The decline of old strategies coupled with the rise of new threats has triggered an intense search for new approaches by the right in Latin America, many of which go significantly beyond parties and elections. That the right is serious about nonpartisan strategies is nothing new in the region. As Atilio Borón reminds us, "in the majority of democratic capitalisms, dominant classes have managed to hold power without the help of a conservative party."[6] While the right's nonpartisan and nonelectoral strategies have always been important in Latin America, the content of these strategies appears to have shifted in the last decade in response to the content of the new challenges that it now faces.

In this chapter, I conceptualize and illustrate three types of nonpartisan and nonelectoral strategies that the right has embraced in recent years: (1) strategies that target state institutions, (2) strategies that focus on civil society, and (3) strategies that emphasize the importance of identity formation. Critical state-centered strategies include attempts to defend liberal representative institutions from the more direct forms of democracy that have proliferated recently under left governments, as well as efforts to defend subnational institutions, many of which the right continues to control despite the national left turn. Civil society also remains an important arena for the right, and not just because of the conservative think tanks and media outlets that scholars have emphasized in the past. In one of the most important developments of the last decade, the right has increasingly come to mimic the kinds of civil society behaviors typically associated with the left—sponsoring social movements, participating in protests and blockades, and coordinating other forms of direct action. In an even deeper fashion, the right has also waded into the politics of identity formation. Given the reality that it will likely lose when conflicts unfold along class lines, the right can and does engage in efforts to deemphasize class conflict and to shift the terms of struggle toward territorial and sectoral identities, political frames that give it a much better chance of success against the left.

Rather than conduct a comprehensive survey across the region, I focus in this chapter on strategies the right has adopted in countries where the left has pursued a radical or contestatory approach rather than a more moderate or incrementalist approach.[7] The challenges that the right faces have been particularly acute in the former set of countries, which I define to include Argentina, Bolivia, Ecuador, and Venezuela. The significance of the threats facing the right in this set of cases makes these countries particularly important for the broader question of how the right has innovated in its search for effective strategies in an era of left dominance.

Traditional Nonpartisan Strategies of the Right

Although the establishment of successful conservative parties has often been a fraught enterprise for the right in Latin America, a number of nonpartisan strategies served in the past as partial substitutes for or complements to party building. The dominant strategy was to make up for the lack of electoral and partisan strength by linking up with powerful institutional and organizational allies, starting with the armed forces.

Particularly after the expansion in the size of urban popular sectors in the early twentieth century, the right was often able to secure military intervention in politics in order to prevent civilian politicians from using the state for redistributive purposes.[8] This was just as important in the countryside, where the opposition of landed elites to agrarian reform in the 1960s and 1970s helped trigger direct military rule in such countries as Argentina, Brazil, and Chile. Subsequently, a combination of factors—including experiences with state-sponsored terrorism by military governments, the end of the Cold War, and the unpredictability of military rule—made direct military governments either far less appealing or far less politically viable for the right. Military-led governments were an important strategy for the right, but they were not the only means through which the military could be used to further its interests. In less visible ways, so long as the military was guided by a national security doctrine that criminalized protest activity, much of which was driven by demands for socioeconomic equality, diffuse military repression of dissent bolstered the right. Also, in some countries, foremost among them Colombia, the right could best defend its interests by turning for protection not to military institutions or military-led rule, but to a range of paramilitary actors instead.[9]

The Catholic Church has been another important partner. Political struggles over the status of the Church in the nineteenth century help explain which countries developed strong conservative parties in Latin America.[10] But even in countries that did not develop such parties, through a number of mechanisms the Church figured prominently in attempts by the right to defend its interests. At the level of doctrine, Catholicism emphasized hierarchical values, charity as the appropriate response to deprivation, and the idea of recompense in the afterlife. Organizationally, the Church was an important component of the "holy trinity" that dominated rural life in much of Latin America; the defense of the status quo by far-flung resident priests enabled landowners to live absentee lifestyles and obviated the need for elites to finance more vigorous forms of state penetration.[11] Beyond dogma and the holy trinity, the Church was also a major landowner, with material reasons of its own to oppose the most potentially significant equity-enhancing proposal of the nineteenth and twentieth centuries: land reform. More recently, the Church has become less useful as an ally for the right, both in economic and social policy dimensions. Internal transformations (i.e., Vatican II) along with external competition (i.e., from Protestantism) have deepened the Church's critique of socioeconomic inequalities and forced it to be more responsive to marginalized communities.[12] With respect to social policy, the Church's failure to stand up to egregious human rights abuses under military rule has weakened its veto power relative to a range of progressive changes from divorce law to same-sex marriage.[13]

Business chambers and associations have also played important roles in the right's traditional strategic orientation. Although some businesses certainly benefited from twentieth-century redistributive reforms that expanded local demand and the size of domestic markets, business as a political actor more often shared with the right a hostility to redistribution and a disinterest in using the state to root out entrenched inequalities. Business organizations were useful to the right both when they were organized "from above" into corporatist structures (i.e., chambers of production and commerce) that had the core purpose of keeping labor in check, and when they developed on their own in a more pluralistic fashion. With respect to corporatist institutions, even when they issued from reformers who were embattled with the right, corporatism as a fundamentally top-down dynamic appealed to important figures on the right who worried deeply in the first half of the twentieth century about Latin America's "social question" and the possibility of revolutionary outcomes. The right also benefited from the creation of a variety of business associations outside the state. Although the scope of most of these organizations was limited to specific sectors, the periodic emergence of more profound threats to private property rights often had the effect of producing more powerful umbrella-wide associations that bridged sectoral differences.[14]

Like corporatism, clientelism can be understood as an extension of material benefits in exchange for independent political voice.[15] As such, clientelism has been a major boon to the right and helps explain Latin America's otherwise puzzling status as the developing region with both the highest levels of inequality and also the lengthiest experience with elections. Thanks to the strength of patron-client relations in the countryside, the extension of the suffrage through the removal of property qualifications and literacy requirements was not always threatening to the right, or incompatible with its ability to defend core interests. In many Latin American countries, clientelism was central to the emergence of conservative parties and therefore cannot be strictly understood as a "nonpartisan" strategy.[16] But clientelism also benefitted the right even when it did not contribute directly to conservative party building. Although clientelistic benefits can perhaps be used to finance certain forms of contentious politics,[17] clientelism more often led marginalized voters to sell votes they might otherwise have cast for politicians with a record of pursuing egalitarian reforms. Against this backdrop, the introduction of conditional cash transfer programs is important not just for their apparently positive impact on social indicators, but also because they appear to offer a form of protection from clientelism—provided they can be insulated from the discretionary interventions of politicians. If successful, the proliferation of these programs and the strengthening of social safety nets more generally pose a potentially frontal challenge to the tool kit the right has traditionally relied upon in Latin America.

Institutional Strengthening, Civil Society Participation, and Identity Formation

The decline in the utility of the right's traditional nonpartisan strategies, as described above, is due not to temporary developments but rather to longer-standing and in some cases structural changes. In the same fashion, the right can have little hope that the new threats it faces in the region are likely to dissipate anytime soon. According to new literature that seeks to explain the left turn, the widespread election of leftist parties was a response to the institutionalization of electoral competition,[18] worsening levels of social inequality,[19] and leftist municipal experiments facilitated by decentralization that were then scaled up to the national level.[20] In the words of Luis Reygadas and Fernando Filgueira, the left turn can be understood as a response to nothing less than the region's "second crisis of incorporation."[21] In those numerous Latin American countries where the right has yet to build successful conservative parties, history offers sobering lessons about how it might respond to the left's recent gains in the electoral arena. According to Middlebrook's study,[22] a history of past organizational strength was the critical factor in explaining whether the right in the 1990s was successful in its party-building efforts. If the absence of a successful conservative party in the past is a major constraint on the ability to produce one now, the right has had to get creative by diversifying its strategies well beyond party building.

State-Centered Strategies

Institutions have historically been important to the right, both under the guise of state institutions like the armed forces and institutional practices like clientelism and corporatism that either enabled it to control decision-making institutions within the state or ensured that these could not be used to subvert its core interests. More recently, an additional state-centered strategy for the right has been to rely on technocrats, who have often used their unelected positions within state institutions to oppose redistributive proposals and thereby to advance the right's core views on socioeconomic inequality. The 1990s saw the emergence of a new breed of technocrats, identified by Jorge Dominguez as "technopols," who vigorously engaged in political life and partisan struggles and who even won elections in their attempt to lead the transition from "the fat to the fit state."[23] Trained in neoclassical economics and armed with doctorates from top US universities, technopols tended to view social expenditure as a threat to the paramount goal of price stability, and to interpret hyperinflation as an experience that harms the poor more than they are likely to benefit from statist policies of redistribution. Although right-leaning technocrats were predominant in the 1990s, the recent turn to the left exposes the fundamental vulnerability for the right of this strategy, which depends on the appointment prerogatives of national governments that are now almost entirely controlled by parties on the left. Furthermore, Rafael Correa's experiment with "techno-populism" in Ecuador[24] suggests that the right has no monopoly on technocracy or technocratic argument.

Rather than abandon all institutional strategies in response to signs that its established institutional strategies have become less useful, the right has instead set its sights on other institutional arenas. For instance, now that it cannot hope that the military will dismiss leftist governments or that technocrats will veto redistributive proposals, the right has sought to defend the institutional roles played by those parts of the state where it still does have a presence—chiefly, legislative bodies and subnational governments.

The examination of recent struggles between left and right in Latin America reveals a deepening conflict between two different models of democracy. Whereas the left has articulated the case for more direct, participatory, and radical forms of democracy (through the creation of new local bodies that are typically tied to the president at the center), the right has often sought to defend liberal representative institutions by trying to protect the constitutional roles played by elected legislatures. For example, the right has argued in Venezuela that Chávez's Bolivarian circles, communal councils, and communes are all at odds with his own 1999 constitution because they transfer resources and authority from elected to unelected bodies.[25] According to the right's analysis, it may well lose most elections to Chavista candidates, but it has even less opportunity to exercise influence within the circles, councils, and communes that Chávez has set up in his push toward a new "geometry of power."[26] In Bolivia, the rightwing opposition to Morales successfully lobbied for constitutional revisions in 2008 that simultaneously introduced a new set of elected legislatures at the departmental level, while reducing the governing authority of other nonelected regional bodies that the right feared would be controlled by the president's indigenous allies.[27] The right in Bolivia has also pushed to use more recent census data in order to redistribute seats from the western highlands to the eastern lowlands in the hopes of thereby boosting its representation in the national legislature. The fear of direct models of democracy can also be seen in Peru, where legislators on the right insisted on changes that reduced the participation of civil society actors relative to elected governmental representatives in the new participatory councils that were established in 2002.[28]

Attempts to use representative institutions as a horizontal check on leftist presidents do not constitute an entirely new strategy for the right in Latin America. Congress was central to efforts by landed elites in Colombia to gut agrarian reform proposals in the 1960s, for example; a similar story unfolded in Brazil, where landowners called in the military when the legislature proved insufficient as a brake on João Goulart's land reform measures. In Chile, a defense of congressional prerogatives was at the centerpiece of the right's attempt between 1970 and 1973 to resist the socioeconomic transformations proposed by Salvador Allende. In Argentina, transitions to democracy in 1973 and 1983 were accompanied by electoral reforms that worsened malapportionment by increasing the number of national legislators who are elected in sparsely populated and conservative provinces. While legislatures have previously been important to the right, that it can no longer so easily call on the military to intervene in response to the inadequacies of congress would presumably mean that there are now stronger reasons for the right to take legislative strengthening seriously. Still, a number of factors impose real constraints on this strategy, including the deep unpopularity of legislatures in most countries, hyperpresidentialist institutions, constitutional provisions for executive decree authority,[29] and the possibility that the right might not win enough legislative seats to make a real difference within those bodies.

If the left's new control over executive institutions has encouraged the right to pay renewed attention to legislative institutions, it has also elevated the potential significance of subnational institutions. Subnational governments can and do provide political shelter for actors on the right when they fail in national elections. This, too, is a strategy with an established pedigree. At the end of the nineteenth century, for example, conservatives in Chile supported decentralization in their battle with the liberal president Manuel Balmaceda; his successful move to expand the scope of the state prompted the beleaguered opposition in congress to strengthen municipal governments as a bulwark against an overweening central government.[30] One hundred years later, in the wake of Chile's 1990 transition to democracy, the right sought to bolster the regional administrative units that were created under Pinochet in the belief that it would not soon capture the national government, and in the expectation that it could win control over at least some regional governments.[31] While subnational governments in the past have been important as political spaces to which the right has retreated when confronted with an adverse national landscape, their utility to the right has extended beyond this strategy. In Brazil, for example, dominance of subnational governments, along with the significant fiscal resources that are controlled by state governors, has operated as one of the chief mechanisms through which the right has exerted influence in the national government.[32] In other words, rather than operating as a platform to which it could retreat when excluded from national institutions, for the Brazilian right, subnational governments have provided the very foundations of national rule. In the past, control over subnational governments has performed multiple functions for the right in Latin America, enabling it to govern in subnational spaces that are valuable to control in their own right, and enabling it to use these subnational spaces in the attempt to exert power nationally.

Thanks to decentralizing reforms that enhanced the stature of subnational governments in the 1980s and 1990s, these governments (both municipal and provincial/departmental) have become more appealing to the right, which helps explain why it has so aggressively opposed the recentralizing changes that several left presidents have been pursuing of late. Subnational governments are now critical for actors on the right, both for those who hope to use them as a toehold to launch national movements (i.e., Venezuela) and for those who want to pursue market-oriented projects in the territorial units that they control (i.e., Guayaquil in Ecuador, Santa Cruz in Bolivia). In the latter set of cases, the demand for territorial autonomy has been articulated as a proposal to sustain the more market-friendly policies that advocates claim are responsible for local economic successes—even as the left of center has turned strongly in the direction of statism. In this sense, the right's demand for territorial autonomy is a fundamentally liberal one, in sharp contrast to the postliberal demand for territorial autonomy that indigenous movements have articulated on the left.[33]

While disagreements over economic policy have driven the right's interest in subnational governments, subnational spaces are appealing not just for those who oppose the left's socioeconomic project but also for those who seek to implement or defend conservative social policies. Salient examples include Mayor Jaime Nebot of Guayaquil, who campaigned against Ecuador's 2009 constitution in part because he argued that it would open the door to abortion, and Panista governors in Mexico who used their control of state governments to impose punitive measures against sexual minorities and to refuse recognition of same-sex marriages celebrated elsewhere in the country.

Despite its appeal, the right's "subnational strategy" faces at least three major shortcomings. First, serious doubts exist about whether the control of subnational institutions will be enough to defend its core interests against national governments that are dominated by the left. On the one hand, subnational governments have been empowered by administrative and fiscal decentralization, which subnational officials on the right can use to do things like fire excess employees from the public sector or institute cuts in fees and taxes owed by businesses. On the other hand, the most important redistributive tools are still national and thus now typically controlled by left-leaning national governments, including individual and corporate income tax rates, land tenure and land titling institutions, and regulatory policies that can be used for redistributive ends. Although the right has sought to defend more market-friendly environments in select subnational jurisdictions, a "one country, two systems" arrangement thus may be untenable in the long run. Similar challenges face social conservatives. Mexico is a case in point, where the federal supreme court ruled in 2010 that states must respect same-sex marriages conducted in Mexico City.

Second, not only might the existing prerogatives of subnational government be insufficient to defend the right's core interests, it is also the case that these prerogatives may be reclaimed by the left politicians who now control the center. For example, Presidents Chávez, Correa, and Morales have been able to claw back for the national government some of the fiscal resources that were previously devolved to subnational governments, though the subnational right in Bolivia has also succeeded in defending and expanding departmental attributes. More generally, while the decentralizing policies that were adopted in the 1980s and 1990s have only infrequently been subject to formal reversal, the resurgence of the center in postdecentralization Latin America has nevertheless put subnational governments on the defensive in a number of dimensions, calling into question their significance as independent governing units.[34]

Third, bracketing concerns about whether the control of subnational governments might prove to be insufficient (now or in the future), the viability of this strategy depends on the ability of the right to actually win subnational elections. Although confidence that it could electorally dominate at least some important subset of subnational governments has animated the right's support for decentralization in the past, the same factors that have prevented the right from competing successfully with the left at the national level may also depress its electoral prospects at the subnational level. Nowhere is this more pronounced or politically significant than in Brazil, where Alfred Montero has documented electoral decline in the same subnational regions that previously served as the right's most dependable redoubt.[35]

Society-Centered Strategies

Holding on tight to those institutional spaces within the state where it continues to win elections despite the left turn (i.e., congress, mayoral and gubernatorial offices) has not prevented the right from also looking beyond the state and beyond institutions. In part because the institutional landscape looks so ominous for the right, it has expended considerable energy in the last decade devising society-centered strategies as well. Sensing the inadequacy or potential impermanence of its presence within legislative and subnational institutions, the right has embraced a number of distinct activities within civil society. While some of what the right has done in this field looks familiar—including the important sponsorship or ownership of foundations, research centers, and media outlets in the attempt to indirectly influence policy outcomes—in other dimensions it has innovated by beginning to borrow more directly from the left's repertoire of contentious politics.

As Kevin Middlebrook concluded for the 1990s, "economic and social elites often exercise more significant influence through privately financed schools and universities, conservative research centers, privately controlled mass communication and cultural institutions than they do through conservative parties."[36] This type of established civil society participation has remained significant in the years since 2000. Consider the key roles played by right-leaning foundations in one of Latin America's most important recent policy debates: the conflict over how to respond to the region's worsening security crisis. According to Claudio Fuentes,[37] growing insecurity has opened up a fissure within civil society between civil rights groups on the left that seek to advance thoroughgoing police reforms, and pro-order coalitions on the right that favor giving the police additional powers to fight crime. In Argentina, for example, the March 2004 kidnapping and death of Axel Blumberg led his father, Juan Carlos, to create the Fundación Axel Blumberg por la Vida de Nuestros Hijos, modeled after Rudolph Giuliani's Manhattan Institute. The foundation emerged as a major critic of police reform efforts, advocating instead for *mano dura* legislation that increased penalties for a series of crimes, imposed restrictions on the use of bail, and reduced the age (to fourteen) at which minors can be tried as adults.[38] A similar dynamic unfolded in Chile, where business executive Agustín Edwards responded to the kidnapping of his son by founding Paz Ciudadana, a pro-order foundation that favors punitive measures over police reform and maintains close relations with rightwing parties.[39]

Concentrated control of the media is another established practice that continues to redound to the right's benefit. As Sallie Hughes and Paola Prado argue, "mass media in most Latin American societies . . . are controlled by a small elite that uses the media's definitional power to further, consciously or unconsciously, a set of class- and family-based interests and ideologies that have helped maintain a status quo of social inequality."[40] Most Latin Americans get their news from broadcast media (radio and television) as opposed to newspapers, which feature greater ideological diversity but are restricted to a wealthier urban readership. In twelve of the sixteen countries studied by Hughes and Prado, just two television networks control over half of the national television market.[41] Lack of ownership diversity translates into tremendous influence for a handful of socioeconomic elites over which stories make the news and how they get reported.[42] In Mexico, owners of the two companies that control 92% of the television market (Televisa and TV Azteca) have successfully fought off reform attempts that would open up access to the broadcast spectrum. Though media control clearly remains an important tactic for the right, Philip Kitzberger argues that elite dominance has lately generated a credibility crisis for the media, particularly in countries marked by backlash against the neoliberal policies that worsened ownership concentration in broadcast media.[43] According to Kitzberger, this crisis has prompted leftist governments to engage in media activism through such practices as direct presidential broadcasts, mandatory airtime for educational programming, and the creation of new forms of state and grassroots media.

While the establishment and control of foundations and media outlets remain important society-centered strategies, the right has also come to embrace forms of participation in civil society that look decidedly leftist. Frustrated by the lack of formal voice that is reflected in its marginalized position within critical decision-making institutions, the right has sought to amplify its voice informally through a range of direct actions, including protests, mass rallies, hunger strikes, and work stoppages. In Argentina in 2008, for instance, opponents of Cristina Kirchner's attempt to finance enhanced state spending by raising taxes on agricultural exports engaged in a series of ultimately successful protests that interrupted the sale and delivery of grains and meat, paralyzing the country. The result was an effective use of the same instrument (road blockades) that had been popularized by the *piqueteros* just a few years before. According to Tasha Fairfield,[44] this rare but important phenomenon of business protest can be understood as an attempt by businesses to "defend their core interests when their structural power is weak and when they lack sources of instrumental power . . . like lobbying." The right has also organized mass rallies, as when Mayor Jaime Nebot brought forty thousand Guayaquileños into the streets on January 24, 2008, to protest Rafael Correa's drive for a new constitution that the mayor argued would scare away foreign investors. Mass rallies have also been organized against Evo Morales by opposition right governors in the four departments of the Bolivian lowlands, in addition to the hunger strikes, regional work stoppages, and acts of civil unrest that wracked Bolivia for much of 2008.[45]

Rather than understand these various episodes of direct action as random or unconnected, in some cases it makes sense to recognize that these actions are coalescing in the form of new social movements on the right.[46] Though scholars have mostly focused on progressive social movements in Latin America by subaltern people who are seeking to change the status quo, movements can also have more conservative goals, including attempts to block the redistributive projects that have followed from left electoral victories. The movements for autonomy in Santa Cruz, Bolivia, and Guayaquil, Ecuador, are two important cases in point. In both places, long-standing business organizations, charity leagues, and nonpartisan civic associations have joined ranks to sponsor coordinated forms of direct action, including signature-gathering campaigns, protests, and rallies designed to channel and articulate opposition to left-leaning national governments. While internal divisions and structural deficits have weakened the Guayaquil movement, in Bolivia the autonomy movement succeeded in forcing Morales to grant a number of important constitutional concessions. More generally, social movements on the right face special opportunities and challenges. On the one hand, financing offered by business associations means that these movements are much better funded than their counterparts on the left. On the other hand, the special roles played by social and economic elites mean that the movements have significant perception problems to overcome before they can draw in nonelite supporters.[47]

Social movement formation on the right has unfolded within the confines of domestic political systems in several countries, but also in forms that are now beginning to span national borders. Just as transnational networks have emerged on the left between advocates of progressive change who have distinct national identities, right movements are building transnational networks as well. One potentially important development in this regard is the International Confederation for Regional Autonomy and Freedom (Confederación Internacional por la Libertad y Autonomía Regional, or CONFILAR). Created in Guayaquil at the end of a 2006 international conference on free enterprise and autonomy, CONFILAR brings together some of the most important national-level organizations active on this topic, including the Comité Cívico Pro-Santa Cruz in Bolivia, the Instituto de Libre Empresa in Peru, the Junta Cívica de Guayaquil in Ecuador, and the Rumbo Propio para Zulia in Venezuela. Through workshops, seminars, courses, and international conferences, CONFILAR hopes to build support for regional autonomy as a bulwark against the statist policies that have emanated from national governments. Pro-autonomy advocates in Guayaquil, for example, have used CONFILAR to network with Bolivian leaders like Rubén Costas (former head of the pro–Santa Cruz committee and subsequently the first elected governor of Santa Cruz), whose successes they hope to imitate. Transnational networking on the right has, in turn, provoked sharp reactions from Chávez, Correa, and Morales, who argue that this transnational network amounts to a new and problematic form of foreign intervention.

Identity Formation

According to the argument so far, the right has responded to the left turn by pursuing a mix of state- and society-centered strategies, some of which have been deployed before and some of which are newly appealing given the nature of the threats it is now facing. In an even more ambitious mode, the right has also pursued its preferred policies by engaging in deeper and ongoing projects of identity formation. Rather than target select state institutions or sponsor civil society organizations, here the strategy has been to engage in discursive and rhetorical practices that seek to transform political identities. As Mauricio Romero argues in a study that explains how elites in the Colombian region of Córdoba created an identity that supported paramilitary expansion,[48] elites in Latin America understand that "identity is not a pre-existing condition that exerts causal influence on collective action, but a changeable result of political interaction." Identity formation is a particularly important and contested arena for the right as it tries to fend off redistributive policies in a region marked by high levels of income inequality and large percentages of the population that live at or below the poverty line. In this context of inequality and poverty, elites realize that they are likely to lose when policy debates are framed in class terms. Those who are poor or economically struggling simply outnumber the rich by too great a margin. In response to attempts by left-leaning governments to frame their conflicts with the right in class terms, the right has often sought to reframe these conflicts as fundamentally territorial or sectoral in nature.

Attempts by the right to activate and accentuate territorial identities and thereby attenuate the socioeconomic or class dimensions of conflict can be clearly seen in the demands for territorial autonomy that have emerged in Bolivia and Ecuador. In Bolivia, the social and economic elites who have coordinated and bankrolled the movement for autonomy in the lowland *media luna* worry about the challenges that Morales's government poses to their control of natural resources, including not just gas and oil but also land. Specifically, property owners in Santa Cruz fear the redistribution of lands to Morales's supporters in a region that escaped the radical agrarian reforms of the 1950s. Given that many residents in Santa Cruz would stand to gain from redistribution, including recent migrants from the highlands, the leaders of this movement have had to work hard to reframe the conflict as one that pits a powerful but remote and neglectful central government against a local, authentic, and creditworthy local government. Beginning in 2005, the pro–Santa Cruz committee embarked on a public relations campaign celebrating *camba* (i.e., lowlander) identities and explaining that all who live in Santa Cruz are *cruceño*, and not just those who were born there.[49] Ecuador has witnessed a similar phenomenon, where the leaders of the autonomy movement routinely emphasize the threats that Correa poses to Guayaquil's unique identity, though this effort has been handicapped by the fact that Correa himself was born in the city. In the attempt to play down class and play up territorial identities, organizations funded by local businesses have financed new textbooks that ask school children in Guayaquil to reflect on what makes their city different from the rest of Ecuador, and special within the nation.

In addition to the territorial option embraced by the right in Bolivia and Ecuador, opponents of leftist governments can also seek to activate sectoral identities in their attempts to prevent redistribution. Like territorial affinities, sectoral affinities can also be used to weaken class affinities. The lengthy 2008 dispute over export tax increases in Argentina mentioned above is a case in point.[50] President Cristina Kirchner explicitly defended the proposal to increase export taxes as a measure that would enable her government to deepen a variety of income support programs for marginalized populations. In response to steadfast opposition to the measure by agricultural producers, Kirchner was quick to resurrect traditional Peronist rhetoric in dismissing her opponents as oligarchs seeking to preserve the wealth that they were able to amass only because of unusually favorable international commodity prices. When the protests by farmers deepened and spread across more of the country, Kirchner then sought to weaken the unity that had characterized the stance of the agricultural sector by using class as a wedge. Specifically, she proposed to lessen the burden of the tax on small- and medium-sized farmers in ways that would shift the entire burden onto larger and wealthier farmers. Kirchner's failure to do so (she was eventually forced to rescind the tax increase altogether) can be taken as a measure of the viability of strategies that emphasize sectoral over class identities.

Conclusion

Strategies that go beyond parties and elections have always been important to the Latin American right. According to the analysis presented in this chapter, however, the right has recently reassessed the relative importance it gives to specific kinds of nonpartisan and nonelectoral strategies. In the institutional realm, for example, actors like the armed forces and arrangements like corporatism are now less important to the right, which has instead responded to the left's commanding control of presidential offices and executive branch institutions by paying more attention to the defense of legislative and subnational institutions. In the societal realm, the right continues to invest intellectual and financial capital in foundations that seek to advance its preferred policy positions on a range of issues, but it has also embraced a more directly confrontational style of politics. Although hunger strikes, mass rallies, and road blockages are most closely associated with progressive groups on the left in Latin America and elsewhere, the right has shown repeatedly in the last decade that these actions can also be deployed effectively in the struggle against redistribution. At the discursive level, the right has also demonstrated a great deal of shrewdness in attempting to broaden support for its positions by directly contesting the class frame that leftist governments use in their battles with the right. Promoting the salience of territorial and sectoral identities that cut across class has emerged as a highly appealing strategy for the right in Latin America.

Having described the range of nonpartisan and nonelectoral strategies that currently animate the right in Latin America, a next research step might be to examine cross-national variation in the pursuit of these different strategies, and to ask whether this variation might be explained as a response to the different types of left-leaning governments that the right is confronting across the region. In the attempt to focus on strategies that are bold and innovative, this chapter privileged the study of what the right is doing in countries where the turn to the left has been the sharpest. Further research might compare the types of strategies that the right has adopted in these countries (Argentina, Bolivia, Ecuador, and Venezuela) with countries where new left governments have been less radical. In other words, how can the various typologies that scholars have recently proposed to understand Latin America's multiple left turns help us understand variation among the right? Using the terminology of Kurt Weyland, Raúl Madrid, and Wendy Hunter,[51] are more radical governments on the left triggering the adoption of more radical strategies on the right, including social movement sponsorship and direct forms of action? Has the right responded to less contestatory leftist experiments by placing greater emphasis on institutional strategies while eschewing contentious styles of politics? Does the concentration or dispersal of authority within the left-leaning parties that Steven Levitsky and Kenneth Roberts emphasize[52] have implications for how the right calculates its response? If, as Juan Pablo Luna argues,[53] we should focus on the level of societal constraints that either liberate or limit leftist governments, can we hypothesize that greater constraints on the left serve to ease the concerns of the right? Integrating in this way the study of the left turn and the right response could generate a promising research agenda.

NOTES

1. Javier Corrales and Michael Penfold, *The Dragon in the Tropics: Hugo Chávez and The Political Economy of Revolution in Venezuela* (Washington, DC: Brookings Institution Press, 2010); Kurt Weyland, "The Rise of Latin America's Two Lefts? Insights from Rentier State Theory," *Comparative Politics* 41, no. 2 (2009): 145–65.

2. For the important argument that conservative party strength has historically bolstered the right's support for democratic rule in Latin America, see Edward Gibson, *Class and Conservative Parties: Argentina in Comparative Perspective* (Baltimore: Johns Hopkins University Press, 1996).

3. Kevin J. Middlebrook, ed., *Conservative Parties, the Right, and Democracy in Latin America* (Baltimore: Johns Hopkins University Press, 2000).

4. Kevin Middlebrook's comments were prescient in this regard. Writing at the end of the 1990s, he noted that "the domestic and international conditions that reassured economic and social elites in late 20th century Latin America will not persist indefinitely," and estimated that "the most significant threat might be the political resurgence of historic opponents on the Left." "Introduction: Conservative Parties, Elite Representation, and Democracy in Latin America," in Middlebrook (2000, 1–50).

5. Alfred Montero, "A Reversal of Political Fortune: The Transitional Dynamics of Conservative Rule in the Brazilian Northeast," *Latin American Politics and Society* 54, no. 1 (2012): 1–36.

6. Atilio Borón, "Ruling without a Party: Argentine Dominant Classes in the Twentieth Century," in Middlebrook (2000, 139–63).

7. Steven Levitsky and Kenneth M. Roberts, eds., *The Resurgence of the Latin American Left* (Baltimore: Johns Hopkins University Press, 2011); Kurt Weyland, Raúl L. Madrid, and Wendy Hunter, eds., *Leftist Governments in Latin America: Successes and Shortcomings* (New York: Cambridge University Press, 2010).

8. In contrast, in some countries the right could not count on the military as an ally, and the armed forces were in fact its chief institutional enemy, as in Peru and Ecuador, where reformist militaries sought to advance socioeconomic reforms that directly targeted "oligarchic" interests.

9. Philip Mauceri, "States, Elites, and the Response to Insurgency: Some Preliminary Comparisons between Colombia and Peru," in *Politics in the Andes: Identity, Conflict, Reform*, ed. Jo-Marie Burt and Philip Mauceri (Pittsburgh, PA: University of Pittsburgh Press, 2004), 146–63.

10. Middlebrook (2000).

11. Osvaldo Hurtado, *Political Power in Ecuador* (Boulder, CO: Westview Press, 1985).

12. Frances Hagopian, "The Catholic Church in a Plural Latin America: Toward a New Research Agenda, in *Religious Pluralism, Democracy and the Catholic Church in Latin America*, ed. Frances Hagopian (Notre Dame, IN: University of Notre Dame Press, 2009), 429–66.

13. Mala Htun, *Sex and the State: Abortion, Divorce, and the Family under Latin American Dictatorships and Democracies* (New York: Cambridge University Press, 2003).

14. Jeffry Frieden, *Debt, Development, and Democracy: Modern Political Economy and Latin America* (Princeton, NJ: Princeton University Press, 1991); Ben Ross Schneider, *Business Politics and the State in Twentieth Century Latin America* (New York: Cambridge University Press, 2004).

15. Jonathan Fox, "The Difficult Transition from Clientelism to Citizenship: Lessons from Mexico," *World Politics* 46, no. 2 (1994): 151–84.

16. In these cases, Middlebrook (2000) uses the apt phrase "party-mediated clientelism."

17. Javier Auyero, Pablo Lapegna, and Fernanda Page Poma, "Patronage Politics and Contentious Collective Action: A Recursive Relationship," *Latin American Politics and Society* 51, no. 3 (2009): 1–31.

18. Mathew Cleary, "Explaining the Left's Resurgence," *Journal of Democracy* 17, no. 4 (2006): 35–49.

19. Evelyne Huber and Fred Holt, "Successes and Failures of Neoliberalism," *Latin American Research Review* 39, no. 3 (2004): 150–64; Kenneth Roberts, "The Mobilization of Opposition to Economic Liberalization," *Annual Review of Political Science* 11 (2008): 327–49.

20. Benjamin Goldfrank, *Deepening Local Democracy in Latin America: Participation, Decentralization and the Left* (University Park: Pennsylvania State University Press, 2011).

21. Luis Reygadas and Fernando Filgueira, "Inequality and the Incorporation Crisis: The Left's Social Policy Toolkit," in *Latin America's Left Turns*, ed. Maxwell Cameron and Eric Hershberg (Boulder, CO: Lynne Rienner, 2010), 173.

22. Middlebrook (2000). However, in a finding that challenges Middlebrook, James Loxton (chap. 5, this volume) demonstrates that some of the most vibrant conservative parties in Latin America today (i.e., Unión Demócrata Independiente in Chile and Alianza Republicana Nacionalista in El Salvador) are relatively new parties, forged during recent experiences with authoritarian rule and without nineteenth-century organizational precursors.

23. Jorge I. Domínguez, *Technopols, Freeing Politics and Markets in Latin America in the 1990s* (University Park: Pennsylvania State University Press, 1997), 29.

24. Carlos De la Torre, "El tecnopopulismo de Rafael Correa" (paper presented at the meeting of the Latin American Studies Association, Toronto, Canada, 2010).

25. At the same time, the anti-Chávez right boycotted the 2005 elections for the National Assembly, effectively abandoning that body to pro-Chávez actors.

26. Carlos Mascareño, "Descentralización, Recentralización y Sociedad Civil," in *Venezuela Vision Plural* (Caracas: Centro de Estudios del Desarrollo, 2005), 146–63.

27. Franz Barrios Suvelza, *Hacia un pacto territorial en Bolivia* (La Paz: United Nations Development Programme, 2008).

28. Stephanie McNulty, *Voice and Vote: Decentralization and Participation in Post-Fujimori Peru* (Stanford, CA: Stanford University Press, 2010).

29. John Carey and Matthew Shugart, *Executive Decree Authority* (New York: Cambridge University Press, 1998).

30. Kent Eaton, *Politics beyond the Capital: The Design of Subnational Institutions in South America* (Stanford, CA: Stanford University Press, 2004).

31. Gary Bland, "Enclaves and Elections: The Decision to Decentralize in Chile," in *Decentralization and Democracy in Latin America*, ed. David Samuels and Alfred Montero (Notre Dame, IN: University of Notre Dame Press, 2004), 94–121.

32. Frances Hagopian, *Traditional Politics and Regime Change in Brazil* (New York: Cambridge University Press, 1996); David Samuels, *Ambition, Federalism, and Legislative Politics in Brazil* (New York: Cambridge University Press, 2003); Alfred Montero, chapter 12, this volume.

33. Deborah Yashar, *Contesting Citizenship in Latin America: The Rise of Indigenous Movements and the Postliberal Challenge* (New York: Cambridge University Press, 2005).

34. Tyler Dickovick and Kent Eaton, "Latin America's Resurgent Center: National Government Strategies after Decentralization," *Journal of Development Studies* (forthcoming).

35. See chapter 12, this volume.

36. Middlebrook (2000, 290).

37. Claudio Fuentes, *Contesting the Iron Fist: Advocacy Networks and Police Violence in Democratic Argentina and Chile* (New York: Routledge, 2005).

38. Kent Eaton, "Paradoxes of Police Reform: Federalism, Parties, and Civil Society in Argentina's Public Security Crisis," *Latin American Research Review* 43, no. 3 (2008): 5–32.

39. Fuentes (2005, 75). Mexico may offer a similar example. According to Diane Davis, business-financed organizations such as the Citizens' Institute for the Study of Insecurity "are now working with some police departments in the Mexico City area to place greater restrictions on individual liberties." "Undermining the Rule of Law: Democratization and the Dark Side of Police Reform in Mexico," *Latin American Politics and Society* 48, no. 1 (2006): 78.

40. Sallie Hughes and Paola Prado, "Media Diversity and Social Inequality in Latin America," in *The Great Gap: Inequality and the Politics of Redistribution in Latin America*, ed. Merike Blofield (University Park: Pennsylvania State University Press, 2011), 109.

41. Ibid., 120.

42. Even in the case of greater ownership diversity, such as the eight broadcast television channels that have emerged in the Dominican Republic, homogeneous views among owners have prevented diversity in media content. Antonio Menéndez Alarcón, *Power and Television in Latin America: The Dominican Case* (Westport, CT: Praeger, 1992).

43. Philip Kitzberger, "The Media Activism of Latin America's Leftist Governments: Does Ideology Matter?," *GIGA Working Papers* 151 (2010): 5–36.

44. Tasha Fairfield, "Business Power and Protest: Argentina's Agricultural Producers Protest in Comparative Context," *Studies in Comparative International Development* 46, no. 4 (2011): 424–53.

45. For more on the right's nonpartisan strategies in Bolivia and Ecuador, see James D. Bowen, chapter 4, this volume.

46. For a study of "uncivil" movements on the right that seek to promote exclusionary policies, see Leigh Payne, *Uncivil Movements: The Armed Right Wing and Democracy in Latin America* (Baltimore: Johns Hopkins University Press, 2000).

47. Kent Eaton, "Conservative Autonomy Movements: Territorial Dimensions of Ideological Conflict in Bolivia and Ecuador," *Comparative Politics* 43, no. 3 (2011): 291–310.

48. Mauricio Romero, "Changing Identities and Contested Settings: Regional Elites and the Paramilitaries in Colombia," *International Journal of Politics, Culture and Society* 14, no. 1 (2000): 53.

49. In a move that likewise illustrates the attempt to reinforce territorial over class divisions, the Santa Cruz business federation broke with its class allies elsewhere in Bolivia by withdrawing from the national business confederation in 2004.

50. Fairfield (2011); Neal Richardson, "Export-Oriented Populism: Commodities and Coalitions in Argentina," *Studies in Comparative International Development* 44, no. 3 (2009): 228–55.

51. Weyland et al. (2010).

52. Levitsky and Roberts (2011).

53. Juan Pablo Luna, "The Left Turns: Why They Happened and How They Compare," in *Latin America's Left Turns: Politics, Policies and Trajectories of Change*, ed. Maxwell Cameron and Eric Hershberg (Boulder, CO: Lynne Rienner, 2010), 23–40.

CHAPTER FOUR

The Right and Nonparty Forms
of Representation and Participation

Bolivia and Ecuador Compared

JAMES D. BOWEN

Most studies of the right in Latin America focus on the representation of rightwing actors within formal political institutions, normally in the form of political parties. Less attention has been paid to alternative ways that the right can influence the political process. The logic of focusing on parties is compelling. Parties provide structure and stability to political life in a way that other institutions do not. But focusing on parties to the exclusion of other important political actors is to take an overly narrow view of how political systems operate in practice. The possibilities for stable democratic governance are strengthened when major societal interests are represented within the formal party system. Nonetheless, the weakness of political parties is a reality in many Latin American countries, with significant impacts on many aspects of political and economic life. Even in political systems with functioning and responsible parties, these parties are only one form of interest representation. Given the historic weakness of political parties in much of the region as well as the more recent debilitation or collapse of political parties and party systems in numerous countries (Peru and Venezuela in the 1990s; Bolivia, Colombia, and Ecuador in the 2000s), it is worth inquiring into how the right is represented in cases where political parties are weak, ineffective, or entirely missing. Once we shift our analytical focus away from political parties, however, we must look at the plethora of actors, interests, and behaviors that shape the nonpartisan right in contemporary Latin America. Following the definition laid out in the introduction to this volume, I define rightwing actors as those who seek to defend the ideological position that the major social cleavages in society are natural and should be outside the purview of the state.

While there is a vast literature on the role of civil society in strengthening democracy, much of it begins from the implicit assumption that civil society groups exist *alongside* functioning parties and political institutions. This line of thinking stresses how strong civil society organizations can improve the quality of formal democratic institutions.[1] When civil society *replaces* parties as the primary locus of political representation and competition, however, we increasingly enter a Huntingtonian world of perceived zero-sum conflicts and praetorianism.[2] Moreover, the lion's share of research on civil society organizations has focused on progressive or leftist causes rather than on rightwing civil society groups.[3] Sustained attention to rightwing civil society organizations has been conspicuously lacking.[4]

Toward that end, this chapter explores nonpartisan forms of rightwing political representation in Bolivia and Ecuador. I have chosen these cases both for their similarities as well as for some striking differences. Both countries have a long history of political instability and weak parties. Both have experienced the collapse and practical disappearance of most of the major political parties that structured political competition in the posttransition era. Prior to the weakening of traditional parties, economic actors normally associated with the right (e.g., business elites and market-oriented technocrats) had increasingly inserted themselves into parties across the political spectrum, blurring the left-right distinction. Presidents who form part of the "new left" in Latin American politics now govern both countries. Bolivia and Ecuador have strong regional divisions that frequently manifest themselves in the form of left-right competition. Finally, both countries have long histories of being economically reliant on natural resource extraction (tin and, more recently, natural gas in Bolivia and oil in Ecuador) and agriculture, and have lagged the rest of the region in industrial development. These similarities allow us to control for a large range of factors that may affect the political behavior of rightwing groups.

A crucial difference that makes these two cases particularly instructive lies in their recent economic histories. Since the 1980s, Bolivia has been at the forefront of the neoliberal revolution in Latin America, while Ecuador has been a regional laggard in this regard.[5] I discuss briefly the causes of this divergence, but my primary interest lies in the consequences that the differing paces of economic reform have for current manifestations of rightwing politics in these two countries. By holding constant many relevant factors, we can more easily investigate the role economic reform plays in producing different forms of rightwing political representation.

Neoliberalism is relevant to the study of the right for multiple reasons. First, at the rhetorical level, left-right politics over the past decade or more has largely been defined by actors' relationship to these reforms. Even in Ecuador, where reform was late and comparatively weak, neoliberalism was the rhetorical centerpiece for most rightwing parties and organizations during the 1980s and 1990s,[6] and the current president, Rafael Correa, has repeatedly campaigned against the perceived evils of Ecuador's "long neoliberal night."[7] Such a focus is thus consistent with this volume's ideological definition of the right. By minimizing the role of the state in economic life, neoliberalism implicitly recognizes that inequalities that occur within a market economy are beyond the purview of political intervention. Even in cases where neoliberal reforms are not aggressively implemented, the ideology is useful in discrediting or delegitimizing leftist alternatives that focus on using state power for more redistributive or egalitarian purposes.

Second, like any development model, neoliberalism generates winners and losers. It empowers some while marginalizing others. In Bolivia and Ecuador, this differentiation has most frequently been studied through the lens of social movements that emerged over the past decades to combat the deepening poverty and inequalities that accompanied neoliberal restructuring.[8] But groups within the dominant class face related pressures. Put most simply, those who rely on access to, or protection by, the state in order retain their privileged status are likely to fare far worse under neoliberalism than those whose access to resources (and accompanying political might) is generated outside the realm of the state (i.e., in the market). Finally, neoliberal reforms and the manner in which they were implemented carry at least part of the causal weight for the implosion of parties and party systems in the two countries, as well as others.[9]

Building from Polanyi's classic work on resistance to market reforms, Silva convincingly argues that popular social movements (and, to a lesser extent, political parties) have successfully pushed back against neoliberal reforms in much of Latin America.[10] There is no reason, however, to confine this sort of analysis exclusively to leftist or popular struggles. The various experiments with neoliberalism that occurred throughout the region produced important challenges not just to the poor and marginalized, but also to the wealthy and powerful. Reactions to the insecurities inherent in unfettered economic liberalism have historically come from the privileged sectors of society and from the ideological right,[11] and scholars have argued that organized business is mainly defensive and reactive to state policy rather than proactive.[12] To the extent that the state cedes many of its economic prerogatives to the market, we should therefore expect a reaction from the right as well as from the left. And just as the behavior of the partisan and nonpartisan left evolved during the transition from import-substituting industrialization to neoliberalism, parties and movements on the right responded as well. Where reforms are deeper and more enduring (as in the case of Bolivia), responses will be more dramatic than in cases (such as Ecuador) where reforms were halting and partial.

In this chapter I develop the general argument that different experiences with neoliberal reform have consequences for rightwing political behavior in countries with weak or collapsed party systems. In the cases of Bolivia and Ecuador, I defend a more specific set of arguments. In Ecuador, rightwing elites are less economically independent of the state such that, in the absence of strong rightwing political parties, (1) many of them are willing to quietly cooperate with a more leftist government such as Correa's, and (2) they will try to work within existing rules to achieve changes, with the understanding that in a fragile political system such as Ecuador's the "rules of game" are often more informal than formal.[13] Meanwhile, in Bolivia, the most prominent rightwing elites are economically dependent on exports and not the state, thus making them (1) more extreme in their opposition to Evo Morales and (2) willing to undermine existing institutions—including the state itself—in order to achieve their goals. Before proceeding, however, I offer a brief analysis of the different timing, degree, and consequences of neoliberal reforms.

The ideological and institutional forms of nonparty rightwing political activism can vary significantly. The Catholic Church (and, increasingly, evangelical churches) can provide both a theological underpinning and institutional vehicle for rightwing mobilization; in some countries conservative forces within the military have led rightwing movements; and the business community is often at the core of rightwing politics (whether partisan or not). In contemporary Bolivia and Ecuador, both the Church and the military have been peripheral to the most important forms of nonpartisan rightwing politics, so the bulk of this chapter focuses on economic actors and the way they organize in the absence of strong and effective rightwing political parties. As Schneider argues, economic actors do not exist in a social and political vacuum, and political activism is part of a portfolio of strategies that organized business uses to defend and advance their collective and individual interests.[14] Given this portfolio of options, I draw connections where appropriate to relevant civil society organizations and what remains of rightwing political parties in the two countries.

Focusing on economic actors also helps to illustrate how rightwing actors operate in the multiple arenas that Kent Eaton describes in chapter 3. As I describe for both the Bolivian and Ecuadorian cases, organized business groups and their political representatives have targeted the state primarily by refocusing their efforts at the subnational level. They have targeted civil society by creating (or throwing their weight behind already existing) social movement organizations that protest the policies of the Morales and Correa administrations. Finally, they have engaged in the politics of identity formation, particularly in Bolivia where business elites in the Santa Cruz region have actively sought to construct and promote regional (and highly racialized) identities that legitimize their resistance to national governments controlled by their leftwing opponents.

Neoliberalism, Backlash, and the Downfall of Rightwing Political Parties

Much as the surge of "new left" politics in the region was shaped by the struggles over economic reforms in the 1980s and 1990s, rightwing groups (particularly those directly tied to the business community) were deeply shaped by neoliberalism, but in complicated and sometimes contradictory ways. Although many studies of leftist movements and parties assume that businesspeople reflexively support neoliberalism, empirical studies have repeatedly shown that this is far from true.[15] Given that neoliberalism, where consistently implemented, deprives state-based actors (like political parties) of much of their capacity to provide protection and distribute rents to well-connected business elites, powerful economic actors often have incentives to try to block these reforms. At the very least, they may seek carve-outs or exceptions that protect specific interests within a larger process of economic liberalization. As Payne demonstrates clearly for the case of Brazil, business elites are often agnostic concerning the institutional structure of particular governments, but are much more concerned about their individual access to government officials.[16] As the state's economic role recedes under neoliberal reforms, such access (as well as the potential economic benefits such access could provide) recedes accordingly, thus creating new challenges for businesspeople.

Bolivia was one of the earliest and most dramatic economic reformers in the region. Facing runaway inflation and a flatlining economy during the mid-1980s (kept afloat largely by the proceeds of the illegal drug trade), political leaders responded with a set of reforms designed to stabilize government finances, liberalize trade policy, and increase the overall competitiveness of the Bolivian economy. In 1985, President Victor Paz Estenssoro, under the tutelage of the planning minister and mining magnate Gonzalo Sánchez de Lozada, imposed by decree a wide-ranging economic reform package that successfully tamed inflation and shifted Bolivia's economy in a decidedly pro-market direction.

While labor, peasant, and indigenous groups predictably opposed most of these measures, several leading business groups (particularly in the lowland department of Santa Cruz) also objected to the rapid and uncompromising nature in which neoliberalism was imposed. While the economic logic of neoliberalism appealed to many industrialists, agro-entrepreneurs, and other businesspeople, the rapid changes emanating from La Paz were a threat to their short-term survival. Paz was successful in insulating his team of economic policy technocrats from outside pressure, however.[17] The primary peak association for Santa Cruz business interests (the Chamber of Industry and Commerce of Santa Cruz) was dominated by importers who stood to be the big winners of trade liberalization, and many of the most productive agro-industrialists were from the local Mennonite population as well as Japanese and Eastern European immigrants who were only weakly connected to national politics and the primary agricultural interest group in the region (the Oriente Chamber of Agriculture). Protectionist interests were thus politically weak at the time neoliberalism was applied and were unable to significantly modify the new economic model. Whatever their objections to economic reform may have been, the long-term result has been a further dramatic weakening of state-dependent business elites and the entrenchment (both economically and politically) of more competitive sectors of the economy. The center of gravity on the Bolivian right has therefore shifted in a dramatically antistatist direction.

While market-dependent actors clearly benefited from the Bolivian reforms, the costs of reform fell hardest on state-dependent businesses and, most dramatically, on the middle and lower (often indigenous) classes. Not surprisingly, these groups responded with the tools at their disposal to defend their collective interests.[18] Among the leftwing activists who led the reaction against neoliberalism (as well as against US-sponsored coca eradication policies in Bolivia) was indigenous and coca growers' leader Evo Morales, who would run unsuccessfully for president in 2002 and eventually win a resounding first round presidential victory in 2005. The social conflicts of the early twenty-first century, culminating in the election of Morales, mark a dramatic backlash against the economic reforms pursued during the previous two decades and delegitimized many of the parties and politicians who had advocated neoliberal reform. In addition to reversing many of these reforms, the election of Morales marked the decisive collapse of the country's political parties. Parties such as the Movimiento Revolucionario Nacionalista, the Movimiento de la Izquierda Revolucionaria, and the Nationalist Democratic Action (Acción Democrática Nacionalista, or ADN), which had dominated electoral politics in previous decades, virtually disappeared. Morales's Movement for Socialism (Movimiento al Socialismo, or MAS) party was hegemonic (at least for the moment) and proceeded to push through a new constitution that significantly enhanced the economic power of the Bolivian state. The only other major political party (or a collection of parties, to be more precise) at that time was the center-right Poder Democrático y Social (PODEMOS), led by former president Jorge "Tuto" Quiroga and closely tied to the old ADN party structure. I will return to PODEMOS below.

In contrast to Bolivia, entrepreneurs in Ecuador were far more successful in blocking and moderating the implementation of neoliberal reforms. While reform was attempted on various occasions going back to the early 1980s, powerful economic interests were better positioned than their Bolivian counterparts to modify reforms in ways that did not undermine core economic interests. The long-run outcome has been that Ecuadorian businesspeople are generally more dependent on the state than their more market-driven Bolivian counterparts. Numerous scholars and commentators describe Ecuador as a regional laggard in terms of economic reform.[19] Even those who disagree with this assessment must couch their description of the Ecuadorian economy carefully. Hey and Klak, for example, who likely overestimate the degree of neoliberal reform in Ecuador, hedge their bets:

Our thesis is that the neoliberal transition in Ecuador has gained hegemonic status, although the implementation process has been characterized by fits and starts rather than a smooth progression. This hegemony does not eliminate quarrels and uncertainty over specific policies, but these occur within an agreed institutional framework and accepted policy paradigm that established the parameters of public choice.[20]

At roughly the same time Bolivia was implementing a dramatic neoliberal restructuring, Ecuador was meandering between reform and retrenchment. Where Bolivia moved to a single uniform tariff of 20%, the Ecuadorian government maintained a complicated system of varied tariffs capped at 90%. Where the Bolivian government froze wages from 1985 to 1987, the Ecuadorians struggled to keep wage increases below inflation. Where the Bolivian government implemented a significant reform of the tax code to simplify and modernize its tributary system, the Ecuadorian government raised taxes and borrowed to plug budget deficits.[21]

The explanation for this sort of partial reform is complex. Perhaps most importantly, Ecuador did not experience the type of hyperinflation and economic implosion faced by the Bolivian government in the mid-1980s. Inflation in Ecuador rarely exceeded 50% annually, and oil revenues continued to provide a backstop for the larger economy. In addition, Ecuadorian businesspeople were better equipped to push back on reforms that threatened their own short- and medium-term interests. Without the pressure of hyperinflation, economic collapse, and the need for dramatic and constant intervention by the International Monetary Fund and other international financial institutions, policy making in Ecuador was less technocratic and more permeable to vested interests. The first serious attempt at reform came during the presidency of León Febres Cordero (1984–88), himself a longtime representative of coastal business elites through his leadership of the Guayaquil Chamber of Industry. Yet the combination of political pushback from powerful economic groups and a series of natural disasters forced Febres Cordero into retreat by the second half of his term.[22]

More sustained economic restructuring occurred under Sixto Durán Ballen (1992–96). Originally with the assistance of rightwing ideological allies in the Partido Social Cristiano (the party of former president Febres Cordero), Durán Ballen was able to create the powerful Consejo de Modernización del Estado (State Modernization Council), which had the independent power to restructure and even eliminate entire government ministries.[23] A series of executive decrees removed domestic and foreign barriers to agricultural markets, privatized public companies, eliminated most price controls, and radically deregulated the financial sector.[24]

The deregulation of financial services led quickly to a financial bubble, as the country's largest *grupos económicos* (economic groups, usually controlled by a single family or small group of families) moved to take advantage of lax oversight of the banking industry. By the end of the decade, a powerful financial crisis had devastated the industry, forced the state to bail out both bankers and depositors (although depositors often got far less than the full value of their accounts), and led to several prominent bankers fleeing the country under the cloud of credible accusations of massive illegalities. The result was the near-total delegitimation of the formal political system and the parties that dominated it (derisively called *la partidocracia*—rule by corrupt political parties—by many Ecuadorians). The country spent the better part of the post–Durán Ballen decade lurching from political crisis to political crisis, with three consecutive elected presidents failing to finish their term in office. Similar to Bolivia, neoliberal reforms (to the extent that they had taken root) were quickly halted with the election of Rafael Correa in 2007.

Correa is a US-educated economist from a middle-class Guayaquil background. The electoral movement (he refuses to call it a "party" because of the dismal reputation that parties have in Ecuador) he leads, Alianza País, is headed by a collection of center-left intellectuals, mostly from Quito and the surrounding highland region. Like Morales, Correa moved quickly to write a new constitution that centralized power in the national government, and in the presidency in particular. Since 2007, Correa has taken advantage of high oil prices (Ecuador's top export and hard currency earner) to fund expansive spending programs to extend basic services and cash transfers to the poor. Similar to the situation in Bolivia, the ascension of a leftist president in Ecuador marked the demise of the country's dominant political parties. Among the largest parties, only the Social Christian Party (Partido Social Cristiano, or PSC) retained significant electoral support, and that support was reduced almost exclusively to the province of Guayas (a coastal province whose capital, Guayaquil, is Ecuador's largest and most economically vibrant city).

To summarize, neoliberal reforms were implemented earlier and more thoroughly in Bolivia than in Ecuador. As a result, the dominant sectors of the Bolivian economic elite are largely tied to market-based activities (particularly export agriculture). By contrast, the profile of Ecuador's economic elite is far more varied with a fairly even mix of both market- and state-dependent actors jockeying for political influence. With the virtual collapse of existing parties in both countries, these actors were forced to find new avenues for representing their interests within the political arena. Given that both the political right (parties and civil society organizations) and economic right (organized business interests) are solidly pro-market in Bolivia, we should expect a more complete rejection of Morales's centralizing political and economic project than in Ecuador, where the political right is generally pro-market in its ideology, but the economic right is deeply divided regarding the concrete implications of Correa's economic reforms.

The Reemergence of the Right

Without reliable and strong allies within the formal political system, rightwing actors in Bolivia and Ecuador have been forced to rely on alternative means of representing their collective interests. In this section I analyze the similarities and differences in patterns of rightwing representation in these two countries by answering five interrelated questions: (1) Who are the key (nonparty) actors on the right? (2) What linkages do these actors have to the state and to the broader society? (3) What political tools do they have at their disposal? (4) What is their perceived basis of legitimacy? (5) What are the consequences of particular constellations of rightwing political forces for stable democratic governance in each country?

Given the lack of popular legitimacy that parties, businesspeople, and neoliberalism suffer in these two countries, the challenges facing a renovated right are fundamentally political rather than simply organizational. Rightwing elites cannot count on mass support either for their collective (business) interests or for their previously proclaimed ideological preferences (neoliberalism). Instead, rightwing actors in both regions have retreated to the subnational level to organize their resistance to Morales and Correa.[25]

Bolivia

In Bolivia, the key rightwing actors are wealthy export-oriented agro-industrial elites located mainly in the eastern region of Santa Cruz. In a subordinate, but important, position are political and economic leaders in other departments of the *media luna* (half-moon) region of eastern Bolivia (Pando, Beni, and Tarija), the departments with significant concentrations of natural gas, one of Bolivia's primary exports. These economic and political elites (they often overlap) are represented by a tightly knit group of business federations (*cámaras de producción*) that overrepresent large enterprises relative to small- and medium-sized firms and are deeply involved in a series of civil society organizations, the Santa Cruz Civic Committee being the most prominent.[26]

Within the formal political sphere, there have been a series of right and center-right parties that have challenged Morales, but none have experienced much electoral success or longevity. Although the focus of this analysis has been on nonparty forms of rightwing political representation, the economic and political elites mentioned above do have ties to rightwing political parties with representation at the national level. These parties have had scant success, however, and tend to be more closely tied to political leaders from the Cochabamba region of central Bolivia. In Evo Morales's two presidential elections, he has easily fought off challenges from two different rightwing parties. In 2005, he defeated former president Jorge "Tuto" Quiroga of PODEMOS in the first round by a comfortable 53.7% to 28.6% margin. In 2009, Morales won an even larger victory over former Cochabamba mayor Manfred Reyes Villa (who represented an alliance of center-right parties under the label Convergencia Nacional) by a margin of 64.2% to 26.5%. Congressional elections have been similarly lopsided, with rightwing parties controlling fewer than one-third of the seats in both the upper and lower houses.[27]

Most recently, the Unidad Nacional (National Unity) party has made important inroads in the MAS stronghold of El Alto, a heavily populated (and predominantly indigenous) area overlooking La Paz. The party's leader, Samuel Doria Medina, is a prominent La Paz businessman and has built what is to date the most effective right-of-center political party in the country. But despite its competitiveness in El Alto, the party has few actual victories, and its durability without Doria Medina is questionable. Given this electoral reality, the desire among rightwing leaders for alternative forms of political representation is understandable.[28] Nonetheless, these parties (or party coalitions) could form the basis of a more formalized rightwing movement in Bolivia, a possibility I discuss in this chapter's conclusion. Given the current weakness of rightwing political parties, the right's links to the state are predictably weak. But rightwing leaders do head many regional and municipal governments in the *media luna* departments from which they exercise considerable influence in pushing for further decentralization of political authority away from the national state. Regional autonomy has thus become the predominant battle cry of the nonpartisan right in Bolivia.

While largely alienated from the national state, rightwing movements enjoy significant support within the broader society in the *media luna* region where they are most prominent. This is demonstrated electorally by the repeated victories of Morales's opponents in referenda on regional autonomy in 2008 and the approval of the new constitution in 2009. By controlling many local government institutions, rightwing parties and movements are able to engage in the time-tested practice of political clientelism to provide concrete benefits to supporters, particularly given the surge in resources made available to local and regional leaders following the decentralizing reforms of the 1990s and early 2000s.[29] Given the relatively high levels of abstention during the controversial 2008 regional autonomy referendum, however, the depth of societal support for the autonomy drive remains an open question.

These regional forces sit uneasily within a larger framework of national rightwing political parties (PODEMOS, Unidad Nacional, and other smaller parties) that operate differently in different parts of the country. In the *media luna* region, particularly Santa Cruz, PODEMOS functions in an essentially corporatist pattern with local economic elites imposing their preferred candidates on the PODEMOS list. In the rest of the country, PODEMOS functions similarly to traditional Bolivian political parties, where a relatively closed group of party elites, currently led by Jorge "Tuto" Quiroga, chooses candidates based primarily on political or clientelist criteria.[30] The party has therefore rarely served as an adequate vehicle for defending the interests of *media luna* elites and is more accurately described as an electoral vehicle to advance the interests of its leaders, particularly Quiroga. Unidad Nacional is mostly confined to the highland region of the country (where Doria Medina's political and economic base resides), and its relationship with the leading sectors of the nonpartisan right is more utilitarian. Were MAS not the hegemonic political force in the country, it is not obvious that autonomy leaders in Santa Cruz and the *media luna* would move easily to support Doria Medina or other Unidad Nacional leaders.

Since the Bolivian right is currently more of a social force than a formal political force, the tools of social movements have been prominent.[31] This is especially true given the reality that the economic elites who lead these organizations derive much of their wealth from agriculture and extractive industries that are land based and thus present fewer opportunities for capital flight, the most obvious tool capitalists can use to undermine unfriendly governments. Organizations like the Comité Cívico pro Santa Cruz (Pro Santa Cruz Civic Committee) and the Santa Cruz Chambers of Commerce and Industry have led mass demonstrations in opposition to the Morales government and in support of greater political and economic autonomy for the region.[32] They have also led hunger strikes, the largest in 2006 to challenge MAS's strategy for circumventing the two-thirds majority needed to approve articles in the new constitution.[33]

Like some social movement organizations on the left, rightwing movements in Bolivia have radical factions that resort to violent tactics to advance their goals. Some of these are linked directly to the civic committees that are the most visible face of the right. The Santa Cruz Youth Union (Unión Juvenil Cruceñista, or UJC), is a far-right movement (claiming about two thousand members) linked to the larger Comité Cívico pro Santa Cruz. They have become the violent enforcers of the many general strikes called by the Santa Cruz Civic Committee, attacked leftist politicians and indigenous activists, and been accused of attempting to assassinate the president. Beyond the UJC, rightwing violence in Bolivia has been on the increase since the election of Morales. The best-known (and perhaps most concerning) case involved Eduardo Rosza Flores and his collaborators. Rosza Flores was of Hungarian-Bolivian ancestry and had fought with the Croatian National Guard during the Balkan Wars of the early 1990s. In April 2009, having returned to Bolivia, allegedly to help organize a paramilitary movement in Santa Cruz and attempt to assassinate the president, he was killed along with two colleagues in a Santa Cruz hotel by government forces. Although the details of this specific case remain controversial,[34] the existence of violent rightwing movements targeting MAS activists and their supporters, particularly in the *media luna* provinces, is well documented.[35] Whether peaceful or violent, rightwing groups in Bolivia have used familiar social movement framing strategies to legitimate their opposition to the Morales government.[36] Given the elite-dominated nature of the Santa Cruz Civic Committee and other rightwing organizations, they face the challenge of presenting themselves as broadly representing the interests of a constituency far larger than themselves.

Given the depth and history of regional identities, it is entirely logical that rightwing movements have attempted to tap into regionalism as a way to legitimate their movement and their unyielding opposition to Morales. The increasing political salience of *camba* identity is not exactly an "invented tradition" in the sense of Hobsbawm and Ranger,[37] but rather the strategic reassertion (with some key adjustments) of long-standing traditions.[38] The reassertion of regional identities is strategic because it emerged as lowland elites gradually lost control of the political process at the national level and were thus forced to retreat to their strongholds in Santa Cruz and surrounding areas. As the Morales government encroached on these strongholds through his proposed constitutional assembly and agrarian reform program, *cruceño* elites responded by refashioning old regional grievances to accord with new political necessities.

As ethnicity became increasingly salient at the national level with a surge of indigenous organizing culminating in the election of Morales in 2006, rightwing elites attempted to tap into the discourse of ethnic inclusion to promote autonomy (if not outright independence) for the departments of the *media luna*. As Fabricant argues in her work on the "*camba* countermovement" in eastern Bolivia,

> new forms of symbolic and cultural politics in Bolivia have everything to do with historical elite investment in extractive industries, such as petroleum, gas, and, more recently, soy. Linguistic distinctions between highlander and lowlander, Indian and mestizo, only bolster territorial claims to land and natural resources by shifting the focus away from economics and onto race and ethnicity.[39]

Such discourses serve multiple purposes. Racial animosities simmer just under the surface of right-left conflicts in Bolivia, and the assertion of *camba* identity draws a sharp distinction between a rightwing elite that is primarily of European extraction (many are even first- or second-generation immigrants) and the current political establishment, which is drawn overwhelmingly from the highland and is largely indigenous and mestizo. *Camba* identity also offers a way to claim continuity with the indigenous traditions of the Guaraní peoples, one of the largest indigenous groups of the lowland region, and thus assert a historical basis for autonomy from a strong central government based in La Paz.

Just as important for the purpose of legitimating a movement, the *camba* discourse works to obscure the identities and interests of the primary beneficiaries of regional autonomy and their historical relationship with the national state. By stressing *cambas'* historic struggle against a centralizing state, these movements and organizations present two (only partially accurate) views of how Santa Cruz became the most prosperous region of Bolivia. The first argument is the classical liberal position that, by privileging the highland region, the state neglected lowland regions, thus in effect encouraging the development of unfettered markets in that region of the country. Where it is necessary to acknowledge the role the state has played in the development of the region, a second argument emerges, emphasizing that the funds for large-scale, state-funded public infrastructure projects came from oil and gas royalties that derive primarily from resources in the *media luna* region. While there is some truth in both of these narratives, they ignore the fact that Santa Cruz economic elites effectively colonized much of the state during the decades prior to the emergence of Morales, and they used this influence to direct a large proportion of the funding Bolivia received in foreign aid and loans toward the development of the lowland region.[40]

In terms of developing stable democratic governance, the current state of right-wing politics in Bolivia is distinctly unhelpful. Most concerning is the near-total lack of institutionalized political representation for the right at the national level. This is partly a self-inflicted wound, as various right and center-right parties governed over a series of economic and political crises during the 1990s and early 2000s and have been roundly rejected by the Bolivian electorate during popular uprisings in the early 2000s and by electoral politics since 2006. It is also an artifact of policies by the Morales administration to further weaken and marginalize its opponents.[41] Bolivia's already-weak formal institutions have been further weakened as the primary conflicts in society over resources and rules of governance play out not in congress or the courts, but increasingly in zero-sum street politics.[42]

Ecuador

In Ecuador, the right is more diverse in its regional origins, political and economic preferences, and political tactics. To a greater extent than in Bolivia, political parties in Ecuador have long been regionally based, and the survival (albeit in a dramatically weakened state) of PSC on its home turf of Guayaquil gives the partisan right more options in Ecuador than in Bolivia. The deinstitutionalization of Ecuadorian politics is dramatic, but less severe than in Bolivia. There are also more fissures within the right in Ecuador in comparison with Bolivia. While the formal, right-wing political opposition is ideologically opposed to the Correa government and strategically uncompromising, the economic right is far more diverse and strategically more pragmatic.[43]

On the coast (particularly in Guayaquil) PSC still largely controls the reins of power, and Guayaquil mayor Jaime Nebot has emerged as the most visible and vocal representative of the partisan right. Nebot is a longtime PSC leader who currently leads a faction of the party under the label Madera de Guerrero. Beyond administering the city of Guayaquil, Nebot works closely with rightwing civil society leaders in the city to lead antigovernment marches and demonstrations demanding greater autonomy for the city and the province of Guayas. Among other rightwing figures with some partisan apparatus behind them, banana tycoon and four-time presidential candidate Álvaro Noboa and the party he leads, the Partido Renovador Institucional de Acción Nacional, represents a more populist and clientelist alternative to PSC. During four presidential campaigns, however, Noboa has failed to successfully mobilize the most important segments of the business community behind his candidacy.[44] During the 2009 presidential election, rightwing business elites appear to have coalesced around the candidacy of Lucio Gutiérrez, who led a short-lived military coup in collaboration with Ecuador's leading indigenous peoples' organizations in 2000. Despite his populist campaign style, Gutiérrez governed in close collaboration with business elites (thus confirming Payne's argument that business is more concerned with access than regime type), and many business-people continue to voice support for him in interviews I conducted in 2008 and 2009. In the most recent (2013) presidential and legislative elections, the right mostly coalesced around the candidacy of Guillermo Lasso, a prominent Guayaquil banker, who came in second to Correa by more than thirty percentage points. Results for the 2013 legislative elections suggest that support for both traditional rightwing parties like PSC-Madera de Guerrero and newer parties like Lasso's Creando Oportunidades was weak. Correa will continue as president with a large legislative majority.

As in Bolivia, weakening political parties means that the energy for rightwing politics must come from nonpartisan sources. And as in Bolivia, the business community has provided much of that fuel. The Ecuadorian business community is far more diverse than its Bolivian counterpart, however. The coastal economy (with its hub in Guayaquil) is primarily geared toward export agriculture and is home to some of the country's largest and most influential financial institutions. The highlands region (with its hub in Quito and an important secondary center in Cuenca) is home to both major exporters (particularly flowers and minerals) and domestically oriented manufacturing and agriculture. The oil sector is concentrated in state hands, with concessions to several multinational firms.

As mentioned above, neoliberal reforms were both late in arriving to Ecuador and only partially implemented, leaving behind a set of economic elites still largely dependent on state protection and rent-seeking behavior—with significant consequences for the way rightwing movements approach the current Ecuadorian government. Rhetorically, they are almost universally opposed to the current Correa administration, but practically, many business elites have cooperated with the government and benefited quite handsomely. Despite consistent complaints that the president's economic policies were hampering economic development,[45] for example, several of the country's largest importers (many with long-standing links to rightwing political parties and the leading chambers of commerce and industry) signed an agreement with the president in 2009 to restrict imports as a way to protect the government's balance of payments and stimulate domestic production.[46] This agreement reflects the degree of business dependence on the state and, correspondingly, the willingness of prominent business groups to do business with a government with which they are generally in open political conflict. Further evidence of the willingness of business associations to cooperate with the Correa government came in 2010, during negotiations over the *Código de la producción*, or production code, which set the government's strategic economic objectives and policies for achieving them. Although the leading peak associations in both Quito and Guayaquil criticized Correa for giving them economic incentives with one hand while undermining their competitiveness with the other, they praised the openness of the government's top negotiator, Nathalie Cely, and eventually dropped their total opposition to the plan.

The willingness of the business community (and the broader spectrum of rightwing parties and civil society organizations) to work within the confines of existing rules was made obvious on September 30, 2010, when President Correa was taken prisoner during a standoff with disgruntled police officers. Instead of taking advantage of the chaos and uncertainty to weaken the president or assist in his removal, the right (both partisan and nonpartisan) closed ranks around the regime in denouncing the attempt to violently remove Correa from office.[47]

Of course, not all business leaders have reached agreements with the Correa administration. Exporters (particularly on the coast, but also in the highly profitable cut flower sector in the highlands) have opposed any sort of agreement that restricts international trade and have taken a much harder line with the Correa government. As such, they are most similar to the agro-export elite in Bolivia. Predictably, the Guayaquil chambers of commerce and industry (as well as several smaller chambers) have participated in organizing efforts led by Mayor Jaime Nebot to oppose much of Correa's economic and social policy agenda. Chamber of commerce and industry leaders in the highlands tread more carefully. While launching rhetorical bombs in the media, they also recognize that many of their most influential members benefit significantly by doing business with the state. Given the surge in oil revenues during the Correa administration and his government's penchant for large-scale spending projects (which the right derides for ideological reasons), the government has been a good customer for many of these businesses.[48]

Although less prominent than their counterparts in Bolivia, the Ecuadorian right has organized a series of small and large civil society organizations (or retooled existing organizations toward more explicitly ideological and political ends). The Junta Cívica de Guayaquil, formed in 1992, has been the most active and vocal in organizing outside the formal party system in Guayaquil. Its activities, however, have generally been in support of the PSC-Madera de Guerrero movement. The Junta Cívica draws its membership from the cities' upper class (a mix of the city's traditional aristocracy and its politically upwardly mobile nouveau riche), but it has successfully mobilized the symbols of regional identity to support mass protests against the Correa government. Others have created hybrid organizations such as the Una Nueva Opción, led by politically prominent businessman Eduardo Maruri (who is also on the board of directors of the Junta Cívica), which seeks to train political leaders but has also run candidates for the country's constitutional assembly and participated in opposition marches in Guayaquil.

In the highlands, rightwing politics has been a distinctly more intellectual affair with shallow roots within the broader society. Prominent economists such as Pablo Lucio Paredes have attempted to mount opposition to the Correa administration based on the enunciation of a clear and consistent center-right ideology. Organizations such as the Corporación de Estudios para el Desarrollo (or Corporation for Development Studies), led by former president Osvaldo Hurtado, have long provided high-quality analysis of political and economic affairs, also from the center-right. More radical rightwing voices are heard within the chambers of commerce and industry even though, as discussed above, many highland businesspeople have also quietly cooperated with the government.

The less unified approach of the Ecuadorian right has its basis primarily in economic interests directly tied to the country's experience as a petro state (since the mid-1960s) and late and tepid neoliberal reformer. The explosion of state resources starting in the 1960s rapidly expanded the size and scope of state activity. Prior to the discovery of oil, the Ecuadorian state was neoliberal by default. It simply lacked the financial and organizational wherewithal to intervene extensively in the political and economic affairs of the various parts of the country. As the state grew, its economic profile increased, and increasingly large swaths of the private sector became suppliers of state-owned enterprises.[49] Although the economic profile of the state shrank under the neoliberal half-measures of the 1980s and 1990s, the state (and the enterprises it controls) is still an important buyer for local companies, particularly those who are uncompetitive internationally. For example, within the insurance industry (which has generally been hostile to Correa's attempt to corral the financial sector), over 60% of revenue is generated by policies written for the government or publicly owned companies.[50]

Given the fragmented nature of the Ecuadorian right, its political tools are relatively weak. Rightwing elites have controlled much of the country's media infrastructure, but this dominance has come under successful attack by the Correa administration. The constitution (approved in 2009) and the recently proposed Ley de Medios (media law) greatly restrict media ownership (e.g., families with significant ownership stakes in financial institutions cannot also own media outlets). Rightwing social mobilization has been a primary strategy in Guayaquil but has had little resonance in other parts of the country. President Correa's family roots in Guayaquil (and the significant popular support he retains there, owing partly to that fact) have complicated the right's attempts to paint him as just another outsider from the highlands trying to subjugate (and take resources from) the more prosperous Guayaquil region. The most successful venue for rightwing politics has been in local government, where PSC continues to possess a virtual stranglehold on all levels of government in Guayas province. Outside the province, though, the organizational and partisan power of PSC (and any other rightwing party or organization) dissipates rapidly.

A key contrast with Bolivia is that, in Ecuador, rightwing mobilization and political activism has been overwhelmingly peaceful. While there has been plenty of aggressive rhetoric, there is no evidence that rightwing groups are organizing something equivalent to the Bolivian UJC. Credible threats of presidential assassination have been scarce. President Correa travels regularly and freely throughout the country, in contrast to President Morales, who is effectively persona non grata in Santa Cruz and other parts of the *media luna*. In fact, in moments of political crisis such as the police mutiny that threatened to overthrow (or kill) Correa in September 2010, much of the right rallied (albeit temporarily) behind the president in opposition to attempts to violently remove him from power.

The politics of rightwing legitimacy is also slightly different in Ecuador than in Bolivia. Regional identities are strong in both countries, with Guayaquil and Santa Cruz elites drawing on long-standing regional grievances to criticize their leftist opponents and mobilize mass support for regional interests. While regional identities overlay racial identities in Bolivia, however, the situation in Ecuador is far more fluid and negotiable. Given Correa's *mestizo* background and the significant weakening of Ecuador's indigenous movement over the past decade, Ecuador's racial politics are less toxic. The Ecuadorian right, particularly in Guayaquil, is thus better equipped than its Bolivian counterparts to credibly claim the mantle of a loyal rightwing opposition to an ascendant leftwing government. While the behavior of the Ecuadorian right is far from pristine, in both discourse and praxis it has generally proven willing to live within the minimal confines of formal democracy.

The weakening of political parties and the deep regional divide that has made rightwing actors powerful on the coast but relatively impotent at the national level do not bode well for the stability of democratic governance in Ecuador. Given the factors discussed above, however, the Ecuadorian right is better placed (and has better positioned itself) to enhance the stability of Ecuadorian democracy than its Bolivian counterparts. At best, the majority of the Ecuadorian right has shown itself willing to defend an embattled (but democratically elected) president in moments of crisis. Moreover, having at least one somewhat viable rightwing party directly under their control likely has served to restrain the worst impulses of some on the right (particularly in Guayaquil). Given the strong popular support that Correa enjoys throughout the country, rightwing forces seem willing to exercise vocal and aggressive opposition while biding their time for a more opportune political moment. Given the chronic instability of Ecuadorian politics since at least the mid-1990s, such patience may be well advised.

Conclusion

This comparison of the nonpartisan right in Bolivia and Ecuador leads us to a few important conclusions. First, I echo the cautionary message of scholars like Berman and Encarnación, who question the positive impact that civil society has on democratic politics.[51] As the two cases discussed here illustrate, the impact of civil society can be incredibly destabilizing (and, as in Bolivia, violent) in the absence of institutionalized linkages to the state (namely, political parties). The links between rightwing civil society organizations and the broader society in both Bolivia and Ecuador are fairly shallow in the sense that rightwing movements use regional (and more in Bolivia than in Ecuador) racial imagery to mobilize popular support in defense of elite interests.[52] The challenge in these two countries, as well as others, is that the pendulum has swung rather dramatically over the past two decades from the overinstitutionalization of political parties (the so-called *partidocracia* in both Bolivia and Ecuador) to the almost-complete collapse of political parties. Civil society organizations on both the right and left can make important contributions to democratization, but only when they exist alongside (rather than in place of) viable, representative political parties.

Second, although the neoliberal reforms of the 1980s and 1990s evoked a predictably strong backlash from the left, arguably leading to the leftist surge of the past decade, the reforms (even where only partially implemented) also had strong—and understudied—impacts on political organizations of the right. As voters abandoned neoliberal parties, the partisan right virtually collapsed. The elites capable of picking up the pieces and promoting a rightwing agenda were primarily business elites organized in various types of civil society organizations (e.g., business associations and civic committees). The interests of these actors were largely defined by their experience with neoliberalism. In Bolivia, where neoliberal reforms occurred earlier and were more thoroughly implemented, the rejection of the Morales government has been near absolute, and the tactics deployed by the right have corresponded to a "by any means necessary" approach to changing the existing government. In Ecuador, by contrast, neoliberal reforms were late and relatively weak. Reforms were successfully resisted in part by business elites who depended on various forms of state protection. Although the rhetoric on the right is almost universally anti-Correa, there has actually been meaningful cooperation in several areas. Moreover, the political tactics of the nonpartisan right reflect a less extreme form of opposition than we see in Bolivia.

Finally, the nature of the nonpartisan right in both countries suggests new places to look for rightwing activism: subnational and transnational politics. Not surprisingly, political actors tend to focus their energies where they have greatest strengths. Where political parties are weak and leftist presidents are strong, it is logical to look beyond political parties and national politics for meaningful rightwing political activism. This pattern would be similar to what scholars observed during the resurgence of the left, when forces "from below" (i.e., grassroots mobilization and local politics) and "from above" (i.e., transnational advocacy) generally preceded successful participation in national politics.[53]

Rightwing movements (and the remnants of rightwing parties) are strongest at the local level in both Bolivia and Ecuador. This strength takes the form of successful candidates for subnational offices as well as local civil society organizations such as civic committees and business associations. Focusing on presidential elections, constitutional assemblies, and national legislatures, therefore, gives us comparatively little leverage in understanding the role that rightwing actors play in these types of settings.

At the transnational level, rightwing groups throughout the Latin American region have successfully evoked the image of Hugo Chávez and (to a lesser extent) Fidel Castro to garner domestic support for resistance to leftwing leaders. Additionally, the behavior of US diplomats in supporting rightwing civil society leaders in places like Venezuela, Honduras, and Bolivia suggests a critical evaluation of the role that outside actors play in supporting or enabling these movements. If the on-going natural resource boom turns bust, rightwing actors may again make common cause with international financial institutions in an effort to constrain or remove leftwing presidents.[54]

Implicitly or explicitly, rightwing organizations defend existing inequalities as natural and appropriate, as defined by Juan Pablo Luna and Cristóbal Rovira Kaltwasser in their introduction to this volume. While the movements and leaders described in this chapter would generally defend that thesis, they currently find themselves on the losing side of battles against nearly hegemonic leftist presidents. As such, it is highly unlikely that we will see rightwing ideologies translate into concrete public policies (at least at the national level) in the near future. What these movements have accomplished, however, is to keep these ideologies alive, often by tying them to other sorts of grievances related to perceived racial or regional biases in national government policies. Given the economic power of rightwing elites, and their entrenched position in the important population centers of Santa Cruz and Guayaquil, it is likely that these ideas will reemerge in the future, perhaps under new leadership not tied to elite economic interests.

Even where political parties are weak they are not irrelevant. My argument about the importance of nonpartisan forms of rightwing political representation is designed to complement, rather than undercut, arguments that stress the need for viable rightwing parties in functioning democratic polities. As the case of Bolivia shows most clearly, rightwing actors will not go unrepresented. Where institutional avenues are perceived to be closed (by force or by choice), rightwing actors will respond in ways destructive not just of formal democracy, but of political order more generally. The long-term viability of democracy in the region thus depends on the ability of rightwing civil society groups to coexist with (or create) a small number of viable political parties.

NOTES

1. Robert Putnam, *Making Democracy Work: Civic Traditions in Modern Italy* (Princeton, NJ: Princeton University Press, 1993).

2. Samuel Huntington, *Political Order in Changing Societies* (New Haven, CT: Yale University Press, 1968).

3. Omar Encarnación, "Civil Society Reconsidered," *Comparative Politics* 38, no. 3 (2006): 357–76.

4. For noteworthy exceptions, see Leigh Payne, *Uncivil Movements: The Armed Right Wing and Democracy in Latin America* (Baltimore: Johns Hopkins University Press, 2000); Kent Eaton, "Conservative Autonomy Movements: Territorial Dimensions of Ideological Conflict in Bolivia and Ecuador," *Comparative Politics* 43, no. 3 (2011): 291–310.

5. Catherine Conaghan and James Malloy, *Unsettling Statecraft: Democracy and Neoliberalism in the Central Andes* (Pittsburgh, PA: University of Pittsburgh Press, 1994).

6. James Bowen, "The Right in 'New Left' Latin America," *Journal of Politics in Latin America* 3, no. 1 (2011a): 99–124; "Multiculturalism, Markets, and Democracy: Elites and Indigenous Movements in Contemporary Ecuador," *Journal of Latin American Studies* 43, no. 3 (2011b): 451–83.

7. Catherine Conaghan, "Ecuador: Correa's Plebiscitary Presidency," *Journal of Democracy* 19, no. 2 (2008): 46–60.

8. Lesley Gill, *Teetering on the Rim: Global Restructuring, Daily Life, and the Armed Retreat of the Bolivian State* (New York: Columbia University Press, 2000); Oscar Olivera, *¡Cochabamba! Water War in Bolivia* (New York: South End Press, 2008); Eduardo Silva, *Challenging Neoliberalism in Latin America* (New York: Cambridge University Press, 2009); Deborah Yashar, *Contesting Citizenship in Latin America: The Rise of Indigenous Movements and the Postliberal Challenge* (New York: Cambridge University Press, 2005).

9. Kenneth Roberts, "Market Reform, Programmatic (De-)Alignment, and Party System Stability in Latin America," *Comparative Political Studies* 20, no. 2 (2012): 1–31; Kurt Weyland, "Neoliberalism and Democracy in Latin America: A Mixed Record," *Latin American Politics and Society* 46, no. 1 (2004): 135–57.

10. Karl Polanyi, *The Great Transformation: The Political and Economic Origins of Our Time* (New York: Beacon Press, 1944); Silva (2009).

11. Hector Schamis, "Distributional Coalitions and the Politics of Economic Reform in Latin America," *World Politics* 51, no. 2 (1999): 236–68.

12. Ben Ross Schneider, *Business Politics and the State in Twentieth-Century Latin America* (New York: Cambridge University Press, 2004).

13. Andrés Mejía Acosta, *Informal Coalitions and Policymaking in Latin America: Ecuador in Comparative Perspective* (New York: Routledge, 2009).

14. Schneider (2004).

15. Kurt Weyland, *The Politics of Market Reform in Fragile Democracies: Argentina, Peru, Brazil, Venezuela* (Princeton, NJ: Princeton University Press, 2002).

16. Leigh Payne, *Brazilian Industrialists and Democratic Change* (Baltimore: Johns Hopkins University Press, 1994).

17. Conaghan and Malloy (1994, 156–57).

18. Olivera (2008); Yashar (2005); Forrest Hylton and Sinclair Thomson, *Revolutionary Horizons: Past and Present in Bolivian Politics* (New York: Verso Press, 2007).

19. Conaghan and Malloy (1994); César Montúfar, *La reconstrucción neoliberal: Febres Cordero o la estatización del neoliberalismo en el Ecuador, 1984–1988* (Quito, Ecuador: Abya-Yala, 2000).

20. Jeanne Hey and Thomas Klak, "From Protectionism towards Neoliberalism: Ecuador across Four Administrations (1981–1996)," *Studies in Comparative International Development* 34, no. 3 (1999): 66–97.

21. Conaghan and Malloy (1994, 140).

22. Montúfar (2000).

23. Pablo Andrade, *La era neoliberal y el proyecto republicano: La recreación del Estado en el Ecuador contemporáneo* (Quito, Ecuador: Corporación Editora Nacional, 2009), 22.

24. Ibid., 24–29.

25. Eaton (2011).

26. Kent Eaton, "Backlash in Bolivia: Regional Autonomy as a Reaction against Indigenous Mobilization," *Politics and Society* 35, no. 1 (2007): 74.

27. All election data come from Bolivia's *Tribunal Supremo Electoral.*

28. Dunia Mokrani Chávez and Pilar Uriona Crespo, "Bolivia: Construcción hegemónica o monopolización de la política: El Movimiento al Socialismo y las posibilidades del proceso de cambio," *Observatorio Social de América Latina* 12, no. 29 (2011): 111–27.

29. Roberto Laserna, "Mire, la democracia boliviana, en los hechos . . . ," *Latin American Research Review* 45, no. 4 (2011): 27–58.

30. José de la Fuente Jeria, "El difícil parto de otra democracia: La Asamblea Constituyente de Bolivia," *Latin American Research Review* 45, no. 4 (2011): 12.

31. Nicole Fabricant, "Defending Democracy? Human Rights Discourse in Santa Cruz, Bolivia," *NACLA Report on the Americas* 44, no. 5 (2011a): 23–28.

32. Nicole Fabricant, "Performative Politics: The Camba Countermovement in Eastern Bolivia," *American Ethnologist* 36, no. 4 (2009): 768–83; "A Realigned Bolivian Right: New 'Democratic' Destabilizations," *NACLA Report on the Americas* 44, no. 1 (2011b): 30–31.

33. Fabricant 2011a.

34. For greater detail on controversy surrounding this case, see Miguel Centrellas, "Bolivia," in *Countries at the Crossroads: An Analysis of Democratic Governance* (Washington, DC: Freedom House, 2011), 89–110.

35. Fabricant (2009; 2011b); Mokrani and Uriona Crespo (2011).

36. Payne (2000).

37. Eric Hobsbawm and Terence Ranger, eds., *The Invention of Tradition* (New York: Cambridge University Press, 1983).

38. The term *camba* was once a generic derogatory reference to the indigenous peoples of lowland Bolivia (but, crucially, not the indigenous peoples of the Andean highlands). Over the second half of the twentieth century, the term was refashioned in both high and popular culture to refer to a specific form of lowland *mestizaje* that explains the exceptionalism of the lowland region with reference to the mixing of the regions Spanish and pre-Hispanic peoples. See Kathleen Lowrey, "*Bolivia Multiétnico y Pluricultural*, Ten Years Later: White Separatism in the Lowlands," *Latin American and Caribbean Ethnic Studies* 1, no. 1 (2006): 66. See also chapter 3, this volume.

39. Fabricant (2009, 769).

40. Eaton (2007) Fabricant (2011b).

41. Centrellas (2011).

42. Fabricant (2011b).

43. Mario Unda, "Ecuador 2010: El año 4 de la revolución ciudadana," *Observatorio Social de América Latina* 12, no. 29 (2011): 137–49.

44. Mario Unda, "Hacia la segunda fase de la revolución ciudadana" (unpublished manuscript, 2009).

45. Specific complaints usually involve some combination of Correa's decision to pursue a unilateral; partial default of Ecuador's "illegitimate" debt in 2008; the rapid rise in government spending and regulation since Correa took office; and the use of formation of strategic alliances with countries such as Venezuela, Cuba, and Iran.

46. República del Ecuador, "Acuerdo Voluntario entre le Gobierno Nacional de la República del Ecuador y los Importadores a fin de Salvaguardar la Balanza de Pagos" (report, Quito, Ecuador, January 16, 2009).

47. Unda (2011).

48. Personal interviews with Blasco Peñaherrera (Quito, Ecuador, June 12, 2009) and Sebastián Borja (Quito, Ecuador, June 2, 2009).

49. Eaton (2011).

50. Personal interview with Gabriela Calderón (Guayaquil, Ecuador, June 24, 2009).

51. Sheri Berman, "Civil Society and the Collapse of the Weimar Republic," *World Politics* 49, no. 3 (1997): 401–29; Encarnación (2006).

52. Eaton (2011).

53. Alison Brysk, *From Tribal Village to Global Village: Indian Rights and International Relations in Latin America* (Stanford, CA: Stanford University Press, 2000); Margaret Keck and Kathryn Sikkink, *Activists beyond Borders: Transnational Activists Networks in International Politics* (Ithaca, NY: Cornell University Press, 2002); Donna Lee Van Cott, *The Friendly Liquidation of the Past: The Politics of Diversity in Latin America* (Pittsburgh, PA: University of Pittsburgh Press, 2000); *From Movements to Parties in Latin America: The Evolution of Ethnic Politics* (New York: Cambridge University Press, 2005).

54. This is not a call for conspiratorial theorizing, but rather an attempt to draw attention to the myriad ways that transnational actors influence domestic politics in small, dependent countries.

CHAPTER FIVE

The Authoritarian Roots of New Right Party Success in Latin America

JAMES LOXTON

The electoral right has traditionally been weak in most Latin American countries. Much of this fact can be explained by the availability of nonelectoral modes of interest representation for rightwing actors. So long as these actors could directly influence policymakers—and, if all else failed, encourage coups in order to install more pliable rulers—they had little reason to pursue seriously electoral politics. Gibson noted this point in his analysis of the relationship between conservative parties and democratic stability.[1] Rightwing actors, he argued, tended to back coups less often when strong conservative parties existed that could represent their interests. Yet Gibson argued that the opposite was also true: "When opportunities exist for direct access by conservative leaders to state power or policy making, they abstain from party-building efforts."[2] Seen in this way, there appears to be an inverse relationship between the electoral and the nonelectoral right: insofar as one is relatively strong, we can expect the other to be relatively weak.

This chapter analyzes the relationship between the electoral right and one variant of the nonelectoral right: the nondemocratic right. To what extent are the electoral and the nondemocratic right inversely related? I address this question by analyzing the formation of new right parties in Latin America in the midst of the third wave of democratization. In the 1980s and 1990s, the transition to democracy was accompanied by an unprecedented burst of rightwing electoral activism. The clearest manifestation of this activism was the formation of new rightwing parties, which occurred in several countries in the region. The formation of such parties was fully in line with the notion of an inverse relationship between the nondemocratic and the electoral right. As coups became prohibitively costly owing to international pressure and other factors, rightwing actors suddenly had a strong incentive to create partisan vehicles of interest representation. When we compare the success of these new parties, however, a surprising pattern emerges: virtually all of the new right parties that enjoyed sustained electoral success had strong links to former dictatorships. These were "authoritarian successor parties"—political parties founded by high-level incumbents of former authoritarian regimes that participate in democratic elections.

While we might expect parties led by individuals closely associated with defeated dictatorships to repel voters following a transition to democracy, authoritarian successor parties were in fact remarkably successful in several countries in Latin America.

What explains the success of authoritarian successor parties, and what does this success imply about the relationship between the nondemocratic and the electoral right? I argue that there is a dual relationship between the nondemocratic and the electoral right: the relationship is negative when we consider the *emergence* of right-wing parties, but positive when we consider the *performance* of such parties. In other words, rightwing actors do not have a strong incentive to engage in party building so long as viable nondemocratic alternatives exist; however, once these actors are forced to enter the democratic game, the parties they build are more likely to thrive if built on a nondemocratic foundation.

To make my argument, I divide this chapter into four sections. In the first section, I argue that rightwing actors in Latin America traditionally had few incentives to engage seriously in party building, given the viability of nondemocratic alternatives. With the third wave of democratization, however, the coup option became prohibitively costly, which prompted a burst of rightwing electoral activism. In the second section, I examine this electoral activism, focusing in particular on the formation of new right parties. I highlight the surprising phenomenon of authoritarian successor parties and describe some prominent examples. In the third section, I argue that the electoral success of authoritarian successor parties can be explained in terms of what I call "authoritarian inheritance." Authoritarian successor parties often inherit a number of valuable resources from former dictatorships that can help them to prosper under democracy, including clientelistic networks, organizational infrastructure, privileged relations with business elites, a well-known and popular party brand, and leadership cohesion born of joint struggle. In the conclusion, I consider the effects of authoritarian successor parties on democracy and argue that, paradoxically, the existence of electorally viable rightwing parties with strong roots in former dictatorships may in fact contribute to democratic stability.

The Electoral and the Nondemocratic Right:
Inversely Related?

It is no secret that rightwing actors have frequently supported coups in Latin America. Although there are examples of leftist or "populist" soldiers seizing power (e.g., Torrijos in Panama, Velasco Alvarado in Peru), coups have for the most part been a rightwing phenomenon. Until recently, the violent overthrow of elected governments remained a viable option for actors who felt threatened by the rise of leftist or popular forces. Economic elites, in particular, traditionally had little difficulty finding the ear of sympathetic members of the armed forces when they felt their interests to be imperiled by threats from below. Indeed, one of the "established political facts" of the region is that "alliances between upper-class economic and social groups and the armed forces have historically been a major cause of military intervention in Latin America."[3] This relationship between rightwing actors and the armed forces reached its nadir in the aftermath of the Cuban Revolution, when rightist authoritarian regimes came to or retained power in nearly every country in the region. By the 1960s and 1970s, "most of the groups included under the Right were clearly antidemocratic."[4]

Nevertheless, in some Latin American countries, coups have been much less common than elsewhere. As Gibson famously argued, where electorally viable conservative parties existed, economic elites typically lacked a strong incentive to engage in antidemocratic conspiracies.[5] Since conservative parties provided a viable *electoral* means of interest representation, coups were a less essential part of these actors' political repertoire. Thus, while countries with strong conservative parties like Chile, Colombia, and Costa Rica experienced relatively few coups during the twentieth century, those without such parties like Argentina, Bolivia, and Peru experienced them repeatedly. Countries with strong conservative parties were not immune to coups, as illustrated by the breakdown of democracy in Chile in 1973. The frequency of coups during the twentieth century, however, was far lower in countries with strong conservative parties than in those lacking such parties.[6]

Understood in this way, the electoral and the nondemocratic right appear to be inversely related: insofar as one is relatively strong, we can expect the other to be relatively weak. The logic of this argument is straightforward. If electorally viable rightwing parties exist and provide adequate means of interest representation, why encourage coups? Conversely, if rightwing parties are weak but the coup option remains viable, why build parties? Each of these situations can be considered a kind of equilibrium. In both the "weak electoral right, strong nondemocratic right" and the "strong electoral right, weak nondemocratic right" situations, actors lack a strong incentive to alter their position with respect to electoral politics. Given that these different equilibria appear to have resulted from unique and nonreplicable historical circumstances,[7] the implications for countries with a weak electoral right but strong nondemocratic right are disheartening. Barring some kind of disruptive exogenous shock, we would predict them to remain coup-prone indefinitely.

In the 1980s and 1990s, such a disruption was produced by the third wave of democratization.[8] The third wave was the result of several factors, many of them specific to individual countries. One crucial factor, however, was common throughout Latin America and constituted an exogenous shock: a change in the international environment. This change was composed of several parts, including the emergence of transnational advocacy networks, the growing importance of the Organization of American States, and the newly democratic orientation of the Catholic Church. But perhaps the most important factor was a shift in US foreign policy. During the Cold War, the United States tolerated, and sometimes actively encouraged, coups and authoritarian rule in Latin America. Beginning with the presidency of Jimmy Carter (1977–81), however, the United States began to support democracy in the region—a position that it has held more or less consistently ever since. As Huntington put it, "In effect, under Carter, Reagan, and George H. W. Bush the United States adopted a democratic version of the Brezhnev doctrine: within its area of influence it would not permit democratic governments to be overthrown."[9] This had a powerful impact on the calculations of actors who had previously depended on nondemocratic options in order to represent their interests: "Its positions have raised the costs of coups to potential coup players. Under such circumstances, some players that would otherwise have probably supported coups have not done so. The threat of sanctions by the United States . . . makes the expected benefit-cost ratio of supporting a coup unfavorable."[10]

This pro-democracy shift in the international environment had a profound effect on the Latin American right. The coup option, long a key part of the right's political repertoire, became prohibitively costly. The reaction to this shift both supports and challenges the notion of an inverse relationship between the nondemocratic and the electoral right. On the one hand, the right largely forewent coups[11] and made an unprecedentedly serious turn to electoral politics. On the other hand, the most successful of the newly formed right parties were those with deep roots in former authoritarian regimes. How do we make sense of this apparent contradiction? The next two sections attempt to answer this question.

Authoritarian Successor Parties

In the context of the "left turn" of the late 1990s and the first decade of the twenty-first century, it is hard to believe that until recently it was the right that appeared ascendant in Latin America. Yet in the years immediately following the third wave, it was widely believed that the right was, and would remain for the foreseeable future, the most dynamic political sector in the region. Chalmers et al. captured this sentiment when they wrote that a "focus on the Right is needed because it has, over the last decade or so, expanded its support among the Latin American public," while "the Left seems to be in disarray."[12] O'Donnell and Schmitter had famously argued that the right must be "'helped' to do well" in new democracies.[13] But in Latin America in the immediate aftermath of the third wave, the right did well without needing much help, winning office or wielding major influence nearly everywhere.

This could be seen in the election of several rightwing "neo-populist" presidents (e.g., Fernando Collor de Mello in Brazil, Alberto Fujimori in Peru),[14] as well as with the return to prominence of a number of traditional rightwing parties after a period of relative dormancy during the authoritarian period (e.g., the Liberal and National Parties in Honduras and the Social Christian Party in Ecuador). In Mexico, a twist on this process played out, as the decades-old—but electorally marginal—National Action Party (Partido Acción Nacional, or PAN) was revamped by so-called Neo-panista leaders into a party capable of winning the presidency and in the process, toppling the country's authoritarian regime.[15]

But the most conspicuous manifestation of this turn to electoral politics was the formation of *new* rightwing parties in several countries. In the years following the onset of the third wave, such parties emerged to represent the interests of actors who had previously depended on nondemocratic alternatives, leading some to speak of a "new right" in Latin America. Several of these parties quickly became electorally relevant and appeared to have promising futures. Notable examples include the Independent Democratic Union (Unión Demócrata Independiente, or UDI) and National Renewal (Renovación Nacional, or RN) in Chile; the Nationalist Republican Alliance (Alianza Republicana Nacionalista, or ARENA) in El Salvador; Nationalist Democratic Action (Acción Democrática Nacionalista, or ADN) in Bolivia; the Liberal Front Party (Partido da Frente Liberal, or PFL) in Brazil; the Union of the Democratic Center (Unión del Centro Democrático, or UCEDE) in Argentina; the Liberty Movement (Movimiento Libertad, or ML) in Peru; the Nationalist Republican Liberal Movement (Movimiento Liberal Republicano Nacionalista, or MOLIRENA) in Panama; and the National Advancement Party (Partido de Avanzada Nacional, or PAN) and Guatemalan Republican Front (Frente Republicano Guatemalteco, or FRG) in Guatemala. These parties did not enjoy similar levels of success. While some demonstrated a capacity to win large shares of the vote over a prolonged period of time, others failed and quickly disappeared from the political map. In itself, this was unremarkable, given the difficulties of party building and the high failure rate for new parties in general. When we examine the *kinds* of parties that succeeded, however, an unexpected pattern emerges: virtually all of the successful new right parties were authoritarian successor parties.

Authoritarian successor parties are parties founded by high-level incumbents of former authoritarian regimes that participate in democratic elections.[16] Parties that fit this description are a startlingly common phenomenon, yet they have received little scholarly attention in the context of Latin America.[17] Broadly, authoritarian successor parties can be divided into two groups. The first are former "official" parties from single-party dictatorships that continue to compete in elections after a transition to democracy.[18] These are instances of what Shefter calls "internally mobilized parties," or parties "founded by politicians who . . . occupy leadership positions in the prevailing regime."[19] The clearest examples of this kind of authoritarian successor party are ex-communist parties in Eastern Europe and the former Soviet Union. In Latin America, examples include the Institutional Revolutionary Party (Partido Revolucionario Institucional, or PRI) in Mexico, the Sandinista National Liberation Front (Frente Sandinista de Liberación Nacional, or FSLN) in Nicaragua, and the National Conciliation Party (Partido de Conciliación Nacional, or PCN) in El Salvador.[20]

The second kind of authoritarian successor parties are what we might call "inside-out" parties. The founders of these parties are authoritarian incumbents who are displaced from their leadership positions, and only *then* choose to form parties and participate in democratic elections. This kind of authoritarian successor party straddles the line between Shefter's categories of "internally mobilized" and "externally mobilized,"[21] the latter of which are "established by leaders who do *not* occupy positions of power in the prevailing regime and who seek to bludgeon their way into the political system by mobilizing and organizing a mass constituency." On the one hand, these parties are created by individuals who used to occupy leadership positions in the prevailing regime, as in the case of internally mobilized parties. On the other hand, they are only formed after their founders have been displaced and thus find themselves without political office, as in the case of externally mobilized parties. Owing to an unplanned transition to democracy or an internal shuffle within the authoritarian regime, these former insiders suddenly find themselves on the outside and, in response, form parties in order to "bludgeon" their way back into the political system.

The phenomenon of authoritarian successor parties has received considerable attention in the context of the postcommunist world.[22] These scholars have attempted to understand how parties associated with repressive—and largely reviled—dictatorships could survive the transition to democracy. Understandably, one of their major findings is that in order to be successful, communist successor parties had to make a symbolic break with the past. This implied replacing old leaders with new faces, changing their "name, symbols, and historical justifications," and "denouncing former misdoings and crimes."[23] In Latin America, such a break with the past sometimes occurred. In Brazil, for example, Power asserts that after democratization politicians with links to the country's former authoritarian regime (1964–85) usually sought to "obfuscate their political past."[24] Surprisingly, however, many authoritarian successor parties in Latin America made no such break with the past. Far from replacing old leaders, changing historical symbols, and denouncing past deeds, these parties were often led by prominent figures from past dictatorships (including heads of state), drew on symbols associated with the old regime, and explicitly extolled the memory of that regime.

The most successful new rightwing party in Latin America and a clear instance of authoritarian succession is El Salvador's ARENA.[25] ARENA was formed in 1981 by the former deputy chief of military intelligence and death squad leader Roberto D'Aubuisson in the context of civil war and a partial transition to democracy. The civil war pitted the leftist Farabundo Martí National Liberation Front (Frente Farabundo Martí para la Liberación Nacional, or FMLN) guerrillas against the armed forces and allied paramilitaries, or "death squads." Nominally independent, these death squads were in fact directly linked to the infrastructure of the country's decades-old authoritarian regime, including the armed forces and members of formally disbanded pro-regime organizations.[26] After a reformist military government took power in October 1979, many newly marginalized regime hardliners reinvented themselves as death squad leaders. With El Salvador under pressure from the United States to democratize, ARENA was formed in order to participate in the 1982 elections for a constituent assembly. Despite the fact that it was an "anticommunist, antireformist terrorist organization,"[27] the party came in second place with 29.5% of the vote. Although it eventually moderated its public image, in its early years the party's "capacity for violence against the left was an important theme of . . . ARENA campaigns"; it ran D'Aubuisson as its presidential candidate in 1984 and continued to engage in death squad activities on the side.[28] In the following decades, ARENA won the presidency in four consecutive elections (1989, 1994, 1999, and 2004) and oscillated between one-third and one-half of votes in legislative elections, becoming El Salvador's "dominant political party."[29]

Another strikingly successful new right party with authoritarian roots is UDI in Chile. UDI was formed in 1983 by "loyal supporters of the Pinochet regime"[30] and has been described as "the military regime's direct heir."[31] Like ARENA, the party was formed after a shift within the authoritarian regime displaced—temporarily—many of Pinochet's most prominent political and economic policymakers.[32] The founders of UDI were former high-level officials of the Pinochet regime, most notably Jaime Guzmán, "the regime's main civilian adviser," and Sergio Fernández, the minister of the interior and "head of cabinet" in Pinochet's government from 1978 to 1983.[33] UDI supporters were found at all levels of the authoritarian regime, but were particularly widespread at the municipal level, earning it the nickname the "party of the mayors."[34] In the early years after democratization, UDI openly proclaimed its loyalty to the former regime, holding annual celebrations on September 11 to commemorate the 1973 coup and adamantly resisting reforms to the military regime's 1980 constitution.[35] UDI has enjoyed tremendous electoral success: in the founding elections of 1989, it won 9.8% of votes for the chamber of deputies and then expanded in subsequent electoral cycles. In 2001, it won 25.2% of votes in the election for the chamber of deputies, making it the single most voted-for party in Chile—a position that it has maintained in all subsequent legislative elections. In 2010, UDI also reached the executive branch as part of a coalition government led by RN candidate Sebastián Piñera.

A third successful authoritarian successor party was ADN in Bolivia. ADN was formed in 1979 by General Hugo Banzer, the country's dictator from 1971 to 1978. After being overthrown in a palace coup, the former dictator decided to form his own party in order to participate in future elections. ADN was peopled by former incumbents of the Banzer dictatorship, including: "(1) professional politicians who had defected from other parties to serve during the Banzer administration; (2) notable businessmen who had served in Banzer cabinets; [and] (3) young technocrats who had manned a variety of bureaucratic positions in the Banzer administration."[36] Although Banzer was reportedly concerned about "overcom[ing] the stigma of his past authoritarian rule by securing election as a democratic president,"[37] he did not deny—nor could he have, realistically—his status as a former dictator. He openly campaigned on nostalgia for the old regime, using *Banzer vuelve*—"Banzer returns"—as a campaign slogan in the 1980s.[38] ADN became one of the three pillars of Bolivia's "three-party dominant multiparty system."[39] The party was electorally successful: it won 14.9% in its first election in 1979; oscillated between 20% and 30% of votes in the 1985, 1989, 1993, and 1997 legislative elections; and won a plurality of votes in the 1985 and 1997 presidential elections with Banzer as its candidate.[40] ADN also participated in two coalition governments (1985–89 and 1989–93), and Banzer himself won the presidency in 1997.[41] Yet ADN was not an institutionalized party; rather, it was thoroughly personalistic, with the bulk of its supporters "Bánzeristas first and Adenistas only secondarily."[42] The result was that, when Banzer died in 2002, the party quickly collapsed. Still, for two decades, ADN, a clear example of an authoritarian successor party, was arguably the most important party in Bolivia.

These examples illustrate the surprising phenomenon of successful rightwing authoritarian successor parties in Latin America. They are not isolated instances. Other examples include PFL in Brazil, a splinter of the "official" party of the former authoritarian regime (1964–85);[43] FRG in Guatemala, the party formed in the late 1980s by ex-dictator (1982–83) General Efraín Ríos Montt;[44] various partisan incarnations of Fujimorismo in Peru, which grew out of the competitive authoritarian regime of Alberto Fujimori (1992–2000);[45] and perhaps also RN in Chile, which is something of a hybrid between a revamped traditional party and an authoritarian successor party.[46] Two other examples include PCN in El Salvador and the Social

Christian Reformist Party (Partido Reformista Social Cristiano, or PRSC) in the Dominican Republic. PCN was the "official" party created by El Salvador's military rulers in 1961, while PRSC was founded in 1963 by Joaquín Balaguer, a high-level functionary of the dictatorship of Rafael Trujillo (1930–61).[47] Although PCN and PRSC cannot be classified as new parties, they are clear instances of authoritarian succession and help to illustrate the pattern of rightist parties with dictatorial roots flourishing under democracy.

This pattern of successful authoritarian successor parties becomes especially striking when compared to the experience of new rightwing parties *without* links to former dictatorships. These parties, virtually without exception, collapsed soon after being formed. Two paradigmatic examples are UCEDE in Argentina and the Liberty Movement in Peru.[48] Neither was founded by high-level incumbents of its country's most recent authoritarian regime, and each went to great lengths to emphasize its democratic credentials. After its creation in 1982, UCEDE became the country's "fastest-growing political party, and its third electoral force," and many believed that it was destined to become Argentina's "long-sought democratic mass conservative party."[49] The creation of Mario Vargas Llosa's Liberty Movement in 1987 was met with similar fanfare, and the party performed well in the 1990 general election.[50] Both UCEDE and the Liberty Movement quickly disintegrated, however, after newly elected "populist" presidents—Carlos Menem in Argentina and Alberto Fujimori in Peru—made sharp turns to the right, aping these parties' programs and appointing some of their leaders to governmental posts.[51] Overall, one is hard-pressed to find a single example in Latin America of an electorally successful rightwing party formed since the third wave that was not constructed upon a nondemocratic foundation.[52]

The relative success of so many authoritarian successor parties is surprising. Simply put, this is not how we usually think about democratization. We accept that certain groups, such as the military or economic elites, may resist a transition to democracy for fear of losing privileges in the new regime. Mindful of this threat, democratization scholars have argued that it is important to secure the vital interests of such groups through carefully crafted pacts. But we assume that what Bermeo calls "ordinary people"[53] will generally favor democracy. The existence of successful authoritarian successor parties poses a challenge to this assumption. Instead of saying "good riddance" to former dictatorships after a transition to democracy, millions of Latin Americans have opted to vote for parties led by individuals who previously ruled them in an authoritarian—and often highly brutal—manner. What allowed these authoritarian successor parties to flourish in Latin America while their counterparts elsewhere, with better democratic credentials, all failed?

Authoritarian Inheritance and Democratic Success

Party building is always difficult, but the founders of rightwing parties face an especially daunting task. As Luna and Rovira Kaltwasser note in their introduction to this volume, if the right is a political position distinguished by the belief that the main inequalities between people are natural and outside the purview of the state, we can expect its natural constituency to be relatively small in a region as unequal as Latin America. Even if we do not adopt Gibson's sociological definition of rightwing parties (or, to use his term, conservative parties),[54] one of his key insights is consistent with the ideological definition of the right used in this volume: a party that views inequality as natural and outside the purview of the state is likely to have a natural affinity to the "the upper strata of society." Parties cannot win elections, however, with the votes of the upper strata alone. Thus, in order to be successful, rightwing parties must build an electoral coalition that transcends their elite core constituency.

Various strategies have been employed by successful rightwing parties around the world in order to achieve this goal, such as clientelism and the emphasis of crosscutting issues like economic performance and "order." Yet employing these strategies effectually poses serious difficulties for new right parties. A new party is unlikely to have immediate access to state resources, for example; how, then, is it to finance clientelism? Similarly, establishing a reputation for competent economic stewardship or the effective maintenance of law and order will take time and effort; what is to prevent party leaders from defecting during this difficult start-up period? Drawing on existing literature and illustrative examples, in this section I argue that authoritarian successor parties may be able to overcome the difficulties of rightwing party building as a result of their access to "authoritarian inheritance." Authoritarian successor parties often inherit a number of resources from former dictatorships that allow them to prosper where other parties—parties with better democratic credentials—would be likely to fail. Below I discuss five resources that these parties may inherit: clientelistic networks, organizational infrastructure, privileged relations with business elites, a well-known and popular party brand, and leadership cohesion born of joint struggle. The upshot is that authoritarian roots, far from being an albatross, may in fact be the key to new right parties' success under democracy.

Resource 1: Clientelistic Networks

Clientelism is an appealing strategy for rightwing parties seeking to win the support of a mass electorate. Although poorer voters may be repelled by a rightwing party's views on inequality, they may still be convinced to vote for the party in exchange for the selective distribution of material benefits. Despite its obvious attractiveness to rightwing parties, employing a strategy of clientelism is no easy task. Among the challenges it poses is to construct a "clientele," or a sizeable group of individuals locked into a stable relationship of dependency with their patron. For this, the patron must become known to his clients and be viewed as reliable, and clients must come to expect and depend on payoffs from their patron. Authoritarian successor parties are often born with an advantage with respect to clientelism. Few authoritarian regimes seek to hold onto power through force alone. Instead, they attempt to legitimize themselves and to construct popular support through various means, including the selective distribution of material goods to their supporters. If an authoritarian successor party is able to transfer to itself the clientelistic networks produced through this practice, it inherits a highly valuable resource.[55]

The case of Chile under Pinochet—and UDI after the transition to democracy—clearly illustrates the potential importance of this resource. During the authoritarian period (1973–90), the military regime "sought to win the support of the poorest sectors through clientelist policies, deliberately distributing economic resources, particularly through municipalities, so as to create and increase support for the military regime."[56] After the transition to democracy, many of the mayors responsible for the distribution of this material largess joined UDI and ran for congress in the same municipalities that they had governed during the dictatorship. Successfully transferring to themselves the loyalties generated by clientelism during the dictatorship, many of these former mayors were elected to congress. Of the fourteen UDI members elected to the lower house of congress in 1989, ten had been mayors during the authoritarian regime. According to many observers, the fact that UDI inherited a clientele of impoverished voters was a decisive factor in the party's early success.[57] As Klein puts it, "In the end, the network of clientelism and patronage, which the party was able to establish because of its privileged position during the military regime, primarily explains the UDI's electoral successes in the shantytowns since 1989."[58] A similar process played out in Brazil, with PFL and other parties inheriting the "political networks and clienteles" constructed by the military's official party during the authoritarian regime.[59]

Resource 2: Organizational Infrastructure

Parties constructed upon the infrastructure of preexisting organizations have an advantage over parties built from scratch.[60] The reason that preexisting organization is advantageous is straightforward: "Organization building does not come naturally or automatically to political actors. It is a difficult, time-consuming, costly, and often risky enterprise."[61] Yet some kind of organization is necessary if parties are to choose candidates, develop a platform, maintain a territorial presence, fundraise, run campaigns, and so forth. Even the effective employment of clientelism requires a significant amount of organization.[62] If parties can draw on and "retrofit" organizations initially designed for different purposes, such as labor unions or religious organizations, they are spared much of the work of organization building and can hit the ground running. Authoritarian successor parties often inherit the organizational infrastructure of former dictatorships and are thus born with a significant advantage. While one might expect organizations originally designed for antidemocratic—and often violent—purposes to be of little use after democratization, such organizations have demonstrated remarkable agility and have proven to be a valuable resource for authoritarian successor parties.

Perhaps the most startling example of such agility can be seen in the relationship between death squads and ARENA in El Salvador. As described above, ARENA grew directly out of the death squad networks that in the 1980s "carried out a deadly campaign of targeted assassinations, interrogations, and generalized violence."[63] Clearly, these organizations were not designed with democratic purposes in mind. After the foundation of ARENA, however, they proved to be a remarkably effective means of getting out the vote. This partially involved the "direct intimidation" of voters,[64] especially in the 1980s before full democratization had occurred. But this inherited organizational infrastructure was also employed for more legitimate purposes. For example, ARENA managed to transfer "the loyalties of many members of the rural paramilitary networks from the military to the party, creating a base from which to mobilize turnout for rural and urban rallies."[65] In addition, this inherited organization could be drawn on in order to employ clientelism more effectively.[66] In Guatemala, the so-called civil defense patrols, which were created during the Ríos Montt dictatorship in rural areas in order to assist the military in its fight against guerrilla forces, appear to have played a similar supporting role for FRG.[67]

Resource 3: Privileged Relations with Business Elites

Maintaining a party organization and campaigning during elections is expensive. It is of great utility to parties, therefore, to have the support of business elites who can make important financial contributions to party activities. Yet, historically, as Gibson notes, "Latin American business has remained an aloof ally in the electoral struggles of conservative parties," preferring to focus its political action "directly on the state, either through firm-state contacts or through corporatist institutions."[68] In practice, this focus on the state has often resulted in intimate ties between business elites and authoritarian regimes. Authoritarian successor parties have the potential to alter the pattern of business wariness toward parties. While new rightwing parties without authoritarian roots must convince business elites of their credibility and usefulness, authoritarian successor parties may be spared this labor. By virtue of the reputation they inherit from "trustworthy" former authoritarian regimes, business elites may be more willing to give them the benefit of the doubt and to support them from the moment of their formation. If they do, authoritarian successor parties are born with a clear advantage over other rightwing parties.

This dynamic clearly played out in the cases of UDI in Chile, ARENA in El Salvador, and ADN in Bolivia. In Chile, business elites were intensely loyal to the Pinochet regime, largely because of the traumatic memory of the 1970–73 government of Salvador Allende.[69] After the transition to democracy, UDI, because it "came to represent the dictatorship's economic and political legacy," enjoyed "special allegiance from . . . business interests."[70] This allowed the party to tap these groups for financial resources and then distribute them to poor voters in the form of clientelistic payouts.[71] In El Salvador, ties between the authoritarian regime and business elites had traditionally been extraordinarily close, but were severed after a reformist military government took power in October 1979. Suffering an "unprecedented political and economic exclusion from national power,"[72] many of these elites chose to transfer their loyalties to the country's death squads and, subsequently, to the death squads' partisan extension, ARENA. ARENA's privileged access to business elites allowed its election spending to be "in a different league than that of the other parties."[73] In Bolivia, Hugo Banzer enjoyed similar support from business elites during his dictatorship and, following the transition to democracy, managed to transfer much of this loyalty to ADN.[74]

Resource 4: Party Brand

Among the most important resources that authoritarian successor parties may inherit from former dictatorships is a well-known and popular party brand. In order to be successful, parties need partisans in the electorate—individuals who feel an attachment to the party and thus are motivated to turn out and vote for it. A central determinant of partisanship is *party brand*. According to Lupu,[75] a party brand is the image of a party that voters develop by observing its behavior over time. Parties with strong brands come to stand for something that is distinct in the eyes of the electorate, and voters who feel a "comparative fit" between their own views and a particular party's brand are likely to support that party. New parties, however, face at least two challenges when attempting to build a brand. First, they must develop brand content that is potentially attractive to large numbers of voters. Second, they must ensure that the brand is disseminated and becomes widely known among the electorate. Each of these tasks is difficult, given the existence of both traditional parties and other new parties competing for voters' attention. Under such circumstances, party builders may be tempted to abandon the new party before the process of brand development is complete. If a new party can simply inherit an already well-known and popular brand, however, it is born with an advantage. In the case of authoritarian successor parties, such a brand can often be inherited from former dictatorships.

Authoritarian regimes often enjoy considerable popular support. This does not necessarily mean that they have the backing of the majority; they may, however, enjoy the support of a sizeable minority of the population. In Chile, for example, when citizens were given the opportunity in 1988 to vote on whether to extend Pinochet's rule, 44% voted in favor. While it is usually difficult, for obvious reasons, to ascertain popular opinion under authoritarianism, anecdotal evidence suggests that such regimes often have significant support. One reason, as discussed above, is clientelism. Another reason is performance: if authoritarian regimes provide public goods that people value, such as economic growth or political stability, they may win popular support.[76] These factors are likely to be even more highly valued if an authoritarian regime is preceded or followed by (or both) a period of political and economic chaos. Authoritarian regimes that succeed in providing such goods to citizens may end up developing a brand—in the case of Chile, Pinochetismo—that many voters find appealing. If an authoritarian successor party like UDI can transfer this popular brand to itself, it is born with a ready-made partisan base in the electorate.

Consider the example of ADN in Bolivia, where the seven-year (1971–78) dictatorship of Hugo Banzer was preceded *and* followed by high levels of instability. The year prior to Banzer's rise to power was characterized by "an almost comic series of coups and countercoups," while in the four years after his fall Bolivia had "seven military and two weak civilian governments."[77] When democracy finally took hold in 1982, the country suffered an extraordinary economic crisis under the new democratic government of Hernán Siles Zuazo, in which "growth rates were negative, real salaries dramatically deteriorated, and inflation reached 8,000 percent by 1985."[78] The Banzer government, by contrast, was relatively successful: not only was the country politically stable for seven years—a long time relative to the preceding and following periods—but it also enjoyed an economic boom during much of the period. As a consequence, "the extraordinary growth affecting the national economy . . . created popular support for the regime despite its antidemocratic activities."[79] After the disastrous democratic government of Siles Zuazo, Banzer's record must have seemed especially impressive to voters. During its campaigns in the 1980s, ADN openly sought to capitalize on nostalgia for the Banzer dictatorship. In the context of economic and political crisis, the party's slogan of *Banzer vuelve*—"Banzer returns"—was, for many Bolivians, "the rough equivalent of 'Happy days are here again.'"[80]

More recently, some authoritarian successor parties have utilized their dictatorship-derived brands to establish credibility on the issue of public security. With violent crime skyrocketing in Latin America, calls for a *mano dura*[81] response have become increasingly common. Typical *mano dura* policies include the suspension of procedural rights, the use of the military for police work, and the empowerment of the police to make arrests on limited evidence.[82] In theory, any party could advocate such policies; in practice, however, a party led by ex-authoritarians who showed no qualms about such practices in the past is likely to be viewed as especially credible. This connection between authoritarian succession and *mano dura* appeals seems to have benefited El Salvador's ARENA. As Holland demonstrates,[83] the party has made effective use of its death squad origins in order to bolster its "tough on crime" image. For example, it has increasingly invoked the image of Roberto D'Aubuisson, the founder of the party described by one US ambassador as a "pathological killer."[84] The message seems to be that ARENA can be trusted to take a no-holds-barred approach to crime in the present, since it had no problem employing mass violence in the past. In Peru, the same can be observed in the case of *Fujimorismo*, which has also sought to capitalize on the reputation that it earned during the 1990s while fighting the Shining Path insurgency—specifically, the reputation of prioritizing public security over individual rights and showing contempt for human rights organizations[85]—in order to make credible its promises of *mano dura*.[86]

Resource 5: Party Cohesion

Party cohesion is the Achilles' heel of new political parties. While it may be possible for a new party, with time and effort, to build the reputation and network of supporters necessary for electoral viability, this attempt is likely to fail if key leaders defect during the difficult start-up phase of party building.[87] Authoritarian successor parties may be born with an advantage over other new parties in this respect by inheriting sources of party cohesion from former dictatorships. As Levitsky and Way argue, while sources of party cohesion vary, "Bonds of solidarity forged out of periods of violent struggle are perhaps the most robust source of cohesion."[88] By periods of violent struggle, these authors mainly have in mind revolutionary and anticolonial movements. There is good reason to believe, however, that right-wing authoritarian successor parties also may benefit from this source of cohesion.[89] Although most observers perceive the regimes from which these parties grew as murderous dictatorships that suppressed legitimate democratic rule, the protagonists of these regimes, unsurprisingly, see themselves in a different light. In their view, they were soldiers on the front lines of the Cold War who struggled heroically against the imported ideology of Marxism and its totalitarian aspirations for Latin America.

This form of party cohesion born of joint struggle is clearly applicable to UDI, a party that possesses a level of unity and discipline "difficult to find outside Leninist structured left-wing parties."[90] In part, this cohesion is the result of the relatively homogeneous cultural and religious background of UDI leaders.[91] But it also stems from "a common political perspective, which was forged to an important extent in the fires of the struggle against the Popular Unity."[92] In the 1970s, most UDI leaders participated in the Gremialista movement,[93] which party founder Jaime Guzmán described as "the vanguard of the struggle against the Popular Unity.[94] According to Guzmán,[95] they felt obligated to resist the Allende government because they "did not accept that a minority should subject [the people] to a totalitarian and foreignizing doctrine." This perceived battle against totalitarianism took them first into the streets, and then into the halls of power of the Pinochet regime, where they continued their struggle. In April 1991, Guzmán was assassinated by leftist urban guerrillas, resulting in what UDI considers an act of "martyrdom," which to this day serves as a source of inspiration for party members. Like those who participate in revolutionary and anticolonial movements, then, joint struggle against perceived tyranny appears to have served as an important source of cohesion for UDI leaders. In the case of El Salvador's ARENA, which went even further by actually engaging in armed combat against leftist guerrillas (and unarmed civilians), joint struggle also left a legacy of impressive party cohesion.

Conclusion

This chapter set out to determine the relationship between the nondemocratic and the electoral right by examining the formation of new right parties in Latin America since the third wave of democratization. It found that this was a dual relationship: while the nondemocratic and the electoral right are inversely related with respect to the *emergence* of new parties, they are positively related with respect to the *performance* of these parties. In support of the notion of an inverse relationship between the nondemocratic and the electoral right, the chapter argued that the increased cost of coups following the third wave led to a burst of rightwing electoral activism in Latin America, which included the formation of new right parties. Yet the chapter also drew attention to an unexpected positive relationship between the nondemocratic and the electoral right. Surprisingly, virtually all successful rightwing parties formed during this period were authoritarian successor parties.

The main theoretical contribution of this chapter is to demonstrate that resources inherited from authoritarian regimes can be valuable to new parties in the context of democracy. Under some circumstances, authoritarian regimes can bequeath to their partisan successors the tools necessary for sustained electoral success. The precise ways in which this transference occurs, however, can differ. One of the most conspicuous differences among the parties examined in this chapter was the extent to which they were truly institutionalized or merely personalistic vehicles. In some cases, such as ARENA in El Salvador and UDI in Chile, authoritarian successor parties were highly institutionalized and not dependent on an individual leader. In others, like ADN in Bolivia and FRG in Guatemala, parties were little more than personalistic vehicles for former dictators. After these ex-dictators died (e.g., Banzer) or declined in popular support (e.g., Ríos Montt), their parties collapsed, despite having been major electoral players for years. Why is the party organization as a whole sometimes the inheritor of authoritarian resources, while at other times a particular individual is the main beneficiary? A possible answer is that the nature of authoritarian successor parties is determined by the nature of the authoritarian regimes from which they emerge: institutionalized dictatorships bequeath institutionalized parties, while personalistic dictatorships bequeath personalistic parties. For example, UDI grew out of an authoritarian regime in Chile that was unusually interested in institution building. ADN, in contrast, was associated not with the entirety of Bolivia's military regime, which lasted for eighteen years (1964–82), but with the seven-year government of one man: Hugo Banzer.

The main findings of this chapter are unsettling. They raise uncomfortable issues, such as the popularity of dictatorship, and challenge some of our most basic assumptions about ordinary people's support for democracy. Perhaps an even more troubling implication concerns the stability of democracy. Gibson famously argued that democratic breakdown was less likely in countries with strong conservative parties, since these offered economic elites an electoral means of interest representation and thus made coups less necessary.[96] This chapter focuses on a historical period in which the international environment strongly favored democracy in Latin America, thus rendering this argument moot for the time being. If international conditions were to become more permissive, however, it is worth speculating about the effect of authoritarian successor parties on democratic stability. If electorally viable conservative parties promote democratic stability, and if the only instances of such parties formed in recent decades are those with strong links to former dictatorships, then the implication is as clear as it is paradoxical. In such a hypothetical future, could authoritarian successor parties of the right help to safeguard democratic stability by providing elites with an electoral means of interest representation? Could a party like ARENA, which was grew out of organizations initially designed for mass murder, play the unlikely role of democratic savior?

NOTES

1. Edward Gibson, *Class and Conservative Parties: Argentina in Comparative Perspective* (Baltimore: Johns Hopkins University Press, 1996).

2. Ibid., 212.

3. Kevin J. Middlebrook, "Introduction: Conservative Parties, Elite Representation, and Democracy in Latin America," in *Conservative Parties, the Right, and Democracy in Latin America*, ed. Kevin J. Middlebrook (Baltimore: Johns Hopkins University Press), 1.

4. Douglas A. Chalmers, Mario do Carmo Campello de Souza, and Atilio A. Borón, "Introduction: The Right and Latin American Democracies," in *The Right and Democracy in Latin America*, ed. Douglas A. Chalmers, Mario do Carmo Campello de Souza, and Atilio A. Borón (New York: Praeger, 1992), 4.

5. Conservative parties, which Gibson (1996, 7) defines as "parties that draw their core constituencies from the upper strata of society," are close cousins though not identical to rightwing parties, as defined in this volume. While conservative parties are defined sociologically in terms of their upper-class core constituency, rightwing parties are defined ideologically in terms of their views on inequality.

6. The correlation between electorally viable conservatives parties and democratic stability for the period between the advent of mass politics and 1990 is robust: "The average ratio of years under democratic rule to years under authoritarian rule for the four countries with strong legacies of conservative party organization was almost 9 to 1. For countries with weaker legacies of national conservative party organization at the start of mass democracy, the average ratio was 0.7 to 1" (Gibson 1996, 26–27).

7. Gibson (1996, 31–36) emphasizes the nature of elite conflict in the postcolonial period: when conflict was primarily between the city and the countryside, strong national conservative parties emerged to represent the interests of the latter; when conflict was primarily between different regions, conservative fragmentation was the result. Middlebrook (2000, 7–11), for his part, argues that periods of especially intense church-state conflict resulted in the emergence of strong conservative parties to defend the position of the Catholic Church.

8. Frances Hagopian and Scott P. Mainwaring, eds., *The Third Wave of Democratization in Latin America: Advances and Setbacks* (New York: Cambridge University Press, 2005); Samuel P. Huntington, *The Third Wave: Democratization in the Late Twentieth Century.* (Norman: University of Oklahoma Press, 1991).

9. Huntington (1991, 95).

10. Scott Mainwaring and Aníbal Pérez-Liñán, "Latin American Democratization since 1978: Democratic Transitions, Breakdowns, and Erosions," in Hagopian and Mainwaring (2005, 40).

11. Rightwing coups in Latin America were not completely eliminated, however. Two notable exceptions were the failed coup in Venezuela in April 2002 and the successful coup in Honduras in June 2009.

12. Chalmers et al. (1992, 2–3).

13. Guillermo O'Donnell and Philippe C. Schmitter, *Transitions from Authoritarian Rule: Tentative Conclusions about Uncertain Democracies* (Baltimore: Johns Hopkins University Press, 1986), 62.

14. Kenneth M. Roberts, "Neoliberalism and the Transformation of Populism in Latin America," *World Politics* 48, no. 1 (2005): 82–116; Kurt Weyland, "Neopopulism and Neoliberalism in Latin America: Unexpected Affinities," *Studies in Comparative International Development* 31, no. 3 (1996): 3–31; see also chapter 6, this volume.

15. David A. Shirk, *Mexico's New Politics: The PAN and Democratic Change* (Boulder, CO: Lynne Rienner, 2005).

16. For an earlier use of the term "authoritarian successor party," see Kenneth M. Roberts, "Historical Timing, Political Cleavages, and Party Building in 'Third Wave' Democracies" (paper presented at the Challenges of Party Building in Latin America conference, Harvard University, November 16–17, 2012).

17. There are two notable exceptions: Timothy Power, *The Political Right in Postauthoritarian Brazil: Elites, Institutions, and Democratization* (University Park: Pennsylvania State University Press, 2000); Kenneth M. Roberts, "Latin America's Conservative Party Deficit" (paper presented at the annual meeting of the Latin American Studies Association, San Juan, Puerto Rico, March 15 to March 18, 2006).

18. For a classic account of single-party dictatorships and how they differ from military and personalistic regimes, see Barbara Geddes, "What Do We Know about Democratization after Twenty Years?," *Annual Review of Political Science* 2 (1999): 115–44.

19. Martin Shefter, *Political Parties and the State: The American Historical Experience* (Princeton, NJ: Princeton University Press, 1994), 5.

20. Although this chapter focuses on rightwing authoritarian successor parties, it should be noted that such parties are *not* an exclusively rightwing phenomenon. In Latin America, successful authoritarian successor parties with links to leftist dictatorships include FSLN in Nicaragua and the Democratic Revolutionary Party (Partido Revolucionario Democrático, or PRD) in Panama, which emerged from the Omar Torrijos regime. Robert Claude Harding, *Military Foundations of Panamanian Politics* (New Brunswick, NJ: Transaction, 2001).

21. Shefter (1994, 5).

22. Anna M. Grzymala-Busse, *Redeeming the Communist Past: The Regeneration of Parties in East Central Europe* (Cambridge: Cambridge University Press, 2002); John T. Ishiyama, *Communist Successor Parties in Post-Communist Politics* (Carmack, NY: Nova Science, 1999).

23. Grzymala-Busse (2002, 71–73, 77–79).

24. Many went even further, denying not only their authoritarian roots, but also their links to the right—a phenomenon that Power (2000, 71) calls "right flight."

25. For a detailed discussion of ARENA, see chapter 11, this volume.

26. William Stanley, *The Protection Racket State: Elite Politics, Military Extortion, and Civil War in El Salvador* (Philadelphia: Temple University Press, 1996), 69, 232; Elisabeth Jean Wood, "Civil War and the Transformation of Elite Representation in El Salvador," in Middlebrook (2000, 223–54). Of particular importance was the Nationalist Democratic Organization (Organización Democratica Nacionalista, or ORDEN), a rural paramilitary force created by the regime in the 1960s, with tens of thousands of members throughout the

country. According to Julie Mazzei, ORDEN eventually evolved into "the central nerve system of the country's death squads." *Death Squads of Self-Defense Forces? How Paramilitary Groups Emerge and Challenge Democracy in Latin America* (Chapel Hill: University of North Carolina Press, 2009), 153.

27. Stanley (1996, 219).

28. Ibid., 107.

29. Wood (2000, 243).

30. Marcelo Pollack, *The New Right in Chile, 1973–1997* (New York: St. Martin's, 1999), 198.

31. Manuel Antonio Garretón, "Atavism and Democratic Ambiguity in the Chilean Right," in Middlebrook (2000, 61).

32. The backdrop to these events was the 1982–83 economic crisis and resulting uptick in political opposition. Pinochet responded with a short-lived political "opening" and replaced many prominent government officials. In the words of one former interior minister and UDI founder, "the groups that had arrived in the government with the [new] Minister of the Interior had initiated a systematic displacement of the previous collaborators of the government within the entire public administration." Those who were displaced concluded that "it was indispensable to organize themselves politically, in order to give permanence and projection to the new ideas they advocated." Sergio Fernández, *Mi lucha por la democracia* (Santiago: Editorial los Andes), 194–95.

33. Carlos Huneeus, *The Pinochet Regime* (Boulder, CO: Lynne Rienner, 2007), 196, 226. After Chile's transition to democracy, several other high-profile authoritarian regime incumbents joined UDI, including a number of former Pinochet ministers (e.g., Hernán Büchi, José Piñera, Guillermo Arthur) and even a member of the former military junta (General Rodolfo Stange).

34. Pamela Constable and Arturo Valenzuela, *A Nation of Enemies: Chile under Pinochet* (New York: W. W. Norton, 1991), 289.

35. Ibid., 141–42, 146.

36. Catherine M. Conaghan and James M. Malloy, *Unsettling Statecraft: Democracy and Neoliberalism in the Central Andes* (Pittsburgh, PA: Pittsburgh University Press, 1994), 126.

37. Laurence Whitehead, "Bolivia and the Viability of Democracy," *Journal of Democracy* 12, no. 2 (2001): 11.

38. Catherine M. Conaghan, James M. Malloy, and Luis A. Abugattas, "Business and the 'Boys': The Politics of Neoliberalism in the Central Andes," *Latin American Research Review* 25, no. 2 (1990): 11.

39. Eduardo A. Gamarra and James M. Malloy, "The Patrimonial Dynamics of Party Politics in Bolivia," in *Building Democratic Institutions: Party Systems in Latin America*, ed. Scott Mainwaring and Timothy R. Scully (Stanford, CA: Stanford University Press, 1995), 420.

40. Owing to Bolivia's unusual electoral system, which allowed congress to choose the president if no candidate won a majority of the popular vote, in 1985 Banzer was denied the presidency despite having won a plurality.

41. In July 2001, Banzer was diagnosed with terminal cancer. He subsequently resigned the presidency and handed power to his vice president, Jorge Quiroga, who completed his term.

42. Gamarra and Malloy (1995, 418).

43. After seizing power in 1964, the Brazilian military created the National Renewal Alliance (Aliança Renovadora Nacional, or ARENA) as the regime's official party. In 1985, PFL

split off from the official party; however, it remained "the true heir of the old ARENA party" (Power 2000, 80). PFL has been tremendously successful under democracy: "in terms of consistent access to political power, the PFL has been the greatest success story among the political parties of the New Republic, and it remains thoroughly dominated by veterans of the military regime" (Power 2000, 81).

44. During Ríos Montt's dictatorship, the Guatemalan military unleashed a "scorched earth" campaign against civilians suspected of aiding the country's guerrillas, which resulted in tens of thousands of deaths—and converted Ríos Montt into a "popular hero." Virginia Garrard-Burnett, *Terror in the Land of the Holy Spirit: Guatemala under General Efraín Ríos Montt, 1982–1983* (New York: Oxford University Press, 2010), 9. The ex-dictator was able to channel this popular support into FRG, which became a major political player during the 1990s and early 2000s. FRG enjoyed at least fifteen years of electoral success before entering into decline. In the extraordinarily unstable context of Guatemalan party politics, FRG became not only an electoral success, but also, arguably, the country's most stable party since democratization. For a discussion of the instability of the Guatemalan party system, see Omar Sánchez, "Guatemala's Party Universe: A Case Study in Underinstitutionalization," *Latin American Politics and Society* 50, no. 1 (2008): 123–51.

45. In the 2006 and 2011 elections, the Alliance for the Future and Force 2011 coalitions, respectively, represented Fujimorismo. In 2006, Fujimorismo became the fourth-largest force in congress. In 2011, it became the second-largest force in congress, and its presidential candidate, Keiko Fujimori, won 48.5% in the presidential runoff election. In addition to its electoral success, Fujimorismo appears to be undergoing an unexpected process of party institutionalization. See Steven Levitsky, "Peru: Challenges of a Democracy without Parties," in *Constructing Democratic Governance in Latin America,* 4th ed., ed. Jorge I. Domínguez and Michael Shifter (Baltimore: Johns Hopkins University Press, 2013), 286–90, 303–5; see also chapter 7, this volume.

46. On the one hand, RN "mainly recreated the National Party," an older party formed in 1966 through a merger of the traditional Conservative and Liberal Parties, as well as the smaller National Action Party. J. Samuel Valenzuela and Timothy R. Scully, "Electoral Choices and the Party System in Chile: Continuities and Changes at the Recovery of Democracy," *Comparative Politics* 29, no. 4 (1997): 514. RN's connection to the National Party can be seen not only in its name, but also in the fact that several of its early leaders—such as Sergio Onofre Jarpa, Andrés Allamand, and Sergio Diez—had all belonged to the National Party prior to the 1973 coup. On the other hand, many of the party's leaders had occupied positions in the dictatorship, most notably Jarpa, who was Pinochet's minister of the interior between 1983 and 1985. While less closely linked to the dictatorship than UDI, nearly half of all RN deputies in the 1990s had held positions in the military regime (Huneeus 2007, 443).

47. PCN has been El Salvador's third-most important political party (after ARENA and FMLN) during most of the democratic period, while PRSC enjoyed considerable electoral success after the Dominican Republic's democratic transitions in 1978 and 1996.

48. For UCEDE, see Gibson (1996). For the Liberty Movement, see José Carlos Requena, *"Una gran ingenuidad": El Movimiento Libertad, 1987–1989* (Lima: Mitin Editores, 2010).

49. Edward Gibson, "Democracy and the New Electoral Right in Argentina," *Journal of Interamerican Studies and World Affairs* 32, no. 3 (1990): 180, 183.

50. In 1990, the Liberty Movement ran as part of the Democratic Front (FREDEMO) coalition, which also included two older parties, Popular Action and the Christian People's Party. Since the parties in FREDEMO all ran on a single list, it is not clear what percentage each party received in the legislative election. Though he ultimately lost the 1990 presidential election to Alberto Fujimori, Vargas Llosa received 37.6% of votes in the second round, and FREDEMO won 30.1% of the vote in the election for the legislature.

51. Susan C. Stokes, *Mandates and Democracy: Neoliberalism by Surprise in Latin America* (New York: Cambridge University Press, 2001), 45–47, 110–11.

52. A partial exception is the National Advancement Party in Guatemala, a rightwing party formed in the late 1980s. Under the leadership of Alvaro Arzú, the party became a major party in the 1990s, winning the presidency and becoming one of the largest parties in congress. But it entered into rapid decline in the early 2000s after suffering an internal split and the defection of key leaders. See Sánchez (2008).

53. Nancy Bermeo, *Ordinary People in Extraordinary Times: The Citizenry and the Breakdown of Democracy* (Princeton, NJ: Princeton University Press, 2003).

54. Gibson (1996).

55. For a classic account of how politicians can retain clientelistic networks even after a regime change, see Frances Hagopian, *Traditional Politics and Regime Change in Brazil* (New York: Cambridge University Press, 1996).

56. Huneeus (2007, 274).

57. See, for example, Huneeus (2007); Marcus Klein, "The Unión Demócrata Independiente and the Poor (1983–1992): The Survival of Clientelistic Traditions in Chilean Politics," *Jahrbuch für Geschichte Lateinamerikas* 41 (2004): 301–24; Juan Pablo Luna, "Segmented Party-Voter Linkages in Latin America: The Case of the UDI," *Journal of Latin American Studies* 42, no. 2 (2010): 325–56.

58. Klein (2004, 324).

59. Scott Mainwaring, Rachel Meneguello, and Timothy J. Power, "Conservative Parties, Democracy, and Economic Reform in Contemporary Brazil," in Middlebrook (2000); see also Power (2000).

60. Stathis N. Kalyvas, *The Rise of Christian Democracy in Europe* (Ithaca, NY: Cornell University Press, 1996); Adrienne LeBas, *From Protest to Parties: Party-Building and Democratization in Africa* (New York: Oxford University Press, 2011).

61. Kalyvas (1996, 41).

62. Herbert Kitschelt, "Linkages between Citizens and Politicians in Democratic Politics," *Comparative Political Studies* 33, no. 6/7 (2000): 849.

63. Wood (2000, 240).

64. Leonard Wantchekon, "Strategic Voting in Conditions of Political Instability: The 1994 Elections in El Salvador," *Comparative Political Studies* 32, no. 7 (1999): 819.

65. Wood (2000, 247).

66. Stanley (1996, 241); Wood (2000, 247–48).

67. Sánchez (2008, 134).

68. Gibson (1996, 216).

69. Jeffry Frieden, *Debt, Development and Democracy: Latin America, 1965–1985* (Princeton, NJ: Princeton University Press, 1991).

70. Luna (2010, 333).

71. Ibid.

72. Wood (2000, 251).

73. Ibid., 249; see also Riita-Ilona Koivumaeki, "Business, Economic Experts, and Conservative Party Building in Latin America: The Case of El Salvador," *Journal of Politics in Latin America* 2, no. 1 (2010): 79–106.

74. Herbert S. Klein, *A Concise History of Bolivia,* 2nd ed. (New York: Cambridge University Press, 2011), 228–40; Gamarra and Malloy (1995, 420).

75. Noam Lupu, "Party Brands and Partisanship: Theory with Evidence from a Survey Experiment in Argentina," *American Journal of Political Science* 57, no. 1 (2013): 49–64.

76. The performance of many authoritarian regimes is disastrous, such as in the case of the 1976–83 regime in Argentina. This may explain why the founders of new right parties in some countries choose to distance themselves as much as possible from outgoing authoritarian regimes.

77. Gamarra and Malloy (1995, 404, 409).

78. Conaghan et al. (1990, 17).

79. Klein (2011, 231).

80. Conaghan et al. (1990, 11).

81. The literal translation is "hard hand"; a more accurate translation would be "tough on crime."

82. Alisha Holland, "Right on Crime? Conservative Party Politics and *Mano Dura* Policies in El Salvador," *Latin American Research Review* 48, no. 1 (2013): 44–67.

83. Ibid.

84. Quoted in Jeffry M. Paige, *Coffee and Power: Revolution and the Rise of Democracy in Central America* (Cambridge, MA: Harvard University Press, 1997), 34.

85. Levitsky (2013, 305).

86. FRG also seems to have benefited from its association with its leader's history of mass violence in the 1980s. As Garrard-Burnett (2010, 81) explains, Ríos Montt "enjoyed considerable support among the urban middle class, who valued the sense of personal security they felt under the *pax riosmonttista,*" and even support "in rural areas that had been deeply affected by the violence, where people reflexively credited him with restoring order and authority."

87. This dynamic is clearly illustrated by the failed cases of UCEDE in Argentina and the Liberty Movement in Peru, both of which collapsed after leadership defections during the parties' formative years.

88. Steven Levitsky and Lucan Way, *Competitive Authoritarianism: Hybrid Regimes after the Cold War* (New York: Cambridge University Press, 2010), 65.

89. For an argument about the potential of counterinsurgent struggle to produce elite cohesion, see Dan Slater, *Ordering Power: Contentious Politics and Authoritarian Leviathans in Southeast Asia* (New York: Cambridge University Press, 2010).

90. Pollack (1999, 117).

91. Alfredo Joignant and Patricio Navia, "De la política de individuos a los hombres del partido: Socialización, competencia política y penetración electoral de la UDI (1989–2001)," *Estudios Públicos* 89 (2003): 129–71.

92. Verónica Valdivia, "Los guerreros de la política: La Unión Demócrata Independiente, 1983–1988," in *Su revolución contra nuestra revolución,* vol. II, *La pugna marxista-gremialista en los ochenta,* ed. Verónica Valdivia, Rolando Álvarez, Julio Pinto, Karen Donoso, and Sebastián

Leiva (Santiago: LOM Ediciones, 2008), 145. The Popular Unity was the coalition of leftist parties supporting the government of Salvador Allende.

93. The Gremialistas were a conservative student movement formed in Chile's Catholic University in the 1960s under the leadership of Jaime Guzmán. Guzmán, who was elected senator in 1989, was assassinated in 1991 by leftist extremists. Many of his writings were subsequently collected and published in Guzmán (2008).

94. Jaime Guzmán, *Escritos Personales*, 4th ed. (Santiago: Fundación Jaime Guzmán, 2008), 63.

95. Guzmán (2008, 100).

96. Gibson (1996).

PART THREE

THE ELECTORAL,
NONPARTISAN RIGHT

CHAPTER SIX

From Right Populism
in the 1990s to Left Populism in the 2000s—
and Back Again?

CRISTÓBAL ROVIRA KALTWASSER

In contemporary Latin America, populism is associated with leftwing politics and with figures such as Evo Morales in Bolivia, Rafael Correa in Ecuador, and not least Hugo Chávez in Venezuela. Chávez, after succumbing to cancer in 2013, today represents a cult figure within vast sectors of the left. Populism can give rise to various political projects, however. Depending on the context in which populist forces emerge, they adopt features that lead to the formulation of leftist or rightist politics. A few Latin American countries experienced a wave of rightwing populism in the early 1990s, with the cases of Carlos Menem in Argentina (1989–99), Fernando Collor de Mello in Brazil (1990–92), and Alberto Fujimori in Peru (1990–2000) as the most salient examples.[1] Not without reason, these political leaders attacked "the elite" for their catastrophic economic management and promised to form a "government of, for and by the people." To the astonishment of most observers, once in power these leaders enacted neoliberal reforms programs that were anything but popular and tended to hurt the majority of the population.

The very rise to power of Menem, Collor, and Fujimori represented a puzzle for at least one reason. Until then, Latin American populism was associated with the promotion of economic policies in favor of state development and increasing social spending. Accordingly, researchers like Kenneth Roberts and Kurt Weyland opened a debate about the concept of populism, arguing convincingly that it is a mistake to define the latter on the basis of a specific set of social or economic policies.[2] This debate demonstrated that populism has a "chameleonic" nature; it can be used to support both left- and rightwing projects. More recently, the appearance of leftist populist leaders, such as Evo Morales in Bolivia and Rafael Correa in Ecuador, has reopened the debate over Latin American populism.[3] To shed new light on this topic, this chapter examines the conditions that determine whether populism ends up sustaining the construction of rightist or leftist projects.

We can learn important lessons from the wave of rightwing populism that Latin America experienced in the 1990s. One of these lessons is that if current left-of-center governments are not able to deliver what they have promised and address the problems that are relevant for voters, rightwing actors will have an avenue of attack against the establishment through populist ideology, advancing a program focused on valence issues such as democratic development, economic stability, or public security. Otherwise stated, the use of the populist discourse is not a privilege of the left. Just as the failure of the leftist type of populism promoted by Alan García in Peru in the 1980s paved the way for the rise of the rightist version of populism supported by Alberto Fujimori in Peru in the 1990s, the downfall of contemporary forms of leftist populism in Latin America can lead to the emergence of a new version of rightist populism in the region.

My contribution is structured in three sections. I begin by presenting a minimal definition of populism and clarifying the ways in which populism can lead to the formation of right- and leftwing political projects. In the second section I offer an analysis of the governments led by Menem, Collor, and Fujimori, putting special emphasis on the rise and fall of each of these presidents. To conclude, I develop some tentative ideas regarding the nature of Latin American populism since the third wave of democratization, seeking to address why rightist populism emerged in the 1990s and why leftist populism has come to the fore in the 2000s. In this final section I speculate about the potential rise of a new form of rightwing populism, which will possibly be centered on a critique of the establishment, with a strong emphasis on public security.

Defining Populism and Studying Its Relationship to Left-Right Politics

Populism is a contested concept in the realm of the social sciences. Given that the notion of populism has been used to refer to such a variety of phenomena and scholars do not agree on how to define it, certain authors have questioned its analytical and empirical value. To cope with this problem, one can turn to Giovani Sartori, who has convincingly argued that minimal definitions are the best option when it comes to dealing with contested concepts.[4] Minimal definitions seek to identify some central core that is present in *all* manifestations of a particular phenomenon. Seen in this light, the main challenge lies in determining the defining attributes of a concept—that is, the necessary and sufficient criteria that permit us to develop categories with clear boundaries. With this aim, Cas Mudde has proposed to define populism as "a thin-centered ideology that considers society to be ultimately separated into two homogenous and antagonistic groups, 'the pure people' and 'the corrupt elite,' and which argues that politics should be the expression of the *volonté générale* (general will) of the people."[5]

This minimal concept of populism has several advantages over other alternatives. First, this concept emphasizes that the aspect that all forms of populism share is the reference to a Manichean distinction between "the pure people" and "the corrupt elite," in which there is little space for pluralism. Once "the people" have spoken, nothing should constrain their will. Second, by referring to Michael Freeden's notion of "thin-centered ideology," Mudde's definition makes evident that populism never exists in pure form, but rather it inevitably emerges in association with other ideological positions, which are key for identifying the programmatic aspects of particular manifestations of populism.[6] Third and finally, this minimal approach takes for granted that both "the pure people" and "the corrupt elite" must be seen as empty vessels that are filled by the populist actors in a continuous process of interaction with their constituencies.[7]

It is worth noting that this concept is similar to other concepts that have been developed for studying Latin American populism. For instance, de la Torre maintains that populism is first and foremost a moral discourse that divides society into two ethically antagonistic fields: *el pueblo* and *la oligarquía*.[8] In a similar vein, Hawkins postulates that populism should be conceived of as a Manichean worldview, which assumes that there is a cosmic struggle between good and evil.[9] From this angle, populism has an elective affinity with certain organizational aspects (e.g., the continuous transgression of intermediary institutions aiming to link political leaders with the electorate), but these kinds of organizational aspects are *not* defining attributes of populism. As Hawkins has pointed out, "political organizations such as religious parties and millenarian movements have charismatic leaders and low levels of institutionalization early in their organizational life cycle, but usually we do not consider them as populist."[10]

The definition proposed here differs from the minimal concept developed by Weyland, who argues that populism "is best defined as a political strategy through which a personalist leader seeks or exercises government power based on direct, unmediated, uninstitutionalized support from large numbers of mostly unorganized followers."[11] There are two problems with this concept. First, Weyland takes for granted that populism inexorably implies a particular type of mobilization and organization, although populist actors make use of different approaches when it comes to mobilizing the masses, building political organizations, and developing political alliances.[12] And second, Weyland's concept puts an excessive emphasis on the leader, focusing the analysis on the supply side of populism. By contrast, an ideological definition of populism takes into account both the demand and supply sides of the populist phenomenon, as it emphasizes that the formation and adaptation of the morphology of the populist ideology depend not only on skillful political entrepreneurs but also on constituencies who have emotional and rational motives for adhering to the populist discourse.[13]

Nevertheless, both the definition proposed here and Weyland's definition stress that populism should not be conceived of as a specific set of economic or social policies. By way of illustration, while the populist Tea Party in the United States favors the free market, contemporary populist leftist forces in Latin America oppose neoliberalism, and populist radical right parties in Europe are characterized by their welfare chauvinism. Clearly, the commonality between these different expressions of populism does not lie in the promotion of "irresponsive economic policies."[14] What all these cases have in common is the employment of the *populist ideology*, which relies on the Manichean distinction between the people and the elite to propose that politics should be the expression of an allegedly self-evident general will.

Having laid out my conceptual approach, it is time to consider how populism can lead to the support of both left and right politics, in the sense that this ideological axis has been defined in Juan Pablo Luna and Cristóbal Rovira Kaltwasser's introduction to this volume. Given that populism is a thin-centered ideology or discourse, it inevitably appears attached to other features that determine whether populism ends up maintaining leftist or rightist political projects. Indeed, populism seldom exists in pure form. It always emerges from wider ideational contexts, and in consequence, populism is heavily dependent upon the political opportunity structure in which it materializes. For instance, Mudde has demonstrated that European populist radical right parties are rightwing parties owing to their nativism (i.e., an ethnic and chauvinistic definition of the people, according to which there are natural differences between cultures and the boundaries between them should be strictly respected).[15] In other words, European populist radical right parties assume that not all men and women are equal because they come from different ethnic and racial groups, which should be considered equal on their own merit. From this angle it follows that the main task of the state is to guarantee that only natives inhabit its territories.

The contemporary situation in Latin America seems to be completely different. Populist presidents like Morales in Bolivia or Correa in Ecuador are on the left side of the political spectrum owing to their fervent claim that inequalities between people are the result of the existing relations of power and hence it is time to overcome them through active state involvement. Despite their socialist rhetoric, they are not eliminating private property but rather fostering a systematic expansion of state control over economic activity. They oppose the free market and seek to use public authority to reduce socioeconomic inequalities. Backed by high levels of popular support and the rising prices of the commodities their countries export, these populist leftwing leaders have been able to implement pro-poor policies and enact reforms against the interests of the elites.[16]

Nevertheless, populism appeared in Latin America in a rightwing variant in the 1990s, when figures like Collor in Brazil, Fujimori in Peru, and Menem in Argentina were able to win elections by using the populist discourse and enacting neoliberal policies once in power. Put another way, these presidents should be considered examples of populism not because of their personalism, type of political support, or socioeconomic policies, but rather because of the ideology they professed. The question, then, is whether each of these leaders employed the populist discourse both during elections and in day-to-day politics. After all, it could be the case that they used the populist ideology in their campaign to win the support of disenchanted voters, while in office they might have eschewed the populist discourse in order to avoid the hostility of the economic establishment and secure sociopolitical stability. There is some evidence that a shift from populism to nonpopulism occurred in some of these cases, meaning that the populist label should be applied with some caution when it comes to analyzing Collor, Fujimori, and Menem. Not every one of these presidents *consistently* employed the populist ideology.[17]

Why did the Argentine, Brazilian, and Peruvian electorate vote for leaders who ended up enacting austerity measures and painful reforms that were anything but favorable in terms of economic redistribution? As indicated in the introduction to this volume, this is not a trivial question. Given that high levels of socioeconomic inequality characterize Latin American societies, the right has little chance of winning elections by openly stating its ideas and interests. This is where populism came into play in the 1990s. By attacking the establishment and speaking in the name of "the people," rightwing actors had the possibility of portraying themselves as political outsiders focused on valence issues, such as democratic development, economic stability, or public security. Doing so allowed them to develop a dual electoral strategy: on the one hand, they appealed to upper-class sectors that identified with the right by promoting neoliberal economic policies, and on other hand, they made inroads into lower socioeconomic classes not only by blaming the ruling elites for the dire situation of the country, but also by employing targeted spending programs once in office.

In this sense, the administrations of Collor in Brazil, Fujimori in Peru, and Menem in Argentina can be seen as examples of populism, particularly because of the discourse that these presidents advanced in their campaigns. Their adherence to the right can be distinguished by the implementation of drastic reform programs in favor of the free market. As Lechner has pointed out, a radical defense of neoliberalism implies the support of a model of society in which economic outcomes are seen as natural, and thus the existing inequalities are depicted as the inevitable result of a Darwinian process of selection against which the state can and should do little.[18] Equally important to the rightwing standing of these populist leaders was their alliance with specific pressure groups and upper-class sectors, whose ideas and interests were taken into account and thus crucial for the realization of far-reaching market reform programs.[19] It is not a coincidence that none of these rightwing populist leaders aimed to organize popular sectors and penetrate civil society. In order to not threaten the economic elites by enacting redistributive measures, they mobilized their followers only for voting. In contrast to contemporary cases of leftwing populism, the rightwing populist leaders in question did not have incentives to organize and empower their followers with the aim of driving them to the streets to pressure for reforms against the wishes of the elites.[20]

Comparing Cases of Rightwing Populism in Latin America in the 1990s

The most important similitude between Fernando Collor de Mello, Carlos Menem, and Alberto Fujimori lies in the fact that their coming into power was marked by a period of growing disappointment with the overall performance of the postauthoritarian governments in their respective countries. In effect, the administrations of Sarney in Brazil (1985–90), Alfonsín in Argentina (1983–89), and García in Peru (1985–90) implemented erratic and rather disastrous economic programs, particularly in terms of the capacity to control inflation.[21] The electorate of these countries had good reasons for being disillusioned with the political establishment and the economic results after the return to democracy. Collor, Menem, and Fujimori channeled this collective discontent by employing a populist ideology during the elections.

In other words, the rise of these three leaders was related to a particular sociopolitical situation in which the populist discourse was appealing to a broad variety of social groups who denounced the inability of democratically elected governments to satisfy the citizens' demands. By appealing to "the people," Collor, Menem, and Fujimori not only attacked "the elite" for their alleged incapacity for and disinterest in dealing with the real problems of the society, they also constructed an image of themselves as the only ones able to rescue their countries from the present disaster. This is exactly what Margaret Canovan has called the populist drive to enact the redemptive face of democracy; that is, a secular notion of salvation that implies that only a "government of the people, by the people and for the people" can overcome political alienation and realize the democratic ideal.[22]

Yet, as argued above, not all of these presidents employed the populist ideology consistently. Comparing the three of them, Fujimori was the only one who used the populist discourse in a systematic manner, while Menem was populist during the 1989 election but afterward abstained from exploiting the populist ideology. Some empirical support for this argument can be found in the work of Kirk Hawkins and his measurement of the populist discourse through the speeches of chief executives. A new data set shows that Menem's campaign speech in 1989 was moderately populist,[23] but the populist ideology almost disappeared in his inaugural address and during his time in office.[24] By contrast, Hawkins's data set indicates that Fujimori employed the populist ideology in his speeches in a systematic way until 1995. His discourse became much less populist between 1996 and 2000—a development that is probably related to the increasingly authoritarian tendencies of Fujimori's government.[25]

Unfortunately, Hawkins has not examined the speeches of Collor de Mello. There is nevertheless little doubt that he employed the populist ideology during his political campaign. As several scholars have argued, the Brazilian elections of 1989 were characterized by high levels of political polarization, and Collor used the populist discourse to portray himself as an outsider interested in fighting against corruption, getting rid of the establishment, and modernizing the country.[26] That said, the case of Collor is arguably a midpoint between Fujimori and Menem. I would argue that he was populist during the election, but in government he increasingly avoided the populist ideology. As discussed below, Collor's gradual moderation was possibly related to his growing difficulties to form a stable political coalition, while Menem's sudden moderation was probably linked to his interest in cultivating a good relationship with the economic establishment.

In addition to the use of a populist ideology, these three leaders shared another important feature: once in power, they implemented neoliberal reforms with the aim of controlling inflation and generating economic growth. Even so, the pace and content of the free market reforms varied considerably from government to government. While Fujimori and Menem prompted a drastic reorganization of the economy, Collor was less radical.[27] This is a striking fact because Collor developed a neoliberal program in his campaign, arguing that it was time to modernize and open the economy.[28] By contrast, the campaigns of Fujimori and Menem were based on an ambiguous economic program that was anything but neoliberal. Not by coincidence, Stokes refers to the cases of Fujimori and Menem as prime examples of Latin American presidents making a policy switch once in government.[29]

Another similarity between these three rightwing presidents was their capacity to forge alliances with upper-class sectors and specific pressure groups with the aim of consolidating their power and winning support for the implementation of drastic neoliberal reforms. Namely, Fujimori maintained a privileged relationship with sectors of the military and the business elites; Menem co-opted the rightwing party led by Alsogaray and included some rightwing technocrats into his government; in turn, Collor tried to craft a coalition with business elites and the right in the parliament, although his anti-institutional approach played against him, particularly when the corruption scandals related to his presidential campaign came to light. By attempting to take into account the ideas and interests of elite groups, these presidents put in place a number of strategies to compensate or neutralize losers and to create coalitions of winners.[30]

An important difference between these three cases of rightwing populism was the relationship of the president with the political parties and the congress. It is misleading to assume that populist actors, because of their use of an antiestablishment appeal, are always political outsiders.[31] Populist leaders can emerge from established parties and try to develop political alliances with the aim of staying in power. This was precisely the case of Carlos Menem, a member of the Peronist Justicialist Party (Partido Justicialista, or PJ) who radically reshaped his own party not only to undertake a far-reaching, market-oriented reform program, but also to dismantle traditional linkages with the unions and develop clientelistic linkages with the urban poor.[32] As a result, Menem had the ability to build a pro-reform coalition, which was reflected in a stable legislative majority during his administration.

Similarly, Fernando Collor de Mello was not a political outsider but rather a "maverick" because he gained political prominence in association with an established party and later opted to form his own political party. He started his political career in the National Renewal Alliance Party (Aliança Renovadora Nacional), a rightwing party created to support the military government. Then he created his Party of National Reconstruction (Partido da Reconstrução Nacional) as a personalistic vehicle for his presidential bid.[33] Collor's father was a federal senator from Alagoas, one of the poorest states of the impoverished northeastern region, but Collor himself studied in Rio de Janeiro and Brasilia. This personal trajectory allowed him to bridge the "old" and the "new" Brazil.[34] Nevertheless, Collor did not create a firm base of support on the streets or in the parliament because he naively thought that it was possible to govern insulated from conventional channels of political power.[35]

Quite different was the case of Fujimori, whose career represents a prime example of a political outsider. He was a professor and rector of a small university in Lima, and had never run for office before the presidential elections of 1990.[36] In fact, his meteoric rise to political prominence is directly related to the crisis of the established parties and his ability to cultivate the image of the untainted leader who

TABLE 6.1.
Key characteristics of the Latin American rightwing populist presidents of the 1990s

	Collor	Fujimori	Menem
Employed a populist ideology?	yes	yes	yes
Implemented neoliberal reforms?	yes	yes	yes
Developed alliances with upper-class sectors and specific pressure groups?	yes	yes	yes
Made a policy switch upon taking office?	no	yes	yes
Can be considered as a political outsider?	no	yes	no
Counted with the support of a strong political party in the parliament?	no	no	yes

was above the fray of partisan politics.[37] Although Fujimori obtained 62.4% of the vote in the run-off election against Mario Vargas Llosa, he did not have majority in the parliament, and, based on his electoral support, he decided to follow a confrontational strategy in congress.[38]

Table 6.1 summarizes the similarities and differences between the three presidents. Regarding their common characteristics, all of them employed the populist ideology (although Collor and Menem did so much more during the elections than in government) and implemented free market reforms. In addition, these three presidents developed alliances with upper-class sectors and specific pressure groups (e.g., the military in the case of Fujimori, provincial party bosses in the case of Menem, and business groups in the case of Collor) with the aim of developing coalitions willing to support the neoliberal reforms. Accordingly, these cases can be considered examples of rightwing populism. Concerning their differences, although Collor campaigned on a neoliberal platform, Fujimori and Menem switched to neoliberalism only once they came into power. Furthermore, only Fujimori can be considered as a genuine political outsider, and Menem was the only one with a strong political party behind him.

Fernando Collor de Mello, 1990–92

Twenty-one candidates took part in the Brazilian presidential bid of 1989, with the figures of Lula da Silva from the Workers Party (Partido dos Trabalhadores) and Leonel Brizola from the Labor Democratic Party (Partido Democrático Trabalhista) as the main favorites. Even though Collor started as a relatively unknown contender, he managed to make a strong showing in the opinion polls. His electoral campaign was based on an anticorruption platform, which accentuated his moral discourse about the dire situation of the country. By making use of the populist ideology, he presented himself as a modern politician who did not form part of the establishment and consequently was willing to enact policy reforms in favor of "the people." To the surprise of many observers, he obtained 28.5% of the votes in the first round of the presidential elections, while Lula da Silva came second with 16.1% of the votes.[39] Centrist candidates were eliminated, and the winners polarized the electoral competition.

In the second round of the presidential election, Collor took a clearer rightwing position, whereby he defended neoliberal reforms and portrayed Lula da Silva as a radical leftwing actor who would lead to not only a worsening economic situation but also an increasingly authoritarian state. Collor's strategy turned out to be effective, and he won the second round of the presidential election. But from the start he was a president without a firm party backing or strong base in congress. Although the left dominated neither chamber of congress, Collor did not try to develop an alliance with the center-right. Instead, he resorted to "provisional measures," making executive-legislative relations steadily worse.

This confrontational strategy was successful in the short run because it permitted him to enact a couple of reforms, particularly the so-called Collor Plan, a package of economic reforms seeking to eliminate hyperinflation, to foster privatization of state-owned companies, and to slash public spending through massive public sector job cuts.[40] Nevertheless, these measures did not deliver the expected outcomes. The situation of the economy remained anything but rosy, and Collor's public approval started to decrease at a fast pace.[41] Not all the business sectors were pleased with the economic management of Collor's government, as the free market policies represented a real threat to industrial groups, who began to mobilize against him and commercial liberalization.[42]

Collor aimed to govern by relying on popular support rather than a broader alliance between sectors of the economic and political establishment. This strategy ended up being problematic because the less he was able to satisfy citizens' expectations, the weaker his political position became. As Schneider has argued, because disorganized masses were largely responsible for electing Collor to office, his political support was extremely dependent on the output dimension and thus shallow.[43] Given that he was not able to build sufficient political force through popular mobilization, party coalitions, or elite pacts, the worsening of the economic situation and his decreasing popularity placed him in a vulnerable, isolated position. As a result, he began to rethink his strategy, and at the end of 1991 he succeeded in creating a pro-government bloc in the parliament.[44]

Collor's new approach came too late, however. During the first phase of his administration he made several enemies anxious to weaken his political position. Even though there were a number of scandals in the first two years of his government, the watershed came in 1992, when Collor's own brother accused him of involvement in an extensive corruption scheme coordinated by Collor's former campaign manager.[45] Under these circumstances, the president of the congress initiated a congressional inquiry. Neither on the streets nor in the parliament were there voices defending Collor. Even the conservative elites and former political allies were decisive in both allowing the investigation and, later, voting for his impeachment.[46] Before the senate voted his removal from power, Collor announced his resignation at the end of 1992, and Vice President Itamar Franco assumed the presidency of the country.

As Alfred Montero reveals in chapter 12 in this volume, Collor's rise and fall can be seen as a failed attempt to form a government controlled by the Brazilian traditional right, which has its roots in clientelist networks in rural areas of the country. Compared to the governments of Fujimori and Menem, Collor's administration was the least successful case of rightwing populism that Latin America experienced during the 1990s. Not only was Collor impeached and therefore unable to run for reelection, but also the neoliberal reforms he implemented did not help control inflation or foster economic growth. This means that Collor could not accomplish his electoral promises, and his parliamentary alliance with the center-right parties came too late. Accordingly, neither the popular sectors nor the upper classes attempted to defend him when he has impeached. Collor's rapid rise and dramatic fall demonstrate that waving the populist flag is a risky strategy. While the populist ideology can be useful for winning votes in sociopolitical contexts where the population is deeply disappointed with the establishment, it also leaves the populist leader in a precarious situation because he must show his constituency that he seeks to form a government "of, for and by the people." The corruption scandals and poor results of his government revealed that Collor was a role model neither from a moral point of view nor in terms of output. Under these circumstances, Collor's attack on the elites lost its plausibility and the appeal of the populist ideology simply vanished.

Alberto Fujimori, 1990–2000

At the end of the 1980s, the government of Alan García faced a major crisis on at least two fronts.[47] First, the economic situation of the country was more than precarious, not just because of hyperinflation and economic contraction, but also because of absolute isolation from the international financial community. Second, the Shining Path guerilla movement had increasing power and continuously challenged the capacity of the state to enforce the law and guarantee public order. The presidential elections of 1990 took place in a turbulent climate in which the Peruvian electorate had good reasons for being disappointed with the general situation of the country after the return to democracy.

To understand the rise of Fujimori it is nonetheless important to take into account both structural problems of the country and the dimension of agency. As Tanaka has argued, because the country was experiencing a critical situation, the main political actors and parties opted to be audacious instead of following risk-averse behaviors and taking pragmatic steps.[48] This was particularly evident within the left, which was not able to act together in order to develop a successful strategy for the presidential elections, although several surveys showed that Alfonso Barrantes, the main figure of the United Left (Izquierda Unida), had good chances of winning the electoral contest.[49] As a result, the left presented two presidential candidates and resisted forming a coalition with Alan García's party, the American Popular Revolutionary Alliance (Alianza Popular Revolucionaria Americana).

At the same time, the right also opted for a risky strategy. In contrast to the left, the main parties of the right developed an electoral alliance called the Democratic Front (Frente Democrático) and decided to have a common candidate: the famous writer Mario Vargas Llosa, who made a furious defense of neoliberalism.[50] While the left maintained revolutionary rhetoric and presented more than one candidate, the right advocated a radical modernization plan in favor of the free market and united around one candidate. By abandoning the ideological center, the main political parties provided a fertile breeding ground for the rise of a populist leader like Fujimori.

Alberto Fujimori was an unknown figure who eschewed ideological definition and employed the populist ideology to criticize "the corrupt elite" and to portray himself as the only candidate of "the pure people." Given that the political establishment of the country was highly delegitimized, Fujimori's Japanese heritage turned out to be a positive feature, through which he built the image of both a self-made man and a person who belonged to a cultural minority that—just like the indigenous population—suffered from discrimination.[51] With the support of Protestant Evangelicals and small entrepreneurs, he was able to put together an electoral movement called "Cambio 90." To the surprise of most observers, Fujimori obtained second place in the first round of the election and won a massive 62.4% of the vote to Vargas Llosa's 37.6% in the second round.[52]

The triumph of Fujimori represented a major shock to the political class, but he did not have a party organization behind him, and the main political parties continued to control the parliament. Hence conflicts between the executive and the legislative were bound to happen. Once Fujimori assumed the presidency, he announced a policy measure that took almost everyone by surprise: a draconian adjustment plan in favor of the free market.[53] But in contrast to Collor de Mello's reform package, Fujimori's drastic plan was successful. The implemented measures helped both to overcome hyperinflation and to foster economic growth, which in turn had a positive impact on the president's level of approval in public opinion polls.[54]

Given the absence of a broad political coalition and the adoption of a confrontational strategy with the parliament, Fujimori sought alliances with two kinds of de facto powers: business groups and the military.[55] Moreover, by accurately monitoring the opinion of the electorate through surveys, he knew that his approval ratings were improving. As Carrión has demonstrated, Fujimori's constant support in public opinion polls can be explained by two factors: his ability to defeat hyperinflation and his capacity to undermine the Shining Path guerilla movement.[56] Backed by his approval ratings and the military, in April 1992 Fujimori undertook what has become known as the *autogolpe*, or "self-coup." Fujimori closed the parliament, arguing not only that the congressmen were "unproductive charlatans" and "enemies of the people," but also that there was a need for "government of emergency and national reconstruction."[57] Interestingly, Peruvians were not against this measure—quite to the contrary. Different polls showed that there was extensive popular support for closing the parliament, and Fujimori referred to these data in his public discourses, both at the national and international levels, to argue that the self-coup was a "democratic" exercise.[58]

The closing of the parliament marked a watershed in the country's political development, signaling the beginning of the formation of a competitive authoritarian regime.[59] In effect, Fujimori's power rested in general on the military and in particular on the obscure figure of Vladimiro Montesinos, who was in charge of Peru's intelligence service (Servicio de Inteligencia Nacional), from which he not only bribed parliamentarians, members of the media, and businesspeople, but also waged a dirty war against the opposition.[60] Fujimori's fall was directly related to the September 2000 leaking of a videotape in which Montesinos appeared paying a congressman $15,000 to join the government majority in the parliament.[61] The video demonstrated what many Peruvians knew—that Fujimori's administration ruled by developing a vast network of pressure and corruption. The leaking of the tape generated internal divisions, which led to the final breakdown of the regime. On November 20, 2000, the president faxed his resignation from Tokyo, Japan.

Fujimori's rise to power was related to the dramatic situation that the country was facing at the end of the 1980s and his ability to channel the existing discontent by employing the populist ideology during the elections. Fujimori also used the populist discourse in government to attack the political establishment and to legitimize his antidemocratic measures, such as the closure of the parliament in 1992. As Weyland has persuasively argued, however, Fujimori's success in terms of economic stability and public security brought about new citizen demands, which his regime was not capable of addressing.[62] To put it another way, while Peruvians voters reelected

Fujimori in 1995 because he was able to control hyperinflation and to undermine the Shining Path guerilla movement, they were aware that the means Fujimori employed were anything but honest. Once they started to request more transparency and less involvement of the military, the government entered a blind alley.

Carlos Menem, 1989–99

Although the government of Raúl Alfonsín (1983–89) made important contributions to the restoration of democracy in Argentina, it also had a negative impact on the promotion of democratic stability, aggravating the fragile economic situation of the country and thus generating a political climate of anxiety and distrust.[63] In 1988, given that Alfonsín's administration faced problems with the military and was confronted with growing economic difficulties, it decided to move up the presidential election by six months. In essence, two options were on the table. On the one hand, Eduardo Angeloz, the candidate of the Radical Civic Union (Unión Cívica Radical), represented a centrist and prudent leader who argued in favor of state austerity and a gradual opening of the economy. On the other hand, Carlos Menem, the candidate of PJ, symbolized not only the return of Peronism, but also the promise of large wage increases and a moratorium on servicing of external debt.

The populist discourse was present in Menem's campaign, which relied on a defense of the "common people" as well as a radical critique of the establishment in general and the economic elite in particular. In fact, Menem insisted that he would not pay the country's debt "with the hunger of the Argentine people," and he harshly criticized the economic bourgeoisie, exemplified by the conglomerate Bunge y Born.[64] At the same time, instead of developing concrete policy proposals and economic reforms, Menem opted to use the ambiguous concept of a "productive revolution," whereby he promised large wage increases and job expansion.[65] At the end of the day, this electoral strategy was successful. On May 1989, with the support of the middle and lower classes, Menem won the presidential elections with 49% of votes, allowing for the return of Peronism to power.[66]

At the beginning of 1989 the specter of hyperinflation was haunting Argentina again, and both the World Bank and the International Monetary Fund announced that they were not going to release more credits unless the country undertook economic reforms in favor of the free market. Hence Menem's triumph occurred in a critical context. But to the surprise of most observers, he responded to the hyperinflationary crisis with a dramatic policy shift. Although he attacked the elite during his campaign, once in government, Menem opted to form a cabinet with business leaders (including, among others, executives of the Bunge y Born corporation), conservative politicians (e.g., the center-right party controlled by Álvaro Alsogaray),

and market-oriented technocrats in order to enact a far-reaching neoliberal program.[67] One of the main policy reforms was the so-called Convertibility Plan, an
initiative headed by the economist Domingo Cavallo, which by fixing the exchange
rate contributed to establishing macroeconomic stability. The overall result of
Menem's policy switch was to a certain extent quite positive. Not only was hyperinflation controlled and the economy started to grow again, but also, during the first
four years of government, the administration received high approval ratings.[68]

How does one explain Menem's ability to undertake far-reaching neoliberal reforms, even though he had promised to avoid these kinds of policies during the
electoral campaign? It is important to consider three factors. First, since the country
was facing a critical situation and hyperinflation represented a real trauma for Ar-
gentineans, the electorate was prepared to accept harsh measures in order to restore
economic stability.[69] Second, Menem's economic liberalization program was designed strategically in the sense that it involved several compensatory policies (e.g.,
granting unions a share of the privatization) that were crucial for crafting a coalition
with labor and business.[70] Third, Menem managed to have a virtual majority in the
congress, preventing the kind of executive-legislative deadlock experienced by Collor
in Brazil and by Fujimori in Peru.[71]

The more Menem worked to craft a coalition, the less important the populist
ideology became for his administration. Instead of attacking the establishment, he
opted to take into account the interests of congress and the provinces.[72] Menem
ruled not by exploiting the populist discourse, but by developing "old tactics" that
helped him to construct a strong political alliance both within and outside congress
to provide support for economic reform.[73] Yet Argentine society was not blind to the
way in which Menem ruled. While certain groups tolerated or supported the government because they were winners in the neoliberal reforms or were compensated
by clientelist networks, many other groups were highly critical and developed innovative forms of making authorities accountable that relied on vertical—though
nonelectoral—mechanisms.[74] In fact, during Menem's rule it became clear that
there was a critical mass of citizens with high expectations of democracy in Argentina. These citizens came mainly from the urban middle class, and they demanded
better political representation and institutional innovations in order to improve the
quality of democracy.[75]

Not by coincidence, during his second presidential term (1995–99), Menem's
approval rating declined steadily, and the government was confronted with increasing pressure from the civil society, particularly the so-called Movimiento Piquetero.
Similar to what happened to Fujimori in Peru, Menem suffered a kind of "paradox
of success": his very success in achieving economic stability paved the way for the
rise of new social demands (e.g., clean government, fight against unemployment,

etc.), which the government was not able to satisfy.[76] Moreover, although the neo-liberal reforms contributed to generate macroeconomic stability, they had a devastating effect on Argentine society. The middle class became impoverished and fragmented, and the urban poor got more dependent on clientelistic networks.[77] Indeed, many held Menem responsible for the economic debacle that the country experimented in 2001. Although he passed to the second round of the presidential elections of 2003, the opinion polls showed that he would experience an embarrassing defeat against Néstor Kirchner, and under these circumstances he abandoned the race.[78]

From Right to Left Populism—and Back Again?

The three main rightwing populist actors that were in power in Latin America during the 1990s all experienced rise and fall from power. But today's situation is quite different: the left is using populist ideology. Leaders like Hugo Chávez in Venezuela, Rafael Correa in Ecuador, and Evo Morales in Bolivia have developed a populist discourse that criticizes "the elite" for their support for free market policies, which have been allegedly undertaken against the will of "the people." From this perspective, neoliberal reform programs are seen as the main cause of political alienation, and growing state intervention is defined as a necessary measure to improve the integration of excluded sectors.[79] Additionally, these populist leftwing presidents have condemned the role of the International Monetary Fund, the World Bank, and the United States for their involvement in Latin America, particularly with regard to the promotion of economic deregulation, liberalization, and privatization.[80]

Whereas Latin American populism experienced a marriage of convenience with neoliberalism during the 1990s, today leftwing actors, who adhere to a new model of socialism, advocate Latin American populism. How do we account for this transformation? Why did populism appear in a rightist guise in the 1990s and in a leftist variant after the 2000s? To shed light on this question, below I offer a tentative explanation, which indicates that differences in the Zeitgeist of the 1990s and 2000s are crucial for understanding the emergence of contrasting types of populism in Latin America. In other words, different political opportunity structures set conditions that are more or less propitious for the rise of populism either from the right or from the left.

Following the contentious politics approach, political opportunity structure is conceived here as "consistent—but not necessarily formal or permanent—dimensions of the political environment that provide incentives for collective action by affecting people's expectations for success or failure."[81] According to this conceptualization, resources *external* to leaders and parties are crucial for analyzing why specific political agendas might be more appealing and successful in different periods of time. Populism always refers to the Manichean distinction between "the pure people" and "the corrupt elite," but it offers different views regarding (1) who belongs to "the pure people" vis-à-vis "the corrupt elite," and (2) which problems affect "the pure people." Different political opportunity structures can favor the formation of either rightist or leftist populism.

During the 1990s, the political opportunity structure of most Latin American societies was beneficial for the right. As Kenneth Roberts indicates in chapter 1 in this volume, the end of the Cold War, the transition to democracy, and the process of economic adjustment are key factors when it comes to explaining the predominance of a "conservative modernization project" in the last decade of the twentieth century in Latin America. After all, it seemed that the right had won the battle of ideas: the combination of electoral democracy and market economy was seen as the preferred—and the only viable—model of development. Under these circumstances, the neoliberal ideology and the policies of the Washington Consensus became pervasive in the region. There was little room of maneuver for implementing socioeconomic reforms seeking to go against the tide.

Not surprisingly, populism appeared in combination with a radical defense of neoliberalism. Presidents like Fujimori in Peru and Menem in Argentina used the neoliberal ideology to frame the problems facing their countries and to promote solutions that were allegedly in favor of "the people." By controlling hyperinflation, implementing targeted antipoverty programs, and portraying the defenders of state-led development as selfish elites, Fujimori and Menem were able to obtain an important level of public support. In addition, influential foreign and domestic groups supported these radical neoliberal reforms, which worked toward restoring economic stability but generated unemployment and socioeconomic inequality. Needless to say, this project of "conservative modernization" was implemented in many other countries of the region, resulting in a similar outcome: on the one hand, the consolidation of electoral democracy and the free market and, on the other hand, almost no political leeway for developing political transformations and socioeconomic policies capable of dealing with the uneven distribution of opportunities and the existing inequalities.[82]

Opposition to this conservative modernization project started to grow at the end of the twentieth century, however. One of the first expressions of rising discontent with neoliberalism was the emergence of the so-called Piquetero Movement in Argentina at the end of Menem's government, as well as the electoral triumph of Hugo Chávez in Venezuela in 1998. The episodes of antineoliberal popular mobilization that several Latin American countries have experienced since the beginning of the new millennium relate to both the articulation of social grievances against the negative side effects of free market reforms and the influence of transnational advocacy groups that have promoted new norms, principles, and framings that can be used at the local and national level with the aim of developing alternatives to the neoliberal tenets.[83]

The political opportunity structure of contemporary Latin American societies is currently auspicious for the left. More than twenty years of free market–oriented policies seem not to have been helpful for tackling socioeconomic inequalities. The global commodities boom that has taken place during the 2000s has been beneficial for Latin American economies, and, as a consequence, left-of-center leaders and parties in power had been able to offer material benefits to excluded sectors.[84] This is particularly evident in the case of actors like Hugo Chávez in Venezuela and Evo Morales in Bolivia, who have combined the populist discourse with socialist ideas in order to defend a new type of government in which political power relies on "the people" rather than on "the elite." Their governments have developed a whole range of new policies aiming at fostering the economic and political inclusion of under-privileged sectors in their respective societies.[85] That said, some authors have argued that the socioeconomic policies implemented by these leftist populist presidents are not sustainable and that their political reforms are undermining rather than deep-ening democracy.[86]

Conclusion

The recent history of Latin America demonstrates that populism is ambivalent with respect to left and right politics. After all, populism is a thin-centered ideology that inevitably appears attached to another set of ideas central to developing a political discourse that is appealing to the voters.[87] The current link between populism and leftist politics can thus be seen as a contingent arrangement, implying that changes in the political opportunity structure of Latin American societies might well facili-tate the formation of rightwing populism in the near future. As Carlos Meléndez shows in chapter 7 in this volume, the strong electoral performance of Alberto Fujimori's daughter in the 2011 Peruvian presidential elections was probably related to her ability to combine the populist ideology with a *mano dura* security plat-form—it was no coincidence that she hired former New York City mayor Rudolph Giuliani as an adviser. Many signs indicate that citizen security issues are becoming the Achilles's heel of the left in contemporary Latin America.[88] Accordingly, it would not be surprising if some countries of the region experience a new wave of populism characterized by a "law and order" approach in the coming years.

The analysis offered here of the cases of Collor, Fujimori, and Menem reveals a couple of interesting facts for speculating about the potential rise of a new form of rightwing populism in Latin America. First, the assumption of power of these leaders was directly related to the critical situation that countries like Argentina, Brazil, and Peru were facing at the end of the 1980s. When large sections of the population have emotional and rational motives for adhering to the Manichean distinction between "the people" versus "the elite," there is fertile soil for the rise of political leaders who can increase their electoral odds by relying on the populist ideology to criticize the establishment and to present themselves as the only ones able to rescue their countries from the present disaster. As Nina Wiesehomeier and David Doyle demonstrate in chapter 2 in this volume, many Latin Americans have the impression that their countries are experiencing a crisis of public security. Such perceptions can undoubtedly facilitate the emergence of populist rightwing leaders who can combine the populist discourse with an electoral platform focused on iron fist policies.

Second, although the electoral success of populist forces is linked to their ability to recoding the political space, with its diversity of actors and parties into one single "corrupt establishment," they can change course after their campaigns. Once in office, they can make an alliance with sectors of the establishment in order to have the capacity to secure governability. The more evident and formal this alliance, the less relevant the populist ideology becomes. As the above analysis of Carlos Menem in Argentina has shown, political forces can employ the populist discourse for winning elections, but once in power they might prefer to shun populism with the aim of crafting coalitions that are necessary for undertaking reforms. The assumption of power of populist leaders is related to their capacity to channel dissatisfaction and frustration with the existing state of affairs, while their approval ratings and governmental success are linked to their ability to implement policies that foster the production of common goods (e.g., socioeconomic stability and public security).

This argument has something in common with Susan Stokes's theory on mandates and democracy.[89] According to Stokes, under certain circumstances politicians might violate their campaign promises to enact unpopular policies, which can be best for constituencies and thus help the reelection of politicians. But I am less interested in policy switches than in why politicians might be inclined to employ populist discourse in elections and eschew it once in power. As I have argued in this chapter, both political insiders and outsiders can make use of the populist ideology in campaign, but in office it might seem wiser to avoid it or employ it only occasionally. This is particularly true if they are in favor of enacting reforms that are not opposed by the whole establishment. Populist forces that pose little threat to elites will not invest too much time and energy in organizing grassroots constituencies, building political parties, and employing a confrontational rhetoric.[90] This looks like a promising path for rightwing forces interested in defending iron fist policies in current Latin America.

ACKNOWLEDGMENTS

For helpful comments and suggestions on previous versions of this chapter, the author thanks Matias Dewey, Sofía Donoso, Edward Gibson, Kirk Hawkins, Juan Pablo Luna, Cas Mudde, and Kenneth Roberts.

NOTES

1. A fourth example usually mentioned in the scholarly literature is Abdalá Bucaram in Ecuador, who stayed in power only for a couple of months between 1996 and 1997.

2. Kenneth Roberts, "Neoliberalism and the Transformation of Populism in Latin America: The Peruvian case," *World Politics* 48, no. 1 (1995): 82–116; Kurt Weyland, "Neopopulism and Neoliberalism in Latin America: Unexpected Affinities," *Studies in Comparative International Development*, 31, no. 3 (1996): 3–31; "Clarifying a Contested Concept: Populism in the Study of Latin American Politics," *Comparative Politics* 34, no. 1 (2001): 1–22.

3. Carlos de la Torre, *Populist Seduction in Latin America: The Ecuadorian Experience*, 2nd ed. (Athens: Ohio University Press, 2010).

4. David Collier and John Gerring, eds., *Concepts and Method in Social Science: The Tradition of Giovanni Sartori* (New York: Routledge, 2009); Giovanni Sartori, "Concept Misformation in Comparative Politics," *American Political Science Review* 64, no. 4 (1970): 1033–53.

5. Cas Mudde, "The Populist Zeitgeist," *Government and Opposition* 39, no. 4 (2004): 543. For a detailed discussion of this concept, see Cas Mudde and Cristóbal Rovira Kaltwasser, "Populism," in *The Oxford Handbook of Political Ideologies*, ed. Michael Freeden, Marc Stears, and Lyman Tower Sargent (Oxford: Oxford University Press, 2013), 493–512.

6. Michael Freeden, *Ideologies and Political Theory: A Conceptual Approach* (Oxford: Clarendon Press, 1996).

7. Ben Stanley, "The Thin Ideology of Populism," *Journal of Political Ideologies* 13, no. 1 (2008): 95–110.

8. de la Torre (2010).

9. Kirk A. Hawkins, "Is Chávez Populist? Measuring Populist Discourse in Comparative Perspective," *Comparative Political Studies* 42, no. 6 (2009): 1040–67; *Venezuela's Chavismo and Populism in Comparative Perspective* (New York: Cambridge University Press, 2010).

10. Hawkins (2010, 40).

11. Weyland (2001, 14).

12. Kenneth Roberts, "Populism, Political Conflict, and Grass-Roots Organization in Latin America," *Comparative Politics* 36, no. 2 (2006): 127–48.

13. Cas Mudde and Cristóbal Rovira Kaltwasser, "Voices of the Peoples: Populism in Europe and Latin America Compared" (working paper 378, Kellogg Institute, Notre Dame, Indiana, 2011), 6–7; Mudde and Rovira Kaltwasser (2013).

14. Rudiger Dornbusch and Sebastian Edwards, eds., *The Macroeconomics of Populism in Latin America* (Chicago: Chicago University Press, 1991).

15. Cas Mudde, *Populist Radical Right Parties in Europe* (New York: Cambridge University Press, 2007).

16. Francisco Panizza, *Contemporary Latin America: Development and Democracy beyond the Washington Consensus* (London: Zed Books, 2009), 174–78.

17. It is worth indicating that Kirk Hawkins has developed an interesting methodology to measure populism through the speeches of chief executives, and one of his findings is that the populist discourse is more common in campaign speeches. See Hawkins (2010, chap. 3).

18. Norbert Lechner, *Los patios interiores de la democracia: Subjetividad y política* (Santiago: Fondo de Cultura Económica, 1999).

19. Panizza (2009, 55–63).

20. Roberts (2006, 137).

21. Weyland (1996, 15).

22. Margaret Canovan, "Trust the People! Populism and the Two Faces of Democracy," *Political Studies* 47, no. 1 (1999): 2–16.

23. For an analysis of this data set, see Kirk Hawkins, "Populism and Democracy in Latin America: New Data for Old Questions" (paper presented at the meeting of the Latin American Studies Association, San Francisco, California, May 23–26, 2012).

24. Personal communication with Kirk Hawkins, March 2013.

25. Ibid.

26. See, among others, Peter Flynn, "Collor, Corruption and Crisis: Time for Reflection," *Journal of Latin American Studies* 45, no. 2 (1993): 351–71; Márcio Moraes Valença, "The Politics of Giving in Brazil: The Rise and Demise of Collor (1990–1992)," *Latin American Perspectives* 29, no. 1 (2002): 115–52.

27. Panizza (2009, 54–55).

28. Moraes Valença (2002, 118–19).

29. Susan Stokes, *Mandates and Democracy: Neoliberalism by Surprise in Latin America* (New York: Cambridge University Press, 2001).

30. Panizza (2009, 59).

31. Robert Barr, "Populists, Outsiders and Anti-Establishment Politics," *Party Politics* 15, no. 1 (2009): 29–48.

32. Steven Levitsky, *Transforming Labor-Based Parties in Latin America: Argentine Peronism in Comparative Perspective* (New York: Cambridge University Press, 2003).

33. Timothy Power, *The Political Right in Postauthoritarian Brazil: Elites, Institutions, and Democratization* (University Park: Pennsylvania University Press, 2000).

34. Thomas Skidmore, "Collor's Downfall in Historical Perspective," in *Corruption and Political Reform in Brazil: The Impact of Collor's Impeachment,* ed. Keith S. Rosenn and Richard Downes (Miami, FL: North-South Center Press, 1999), 1–19.

35. Kurt Weyland, "The Rise and Fall of President Collor and Its Impact on Brazilian Democracy," *Journal of Interamerican Studies and World Affairs* 35, no. 1 (1993): 4.

36. Catherine Conaghan, *Fujimori's Peru: Deception in the Public Sphere* (Pittsburgh, PA: Pittsburgh University Press, 2005), 16–17.

37. Roberts (1995, 94).

38. Martín Tanaka, "Chronicle of a Death Foretold? Determinism, Political Decisions, and Open Outcomes," in *The Third Wave of Democratization in Latin America: Advances and Setbacks,* ed. Frances Hagopian and Scott Mainwaring (New York: Cambridge University Press, 2005), 271.

39. Moraes Valença (2002, 125).

40. Francisco Panizza, "Neopopulism and Its Limits in Collor's Brazil," *Bulletin of Latin American Research* 19, no. 2 (2000a): 184–85.

41. For an analysis of the approval ratings of Collor's government, see Argelina Cheibub Figueiredo, "The Collor Impeachment and Presidential Government in Brazil," in *Presidential Breakdowns in Latin America: Causes and Outcomes of Executive Instability in Developing Democracies*, ed. Mariana Llanos and Leiv Marsteintredet (New York: Palgrave Macmillan, 2010), 114–15.

42. Peter Kingstone, *Crafting Coalitions for Reform: Business Preferences, Political Institutions, and Neoliberal Reform in Brazil* (University Park: Pennsylvania University Press, 1999), chap. 5.

43. Ben Ross Schneider, "Brazil under Collor: Anatomy of a Crisis," *World Policy Journal* 8, no. 2 (1991): 321–47.

44. Power (2000, 193–94).

45. Moraes Valença (2002, 141).

46. Skidmore (1999, 12).

47. Conaghan (2005, 18).

48. Martin Tanaka, "From Crisis to Collapse of the Party Systems and Dilemmas of Democratic Representation: Peru and Venezuela," in *The Crisis of Democratic Representation in the Andes,* ed. Scott P. Mainwaring, Ana María Bejarano, and Eduardo Pizarro Leongómez (Stanford, CA: Stanford University Press, 2006), 52–56.

49. Martin Tanaka, "The Left in Peru: Plenty of Wagons and No Locomotion," in *Leftovers: Tales of the Latin American Left*, ed. Jorge Castañeda and Marco Morales (London: Routledge, 2008), 201.

50. Stokes (2001, 49–50).

51. Roberts (1995, 94–95).

52. Tanaka (2005, 271).

53. Weyland (1996, 18).

54. For a detailed analysis of the approval ratings of Fujimori's government, see Julio Carrión, "Public Opinion, Market Reforms, and Democracy in Fujimori's Peru," in *The Fujimori Legacy: The Rise of Electoral Authoritarianism in Peru*, ed. Julio Carrión (University Park: Pennsylvania University Press, 2006), 124–49.

55. Roberts (2006, 139).

56. Carrión (2006, 131).

57. Conaghan (2005, 29–30).

58. Ibid., 32–36.

59. Steven Levitsky and James Loxton, "Populism and Competitive Authoritarianism: The Case of Fujimori's Peru," in *Populism in Europe and the Americas: Threat or Corrective for Democracy?*, ed. Cas Mudde and Cristóbal Rovira Kaltwasser (New York: Cambridge University, 2012), 160–81.

60. Julio Cotler, "La gobernabilidad en el Perú: Entre el autoritarismo y la democracia," in *El Fujimorismo: Ascenso y caída de un régimen autoritario*, ed. Julio Cotler y Romeo Grompone (Lima: Instituto de Estudios Peruanos, 2000), 53–67.

61. Maxwell Cameron, "Endogenous Regime Breakdown: The Vladivideo and the Fall of Peru's Fujimori," in Carrión (2006, 275).

62. Kurt Weyland, "A Paradox of Success? Determinants of Political Support for President Fujimori," *International Studies Quarterly* 44, no. 3 (2000): 481–502.

63. Guillermo O'Donnell, "Argentina, de nuevo" (working paper 152, Kellogg Institute, Notre Dame, Indiana, 1991).

64. Stokes (2001, 46).

65. Sebastián Barros, "The Discursive Continuities of the Menemist Rupture," in *Populism and the Mirror of Democracy,* ed. Francisco Panizza (London: Verso, 2005), 261–62.

66. Ricardo Sidicaro, *Los tres peronismos: Estado y poder económico 1946–1955 / 1973–1976 / 1989–1999* (Buenos Aires: Siglo XXI, 2002), 155.

67. Edward Gibson, "The Populist Road to Market Reform: Policy and Electoral Coalitions in Mexico and Argentina," *World Politics* 49, no. 3 (1997): 357.

68. For an analysis of the approval ratings of Menem's governments, see Daniel Vázquez and Valeria Falleti, "Política económica, deslegitimación democrática y reconstrucción social en Argentina," *Perfiles Latinoamericanos* 29 (2007): 71–109.

69. Weyland (1996, 18).

70. Sebastián Etchemendy, "Old Actors in New Markets: Transforming the Populist/Industrial Coalition in Argentina, 1989–2001," in *Argentine Democracy: The Politics of Institutional Weakness,* ed. Steven Levitsky and María Victoria Murillo (University Park: Pennsylvania University Press, 2005), 62–87.

71. Steven Levitsky, "Argentina: Democratic Survival amidst Economic Failure," in Hagopian and Mainwaring (2005, 77).

72. Mark P. Jones and Wonjae Hwang, "Provincial Party Bosses: Keystone of the Argentine Congress," in Levitsky and Murillo (2005, 115–38).

73. Francisco Panizza, "Beyond 'Delegative Democracy': 'Old Politics' and 'New Economics' in Latin America," *Journal of Latin American Studies* 32, no. 3 (2000b): 755.

74. Enrique Peruzzotti, "The Nature of the New Argentine Democracy: The Delegative Democracy Argument Revisited," *Journal of Latin American Studies* 33, no. 1 (2001): 143.

75. Juan Carlos Torre, "Citizens versus Political Class: The Crisis of Partisan Representation," in Levitsky and Murillo (2005, 165–80).

76. Weyland (2000, 498).

77. Maristella Svampa, *La sociedad excluyente: La Argentina bajo el signo del neoliberalismo* (Buenos Aires: Taurus, 2005).

78. Levitsky (2005, 85).

79. Panizza (2009, 174–78).

80. Eric Hershberg, "Latin America's Left: The Impact of the External Environment," in *Latin America's Left Turn: Politics, Policies, and Trajectories of Change,* ed. Maxwell A. Cameron and Eric Hershberg (Boulder, CO: Lynne Rienner, 2010), 233–49.

81. Sidney Tarrow, *Power in Movement: Social Movements and Contentious Politics,* 2nd ed. (New York: Cambridge University Press, 2008) 76–77.

82. Fernando Filgueira, Luis Reygadas, Juan Pablo Luna, and Pablo Alegre, "Shallow States, Deep Inequalities, and the Limits of Conservative Modernization: The Politics and Policies of Incorporation in Latin America," in *The Great Gap: Inequality and the Politics of Redistribution in Latin America,* ed. Merike Blofield (University Park: Pennsylvania State University Press, 2011), 245–77.

83. Eduardo Silva, *Challenging Neoliberalism in Latin America* (New York: Cambridge, 2009), 26–29; Kenneth Roberts, "The Mobilization of Opposition to Economic Liberalization," *Annual Review of Political Science* 11 (2008): 340–41.

84. Steven Levitsky and Kenneth Roberts, "Latin America's 'Left Turn': A Framework for Analysis," in *The Resurgence of the Left Latin American Left*, ed. Steven Levitsky and Kenneth Roberts (Baltimore: John Hopkins University Press, 2011), 10.

85. Pilar Domingo, "Evo Morales, the MAS, and a Revolution in the Making," in *Governance after Neoliberalism in Latin America*, ed. Jean Grugel and Pia Riggirozzi (New York: Palgrave Macmillan, 2009), 113–45; Judy Meltzer, "Hugo Chávez and the Search for Post-Neoliberal Policy Alternatives in Venezuela," in *Post-Neoliberalism in the Americas,* ed. Laura Macdonald and Arne Ruckert (Basingstoke: Palgrave Macmillan, 2009), 89–104.

86. See, for example, Kurt Weyland, "The Rise of Latin America's Two Lefts: Insights from Rentier State Theory," *Comparative Politics* 41, no. 2 (2009): 145–64.

87. Stanley (2008).

88. Deborah J. Yashar, "The Left and Citizenship Rights," in Levitsky and Roberts (2011, 184–210).

89. Stokes (2001).

90. Roberts (2006).

CHAPTER SEVEN

Is There a Right Track in Post–Party System Collapse Scenarios?

Comparing the Andean Countries

CARLOS MELÉNDEZ

Since the breakdown of party systems in the Andean region, literature has characterized its political regimes as "democracies without parties," referring to a profound crisis of political representation expressed by high levels of volatility, extreme fragmentation, and citizen disaffection with politics.[1] This crisis was historically remedied in a personalistic fashion: efficacious, antiparty outsiders achieved popularity after the decay of partisan politics. They have since dominated the political arena in the region. From right to left, Alberto Fujimori in Peru, Álvaro Uribe in Colombia, Hugo Chávez in Venezuela, Evo Morales in Bolivia, and Rafael Correa in Ecuador epitomize the antielitist outsiders that have risen to power without the support of conventional political parties. Instead, their success is based on an antisystemic discourse that challenges established elites on behalf of an ill-defined "people." They have taken advantage of citizens' disillusionment with the political process in order to lead social revolts and even (self-) coup attempts. In democracies that lack political parties, these leaders do not depend on strong, institutionalized political organizations; electoral vehicles highly dependent on their decisions are sufficient. Once in office, their continued success relies on access to state resources that are strategically employed to maintain the loyalty of pragmatic followers.

This political backdrop is not ideal for (re)building political parties, and a number of questions must be addressed in order to overcome the challenges presented. Is it possible to represent a fragmented and disaffected electorate that prefers to endorse unknown, antiestablishment outsiders? Without access to state resources, is the development of successful political organizations feasible? And, more specifically, is it conceivable to build rightwing political projects within political systems controlled by leftist, populist incumbents?

In this chapter, I propose an affirmative answer to these questions based on analysis of Fujimorismo in Peru. In the context of post–party collapse and after more than a decade out of power, Fujimorismo is the political organization that most resembles a political party in this country. The two necessary conditions for its successful electoral comeback in the last presidential elections (its presidential candidate, Keiko

Fujimori, qualified for the runoff) are the development of a nascent political identi-fication at the individual level and the creation of a rightist ideological discourse on public security at the elite level that addresses demands for a state presence in mar-ginalized territories. Rightist movements in Bolivia and Venezuela are studied as negative cases in which rightwing political alternatives fall short of fulfilling these conditions.

Political and Structural Obstacles for Rightwing Parties in the Context of Party System Collapse

In the context of party system collapse, rightwing political organizations must over-come at least four political and two structural obstacles to achieve electoral success (defined by winning national elections or at least qualifying for a runoff). The first political obstacle that rightist parties conventionally face is programmatic: societies with high levels of inequality (as in Latin America) are fertile grounds for leftist po-litical projects that question the status quo (associated with the neoliberal right) and demand "profound," redistributive policies.[2] As Juan Pablo Luna and Cristóbal Rovira Kaltwasser emphasize in their introduction to this volume, it is difficult for the right to obtain electoral relevance if it defends the interests of the wealthiest minority and promarket elites.

A second obstacle emerges when rightwing political organizations do not have the resources to mobilize voters. Rightist organizations that do not have access to public administrations (at either the national or subnational level) have difficulty demon-strating their ability to implement policies and mobilize resources to organize their supporters. This is especially the case in countries governed by leftist projects.

The number of obstacles to the right's electoral success increases within party sys-tem collapse and under regimes with authoritarian practices. Party system breakdown occurs when established political parties are cumulatively unable to obtain a high share of votes during national elections. The resulting process is a gradual decline in electoral relevance.[3] Owing to widespread citizen disaffection with politics, party system collapse is definitively adverse to the formation of an organized and socially rooted political parties. In the Andean region, rightwing organizations face a partic-ular disadvantage because they are more likely to defend the (precollapse) status quo.

These party system breakdowns and crises of representation are followed by the emergence of populist leaders that polarize politics and institute a plebiscitarian form of democracy through the perversion of liberal democratic institutions. This process has a negative impact on political competitiveness and party building.[4] Right- and leftwing antiestablishment political figures in the Andean region have polarized the political arena around two issues: public security (Fujimori in Peru and Uribe in Colombia) and regime change (Chávez in Venezuela, Correa in Ecuador, and Morales in Bolivia). While the creation of a unified opposition based on an anti-incumbent strategy in response to leftist incumbents is important to consider, its development implies ideological diversity and not necessarily the formation of autonomous partisanship.

Additionally, the rise of antiestablishment leaders after the collapse of party systems implies several modifications to countries' respective institutional arrangements and practices that result in authoritarian tendencies and even competitive authoritarian regimes.[5] It is not a coincidence that the presidents following party system collapse promoted new constitutions (and their respective constitutional assemblies) in order to develop new legal frameworks that legitimized their continued electoral support and permitted a concentration of power in the executive.[6] Recent assessments of the state of democracy in the Andean region have emphasized hyperpresidentialism in Venezuela, disequilibrium of power in Ecuador, and concentration of power in the executive branch in Bolivia, all resulting from the political practices of these countries' antiestablishment leaders.[7] Finally, there is a general consensus regarding the profound damage that Fujimori's ruling style had on democratic institutions in Peru.

In addition to political challenges, the successful resurgence of rightwing party politics in Andean countries faces two structural obstacles related to the idiosyncratic characteristics of these societies. First, regional cleavages that divide these countries into territories with distinct social and economic dynamics have a negative impact in the political realm: it is extremely difficult for politics to recover its national perspective when a high degree of regionalism is present. Second, enduring political violence (in Colombia and Peru) significantly decreases the relevance of partisan politics in territories where armed confrontation is the norm because the state does not have complete control over its domain. Not coincidentally, both factors exacerbate the failures of states that are already weak and inefficient.

On the one hand, when peripheral regions lack a political representation of their interests, a polarized discourse emerges and divisions go deep. Subnational polarization aggravates the already-existing crises of representation, creating a collective action obstacle: it is challenging to put together a national political organization (or to forge coalitions) that is capable of overcoming regional barriers. The cases of Bolivia (Oriente versus Occidente), Ecuador (Guayaquil versus Quito), and, to a certain degree, Peru (Lima and the northern coast versus the radical Andean south) are the best examples of these profound, subnational divides.

During the collapse process, political parties attempted to tackle this obstacle through a survival strategy that consisted of "territorializing" electoral support based on regional divisions. The American Popular Revolutionary Alliance (Alianza Popular Revolucionaria Americana) in Peru's northern coast, rightist political organizations in Bolivia's Media Luna, the Ecuadorian populist right in Guayas, and recent opposition alternatives originating in the interior of Venezuela are all examples of this phenomenon.[8] This tactic reflects mounting limitations to the practice of partisan politics in a setting where the concept of the state is ultimately questioned. In the context of party collapse in Andean countries, social claims have emerged from two different groups: indigenous movements that demand political recognition and procapitalist social organizations (especially in Bolivia and Ecuador) that claim economic and political autonomy.[9] Both question the concept of a centralized state that neither recognizes ethnic diversity nor gives political leverage to economically vanguard regions.

However, widespread political violence decreases the chances of the successful recovery of partisan politics. When extrasystemic and radical actors employ military confrontations against the state, political stability, democratic consolidation, and political representation are undermined. This phenomenon not only imposes obstacles to political parties' efforts to organize politics in their respective countries, but also forces them to provide alternative solutions to the violence in order to distinguish their programmatic proposals.

Two cases that exemplify this challenge are Peru in the 1980s and 1990s and Colombia today. In response to widespread political violence, popular rightwing leaders developed a public security platform that addressed the military confrontation against Shining Path in Peru and the Revolutionary Armed Forces of Colombia (Fuerzas Armadas Revolucionarias de Colombia, or FARC), respectively. *Mano dura* policies (e.g., partial states of sieges) in Peru and the politics of *seguridad democrática* in Colombia, benchmarks of Fujimorismo and Uribismo, were employed as a strategy to militarize state presence in areas of confrontation and to strengthen the authoritarian legitimacy of these leaders. While leftist populist leaders focused attacks on the establishment by criticizing neoliberal reforms applied by previous administrations (Chávez in Venezuela, Correa in Ecuador, and Morales in Bolivia), Fujimori and Uribe utilized counterinsurgency strategies and focused on public security to legitimize their brand of rightwing populism and diminish political pluralism in their countries' political systems.

Rightwing political parties in the Andean region must overcome four political and two structural obstacles. First, in an ideological context, rightwing political parties pursue an agenda that is extremely unpopular in societies with high indices of inequality and a weak state presence. Second, when rightwing parties become the opposition (often against leftist populists), they lack resources for electoral mobilization and party formation. Third, it is especially difficult to build political parties in postcollapse scenarios where public discontent is prevalent; social dissatisfaction is generally channeled by leftist projects because rightwing alternatives are acknowledged as (precollapse) status quo defenders. Fourth, populist presidents have weakened electoral competitiveness and limited political pluralism, creating obstacles to (rightist or leftist) party formation. In addition, efforts to rebuild partisan politics face serious structural obstacles because of regional cleavages and political violence within the fragmented and socially heterogeneous countries of the Andean region. Given all of these challenges, how can any political force, let alone rightwing alternatives, generate electorally prosperous parties?

The Andean Region

The purpose of this chapter is to identify the conditions that determine the electoral failure and success of nonincumbent, rightwing political organizations in the Andean region. As stated above, I conceptualize success as a political party's ability to win the presidential election or at least achieve the second majority in a national parliament. I consider the cases of all rightwing political organizations that backed presidential candidates after the collapse of party systems and did not previously belong to government coalitions, including those that survived the collapse and those created afterward. In this sense, I exclude rightist political projects while they were in power (Fujimorismo from 1990 to 2000 and Uribismo from 2002 to 2010) from the universe of cases in order to control for incumbent advantage, although I consider the importance of their previous tenures in my argument.

The cases that fit the previous criteria are the Christian People's Party (Partido Popular Cristiano, or PPC) and Fujimorismo (2001 to present) in Peru; Movimiento Nacionalista Revolucionario (MNR), Nationalist Democratic Action (Acción Democrática Nacionalista, or ADN), Nueva Fuerza Republicana (NFR), Poder Democrático y Social (PODEMOS), Verdad y Democracia Social (VERDES), and Nuevo Poder Ciudadano (NPC) in Bolivia; COPEI, Primero Justicia, and Proyecto Venezuela—which form part of the Mesa de la Unidad Democrática (MUD), an umbrella organization that represents the opposition movement—in Venezuela; the Social Christian Party (Partido Social Cristiano, or PSC), Partido Renovador Institucional Acción Nacional (PRIAN), and Movimiento Creando Oportunidades (CREO) in Ecuador; and Partido Conservador, Partido Social de Unidad Nacional (2010 to present), and Cambio Radical in Colombia. Although my explanation pertains to all political parties in Andean countries, I consider three cases for analysis: one of success (Fujimorismo in Peru) and two failures (rightist political parties in Bolivia and rightwing political organizations that belong to MUD in Venezuela; see

TABLE 7.1.
Rightwing political organizations in the Andean countries

Country	Precollapse right	Postcollapse right
Peru	PPC (Unidad Nacional)	Fujimorismo
Bolivia	Acción Democrática Nacionalista (ADN) Movimiento Nacionalista Revolucionario (MNR) PODEMOS	Poder Democrático y Social (PODEMOS) Nueva Fuerza Republicana (NFR) Verdad y Democracia Social (VERDES) Nuevo Poder Ciudadano (NPC)
Venezuela	COPEI	Primero Justicia Proyecto Venezuela Mesa de la Unidad Democrática (MUD)
Ecuador	Partido Social Cristiano (PSC)	Partido Renovador Institucional Acción Nacional (PRIAN) Movimiento Creando Oportunidades (CREO)
Colombia	Partido Conservador	Partido Social de Unidad Nacional Cambio Radical

Note: MNR originated as an anti-oligarchic political party in the mid-twentieth century.

table 7.1). Before exploring characteristics of each case in depth, I present a general description of the right in the Andean region.

Andean political organizations created before the collapse of party systems throughout the region had strong ideological principles. Although some of them trace their origins to anti-oligarchic political forces (MNR in Bolivia), most supported (and those in power promoted) market-oriented policies. Given the recent resurgence of the left in Latin America and its challenge to neoliberalism, rightwing political organizations that emerged after system breakdowns could not insist on a conventional, pro-market platform. Those who did (PODEMOS in Bolivia and PRIAN in Ecuador), had poor electoral showings and are now ghost organizations. To avoid this demise, rightwing political parties have three alternatives: subsume ideological principles in a regime change agenda, conflate democratization demands with a discourse on regional autonomy, or create an appealing discourse that integrates ideological principles with the electorate's current expectations of the state. I anticipate the latter alternative to have a greater chance of achieving electoral support.

In Bolivia and Venezuela (and in Ecuador to a degree), rightwing forces opted for the first path. Socialist leaders' efforts to concentrate power and reduce political competition in their respective countries and the subsequent damage to representative democratic institutions allowed the rightwing opposition to pursue a democratization agenda based on defense of the rule of law, balance of power, freedom of information, and liberal democracy in general. But this regime-change agenda appears insufficient to mobilize and articulate popular support. While it is useful to unite opposition in electoral junctures, it is not effective over a long enough period of time to build autonomous political organizations (while MUD was relatively successful in Venezuela's 2012 presidential elections, Chavismo won twenty of the twenty-three states that participated in subnational elections held two months later). Furthermore, rightwing opposition parties do not achieve definitive electoral success when they combine democratization demands with claims for regional economic and political autonomy (PRIAN and CREO in Ecuador; VERDES and NPC in Bolivia). While the autonomic platform effectively concentrates electoral support in subnational arenas and in most cases leads to the election of regional figures that emerge as prominent opposition leaders, it is not sufficient within a national political movement.

An alternative strategy is to combine the defense of the status quo (especially in economic terms) with a discourse that implies a specific type of state intervention. Public security and the demand for law and order are fundamental national concerns in the Andean region, particularly in countries with internal social conflicts like Peru and Colombia. An opportunity exists for rightwing political leaders to develop a discourse centered on *mano dura* policies, concentration of power, and promotion of military initiatives, especially when issues related to regime change are not the focus. In Peru, Keiko Fujimori appealed to the memory of the "politics of reconstruction" under her father's mandate (according to polls, public security continues to be the most important concern for Peruvians). Moreover, rightwing leaders attempt to neutralize leftist opposition by emphasizing the shared ideological and formative background of terrorist movements in these countries and formal, pro-system leftist parties. These internal conflicts help explain why the traditional left has become weaker in Colombia and Peru in comparison to other Andean countries: the National Liberation Army (Ejército de Liberación Nacional, or ELN) and FARC in Colombia and Movimiento Revolucionario Túpac Amaru (MRTA) and Shining Path in Peru had common origins with leftwing democratic actors like the sector of M19 embedded in Polo Democrático in Colombia and Partido Socialista and Patria Roja in Peru. I believe the predominant public opinion in favor of *mano dura* in Peru and Colombia cannot be explained without accounting for the influence of political violence (rebellions promoted by leftist radicals), a phenomenon that makes security issues more relevant and neutralizes leftist projects.

In order to identify the conditions for rightwing electoral success in Andean countries, I focus in this chapter on the following cases: Fujimorismo in Peru, VERDES and NPC in Bolivia, and rightist political parties that belong to MUD in Venezuela. Using empirical evidence such as survey and electoral data (used to support the arguments when possible), I consider Fujimorismo a case of rightwing party-building success and the remaining two cases of party-building failure.

Peru

Today, Fujimorismo is a protopolitical party: it has transformed itself into a social movement–like political organization with a solid constituency and active social base.[10] In the presidential elections held in April 2011, Keiko Fujimori (the daughter of former president Alberto Fujimori) won 23.5% of the total vote in the first round and participated in the run-off election held two months later with nationalist leader Ollanta Humala (who won 31.6% of the vote in the first round). In a narrow victory, Humala received 51.4% of the valid vote while Fujimori obtained only 48.5%. It was one the most competitive elections in Peruvian history. What is really intriguing is that Fujimorismo was able to construct a political identification that conquered the hearts and minds of a significant portion of the electorate despite lacking an institutionalized political party, being out of office for more than a decade, and being politically stigmatized following the prosecution and imprisonment of its principal leader—Alberto Fujimori—and several of his collaborators owing to their crimes related to the violation of human rights and corruption.

I attribute the relatively successful reemergence of Fujimorismo in Peru's political system—as compared to other rightwing projects in Peru (e.g., PPC) and the Andean region—to two phenomena: the successful expansion of the rightist platform from an exclusive focus on the economy to a more balanced emphasis on public security and the ability to mobilize the electorate and to shape a strong political identification among its followers. Additionally, previous experience in power helped demonstrate Fujimorismo's effectiveness in public administration. Presidents that followed Alberto Fujimori's tenure in office were not critical of his party's main goal—a dual emphasis on improving social programs and combating threats to public security—thus limiting its political stigmatization after his downfall (especially with regard to corruption and authoritarianism). Below I focus on the recovery of Fujimorismo as a positive case of rightwing political reemergence.

The Successful Revival of Fujimorismo

Although four political organizations pursued a rightwing agenda (Fujimorista Fuerza 2011,[11] Peru Posible, PPC, and Solidaridad Nacional), in the most recent presidential elections, Keiko Fujimori distinguished her campaign from the rest. While Kuczynski and Toledo debated the benefits of economic growth, Fujimori pursued a different platform. Her campaign to improve state services in the country's interior, especially in terms of public security, marked an important difference from the rest of the electoral supply. Her father's previous experience as president

(1990–2000), and in particular his focus on strengthening state infrastructure and defeating the Shining Path, made Keiko Fujimori's political platform credible.

A personalistic organization like Fujimorismo depends greatly on its political head. With Alberto Fujimori convicted of human rights violations and crimes related to corruption, his daughter had the best chance of taking advantage of his electoral capital.[12] Moreover, Fujimorismo was excluded from the democratic transition after the termination of Alberto Fujimori's authoritarian regime and was not allowed to participate in the National Accord, a multiparty consensus meant to guide the country in the next decades.[13] This political exclusion stigmatized local Fujimorista leaders, and the effect at the grassroots level was so extreme that Fujimorista politicians refer to this period (2000–2006) as "La Resistencia" (The Resistance) and consider it key to forging loyalties between their elites and political base.[14] Marginalization successfully united Fujimoristas and permitted the construction of a coherent political identification.

In the process of building a political party, it is important to develop a discourse at the individual level. Fujimorismo constructed a sympathetic "memory" of Alberto Fujimori's government and its legacies. Qualitative work with rank-and-file Fujimoristas exemplifies their unique interpretation (and justification) of issues related to the authoritarian regime. According to Fujimoristas, "justice" does not mean to dwell on human rights violations. Instead, it relates to the poor population's access to social services. Similarly, authoritarianism is interpreted as "order," not a disturbance of the balance of power. Fujimorismo's grassroots organizations created their own interpretation of the recent past. Now they have martyrs (Alberto Fujimori), a cause (Fujimori's freedom), defenders (Alberto Fujimori's collaborators), a *mano dura* ideology, and followers who identify strongly with the Fujimorista political project.[15] Keiko Fujimori's presidential candidacy activated these triggers and converted this social support into a political identification. A political cleavage was created between pro-Fujimorismo and anti-Fujimorismo factions based on the legacy of the fight against Shining Path and the political exclusion experienced after Alberto Fujimori's political demise.[16] With a rightist agenda based on public security issues and the creation of a strong political identity, Fujimorismo achieved the factors adequate to solve social choice and collective action problems that accompany a scenario of party system collapse. The result was an unexpected electoral recovery.

Unlike the other two rightwing candidates in the presidential election (Kuczynski and Toledo), Keiko Fujimori created an alternative rightwing discourse focused on increasing state influence and implementing *mano dura* policies to solve insecurity and disorder problems. PPC (through the electoral coalition led by former finance minister Kuczynsky) and Peru Posible (whose candidate, former president Toledo, focused his campaign in an evaluation of his administration) were not able to move past an economic-centered platform. They were convinced that an elitist coalition with business groups and other conservative sectors would be enough to gain office. According to polls conducted before the first round, Ollanta Humala and Keiko Fujimori were perceived as the candidates best able to promote "law and order" and "peace," while Alejandro Toledo guaranteed "economic continuity." Excluded from the balloting, the PPC coalition had no choice but to endorse Fujimori in order to assure the economic stability that Humala's proposals challenged. Pro-democratic sectors convinced Toledo's Peru Posible to support Humala even though it implied high risks in the administration of the economy.[17]

Political Identification and Rightist Ideological Background of the Fujimorismo

According to polls conducted before the first round of elections, Humala's Partido Nacionalista Peruano led with 24.72% of sympathizers, followed by Fujimorista Fuerza 2001 with 19.5%. Alianza para el Gran Cambio, a rightist coalition led by PPC and promoting Kuczynski's candidacy, enjoyed the support of around 12%; the right-centrist Peru Posible received 6.8%; and the traditional Partido Aprista Peruano only 5.5%. Moreover, 23.39% of the respondents claimed they did not sympathize with any political organization.[18] Significantly, Fujimorismo is the most socially supported rightwing political organization in the country.

These percentages may be inflated by the electoral campaign, however, and should not be taken as a definitive measure of party identification. In order to obtain an accurate measurement, we must analyze two indicators: the presence of a coherent voting intention across multilevel public offices (e.g., national assemblies, regional administrations, and local authorities) and an equally coherent antivote or rejection corresponding to the same party label. In Peru, only Fujimoristas and Apristas meet these two criteria. In the case of Fujimoristas, hard-core supporters represent around 6% of the electorate, while leaning Fujimoristas add an additional 10.4%.[19] Conversely, anti-Fujimoristas, or those who would definitely not vote for a Fujimorista candidate, make up roughly 23% of the electorate (see table 7.2).

In order to ideologically map political preferences, people were asked to place themselves on a ten-point scale (with a score of 1 representing the extreme left and 10 the extreme right). Results were similar to previous investigations. The national mean for this scale is 5.39, which is slightly to the right if a score of 5 is considered the middle point of the continuum. Taking each candidate's electorate separately, support differs noticeably. The ideological mean for Humala's electorate is 4.6 (its standard deviation is 2.6), falling to the left of the middle point. Conversely, Fujimori's elector-

TABLE 7.2.
Percentage of Fujimorista followers and Keiko Fujimori's electorate

Measurement	Category	Percentage
Political sympathizers ("Which political party do you sympathize with?")	Fujimoristas	19.5
Voting intention along three multilevel elections	hard-core Fujimoristas	6.05
	leaning Fujimoristas	10.38
Vote choice in the 2011 presidential elections	voted for Keiko Fujimori (first round)	22.45
	voted for Keiko Fujimori (second round)	35.76

Source: Instituto de Opinión Pública de la Pontificia Universidad Catolica del Perú, June 2011.
National sample of $N = 1,570$.

ate has an ideological mean that is clearly to the right side of the continuum (mean of 6.31) and is moderately less diverse (standard deviation of 2.4). Similarly, PPC sympathizers scored to the right side of the continuum with a mean score of 6.24. The ideological mean for Peru Posible supporters is 5.22, the closest to the national mean of 5.39. As expected, Nacionalistas are rated to the left side of the continuum (4.36) and are the only group that ranked to the left of the ideological spectrum.

Support for democracy is particularly low among Fujimoristas, and the party has been unable to generate a political discourse capable of calming the fear of authoritarianism that it provokes.[20] The fear of authoritarianism was a salient issue during the presidential campaign and, according to various analysts, was ultimately what hampered Keiko Fujimori's election to the presidency.[21] In order to strengthen its political competitiveness, Fujimoristas need to institutionalize their organization and moderate their political discourse in order to attract democratic sectors.

Bolivia

The party system collapsed in Bolivia after the 2002 presidential elections. Gonzalo Sánchez de Lozada (MNR) obtained 22.5% of the valid votes, 1.6 points ahead of Evo Morales's (Movement for Socialism, also known as Movimiento al Socialismo or MAS) 20.9%. Jaime Paz Zamora (Movimiento de Izquierda Revolucionaria, or MIR) received 16.3% of the vote, and Ronald MacLean (ADN) reached just 3.4%. It was the last time that traditional parties were competitive in the electoral arena: the parties forming the base of the "pacted democracy" that governed Bolivia after the democratic transition in the early eighties began to break down after this election.

According to Lazarte, the precollapse Bolivian party system was defined as a system of "three plus four."[22] Three parties (ADN, MIR, and MNR) constituted the main political coalition dating back to 1985, while another four (Conciencia de Patria Condepa; Movimiento Bolivia Libre; NFR; and Unidad Cívica Solidaridad, or UCS) served as temporary partners when they held strategic support. Unlike other cases (Ecuador, Peru, Venezuela), the personalistic organizations that complemented the three primary political parties did not maintain antiestablishment behavior. Although they promised to renew previous political practices and represent the "excluded" (e.g., Condepa and UCS in the late nineties), they forged coalitions with the mainstream political parties. In a context of high levels of poverty, inequality, and ethnic fragmentation, a solid party system emerged based on political alternation. Many scholars considered it an example of a strong democracy in an unexpected scenario.[23]

This form of pacted democracy also implied policy consensus. Despite some nuances, the traditional parties adopted neoliberal reforms as the main guidelines for the national administration. Although MNR had anti-oligarchic origins, it developed an agenda based on neoliberal economic reforms in the 1980s that it applied once in power in the 1990s. Although self-identified as center-left, ADN followed MIR's pragmatism and also assumed neoliberal policies. Including new forces like NFR, which refused to place itself on the ideological spectrum, these parties embraced a neoliberal economic model and ended up representing a traditional right-wing agenda after the decline of mainstream parties in 2002.[24] Before the emergence of MAS, a cohesive and popular critique of the market-oriented policies that governed Bolivia did not exist.

In 2005, the presidential elections divided the country in two directions: stability and change. The antiestablishment and socialist MAS, an articulation of social grassroots organizations, channeled national dissatisfaction with the market-oriented economic model and demanded an agenda based on the nationalization of hydrocarbons and a refounding of the nation through a new Magna Carta.[25] It was not the first time a leftist agenda was represented politically, but its high level of social cohesiveness and radical platform were unprecedented.[26]

As an alternative to MAS, Jorge Quiroga (president after the death of ADN's leader Hugo Bánzer in 2001) in 2005 formed a new political organization—PODEMOS—that was primarily composed of former ADN cadres, citizens' organizations, and corporations. Quiroga promoted a pro-establishment agenda based on adjustments to the current economic model (specifically redistributive economic policies) without severe modifications to Bolivia's economic and political systems.

In the 2005 elections, with the rest of the political parties in decline, Morales defeated his rivals with 53.7% of the valid vote. Quiroga obtained only 28.6%. It was the first time a Bolivian politician received the support of over half the electorate, making unnecessary political pacts to guarantee control in Parliament. Bolivian democracy moved from a coalition-based system to a majority presidential system, a transition that was cemented during Morales's second term.[27]

A Territorial-Ideological Cleavage

The decline of traditional parties had significant consequences in the way politics was practiced and how rightwing issues in particular were represented in Bolivia. First, social identifications emerged as the axis for political articulation: ethnic and regional identities were employed to unify and mobilize support in favor of the government (indigenous organizations supported Morales's promise of a new constitution that guaranteed a plurinational state) or to articulate the opposition's platform (regional organizations demanding autonomic agendas).[28]

Second, and embedded within the last point, the parties' decline made the political divide along territorial divisions more obvious. According to Antezana, the geographic division between Bolivia's Occidente and Oriente is mimicked by their political and ideological differences; the result is a regional cleavage based on electoral performance between 1985 and 2005.[29] Historically, in the *departamentos* of Santa Cruz, Beni, Pando, and Tarija (the Oriente or Media Luna) the political organizations associated with a rightwing agenda—such as ADN, MNR, and PODEMOS—have more electoral success than the political parties that represent a protest agenda (traditionally Condepa, MIR, UCS, and more recently Izquierda Unida, MAS, and Movimiento Indígena Pachakuti). The latter are successful in the Occidente, a region composed of the *departamentos* of La Paz, Oruro, Chuquisaca, Cochabamba, and Potosí. Using electoral districts as units of analysis, it is possible to demonstrate how class and indigenous divisions share this divide: districts with higher indigenous density and levels of poverty (more common in the Occidente) tend to support antiestablishment organizations, while districts with less indigenous density and wealthier populations (more common in the Oriente) generally support rightwing organizations.

Political parties reduced the salience of the territorial divide but did not eliminate it. When they entered into a collapse process (2002 and 2005 elections), territorial polarization became more evident (MAS won majorities in western districts, and the opposition—Quiroga in 2005 and Reyes in 2009—enjoyed more success in eastern districts). While political organizations in the Occidente were able to construct a cohesive political project, however, the Oriente's opposition was highly dependent on temporary candidates that did not base their support on grassroots organizations. While the leftist platform found a vehicle to channel its demands (MAS), the rightist agenda lacked a stable political vehicle to represent it.

Rightwing Mobilization without Parties

Although political parties lost links with society after the party system collapse, it did not mean that society lost its capacity to mobilize. On the one hand, MAS represents a coalition of social, grassroots organizations (traditional unions, indigenous *ayllus*, colonizers) with a tradition of participatory practices and high levels of mobilization.[30] While these groups do not belong organically to MAS, they support the incumbent so long as he or she represents their platform. On the other hand, citizens' organizations coalesced around corporate interests (*cámaras*), and neighborhood organizations supported the Comité Cívico de Santa Cruz, a long-standing regional organization that, in the absence of political parties (ADN, which had a historical base in Santa Cruz, disappeared after 2002 elections), has come to represent the Cruceña agenda.[31]

Comité Cívico de Santa Cruz played a decisive role in Bolivian politics after the collapse of the party system. It was founded in 1950 with a notorious regional agenda centered on demands for social infrastructure. During the 1990s, it mobilized around specific policies related to the economy (in 1999 against the redistribution of land, in 1997 against the mining code, in 1999 in favor of small-scale agricultural organizations, in 2000 in favor of new oil policies) but did not develop a severe critique of the neoliberal platform in Bolivia, perhaps because Santa Cruz, owing to its heterogeneous economy, is considered to be the only region that did not suffer the consequences of neoliberal reforms.

From 2004 to 2006, the Comité was the main political rival to Morales's government. It successfully convoked three massive *cabildos* (popular political meetings organized to make important decisions for the community) that demonstrated both its capacity to articulate discontent with the government as well as the political strength of the Cruceño identity. Its capacity to mobilize its followers represented a veto power that balanced Morales's apparent political monopoly, exemplified by its successful demands for the first-ever election of *prefectos* in 2005 and for autonomous referendum in 2006. As expected, the electoral support for autonomy was huge in the regions of the Media Luna (Beni, 82.4%; Pando, 85.8%; Santa Cruz, 85.6%; Tarija, 84.3%). Nevertheless, support for Jorge Quiroga, its presidential candidate in the 2005 elections, was not great enough to avoid another opposition loss.

Representing a Rightwing Agenda in the Context of Territorial Divide: A Failed Case

Comité Cívico de Santa Cruz did not succeed as the base for rightwing party rebuilding. First, its programmatic platform did not include a role for the state in specific policy areas (e.g., state assistance in social programs). In a context of high dissatisfaction with state performance, a competitive political platform must include initiatives to improve the state's service to citizens. As stated above, even a rightwing proposal should be capable of including a certain type of "state intervention" in its agenda. An argument that restricts the scope of the state will have difficulties appealing to the electorates of the Andean region.

In Bolivia, Comité Cívico de Santa Cruz pursued an autonomic discourse that severely critiqued the centralized state. In its alternative proposal, however, it excluded the possibility of state participation in public affairs. Autonomy meant independence, self-government, and exclusion from the rest of the country.[32] According to the Comité, the market should resolve problems of social and economic inequality. The inability to construct an alternative model that addressed state involvement in providing basic services to citizens significantly diminished the probability of rightwing electoral success in Bolivia.

Second, Comité Cívico de Santa Cruz was successful in politically mobilizing the Cruceño's regional identity, but that does not mean it was able to articulate a cohesive political identification that could serve as the base of an electoral project.[33] Rubén Costas (the Comite's president in 2003 and 2004) painted himself as the principal political opposition to Morales's administration. He was one of the principal promoters of the autonomic referenda and *prefecto* elections and actually was elected as *prefecto* of Santa Cruz in 2006. He was subject of revocatory action but stayed in office thanks to the 66% of electoral support that he received. In 2010, Costas was elected as the first governor of Santa Cruz under the new autonomic legal framework. The extent of his political control is open to dispute, however. Although he formed a rightwing coalition with former ADN and PODEMOS cadres and civic figures that achieved popularity during the Comite's mobilizations, VERDES (the name of this new political coalition) has not been able to monopolize political representation of the opposition, not even in Santa Cruz.

Germán Antelo, president of Comité Cívico de Santa Cruz in 2005–6 and a former ally of Costas, recently created a new political organization, NPC, that aims to dispute VERDES's hegemony in Santa Cruz. Antelo critiques Costas's attempt to actively hinder the emergence of alternative political leadership in the region. In fact, Antelo considers Costas to be the "Morales of the Media Luna" and has accused him of using state resources for various pro-VERDES activities and to coerce his political opponents.[34]

Although the Comité was able to mobilize thousands of citizens against Morales, its promoters were not able to create a solid political organization that, at the very least, represented the Media Luna. Divided by their two main political voices (Costas and Antelo), the opposition in the Oriente has had difficulty establishing coalitions with opposition leaders from other regions of the country (such as Juan del Granado from La Paz or Samuel Doria Medina from Cochabamba). Without a political identification distinct from a regional one, the oppositions' alternative projects are unable to gain widespread electoral relevance.

Venezuela

Since the successful electoral emergence of Hugo Chávez (elected president in 1998 with the support of 56.2% of the electorate), traditional political parties like the social democratic Acción Democrática and the Christian democratic COPEI have not been competitive in the electoral arena. Internal disputes, unwillingness to renew their political leaders, and extreme party institutionalization that inhibits the inclusion of emerging social sectors in their support base are argued to be the principal factors resulting in their electoral deterioration.[35] In the first three (of four) presidential elections in which Hugo Chávez participated, no opposition candidate obtained more than 40% of the electorate's support. Henrique Salas (Proyecto Venezuela) in 1998, Francisco Arias (La Causa R) in 2000, and Manuel Rosales (Un Nuevo Tiempo) in 2006 each failed in their attempts to beat Chávez. Henrique Capriles, a member of the center-right Primero Justicia and his latest electoral rival, was more competitive than his predecessors (receiving 44% of the valid vote) but still was unable to successfully challenge Chávez.

In the Venezuelan opposition there are two types of political organizations. After the collapse of the party system, some political parties managed to survive and maintain their ideological positions. Acción Democrática, COPEI, and, to a lesser degree, La Causa R lost not only followers but also important political cadres that migrated to new political projects. But they managed to launch renovation movements within their organizations—the first two relatively more successful than the third—that have allowed them to maintain their presence in the electoral arena and participate in the opposition's unification efforts without abandoning their programmatic traditions. The case of Acción Democrática is interesting in the sense that its political elites are still electorally competitive in some regional arenas.[36]

The second type of political organization refers to those created after the party system collapse, basically in a context of political polarization with the Chavista regime. Un Nuevo Tiempo, Proyecto Venezuela, and Primero Justicia are the most prominent examples. Although they do not share the same ideological backgrounds (Proyecto Venezuela claims to represent Christian Democrats, Primero Justicia considers itself a "centrist-humanist" organization, and Un Nuevo Tiempo aligns itself with the center-left), they are notoriously anti-Chavista parties that have emerged at the subnational level. Un Nuevo Tiempo started as a political platform for former governor Rosales in Zulia. Proyecto Venezuela has a strong presence in the state of Carabobo and has created a regional movement called Proyecto Carabobo. In the case of Primero Justicia, although it was originally a nonprofit organization, it has since developed into a political movement. In 2008, its main political figure, Henrique Capriles, was elected governor of the state of Miranda.

While the traditional parties that survived the collapse are highly ideological and experienced organizations, the latter represent anti-Chavista movements that have capitalized on electoral strongholds in specific regions in order to become nationally relevant. Significantly, they do not limit their projects to subnational boundaries. Unlike Bolivia's current rightwing organizations that are politically unable to overcome their regional identities, Venezuelan opposition parties use regional politics to gain experience in the pursuit of a competitive image in the national arena. The fact that Venezuela does not have a well-defined territorial divide (in contrast to Bolivia and Ecuador) makes this strategy more feasible.

Regime Change Agenda and Opposition

Fragmentation across the opposition is an obstacle to electoral success and the creation of a viable alternative to Chavismo. Although political polarization with Chavismo creates an opportunity to join forces, it is not until opposition parties relegate their ideological differences to a secondary level that they are able to collectively increase their electoral support. Chavez's regime uses plebiscitarian institutions and participatory mechanisms to maintain popular support and has rapidly entered an authoritarian zone.[37] A complete lack of respect for the balance of power, autonomy of legislative and judicial powers, and the liberty of press qualify it as a competitive authoritarian regime.[38] Chávez's Socialismo del Siglo XXI is characterized by the state's dominant role in the administration of strategic areas of the economy and subsidies targeting low-income sectors.[39]

The fragmented opposition has two options to unite around ideological tenets: articulate the opposition based on an alternative development model to Chavismo or develop an agenda based on regime change and focus on strengthening representative democratic institutions. The ideological diversity of the opposition makes the first alternative unlikely: from traditional (Acción Democrática) and new (Un Nuevo Tiempo) social democrats to neo-Marxists (La Causa R) and traditional (COPEI) and new Centro-humanistas (Primero Justicia), it is too difficult to agree on a programmatic agenda concerning basic issues like the role of the state in the economy and market-oriented reforms. Although the popularity of Chavista policies has created common agreement regarding the value of state intervention in some strategic areas (even the rightwing traditional COPEI acknowledges in its statutes that "the human being is limited, and needs from the state to help him to overcome his limitations"), profound ideological differences based on past political conflicts still exist.

Disregarding ideological principles as a basis for unification, the opposition has attempted to create a political platform based on a regime-change agenda, capitalizing on a political and cultural cleavage that divides Chavismo (leftist and personalistic) from anti-Chavismo (nonpersonalistic).[40] Mesa de la Unidad Democrática was the latest attempt to unite opposition parties (social democrats, Christians, center-right elites) in order to launch a single presidential candidate in the 2012 elections. In response to previously unsuccessful experiences (Concertación Democrática in the 2006 presidential elections and the unified 2004 opposition to the presidential referendum), this coalition created a political agenda broad enough to minimize its programmatic differences, rejected the possibility of antidemocratic strategies to seize power (e.g., extraconstitutional measures led by de facto powers like the 2002 coup by the Federación de Cámaras y Asociaciones de Comercio y Producción de Venezuela, or FEDECAMARAS), and discarded tactics that depended exclusively on the mobilization of civil society (e.g., social movements replacing political parties). Additionally, opposition parties within MUD agreed on procedures to elect their candidates at all levels of government (presidential, parliamentary, and local). The realization of the presidential primaries in February 2012 was both a democratic exercise and an opportunity to experiment with programmatic discourses that were attractive to the electorate.

Representing a Rightwing Agenda in the Context of Political Polarization: A Failed Case

In Venezuela, MUD's principles are defined broadly enough (defense of the rule of law and civil liberties, promotion of human development, and pursuit of political change) that the democratization agenda is emphasized over specific programmatic objectives. Nevertheless, rightist precandidates have been able to transmit their particular programmatic proposals and maintain their ideological preferences. Henrique Capriles (Primero Justicia) won the primaries with a discourse that combined a democratization agenda with public security proposals.[41]

As mentioned above, one of the requirements for rightwing electoral success is the development of a political discourse that articulates citizens' demand for state intervention within the constructs of conservative values. Public security became a central issue in Capriles's 2012 electoral campaign in the primaries, addressing a problem (Caracas is the second-most violent city in Latin America following Ciudad Juarez, and Venezuela's national crime rate is one of the most highest in the continent) that has become especially prominent during Chávez's tenure. *Mano dura* policies to solve security problems and strategies to decrease economic vulnerability to international financial crises, framed around a democratization agenda, promised to meet one of the two conditions necessary for electoral success during the primary campaign.[42]

During the general election, however, Capriles's proposals on security were limited to the capital, Caracas. Nationally, he emphasized employment plans and social services in order to compete with the main pillars of Chavez's political platform. His moderate discourse did not create a distinguishable alternative to Chavez's in the context of state intervention; his rivals framed his platform as a simple "copy" of government initiatives.[43]

Primero Justicia (and other rightwing and center political organizations in Venezuela) has not yet developed a political identification to mobilize followers at the grassroots level. According to Latin American Public Opinion Project survey results, most Venezuelans (between 60% and 70% in the last six years) identify themselves neither as Chavistas nor as part of the opposition. Only 5% consider themselves to be Primero Justicia sympathizers, a percentage similar to what Un Nuevo Tiempo received in previous years.[44] Social mobilization is thus motivated by anti-Chavismo, not political empathies associated with specific political organizations. COPEI's identity has not recovered from the several breakaway movements it suffered in the last two decades, and new opposition alternatives like Primero Justicia are still strongly based on regional administrations that complicate the formation of party identities capable of reaching the national level. I propose an argument whereby political identification must exceed subnational and territorial identities (Bolivia is an extreme example of the right's inability to accomplish this condition) and should be grounded on support for a political organization that has developed a clear and valid ideological proposal as a national project. Public support of Primero Justicia is related to inchoate political attachments under the larger umbrella of anti-Chavismo. It has failed to develop a political project at the national level.

Henrique Capriles and Primero Justicia, the leaders of the opposition block, failed to maintain a rightist platform that justified state intervention within the confines of their ideological tenets and ended up promoting a light replica of Chavismo's social policies during the 2012 presidential campaign. Additionally, an anti-regime political identity turned out to be a more powerful identification than membership to a specific party organization. Opposition votes in Venezuela do not seem to stabilize as an enduring political affiliation. Two months later, in subnational elections, the opposition could not maintain the 44.3% of electoral support that Capriles received in the October presidential election. MUD candidates, including Capriles's candidacy for reelection as governor, won in only three out of twenty-one states.

This evidences the need to develop long-standing political identifications and platforms that exceed regime-change demands. Considering that anti-Chavismo is the glue that connects ideologically diverse parties, Hugo Chávez's death will have severe consequences for the autonomous emergence of rightwing parties like Primero Justicia. Although it is still possible that Primero Justicia, Capriles's political base, will be able to capitalize on his electoral support, the rebuilding of a rightwing political organization in Venezuela will not be immediate.

Conditions That Explain Rightwing Electoral Success

Based on an inferred analysis of the cases developed, I propose two necessary conditions to achieve a successful rightwing political project: the creation of a political identification capable of engaging portions of the electorate as loyal followers (partisanship in the case of institutionalized parties or the development of long-standing psychological attachments to political elites if parties do not exist) and the development of a political platform that combines ideological tenants with state intervention in areas apart from the economy (such as public security). Achieving these conditions should effectively neutralize the political and structural obstacles described above.

These conditions represent the capacity a political organization develops to solve collective action and social choice problems. The former involves parties' capacity to develop administrative-organizational infrastructure that permits office-seeking politicians to band together and reach out to the electorate through political machines within a given territory. The latter relates to politicians' ability to organize their platforms based on clear issue positions that help voters identify their programmatic offer. In a context of democracies without parties, political vehicles that are able to accomplish these two functions tend to be in a better position to build or rebuild political parties and reach electoral success.

Regarding the first condition, partisanship—understood as a long-standing psychological attachment to a political organization that is not affected by day-to-day politics[45]—is the crystallization of a political cleavage at the individual level and implies maintained development over an extended period of time.[46] Partisanship-like political attachments (or nascent partisanship) are different from opinions on platforms, vote intentions, or performance evaluations. Additionally, partisanship should differ from regionalist "social identities"[47] (like *cruceños* in Bolivia) and "anti-regime" positions (like anti-Chavismo in Venezuela) in order to avoid the development of diffuse links between citizens and political projects.

Building partisanship fosters political mobilization (the collective action function), rather than mere regime opposition or regionalism, and neutralizes political obstacles. Successful rightwing mobilization requires an electoral vehicle that, institutionalized within a formal party organization or in the process of shaping one, can galvanize followers through the creation of a stable identification with its project. In this sense, rightwing organizations should mobilize supporters independently of state resources (otherwise it is simply a clientelistic project) and should not depend on the decisions of a particular leadership (in which case it is nothing more than an ephemeral, personalistic vehicle). It is also critical to transcend regional cleavages that complicate the development of solutions to collective action problems for national political projects.

Regarding the second condition, rightwing organizations should be able to define an appealing political platform that includes a role for the state that is coherent with their principles. The crisis of political representation is due to severe dissatisfaction with the state's capacity to provide services to its citizens.[48] In order to reconstruct political linkages between politicians and the electorate, political elites should develop programmatic platforms that consider the state's role in salient social demands.

Developing a rightist political platform focused on public security (the social choice function) overcomes the limitations of a rightwing platform centered on the economy, gives the opposition a programmatic issue around which to coalesce, and makes political organizations more competitive in the electoral arena. A successful rightwing project needs to develop a political platform that is attractive in the context of the crisis of democratic representation. If political disaffection in the Andes is explained, among several factors, by the ineffective performance of incumbents and the incapacity of the state to deliver goods appropriately to its citizens, even a rightwing platform—in theory adverse to state intervention—should create a discourse to strengthen the link between the state and its citizens (albeit in a fashion compatible with conservative principles). One potential opportunity to integrate state intervention into a rightist political platform is through a discourse on public security. Especially when political violence is present, rightwing actors are better positioned to advance a public security agenda because connections between institutionalized, leftwing parties and extreme leftist organizations discredit the left's solutions (Colombia and Peru). It is also possible to foster a security program in the context of violence that lacks political origins, such as criminality and disorder (Venezuela).

Conclusion

Post–party system collapse creates several challenges for the (re)building of political parties in general and rightwing political parties in particular. In addition to the political obstacles that the opposition faces (its limited constituency and its lack of resources for mobilization), rightist organizations are particularly challenged owing to widespread political disaffection. This is the case in all Andean political systems.

The diminished political competitiveness in some countries (Bolivia, Ecuador, and Venezuela) adds yet another political barrier. The possibilities of developing political organizations are complicated by rightwing platforms' attempts to maintain the pro-market oriented status quo, precisely the policy questioned by the left. Finally, subnational cleavages (Bolivia, Ecuador, and Venezuela) and political violence (Colombia and Peru) severely hamper the formation of institutionalized rightwing political parties.

It is not impossible for rightwing political projects to achieve electoral success, however. In my analysis of three cases, I outline an argument supported by a functionalist view of political parties. In democracies without parties, political organizations must find a way to solve collective action and social choice problems, as well as overcome the obstacles imposed in the postcollapse context. Rightwing political projects that propose strategies to accomplish these major tasks tend to be in a better position to reach electoral success.

Rightwing political projects that are capable of shaping (nascent) partisanship and developing a political platform that—without contradicting their ideological principles (e.g., market-oriented policies)—emphasize state intervention (e.g., public security) are able to surmount the political and structural obstacles they face and reach high levels of stable electoral support (fig. 7.1). Accordingly, we can categorize the successful revival of Fujimorismo as the rebuilding of a political force after more than a decade of exclusion from government and lack of access to state resources. Fujimorismo has developed an enduring psychological attachment with rank-and-file members (a nascent partisanship) who identify with its main objectives: pragmatism in public affairs; defense of Alberto Fujimori's administration (1990–2000); and opposition to leftist, liberal elites (especially human rights activists). An electoral mobilization strategy that involves an emerging political identification and a platform focused on state intervention in security (and the construction of a political memory that justifies Alberto Fujimori's crimes) explains its electoral recovery and Keiko Fujimori's qualification in the second round of the Peruvian elections. But the party's opposition to democratic values inhibited her from obtaining the support needed to beat leftist leader Ollanta Humala.

In the case of Bolivia and Venezuela, rightwing alternatives have not been able to present a successful strategy. In Bolivia, contemporary rightist projects (VERDES and NPC) have not been able to transform social identities (especially regional identities in Santa Cruz) and anti-regime opposition into sustained support for a national project, nor have they been capable of elaborating a programmatic discourse that moves beyond anti-regime confrontation. Rightist support has traveled from one ephemeral candidacy to another (Quiroga of PODEMOS, Reyes of NFR) and has not established itself within a formal organization. In Venezuela, rightist orga-

Graph 1: Necessary Conditions for Rightwing Political Parties' Electoral Success

		Political Identification Collective Action Function	Political Platform Social Choice Function	Output
Political Obstacles 1) Limited constituency 2) Lack of access to mobilization resources 3) Political disaffection 4) Lack of political competitiveness				
Structural Obstacles A) Regional cleavages B) Political violence	Peru: Fujimorismo	Nascent Partisanship	Public Security	SUCCESS
B	Colombia: Uribismo	Nascent Partisanship?	Public Security	
Obstacles 1 2 3	Venezuela: MUD	Anti-Regime Regionalism	Anti-Regime Neoliberalism Public Security	FAILURE
4A	Bolivia: Verdes + NPC	Regionalism Anti-Regime	Neoliberalism Regionalism Anti-Regime	FAILURE
	Ecuador: CREO	Anti-Regime Regionalism	Neoliberalism Anti-Regime	

Figure 7.1. Necessary conditions for rightwing political parties' electoral success.

nizations that belong to the opposition's broad coalition (MUD) have adhered to a regime-change agenda as its main strategy, a method that is not conducive to the formation of a long-standing political identification. A poor showing in subnational elections, held two months after the 2012 presidential ones, demonstrates the opposition's limited success within regional enclaves. In terms of a programmatic platform, Primero Justicia combined a general political platform with an agenda in favor of public security during the primaries. During the 2012 and 2013 general elections, however, Capriles could not establish a discourse that involved state intervention in a manner distinct from Chavismo. The strategies in these countries led rightwing alternatives to electoral failure.

Finally, I believe the findings based on these three cases are valid for the Andean region in general and could possibly be tested more broadly in Latin America. In Colombia, the political organization that Álvaro Uribe originally created—Partido de la U—was not totally dependent on his decisions; it was dominated by experienced political brokers from traditional parties, as described by Laura Wills-Otero in chapter 8 in this volume. When Uribe left office after two terms, political party dynamics mattered more than the Uribista inertia. Although weakened, traditional party identifications are still relevant in Colombia, especially among political organizers who control the political machines at subnational levels. The current president, Juan Manuel Santos—elected by Partido de la U but a former cadre of Partido Liberal—has played down the merits of *seguridad democrática* policies in favor of his original political party line. Uribe has been forced to create his own personalistic party (Centro Democrático) in order to capitalize on a public opinion mood in his favor that has (yet) to become a solid political identification. Meanwhile, rightwing alignments have generally returned to the traditional parties that recovered a degree of electoral competitiveness after the exit of Álvaro Uribe and recent political reforms.[49]

An initial overview of Ecuadorian politics paints it as another case of failed rebuilding of rightwing political parties. Rightist organizations have not progressed from personalistic, electoral vehicles (PRIAN) to ideologically based organizations. CREO, the newly formed party that launched the presidential candidacy of banker Guillermo Lasso against Rafael Correa, must evolve into a programmatic and institutionalized party. Traditional rightwing elites (PSC and PRIAN) have not been able to overcome regional cleavages (between the capital and coastal provinces) nor create a programmatic platform that exceeds demands for autonomic recognition or regime change. Upcoming elections will determine the potential of CREO's electoral caudal: whether it represents a mere anti-Correa vote or is capable of maintaining electoral support from one election to another. The arguments explained in this chapter are suggestive of a more profound debate about the prospects of the right in the convulsive Andean region.

ACKNOWLEDGMENTS

The author acknowledges the valuable suggestions of the editors of this volume, as well as of Anna Callis, Jennifer Cyr, Alfonso Ferrufino, Ezequiel González-Ocantos, and Martin Tanaka.

NOTES

1. For democracy without parties, see Maxwell Cameron and Steven Levitsky, "Democracy without Parties? Political Parties and Regime Change in Fujimori's Perú," *Latin American Politics and Society* 45, no. 3 (2003): 1–33. For the crisis in political representation, see Scott Mainwaring, "State Deficiencies, Party Competition, and Confidence in Democratic Representation in the Andes," in *The Crisis of Democratic Representation in the Andes*, ed. Scott Mainwaring, Ana María Bejarano, and Eduardo Pizarro (Stanford, CA: Stanford University Press, 2006), 295–345.

2. See Steven Levitsky and Kenneth M. Roberts, eds., *The Resurgence of the Latin American Left*, 1st ed. (Baltimore: Johns Hopkins University Press, 2011). Growing public opposition to market-oriented reforms (starting in the 1990s) and the 1998–2002 economic crisis triggered a wave of leftist victories.

3. For established political parties that together are unable to field a first- or second-place finisher, see Jason Seawright, *Party-System Collapse: The Roots of Crisis in Peru and Venezuela* (Stanford, CA: Stanford University Press, 2012). Regarding the inability to obtain high share of votes during national elections, Edurne Zoco operationalizes a collapse of a party system

as a situation in which new political organizations together obtain more than 45% of the votes over the course of two consecutive elections. "The Collapse of Party Systems in Italy, Peru, and Venezuela" (PhD thesis, University of Notre Dame, 2008).

4. For populist leaders and their polarization of politics, see Michael Coppedge, *Venezuela: Popular Sovereignty versus Liberal Democracy* (Notre Dame, IN: University of Notre Dame, 2002). For the perversion of liberal democratic institutions, see René Mayorga, "Outsiders and Neopopulism: The Road to Plebicitary Democracy," in Mainwaring et al. (2006, 132–69). For a more profound characterization of populist leaders, see chapter 6, this volume.

5. Steven Levitsky and Lucan A. Way, *Competitive Authoritarianism: Hybrid Regimes after the Cold War*, 1st ed. (Cambridge: Cambridge University Press, 2010).

6. Ana María Bejarano, *Precarious Democracies: Understanding Regime Stability and Change in Colombia and Venezuela* (Notre Dame, IN: Notre Dame University Press, 2011).

7. For a recent assessment, see Maxwell Cameron and Juan Pablo Luna, "El Estado de la Democracia en la Región Andina," in *Democracia en la Región Andina*, ed. Maxwell Cameron and Juan Pablo Luna (Lima: Instituto de Estudios Peruanos, 2010), 12–46.

8. For party appeal to the whole territory, see Jennifer Cyr, "From Collapse to Comeback? Explaining the Fates of Political Parties in Latin America" (PhD thesis, Northwestern University, 2012). Cyr considers persistence in the public debate—the capacity of a party to voice its opinion on different policies—as another party's strategy to remain influential.

9. Felipe Burbano, "Las Luchas Territoriales en Ecuador y Bolivia: Identidad, Nación y Estado," in *Desarrollo, Desigualdades y Conflictos Sociales: Una Perspectiva Desde los Países Andinos*, ed. Marcos Cueto and Adrián Lerner (Lima: Instituto de Estudios Peruanos, 2011), 89–122. See also chapters 3 and 4, this volume.

10. Steven Levitsky, "A Surprising Left Turn," *Journal of Democracy* 22, no. 4 (2011): 84–94.

11. Fuerza 2011 was the electoral vehicle that launched Keiko Fujimori's candidacy; PPC sponsored a broader alliance that supported Pedro Kuczynski's campaign; Peru Posible is the center-right political party founded by Alejandro Toledo; and Solidaridad Nacional is an "independent" organization created by Luis Castañeda, former mayor of Lima.

12. During the 2006 elections, former legislator Martha Chávez, a well-known hardline Fujimorista, reached only 7% of the vote.

13. In the periods of July 2000 and July 2001, 103 constitutional accusations were presented against Fujimorista congressmen. In the periods July 2006 and July 2010, there were only two. Adriana Urrutia, "Que La Fuerza (2011) Esté Con Keiko: El Fujimorismo, Su Organización y Su Estrategia de Campaña," in *Post-Candidatos: Guía Analítica de Sobrevivencia Hasta las Próximas Elecciones*, ed. Carlos Meléndez (Lima: Mítin Editores, 2011), 91–120.

14. Personal interview with Keiko Fujimori, Lima, February 11, 2013.

15. Urrutia (2011).

16. Levitsky (2011).

17. Ipsos-Apoyo, March 21, 2011, national sample ($N = 2,000$); see http://www.ipsos.pe/sites/default/files/opinion_data/avance-humala-ppk.pdf.

18. Data are provided by Pontificia Universidad Catolica del Perú based on a national representative survey ($N = 2,000$) conducted in May 2011.

19. In order to get a concise measurement of Fujimorista identification, I use the label "hardcore Fujimoristas" for those individuals who would *definitively* vote for a Fujimorista candidate in each of these three elections (for mayor, regional president, and congress), and "leaning

Fujimoristas" for those individuals who would *probably* vote for a Fujimorista candidate in each of the aforementioned elections. Individuals who do not meet either of these criteria are considered "non-Fujimoristas."

20. According to the Fujimorista discourse, human rights organizations are considered their "political rivals." This is a clear example of Fujimoristas' positions on certain democratic issues.

21. Martín Tanaka, "A Vote for Moderate Change," *Journal of Democracy* 22, no. 4 (2011): 75–83.

22. Jorge Lazarte, *Derrumbe de la "Res-publica": Los Procesos Electorales en Bolivia: 2002, 2004 y 2005* (La Paz: Plural Editors, 2008).

23. John Crabtree and Laurence Whitehead, *Towards Democratic Viability: The Bolivian Experience* (New York: Palgrave Macmillan, 2001).

24. Mercedes García-Montero, "Bolivia," in *Partidos Políticos de América Latina: Países Andinos*, ed. Manuel Alcántara and Flavia Freidenberg (México City: Fondo de Cultura Económica-Instuto Federal Electoral, 2001), 33–148.

25. Pablo Stefanoni, *Qué Hacer con los Indios . . . y Otros Traumas Irresueltos de la Colonialidad* (La Paz: Plural Editores, 2010).

26. Carlos Toranzo, *Rostros de la Democracia: Una Mirada Mestiza* (La Paz: ILDIS-Friedrich Ebert-Plural, 2006).

27. Mayorga (2012).

28. Kent Eaton, "Indigenous Mobilization Backlash in Bolivia: Regional Autonomy as a Reaction Against," *Politics and Society* 35 (March 2007): 71–102.

29. Mario Antezana, *Bifurcación electoral entre oriente y occidente: Variables de influencia en el comportamiento electoral* (La Paz: Plural, forthcoming).

30. Raúl Madrid, "The Rise of Ethnopopulism in Latin America," *World Politics* 60, no. 3 (2008): 475–508.

31. Martin Sivak, *Santa Cruz: Una Tesis. El Conflicto Regional en Bolivia (2003–2006).* (La Paz: Plural Editores, 2007).

32. Ibid.

33. For the Comité's success in politically mobilizing *cruceño*'s regional identity, see Nelson Jordán and Claudia Peña, *Ser Cruceño en Octubre* (La Paz: Fundación PIEB, 2006).

34. Interview with Germán Antelo, Santa Cruz, Bolivia, September 20, 2011.

35. Michael Coppedge, *Strong Parties and Lame Ducks: Presidential Patriarchy and Factionalism in Venezuela* (Stanford, CA: Stanford University Press, 1994).

36. In the last parliamentary elections (September 2010), Acción Democrática obtained the 8.1% of the valid vote, which is the third party of the opposition coalition.

37. Michael Penfold-Becerra, "Clientelism and Social Funds: Evidence from Chávez's Misiones," *Latin American Politics and Society* 49, no. 4 (2007): 63–84, doi:10.1111/j.1548-2456.2007.tb00392.x.

38. Ana María Bejarano, *Precarious Democracies: Understanding Regime Stability and Change in Colombia and Venezuela* (Notre Dame, IN: Notre Dame University Press, 2011).

39. Kirk A. Hawkins, *Venezuela's Chavismo and Populism in Comparative Perspective*, 1st ed. (Cambridge: Cambridge University Press, 2010).

40. Pierre Ostiguy, *The High and the Low in Politics: A Two Dimensional Political Space for Comparative Analysis and Electoral Studies* (Notre Dame, IN: Kellogg Institute, 2009).

41. Maye Primera, "Henrique Capriles Gana las Primarias de la Oposición Venezolana," *El País*, February 13, 2012, http://internacional.elpais.com/internacional/2012/02/13/actualidad /1329101950_177206.html.

42. According to the Latin American Public Opinion Project, corruption and public security are the two worst evaluated aspects of Chavez's government, according to surveys conducted in 2006, 2008, 2010, and 2012. For *mano dura* policies, see Margarita López-Maya, "Venezuela: Hugo Chávez and the Populist Left," in Levitsky and Roberts (2011, 213–38).

43. Cyr (forthcoming).

44. Jennifer Cyr, "Que veinte años no es nada: Hugo Chávez, las elecciones de 2012 y el continuismo político venezonlano," *Revista de Ciencia Política* (Santiago), 33, no. 4 (2013): http://dx.doi.org/10.4067/S0718-090X2013000100018.

45. Donald Green, Bradley Palmquist, and Eric Schickler, *Partisan Hearts and Minds* (New Haven, CT: Yale University Press, 2004).

46. Ostiguy (2009).

47. Although a partisan identity can be social, see Green et al. (2004) and Cyr (forthcoming).

48. Mainwaring (2006).

49. For the importance of Uribismo, see Fredy Barrero and Carlos Meléndez, "Consideraciones Sobre la Gobernabilidad Como Determinante del Comportamiento Electoral en Colombia: Elecciones Presidenciales de 2010," *Colombia Internacional* 74 (July 2011): 59–87.

CHAPTER EIGHT

Colombia

Analyzing the Strategies for Political Action of Álvaro Uribe's Government, 2002–10

LAURA WILLS-OTERO

In 2010, Colombia was classified as the most unequal country in Latin America after Guatemala. That year, 10% of the population concentrated 49.1% of the national income, 19% was classified as poor, and 6.4% was considered indigent.[1] In this context, where the "natural constituency" of the left is the majority of the population, it is reasonable to expect that left-of-center parties and leaders prone to putting forward redistributive appeals would emerge and consolidate as solid political options that eventually win elections. Even so, governments in Colombia have been identified more with policy agendas that are closer to the ideological right. The question I address in this chapter follows the observation presented in this volume's introduction and posits a puzzle: if the "natural constituency" of the right comprises the minority of the population, how can the right be so influential in Colombia? Or, alternatively, if the "natural constituency" of the left is the majority of the electorate, why is the left not in power at the national level? I argue that a long-lasting bloody armed conflict between the government and leftwing guerrilla groups explains this outcome to a large extent. Because of this conflict, public security—a major concern for most of the population—has been prioritized in governments' policy agendas. On the contrary, issues related to redistribution have occupied a secondary place in the governments' political agendas, despite the high levels of inequality and public demands to deal with it. In addition, institutional constraints marginalized the legal left from the electoral and political arenas for a long period of time. This condition fed the armed conflict. Finally, in a more recent period (2002–10), governments' relative connivance with rightwing paramilitary groups has strengthened the right in power.

In this chapter I analyze the two consecutive governments of Álvaro Uribe, a rightist political leader who won the presidential election in 2002 and again in 2006. This government is an example of how the right in Colombia has found fertile ground for electoral victories. Armed conflict between the government and leftwing guerrilla groups as well as the legal political left's historical weakness are factors that have allowed the right to be successful for a long period of time. In addition, a combination of strategies, or "vehicles," has been instrumental for rightist leaders to gain political leverage. They have been able to compete and gain power through both institutionalized (traditional) political parties and through nonpartisan movements or coalitions. In addition, rightist leaders have engaged in political action not based on electoral politics. Tight relations with business and media conglomerates, technocratic and international networks, and the armed forces have increased the political leverage of the right. The electoral victories of Uribe illustrate this political leverage. In 2002 he won through the antipartisan movement Primero Colombia, and later on, in 2006, he was reelected with the support of his own creation, the Partido Social de Unidad Nacional (PSUN), or Partido de la U. Uribe's period was permeated by a militaristic, confrontational, and warlike mentality, which contributed to both his and his party's qualifications as rightwing actors. During his years in office, a great part of the national budget was allocated to strengthen the military and police for the purpose of confronting insurgency. Public security issues were prioritized in Uribe's agenda. In addition, neoliberal economic policies (opening the economy and free trade, privatizations, etc.), along with an assistentialist social approach, characterized the government and the party that supported it, as actors positioned to the right of the ideological spectrum.

This chapter begins with a brief contextualization of the recent political history of the country and underlines the historical marginalization or political exclusion of the left as a consequence of both the armed conflict and institutional constraints. I then focus on Uribe's government and inquire into the strategies that the rightist leader employed to increase his electoral possibilities and popularity. Electoral and nonelectoral strategies are identified as vehicles that helped him to gain wide popular support. Finally, I summarize Uribe's programmatic platform.

Contextualization: The Historical Exclusion of the Left

During the late 1990s, some center-left leaders and parties triumphed in presidential elections in different Latin American countries and little by little started to gain (wide) backing in legislative assemblies.[2] Even though such progress presented as a generalized phenomenon throughout the region, some countries—including Colombia—broke this pattern and elected right-of-center governments. Throughout its national history, Colombia has elected more governments that identified with the theoretical assumptions that nourish right-of-center positions (i.e., small government, pro-market reforms) than governments that move closer to the left (i.e., big government, redistribution). The simplest explanation has to do with the political hegemony of the traditional parties since their creation in the mid-nineteenth century (1849) up through the first years of the twenty-first century. The Liberal Party (Partido Liberal, or PL) and the Conservative Party (Partido Conservador, or PC) emerged

as elite organizations that fundamentally represented the interests of the most privileged classes and, to a great extent, the landlords of the society.[3] For over 150 years
(until 2002), these two parties not only won all the presidential elections, but they
also consistently obtained the majorities in collegiate bodies. As I explain below,
their success was possible in part because of the institutional design that privileged
these parties to the detriment of other political options.

Over time these parties, especially PL, have transformed into and have become
more inclusive organizations. During different stages of its trajectory, leaders of PL
made efforts to incorporate and respond to the interests of middle and lower classes.[4]
Despite these attempts, in Colombia—unlike in other Latin American countries—it
was not possible to consolidate grassroots parties that gathered the interests of the
working classes.[5] Until the late 1950s, the Colombian Communist Party (Partido
Comunista Colombiano, or PCC) had been the only expression of the Colombian
left that was able to attract some sectors of the working class.[6] But PCC's political
actions were marred when governments in power actively persecuted its militants.
Moreover, the institutional rules designed to overcome a dictatorship in place from
1953 to 1957—that is, the National Front Pact—made it difficult for parties other
than PL and PC to form and compete for political power.[7] These conditions produced fertile ground for the already-existent peasant's *autodefensas* to be transformed
into revolutionary guerrilla groups during the 1960s.[8] The Revolutionary Armed
Forces of Colombia (Fuerzas Armadas Revolucionarias de Colombia, or FARC), the
National Liberation Army (Ejército de Liberación Nacional, or ELN), and the Popular Liberation Army (Ejército Popular de Liberación, or EPL) were founded during
that time (1964), though their origins go back to the late 1940s.[9] These groups opted
for armed struggle when they realized that transforming society by electoral means
was impossible.[10] From the moment these groups consolidated, all legitimate attempts
to constitute leftwing parties were doomed to be discredited and marginalized.[11]
Leftist expressions were not the only ones marginalized from political competition,
however. Other parties that had occasionally formed and participated in elections
also suffered the consequences of a restrictive political system that was exacerbated
during the National Front (1958–74) and that lacked guarantees for the development
of free and fair elections.[12] Such restrictions prolonged the hegemony of PL and PC.

In the early 1970s, the National Front came to an end. In 1974, presidential competitive elections were again inaugurated, and different (and contradictory) sectors
of the left united and participated in the contest. Four years later, the legitimate
(but weak) leftist alliance broke and lost strength. In 1978, the liberal presidential
candidate Julio César Turbay won elections. A few months after his inauguration,
he issued the *estatuto de seguridad*, or "security statute," which allowed him to per-
secute the guerrillas. Under the *estatuto de seguridad*, democratic liberties and civic

rights were dramatically cut, and the closed nature of the political system was prolonged. The armed conflict intensified, and leftist expressions, both legal and illegal,
were repressed. In 1982, the new government of the conservative Belisario Betancur
(1982–86) fostered peace dialogues with FARC and the urban guerrilla M-19, and in
1984 they agreed to a truce. Notwithstanding these efforts, peace negotiations failed
when M-19 broke the truce in 1985 and took over the Palace of Justice in Bogotá in
November that year. Two years later, in 1987, FARC went back to the armed struggle,
in part because of the genocide committed against militants of the Patriotic Union
(Unión Patriótica, or UP), a political party founded in 1985 as part of the peace agreements with the government. Many of its leaders—around three thousand of them,
including two presidential candidates and several congressional representatives, city
council members, and mayors—were murdered between 1984 and 1997.[13]

In the late 1980s, the armed conflict intensified and the number of actors increased.
The *autodefensas*, or paramilitary groups, were formed in reaction to the very existence of the guerrillas. Their goal was to protect landowners' properties through
direct confrontations with the guerrillas and the displacement (or killing) of their
support bases (i.e., peasants). Paramilitaries were increasingly linked to drug traffick-
ing, which they used it as the means to fund their structures and activities. Many of
the *autodefensas'* founders were landowners who counted on the permissiveness of
civic authorities and the military.[14] These networks between landowners, drug traffickers, private armies, and the militaries fed a dirty war against the left: guerrilla
groups, UP's militants, and social activists all constituted war objectives.[15]

Despite this context, in the late 1980s, it was possible for the government to negotiate peace agreements with four guerrilla groups.[16] Peace negotiations ended up with
the formation of a national assembly in 1990, which approved a new constitution in
1991. Demobilized members of the former insurgent groups (forming an alliance
between the Alianza Democrática Movimiento 19 AD-M-19) occupied 27% of the
seats in the assembly and consolidated as influential actors in this process. As a result,
the legitimate left started winning spaces within the political system by electing candidates for governor and mayor to congress and to executive office at the regional and
local levels. In spite of this advance, the conflict continued. Guerrilla groups (i.e.,
FARC and ELN), paramilitaries, and drug traffickers kept fighting. The number of
victims that suffered the consequences of the confrontations increased. According to
official sources, more than one million peasants were forcibly displaced from their
lands between 1995 and 2003, and a number of massacres were committed where
guerrillas or their "collaborators" were installed.[17] Leftist expressions (i.e., social activists, political movements, and parties) were associated with the illegitimate guerrillas. This weakened once again the legitimate options that had arisen from the 1991
constitution. In addition, leftwing legitimate parties started to operate with the same

logic applied as the traditional parties—internal fragmentation—thus limiting the possibility of setting themselves up as solid and unified political actors.[18]

In Colombia, the left has found severe limitations on its rise. Institutional limitations explain the emergence of leftist groups that opted for armed struggle. In addition, the uneven distribution of wealth and the lack of official initiatives to bring forward redistributive reforms have fed the conflict between insurgent groups and the government. In this scenario, the right has predominated. The context of war has justified different governments in prioritizing this issue in their agendas. But the strategies have varied between peace negotiations with subversive actors and military confrontations. At the end of the twentieth century, then-president Andrés Pastrana (1998–2002) pursued peace talks with FARC. His initiative failed, however, and the prospects to peacefully end the war with this group vanished. Presidential candidate Álvaro Uribe emerged after this failure in 2002, postulating the idea of militarily confrontation with insurgent actors, primarily the guerrilla groups FARC and ELN. Any political expression related to these actors, Uribe argued, should be militarily (armed actors) or electorally (legitimate opposition) silenced.

Uribe's rise to power represented the country's political shift further from the center, toward which previous governments (1991–2002) had tried to move closer.[19] Actions aimed at ensuring public order (military confrontation of insurgent groups), neoliberal economic policies (opening the economy and free trade, privatizations, etc.), and an assistentialist social approach characterized the government and the party that supported it, as actors positioned to the right of the ideological spectrum. Uribe's electoral success cannot be explained without analyzing the different strategies that he used to consolidate himself as a popular leader able to get support from a wide variety of social sectors. His candidacy through an antipartisan movement (Movimiento Primero Colombia), the creation of a new party during his first government (PSUN), links with media and business conglomerates, and a certain connivance with rightwing paramilitary groups seem to be factors that explain Uribe's popularity over the two consecutive governments.

The Right's Vehicles: Electoral and Nonelectoral Strategies

Álvaro Uribe won the first round of the 2002 presidential elections with 53% of the vote. His campaign revolved around the need to militarily confront and weaken the criminal organizations present throughout the length and breadth of the national territory,[20] which would allow the government to recover its legitimate monopoly of the use of force. "Democratic security policy" became the main slogan of the campaign and, later on, the main policy of the government. This idea was presented as an alternative to the frustration generated by former president Andrés Pastrana's agenda, which had aimed at negotiating a way out of the conflict.

Both during and after the campaign, this agenda and its promoting leader obtained wide popular approval. Over the eight years that his administration lasted, the president maintained unprecedented levels of approval, close to 70%.[21] There are several factors that explain the success of a rightist leader in a context where the majority of the population belongs to the "natural constituency" of the left. A combination of both electoral and nonelectoral strategies has been instrumental for the right to gain political leverage and to win power at the national, regional, and local levels.

Electoral Vehicles

Winning the presidential election was the first step to shaping public policy. To achieve this goal, Uribe made a bet: he decided to leave the party where he forged his political career—PL—and to present himself as an outsider through his new political movement, Primero Colombia. On the basis of antiparty and antipolitics discourse, Uribe portrayed himself as a renovating option that would solve the problems that traditional parties had not solved. A severely fragmented party system, which was both highly volatile and incapable of representing the interests of all social sectors, generated widespread public discontent and political instability.[22] These weaknesses were further aggravated by corruption scandals associated with deeply rooted clientelist practices that were fostered fundamentally by the leaders of the traditional parties. The possibility of voting for someone who promised to attack corruption arose as a viable option for a great part of the electorate. In addition, Uribe's proposal to put an end to the armed conflict through confrontation congregated a broad electorate, since the high level of insecurity caused by the conflict was a major concern for most of the population.

With the election of Uribe to the presidency in 2002, a milestone was marked in the political history of the traditional PL and PC parties.[23] For the first time in history, these two parties lost the presidential election as well as their legislative majorities. In presidential elections, the liberal candidate obtained 31.8% share of the votes while Uribe won in the first electoral round (53% of the votes) with the new Primero Colombia movement. In legislative elections, PL suffered the most: it went from obtaining nearly 50% of votes (or more) to only 25% that year. The votes and seats this party, together with the PC, failed to obtain were diverted toward a multiplicity of new, independent movements and other political options that, just like the presidential candidate, declared themselves antiparty. The weakening of PL and PC, also explained by their internal fragmentation, prevented them from presenting themselves as unified parties acting as coherent organizations. During the first four-year period from 2002 to 2006, several liberals dissented from what the party leaders established and voted for legislative projects in opposition to the party line. This situation is exemplified in the discussion that arose regarding a constitutional reform presented by the government, which proposed the possibility of immediate presidential reelection. A group of nine senators and some liberal representatives supported the initiative, thus distancing themselves from the decisions of the leaders of the party. Their support led the party's leadership to sanction those legislators. The event set an important precedent for the formation of a new party that would institutionalize the Uribismo. Several legislators, especially from PL but also from other political movements, decided to create a new party under the strong leadership of Uribe.[24] PSUN was formed in August 2005.[25]

A new party that brought together all those who supported the chief executive would prove useful in facilitating approval of even the most decisive projects. It would also serve to obtain support in an eventual campaign aimed at achieving his reelection. For its members, being part of an organization endorsed by such a popular leader would help them obtain recognition and votes in the legislative elections of March 2006 and in the regional elections of 2007.[26] In 2006, out of twenty-one senators elected by the new party (20.58%), seventeen had been elected by other entities in 2002 (mostly by PL), either as senators or as representatives to the chamber.

During Uribe's period, PSUN participated in presidential and legislative elections in 2006 and 2010, as well as in the local elections of 2007. The party has quickly managed to present itself as a strong electoral option capable of competing successfully in elections. In the legislative elections of 2006, PSUN obtained the most seats in the senate, and it followed PL in the lower chamber. In 2010, PSUN's performance improved. It occupied the first place in both the senate and chamber of representatives. Table 8.1 shows legislative results in 2006 and 2010. In the first presidential election in which the party competed (2010), PSUN won by choosing Juan Manuel Santos in the second electoral round with 69.12% of the votes. Regarding regional elections, PSUN participated for the first time in 2007. That year it won seven out of thirty-two governorships, and 101 out of 1,103 mayoralties. Four years later, in 2011, it won only four governorships and 260 mayoralties.[27]

PSUN's electoral success cannot be explained without analyzing an electoral reform introduced in 2003 and applied for the first time in that year's regional election. The rules for electing legislative representatives were modified for the purpose of unifying the previously fragmented political parties. The expected outcome was to create a few collectivities that were strong in electoral terms. To achieve cohesion, single lists decided on by party replaced the multiple closed lists that had been pre-

TABLE 8.1.
Legislative elections of 2006 and 2010

Political party/movement	2006 (%)	2010 (%)
Liberal Party	15.52	13.37
Conservative Party	16.13	17.11
Partido de la U	17.49	21.30
Cambio Radical	13.3	6.09
Polo Democrático Alternativo	9.74	6.53
Movimiento Independiente de Renovación Absoluta	2.35	2.50
Alas-Equipo Colombia	4.68	0.29
Convergencia Ciudadana	6.25	NA[a]
Colombia Democrática	2.85	NA
Colombia Viva	2.46	NA
Partido de Integración Nacional[b]		6.68
Partido Verde		3.50
Compromiso Ciudadano por Colombia		1.40
Other		0.22
Votes for unelected parties	6.06	1.67
Blank votes	3.17	3.69
Total	100	100

Source: National Office of Civil Registry, 2006 and 2010.

[a]NA, not applicable.

[b]The Partido de Integración Nacional resulted from the coalition of three parties: Colombia Viva, Colombia Democrática, and Convergencia Ciudadana.

sented before. The formula used to distribute congressional seats and the definition of an electoral threshold also made the possibility of obtaining said seats more demanding.[28] Before the reform, candidates who managed to obtain seats did so through party factions, and they obtained a small number of votes. After the reform, the necessity to obtain more votes motivated the candidates to join together and to present themselves in attractive party lists. In this context, the creation of a new party, PSUN, led by a popular figure and composed of traditional politicians with established electoral capacity, constituted an attractive possibility. The new rules created this incentive. For liberals and other politicians, to form PSUN was an individual electoral strategy to prevent electoral failure, which could come about as a result of remaining in a seriously weakened and discredited party. A party that had the support of a popular leader like Uribe could help politicians to get elected in either national or regional elections.

PSUN emerged in 2005 within the framework of a new institutional design and under the leadership of Uribe. This happened in 2002 after the traditional parties had suffered the worst electoral results in their whole history and once the rules of the game were modified. The new party was instrumental for the government to put forward its programmatic agenda. In addition to reform of the electoral system, the constitutional court in October 2005 declared immediate presidential reelection to be legally acceptable. The president could therefore aspire to the post again, but to achieve electoral and legislative success, it was important to count on a strong party. The foundations of PSUN thus came about in a strategic moment.

PSUN is the only political party in Colombia's history that has managed to obtain more votes and posts than either PL or PC. Taking this fact into account, an interesting question arises: To which electorate does the party appeal, and why has it been so successful in electoral contests? Part of the answer lies in the fact that PSUN has successfully managed to capture voters from different social classes, origins, and age groups—as well as from the parties that gave it its origin. PSUN successfully appealed to the median voter, which might explain the popularity of its major promoter—Uribe. Figure 8.1 shows that most of PSUN's sympathizers (52.2%) are from the lowest classes of the social spectrum. Nonetheless, the party also has wide support among the middle class (40.2%), as well as not insignificant support from the upper classes (7.6%).

PSUN, however, like all the other parties, finds the largest part of its electoral support in the cities. Over 75% of its sympathizers live in urban centers. But the percentage of people who support the party and live in the countryside is considerable. In fact, after PL, PSUN is the party with the most sympathizers in rural areas. These sympathizers represent 30.4% for PL, and 24.3% for PSUN. Finally, after PL, PSUN

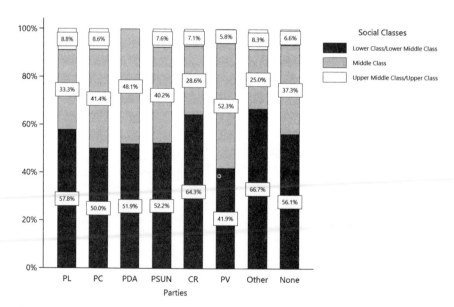

Figure 8.1. Party affiliation by social class (self-perception). *Source:* AmericasBarometer by the Latin American Public Opinion Project

is the party with the most sympathizers in the sectors with the least educated voters. Figure 8.2 shows the ideological self-location of citizens who sympathize with the main political parties in Colombia. It shows that PSUN sympathizers locate themselves furthest to the right on the ideological spectrum.

PSUN has a broad and heterogeneous electoral base. Party sympathizers come from different social classes, various educational levels, and urban centers as well as rural areas. Even so, it seems clear that PSUN identifies itself with the ideals located on the right of the ideological spectrum, and that one of the strategies the party has employed to achieve high voter turnout is to captivate all kinds of voters. PSUN's electorate is close to the median voter, which has helped Uribe, PSUN's most important promoter, increase his popularity through elections. The creation of an anti-partisan movement (Primero Colombia), and the goal to institutionalize the Uribismo through the creation of a new party (PSUN), constituted the electoral vehicle that was useful for Uribe to reach and increase power. Nonelectoral vehicles were also important to consolidate Uribe as a popular leader and to advance his political agenda. Below I describe these vehicles, with an emphasis on links with business and media conglomerates, as well as the connivance with rightist paramilitary groups.

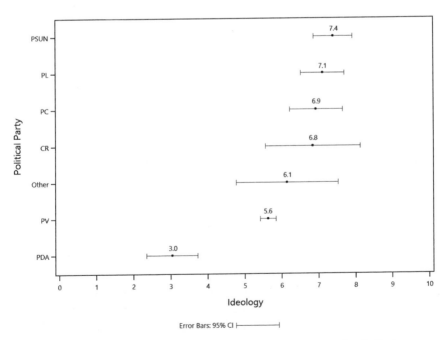

Figure 8.2. Ideology by party affiliation. *Source:* AmericasBarometer by the Latin American Public Opinion Project

Nonelectoral Vehicles

In addition to winning elections and institutionalizing the Uribismo through the creation of PSUN, Uribe engaged in political action not based on electoral politics. He pursued the support of powerful political and nonpolitical actors. Traditional politicians who had long careers in the public sector occupied a significant number of cabinet posts. Technocrats linked to the private sector held another portion of these posts. Business conglomerates and international networks provided the president economic resources to advance both his electoral campaign and his political agenda. Media conglomerates supported and defended the government's actions, with a few exceptions. In addition, the president established tight relations with the armed forces and with politicians linked to paramilitaries. All these links increased the political leverage of the rightist government of Álvaro Uribe. Below, I show information that sheds some light about the nonelectoral strategies Uribe used to increased his power and augment his popular support.

The Ministers' Cabinet: Traditional Politicians and Specialized Technocrats

During his eight years in government, Uribe appointed thirty-seven ministers who came from different sectors.[29] Some of them were traditional politicians who had occupied elected offices or cabinet posts over different governments. These ministries enjoyed local electoral strongholds and were popularly recognized. Most of them identified with PC or with PSUN. This selection was useful for Uribe to increase his political power at the regional level, and a number of technocrats linked to the private sector (i.e., business and media) occupied cabinet posts. The combination of profiles helped the president to permeate and get closer to all possible sectors, both public and private. Table 8.2 summarizes the ministers' profiles during Uribe's administration.

Business and Media

As in other countries, in Colombia, business conglomerates—both national and international—mostly control the media. During Uribe's government, the relationship between both sectors was important. The president established close links with business conglomerates to ensure material and financial resources. In return, he granted benefits (e.g., lower taxes) through political decisions. For their part, media owners supported Uribe's administration through a favorable presentation of the news. Opposition found few spaces in either the written or oral press to voice com-

TABLE 8.2.
Origins of Uribe's ministers

Origin/trajectory	Electoral trajectory	Nonelectoral trajectory	Total
Public sector	8	15	23
Private sector/business		14	14
Total	8	29	37

Source: Congreso Visible, www.congresovisible.org.

plaints and to hold the government accountable for its actions, which helped the president maintain high levels of approval during his eight years in government.[30] Business conglomerates were also major donors of funds for Uribe's two presidential campaigns. Although other candidates also received donations from business entities, Uribe's campaign received the largest share of money.[31] In exchange for these donations, Uribe favored these conglomerates in various ways. He aided entrepreneurs in the massive purchase of land at low prices in the Caribbean coast,[32] for example, and he granted them a significant number of contracts with the state in different sectors: infrastructure, finance, services, and the food industry, among others.[33]

Links between Politicians and Paramilitaries

Empirical evidence shows that since the mid-1990s illegal armed groups (i.e., guerrillas, paramilitaries, and drug traffickers) have permeated Colombian political institutions and have exercised great pressure and influence on decision-making processes and policies in both at the national and local levels.[34] In 1996, for example, a scandal exploded in which it was revealed that one of the most powerful drug cartels (the Cali) funded the presidential campaign of Ernesto Samper in 1994. In 2002, paramilitaries and drug traffickers supported 34% of elected congressmen. According to López, eight out of ten of those legislators were part of Uribe's government coalition.[35] Four years later, in 2006, almost all of them were reelected. They kept the same share of power within the government coalition,[36] and they were instrumental in advancing its political agenda (e.g., presidential immediate reelection reform).[37] In 2006, scandalous links between paramilitaries and congressmen were revealed, leading to what became known as the "paramilitary scandal." Many legislators were removed from office and convicted. Others kept their posts. Evidence shows that a number of politicians linked to paramilitaries won elections at the local level in 2007 and 2011.[38] A portion of these politicians belonged to parties endorsed by Uribe. Electoral and nonelectoral vehicles helped Uribe to reach power, and to increase and keep it during eight years.

Political Platform and Policy Outcomes

The programmatic platform of the administration of Álvaro Uribe was permeated by the central objective he had insisted on ever since the 2001–2 campaign: to defeat through military force outlawed armed groups and to recover the legitimate monopoly on the use of force for the government. Uribe's discourse was translated into his democratic security policy, which constituted the central axis of both his terms in office. To recover territorial control, to ensure security for the population, and to put an end to terrorism were the central objectives proposed and executed by the president.[39]

During eight years of government, the military and police force grew in size and presence throughout the national territory, and the budget allocated for this buildup increased substantially. According to a report from 2007, there was a shift from an expenditure of 2% of gross domestic product (GDP) in 1990, to 6.35% of GDP in 2008.[40] The strengthening of the armed forces was useful for the government to confront the guerrilla groups FARC and ELN, which suffered significant losses and were debilitated in different regions were they had strongholds. Regarding the paramilitary groups, or *autodefensas*, Uribe promoted a softer policy. He attempted to bring about a political agreement that fostered these groups' demobilization. In order to fulfill this goal, it was necessary to generate the conditions that guaranteed paramilitaries' security and their successful reintegration into the civil society. In 2005, the congress approved the Justice and Peace Law (law 975 of 2005). Around four thousand paramilitaries demobilized between 2003 and 2010.[41] Despite the apparent accomplishments, denunciations of human rights violations perpetrated by the military and police forces and false paramilitary demobilizations, among many other accusations, raised questions regarding the legitimacy of the government's actions.[42]

In the economic sphere, Uribe's programmatic agenda established the need to reactivate the economy and to achieve greater economic growth.[43] To reach these goals, his new agenda combined neoliberal monetary strategies with statist policies.[44] With respect to the former, the government fostered private participation in the infrastructure, mining and public service sectors, as well as the generation of incentives in order to attract foreign investment. Assets of Ecopetrol, Colombia's largest oil company; several electric energy- and gas-distributing companies (Ecogas); telecommunication companies (Telecom); financial entities; and other institutions were sold.[45] The mining and hydrocarbon sectors became instruments for attracting the investment of foreign exploiting companies. According to a report from Fedesarrollo, "by 2006 it was estimated that mining without hydrocarbons covered 28% of total foreign direct investment." In general, mining represents about 2.3% of the nation's revenue.[46] As for trade policy, opening the economy and deregulating capital and

service markets were established as the administration's main initiatives.[47] The sign-
ing of the Free Trade Agreement with the United States—which Uribe's government
failed to ratify—as well as other bilateral and regional trade agreements, occupied a
great part of the president's legislative agenda.

Regarding social development, the fundamental guiding principle for policy
would be the need to achieve a more equitable society with better income distribution.[48] For this purpose, the government decided to confront three main challenges:
(1) increase the efficiency of social spending so that greater resources would translate
into better results, (2) enhance the focus of spending so as to ensure that resources
would reach those most in need, and (3) consolidate a system of social protection so
that economic crises did not completely compromise the future possibilities of the
most vulnerable groups.[49] These challenges would apply in the three fundamental
sectors of education, health, and public services, with the central objective being to
increase both their coverage and their quality. The fulfillment of these goals was
precarious, given the financial incapacity of the government to provide public coverage to these services in all departments and municipalities. In some sectors (e.g., education) the coverage grew but the quality did not.[50] In addition, upon finalization of
his administration, corruption was revealed that proved that the "entrepreneurs of
health" had been reaping financial benefits at the expense of the public interest.[51]

One of the permanent actions that the president undertook during the eight years
he was in office, and that he defined as a tool to develop his government agenda, was
to hold "community meetings" (*consejos comunales*) in different regions of the country.
Every Saturday, Uribe would meet with citizens who made claims regarding their
most pressing needs. The president, accompanied by members of his ministerial
cabinet, responded to petitions, on many occasions ordering social spending to relieve
the problems highlighted. The solutions offered were short term, assistentialist, and
particularist.[52] But Families in Action, a plan of conditioned transferences designed
to alleviate poverty among the most vulnerable families, did constitute a significant
social policy.[53] During the Uribe administration, the number of families receiving
these transfers increased. The total number of beneficiaries increased from 83,726 in
2001 to 1,559,369 in 2007.[54] Social public spending destined for the program rose
with respect to previous administrations. Nevertheless, the greater social spending
did not result in a significant decrease either of poverty, or of inequality in the country. Figure 8.3 shows the evolution of social spending per capita throughout this
period in Colombia and other countries of the Latin American region. Even though
this spending has increased in Colombia, it is lower than in other countries in the
subcontinent. The poverty index decreased about six percentage points throughout
Uribe's administration, from 53.5% in 2002 to 47.9% in 2009.[55] Although this can be
considered an accomplishment, the level of poverty remained quite high. Indigence

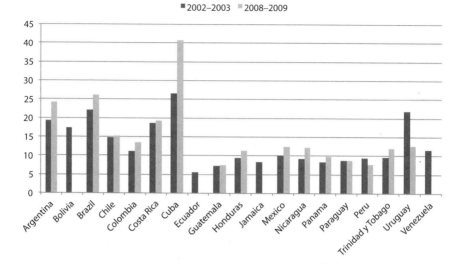

Figure 8.3. Social public spending per capita in nineteen countries in Latin America and the Caribbean, 2002–3 and 2008–9. *Source:* Adapted from data provided by the Economic Commission for Latin America and the Caribbean, 2002–9

was also reduced, but by a lower proportion. Finally, the level of inequality measured by the Gini coefficient remained almost the same between 2002 and 2009 (0.58/1). Colombia was one of the three most unequal countries of the region in 2009 (after Honduras and Guatemala).

The platform for Álvaro Uribe's two terms of office (2002–10) was permeated mainly by rightwing ideology. Economic policies revealed the objective of reducing the size of government through privatization of public enterprises and services, as well as through the continuation of market opening and the call for multinational companies to invest in the country. Yet social policies were above all assistentialist in nature, and many of them aimed to resolve specific demands in a particularist manner (e.g., community meetings and Families in Action). For some analysts, initiatives like the programs of conditioned transferences, as in the case of Families in Action in Colombia, are nothing more than "mechanisms of legitimacy of political regimes . . . [to] ensure the consolidation of the neoliberal order."[56] These programs, they argue, are instrumental in justifying the structural reforms that have been undertaken in the economic sphere since the early 1990s. Beyond solving or overcoming poverty, what they primarily seek is to alleviate somewhat the effects produced by orthodox measures.

Unlike other countries in Latin America, however, the war that has been waged in Colombia between insurgent actors and the government since the mid-twentieth century has had an impact on the programmatic agendas of the different administrations.

The Uribe administration's militaristic and confrontational approach to dealing with the armed conflict has characterized it as a rightwing government and, for many social sectors, an extreme rightwing one. Uribe decisively confronted the guerrilla groups—FARC and ELN—but he advanced negotiations with the rightwing paramilitaries. Many of them demobilized, reintegrated into the civil life, and guaranteed political power—electoral and nonelectoral—at the regional and local level. As I mentioned above, a significant number of politicians—mainly legislators—who were supported by Uribe, had links with active or demobilized paramilitaries. These links among Uribe, politicians at different levels, and paramilitaries constitute one of the vehicles that the president used to accumulate power. Despite massive demobilizations of paramilitaries, a significant number of bands did not dissolve their armed structures and continued their fight (e.g., the so-called *bandas criminales*).

One aspect that occupied a great part of the president's agenda during both his first and second terms of office was a political reform proposal that would lead to a change in the rules of the electoral system and bring about the possibility of immediate presidential reelection (2006) and a second reelection in 2010. The discussion over these possibilities occupied a great part of the legislative agenda and led to a slowdown of the general functioning of the congress. Immediate reelection was approved, and Uribe aspired to a second term in 2006. The project of the referendum to reform the constitution and to approve the possibility of a second reelection was sanctioned as law by the president in September 2009. Later, in February 2010, the constitutional court declared the law unconstitutional, thus impeding the reform.[57]

During Uribe's second term, the government counted on the support of a majority coalition in the legislative assembly formed by PSUN and PC. This coalition helped it achieve the viability of several projects, and these parties served the president to successfully constitute himself as a powerful and popular leader.[58]

Conclusion

The ideological right is powerful in Colombia, despite the fact that it is one of the most unequal countries in Latin America and the world. The long-lasting armed conflict between the government and the leftwing guerrilla groups explains to a large extent this power. The left has been traditionally associated with insurgent armed groups, and citizens' demands toward the improvement of public security have decreased its electoral chances. The right has pursued the strengthening of the military forces in order to confront the guerrillas and to recover the monopoly on the legitimate violence.

A restrictive political system in place until the early 1990s, when parties other than the traditional PL and PC found few spaces to compete electorally (e.g., leftist parties among others), is another variable that accounts for this phenomenon. In this context, *rightist* leaders have found fertile ground to access power, in some occasions through nonpartisan strategies. This was the case of Uribe in the 2002 electoral campaign. A former politician from the liberal party, Uribe decided to create a new political movement that allowed him to present himself as an "outsider" who would fight against the shortcomings that previous presidents were unable to solve. The unresolved armed conflict and corruption scandals that affected traditional politicians gave Uribe enough leeway to win the presidential election. Later on, when he consolidated his popularity, he decided to support the creation of a new party that would support him in congress during his second term (2006–10). The new party—PSUN—won a significant share of power in 2006 legislative election. Four years later, in 2010, PSUN became the strongest party in congress, and the presidential candidate supported by the party and Uribe won the election. With the triumph of Juan Manuel Santos, the former president hoped to consolidate the Uribismo by giving continuity to his programmatic agenda. In particular, he wanted to continue the military fight against the guerrilla groups. As soon as Santos took office, however, he distanced himself from Uribe when Santos decided to prepare the terrain to initiate peace dialogues and negotiations with the strongest guerrilla group, FARC. This decision moved the president and his party closer to the center on the ideological spectrum and generated a deep divide between Uribe and Santos. At the same time, peace negotiations between the government and the guerrilla opened windows of opportunities for the illegal left to become a legitimate actor that might access political power through institutionalized means. In the eventual scenario where peace negotiations end up with the successful demobilization and reintegration of FARC into civil and political life, the left will find new spaces to participate in the political system. This will be possible as long as the guerrilla negotiators become confident that combatants will be provided with enough security guarantees to survive in a new legal life. If armed conflict comes to an end, a new scenario for the right and for the left will be in place. Redistributive policies would become key issues in a postconflict period, and the strengthening of the military forces would be reduced. This scenario would change governments' public agendas as well as the population's demands.

ACKNOWLEDGMENT

The author thanks Christian Iván Benito for his outstanding research assistance.

NOTES

1. Comisión Económica para América Latina y el Caribe, "Panorama social de América Latina 2011" (Santiago, 2011).

2. Venezuela, Hugo Chávez, 1999 (Movimiento V República); Brazil, Luis Inácio "Lula" da Silva, 2002 (Partido dos Trabalhadores); Argentina, Néstor Kirchner, 2003 (Partido Justicialista); Uruguay, Tabaré Vásquez, 2004 (Frente Amplio); Bolivia, Evo Morales, 2005 (Movimiento al Socialismo); Ecuador, Rafael Correa, Alianza Patria Altiva y Soberana; Nicaragua, Daniel Ortega, 2007 (Frente Sandinista de Liberación Nacional); among others.

3. Differences between these parties fundamentally involved their position regarding the role the church should play, the centralization of power, and economic development—whether promoted from inside the country or through foreign trade. PL was anticlerical and defended a federal type of government and favored free trade. PC, however, was clerical, defended centralized government, and favored internal industrial development. Ronald P. Archer, "Party Strength and Weakness in Colombia's Besieged Democracy," in *Building Democratic Institutions: Party Systems in Latin America*, ed. S. Mainwaring and T. Scully (Stanford, CA: Stanford University Press, 1995), 164–99; Robert Dix, *The Politics of Colombia* (New York: Praeger, 1987).

4. Former president Alfonso López Pumarejo (1934–38 and 1942–45) advanced constitutional reforms designed to include new social rights and to increase state intervention in the economy. He also made unsuccessful efforts to carry out an agrarian reform that would redistribute landowners' holdings. The 1948 liberal presidential candidate, Jorge Eliécer Gaitán (who was killed in 1949), appealed to working classes and had sympathy with the Colombian Communist Party (Partido Comunista Colombiano, or PCC). He identified himself with the left and promoted policies aimed at reducing social inequalities. During the second half of the twentieth century, some other liberal leaders were closer to the left of center than to the right of center. Former president Ernesto Samper Pizano (1994–98) and three-time presidential candidate Horacio Serpa Uribe defended ideas of the so-called social democracy. Within the Conservative Party it has been less common to find progressive initiatives in tune with leftist ideas.

5. Ruth Berins Collier and David Collier, *Shaping the Political Arena: Critical Junctures, the Labor Movement, and Regime Dynamics in Latin America* (Princeton, NJ: Princeton University Press, 1991).

6. Mauricio Archila and Jorge Cote, *Una historia inconclusa: Izquierdas políticas y sociales en Colombia* (Bogotá: CINEP, 2009); Marco Palacio, *Entre la legitimidad y la violencia: Colombia 1875–1994* (Bogotá: Norma, 1995); "La solución política al conflicto armado, 1982–1997," in *Armar la paz es desarmar la guerra*, ed. A. Camacho Guizado and F. L. Buitrago (Bogotá: CEREC-DNP-PNUD, FESCOL, IEPRI, Presidencia de la República, 2000), 345–401.

7. Restrictions of the political system became evident in the rules created within the framework of the National Front agreement, in which the traditional parties agreed to share power in an equitable manner, as well as to alternate the presidency over the course of sixteen consecutive years (1958–74); see Jonathan Hartlyn, *Politics of Coalition Rule in Colombia* (Cambridge: Cambridge University Press, 1998).

8. Peasant's *autodefensas* emerged in the second half of the 1940s, when militants and PCC sympathizers took up arms to struggle against the conservative government of Mariano Ospina Pérez (1946–50). Theses peasants' *autodefensas* (1940s) would later be transformed in revolutionary guerrilla groups (1960s). Ana María Bejarano, *Precarious Democracies: Understanding Regime Stability and Change in Colombia and Venezuela* (South Bend, IN: Notre Dame University Press, 2011); Juan Guillermo Ferro and Graciela Uribe, *El orden en la Guerra. Las FARC-EP: Entre la organización y la política* (Bogotá: Centro Editorial Javeriano CEJA,

2002); Andrés Peñate, *El sendero estratégico del ELN: Del idealismo guevarista al clientelismo armado* (Bogotá: Centro de Estudios sobre Desarrollo Económico, Universidad de los Andes, 1998).

9. Ferro and Uribe (2002).

10. Archila and Cote (2009); Peñate (1998).

11. Bejarano (2011).

12. The Alianza Nacional Popular, a political movement founded in 1961 by the former dictator Gustavo Rojas Pinilla, was an example of political exclusion during the National Front. Dissidences from the traditional parties were also marginalized. The Movimiento Revolucionario Liberal was one case.

13. Roberto Romero, *Unión Patriótica Expedientes contra el olvido* (Bogotá: Centro de Memoria, Paz y Reconciliación, 2011).

14. Mauricio Romero, *Paramilitares y autodefensas, 1982–2003* (Bogotá: Planeta y IEPRI, 2003).

15. Archila and Cote (2009).

16. The following guerrilla groups signed peace agreements with the liberal government of Virgilio Barco-Vargas (1986–90) and demobilized: M-19, EPL, PRT, and the indigenous Quintín Lame.

17. For forcible displacement of peasants, see Presidencia de la República, "Red de Solidaridad Social de la Presidencia de la República," 2003. For massacres, see Comisión Nacional de Reparación y Reconciliación, "Memoria Histórica" (Bogotá, 2011).

18. Adolfo Álvarez and Hernando Llano, "La Alianza Democrática M-19: ¿Una tercera fuerza frustrada?" *Revista Foro* 24 (1994): 63–65; Eduardo Pizarro-Leongómez, "La crisis de los partidos y los partidos en la crisis," in *Tras las huellas de la crisis política*, ed. F. Leal (Bogotá: Tercer Mundo Editores, FESCOL-IEPRI, 1996), 205–34; Eduardo Pizarro-Leongómez, Francisco Gutiérrez, and Alvaro Villarraga, *La oposición política en Colombia* (Bogotá: Fescol, IEPRI, 1996). In 2003, 2007, and 2011, leftist candidates had won the mayoral elections in Bogotá. In presidential elections, leftist candidates had occupied the third, second, and fourth places in 2002, 2006, and 2010, respectively.

19. César Rodríguez Garavito, "La izquierda democrática en Colombia: Orígenes, características y perspectivas," in *La nueva izquierda en América Latina: Sus orígenes y trayectoria futura*, ed. P. Barrett, C. R. Garavito, and D. Chávez (Buenos Aires: Norma, 2005), 191–238.

20. Uribe decided that FARC and ELN were terrorist groups, not leftist guerrilla groups. He qualified them as criminal organizations that lacked any possibility to join the legitimate order. The candidate's campaign slogan was "A firm hand and a big heart," which summarized a proposal aimed at duplicating the number of police and professional soldiers to create an organization of "cooperating" citizens (or network of informants) who would collaborate with the forces of the order and, at the same time, invest in humanitarian assistance. Daniel Zovatto, "Uribe: Mano firme y corazón grande," *Nueva Mayoría*, June 2, 2006, http://www.nuevamayoria.com/analisis/zovatto/zovatto050602.htm.

21. Miguel García Sánchez and Laura Wills-Otero, "El poder de la television: Medios de comunicación y aprobación presidencial en Colombia," in *Medios, democracia y poder*, ed. A. Rettberg and O. Rincón (Bogotá: Universidad de los Andes, 2011), 135–57.

22. Scott Mainwaring, Ana Maria Bejarano, and Eduardo Pizarro-Leongomez, *The Crisis of Democratic Representation in the Andes* (Stanford, CA: Stanford University Press, 2006);

Laura Wills-Otero, "Latin American Traditional Parties: The Impact of Parties' Internal Features on their Electoral Performance" (PhD diss., Department of Political Science, University of Pittsburgh, 2010).

23. The competition was between Álvaro Uribe Vélez and Horacio Serpa Uribe from PL. PC did not present a candidate.

24. Álvaro Uribe Vélez had not been a member of PSUN. Nevertheless, PSUN was his main promoter and defender.

25. PSUN was also the result of the fusion of two factions of Uribe followers who already established a legal party: the Nuevo Partido and the Movimiento Democrático por la Seguridad Social. "Nació el hijo político de Uribe," *El Tiempo*, September 1, 2005, http://www.eltiempo.com/archivo/documento/MAM-1757816.

26. Felipe Botero, ed., *Juntos pero no revueltos? Partidos, candidatos y campañas en las elecciones legislativas de 2006 en Colombia* (Bogotá: Centro de Estudios Socioculturales, Universidad de los Andes, 2009).

27. Misión de Observación Electoral, "Resultados elecciones 2011: Locales y Departamentales" (Bogotá, 2011).

28. Before 2003, the formula for assigning posts was that of quotients or largest remainders, technically known as the Hare formula. With this formula, seats could be won with just a small number of votes. In 2003, this system was replaced by the d'Hondt allocation figure or formula, which raises the threshold of votes required to win a seat. See Wills-Otero (2010).

29. During Uribe's tenure, the cabinet was composed of thirteen ministries. He merged some offices when he assumed the presidency in 2002.

30. García Sánchez and Wills-Otero (2011).

31. Votebien, "¿Quien financió a Álvaro Uribe?," October 14, 2002, http://www.terra.com.co/elecciones_2002/cubrimiento_especial/financiacion/26-09-2002/nota68713.html.

32. Iván Cepeda, "Gobierno Uribe favoreció a empresarios antioqueños en compra masiva de tierras en Montes de María," *Ágora*, September 2, 2011. http://congresovisible.org/agora/post/gobierno-uribe-favorecio-a-empresarios-antioquenos-en-compra-masiva-de-tierras-en-montes-de-maria/2309/.

33. Lina M. Marín Moreno, "Las empresas que aportaron al proyecto de referendo para la reelección podrían ser corresponsables en violación de topes," *La Silla Vacía*, March 23, 2009, http://www.lasillavacia.com/historia/75.

34. Claudia López, ed., *Y refundaron la patria . . . De cómo mafiosos y políticos reconfiguraron el Estado colombiano* (Bogotá: Corporación Nuevo Arco Iris, 2010).

35. Ibid.

36. For share of power within the government coalition, see ibid, 33. Guerrilla groups exercised another kind of influence in the electoral process. See Miguel García, "Sobre balas y votos: Violencia política y participación electoral en Colombia, 1990–1994," in *Entre la persistencia y el cambio, reconfiguración del escenario partidista y electoral en Colombia*, ed. D. Hoyos (Bogotá: Editorial Universidad del Rosario, 2007), 84–117. FARC sabotaged local elections there where they had power. They also threatened, kidnapped, and assassinated a number of regional politicians and congressmen.

37. Daron Acemoglu, James A. Robinson, and Rafael Santos, *The Monopoly of Violence: Evidence from Colombia* (Cambridge, MA: National Bureau of Economic Research, 2009).

38. Verdad Abierta, "¿Una nueva generación de parapolíticos?," *Paramilitarismo y conflicto armado en Colombia*, October 31, 2011, http://www.verdadabierta.com/component/content /article/63-nacional/3633-iuna-nueva-generacion-de-parapoliticos.

39. "The general objective of the Policy of Defense and Democratic Security is to reinforce and guarantee the State of Right throughout the national territory, by means of the strengthening of democratic authority." Presidencia de la República, Ministerio de Defensa Nacional de Colombia, "Política de Defensa y Seguridad Democrática" (Bogotá, 2003).

40. Fernando José Isaza and Diógenes Campos, "Algunas consideraciones cualitativas sobre la evolución reciente del conflicto en Colombia," in *Mimeo* (Bogotá: Universidad Jorge Tadeo Lozano, 2007).

41. Observatorio de Procesos de Desarme, Desmovilización y Reintegración, "Los procesos de Desarme, Desmovilización y Reintegración: Buenas prácticas y retos" (Universidad Nacional de Colombia, Bogotá, 2010).

42. Amnistía Internacional, "Amnistía Internacional revela informe sobre DDHH en Colombia," *dh Colombia, Red de Defensores No Institucionalizados,* May 28, 2008, http://www .dhcolombia.info/spip.php?article585; El Espectador, "Acusan a Uribe de violar los derechos humanos" *El Espectador*, September 17, 2008, http://www.elespectador.com/noticias/politica /articulo-acusan-uribe-de-violar-los-derechos-humanos; Samuel Logan, "Uribe's Reality Check," blog entry, April 5, 2007, http://www.samuellogan.com/articles/uribes-reality-check .html; Tim West, "Right Wing Wins Colombian Elections—Workers Must Prepare to Fight," *League for the Fifth International*, August 17, 2010, http://www.fifthinternational.org/content /right-wing-wins-colombian-elections-workers-must-prepare-fight. Other denunciations had to do with violations of the sovereignty of neighboring countries.

43. In the term that preceded Álvaro Uribe's, the indicators of economic growth were weak in comparison to the national historical tendency. In 2000, 2001, and 2002, the GDP was 2.9%, 1.5%, and 1.9%, respectively. Unemployment in the main cities was 17.2%, 18.2%, and 17.6%, respectively. Inflation, however, was 8.8%, 7.7%, and 6.9%, respectively. Data from the National Administrative Department of Statistics (Dane) and the National Planning Department.

44. Francisco Javier Giraldo Isaza, "Balance económico de la administración Uribe primer período: 2002–2006," *Apuntes del Cenes* (2007): 93–116. The title the president gave to his 2002–6 development plan was "Towards a Communitarian State," which embodied his integral plan of government. From 2006 to 2010, the plan was called "Communitarian State."

45. Carlos Caballero Argáez, "Al César lo que es del César," *El Tiempo*, April 15, 2006; Juan Guillermo Londoño, "¿Por qué Ecopetrol se abre a privados?," *El Tiempo*, June 26, 2006.

46. Mauricio Cárdenas and Mauricio Reina, "La minería en Colombia: Impacto socioeconómico y fiscal" (Fundación para la Educación Superior y el Desarrollo, Bogotá, 2008).

47. Departamento Nacional de Planeación, "Bases del Plan Nacional de Desarrollo 2002–2006: Hacia un Estado Comunitario" (Bogotá, 2003).

48. Social indicators for the years preceding the Uribe administration were as follows: the poverty level reached 55% in 2000, 55.2% in 2001, and 57% in 2002. Inequality, measured with the Gini coefficient, was 0.56, 0.55, and 0.57 in 2000, 2001, and 2002, respectively. Data from the National Administrative Department of Statistics (Dane) and the National Planning Department.

49. Ibid.

50. Alexis V. Pinilla Díaz, "Breve mirada sobre la revolución educativa en Colombia" (Foro Latinoamericano de Políticas Educativas, Bogotá, 2006). In the educational sector, the government found enormous resistance from students and teachers who did not agree with initiatives directed to privatize public education.

51. Juanita León, "Robledo y Coronell lograron poner a Saludcoop contra la pared," *La Silla Vacía*, May 12, 2011, http://www.lasillavacia.com/historia/robledo-y-coronell-lograron -poner-saludcoop-contra-la-pared-24282; Semana, "Supersalud interviene la EPS Saludcoop," *Semana*, May 12, 2011, http://www.semana.com/nacion/articulo/supersalud-interviene-eps -saludcoop/239664-3.

52. Regarding these solutions, studies show that community councils entailed "populist" expenditures. In municipalities where such meetings were held during Uribe's first term, for example, spending in the amount of $14.1 million was allocated for transport infrastructure (in the meetings) in addition to that of municipalities in which they did not take place. Luis Bernardo Mejía Guinand, Felipe Botero, and Juan Carlos Rodríguez-Raga, "¿Pavimentando con votos? Apropiación presupuestal para proyectos de infraestructura vial en Colombia, 2002–2006," *Colombia Internacional* 68 (2008): 14–42.

53. The programs of conditioned transferences are currently important programs in the fight against poverty in most countries of the Latin American region.

54. César García Trujillo, "Los programas de transeferencias condicionadas: Mecanismos de legitimidad política en América Latina: El caso de Familias en Acción" (Facultad de Ciencias Sociales y Relaciones Internacionales, Universidad Javeriana, Bogotá, 2009).

55. Economic Commission for Latin America and the Caribbean, 2002–9.

56. Ibid.

57. Congreso Visible, "Congreso Visible: Balance del cuatrienio 2006–2010," in *Boletín Congreso Visible* (Bogotá: Universidad de los Andes, 2010).

58. At the end of the government, serious corruption scandals involving legislators, ministers, and other public officials were revealed, which also diverted the attention from legislative activity. The scandals included the so-called parapolitical phenomenon, in which several members of congress were removed from their posts for being linked to the paramilitaries; the purchase of congressional votes by the executive branch in order to obtain the approval of the presidential reelection project; the "bugging" or illegal hacking of telephones of different public officials from the opposition and journalists, among other people, by the Administrative Department of Security; and the allocation of millions of dollars' worth of resources to privileged sectors through the Agro Ingreso Seguro policy of the Ministry of Agriculture.

PART FOUR

THE PARTISAN RIGHT

CHAPTER NINE

Mexico

The Partido Acción Nacional as a Right Party

STEVEN T. WUHS

Mexico's right party was hidden in plain sight for almost twenty years. As Mexico slowly edged toward democratic change in the 1980s and 1990s, the National Action Party (Partido Acción Nacional, or PAN) emerged as Mexico's democratic alternative to the incumbent and authoritarian Institutional Revolutionary Party (Partido Revolucionario Institucional, or PRI). As a party, it promised good governance, responsible stewardship of the economy, and democracy—an appealing program for Mexican voters weary of one-party rule and, by the 1980s and 1990s, stung by repeated economic crises. In 2000, PAN's presidential candidate Vicente Fox defeated the PRI candidate, a feat repeated in 2006 by PAN candidate Felipe Calderón Hinojosa. PAN's two terms in the federal executive (accompanied by many victories in state-level elections and the emergence of deep regional attachments to the PAN) revealed other dimensions of the party's program to Mexican voters—ones that some PAN members and many Mexican citizens found considerably less appealing than its democratic credentials. The problem for PAN is that these dimensions relate to its long-standing identity as a party of the right.

In this chapter I explain the complexity of PAN's "right" character, and highlight the effect of one-party rule and protracted transition on both the programmatic identity of the party and the perception of that programmatic identity. In doing so, I argue that PAN's underlying left-right ideological position was for decades clouded by a crosscutting issue—the support of democracy—that was the dominant issue for Mexican parties and voters for the final twenty years of PRI's decades-long rule (1929–2000). PAN's electoral success during the transition period was thus not a function of its left-right ideological profile. Instead, it depended on the party's ability to present itself not as the right party it was, but as a political alternative (an agent of good governance or a democratizing force). This chapter charts PAN's development and transformation *as a party of the right* over the course of the twentieth century, while placing particular attention on the sometimes-difficult relationship between its ideological and electoral selves. Drawing on primary and secondary data, I also consider the current contours of PAN in Mexican politics and its prospects in the context of an increasingly traditional "left-right" Mexican ideological landscape.

Party Foundation, Ideals, and Experience under Authoritarianism

The Partido Acción Nacional was at its foundation and remains today a right party, though its particular brand of right does not easily fall into the categories of either "the old right" (European Christian Democratic parties, for example) or "the new right" (e.g., Chile's Renovación Nacional or Colombia's Partido de la U). It has consistently supported the idea that the "main inequalities between people are natural and outside the purview of the state."[1] It also falls on the right according to other measures. Coppedge places PAN on the center-right on the basis of its stances on public security, morality, and the economy, as Bruhn confirms through an analysis of party manifestoes.[2] And, consistent with Gibson's approach, PAN also draws support from the upper strata.[3] Yet PAN also features a complicated set of overlapping and competing internal interests through the authoritarian, transition, and democratic periods that shaped its eventual identity as a pro-democratic alternative—not the typical profile of a right party.

Religious and Liberal Origins

Catholic associations and ideologues were crucial to the foundation of PAN in 1939. These actors mobilized in response to anticlerical reforms of the administration of President Lázaro Cárdenas (1934–40) that secularized public education and expropriated Church landholdings while also politically isolating the Church hierarchy. In response to government actions, Catholic groups like Acción Católica Mexicana (Mexican Catholic Action) and the Asociación Católica de la Juventud Mexicana (Catholic Association of Mexican Youths), without the consent of the Catholic Church, collaborated in the foundation of PAN and contributed key elements of its core principles and strategic dispositions.[4] While other ideological and political streams were present at the party's foundation, the early secondary literature on PAN emphasized its Catholic origins, calling the party a restorationist ally of the archconservative Unión Nacional de Padres de Familia (National Union of Parents) and a strategic ally of the Unión Nacional Sinarquista (National Sinarquist Union).[5] In its first decades its leaders sought not to proselytize the general electorate, but rather to retreat to their ideals—to a monastic, contemplative existence. Borrowing from the leaders of the time, PAN scholars often discuss this period in party history using biblical metaphors— PAN was "crossing the desert," for example.[6]

Other accounts of party formation emphasize the party's liberal orientation, referring in this case to economic liberalism.[7] Rather than focus on the Catholic social base of the party at its foundation, these arguments point to the liberal credentials of founder Manuel Gómez Morin and his influence on the party, as well as the political-economic juncture at which PAN was formed, specifically the actions that Cárdenas's Mexican Revolutionary Party (Partido Revolucionario Mexicano, or PRM) government took to alleviate poverty and address questions of social inequality (and PAN's opposition to it). Three elements of his program were crucial. First, agrarian reform radically restructured the Mexican countryside and created new communal structures, the *ejidos*. While rural poverty persisted long after the reform, that reform effectively ended the *latifundio* structure in Mexico. Second, this *sexenio* also featured national leadership intent on improving working-class conditions through social legislation.[8] Cárdenas's goal was to deepen the early postrevolutionary social reforms (pensions for government employees and the passage of a federal labor law that addressed workers' compensation) through the passage of a social security law and the creation of social insurance for private sector workers. While those efforts themselves faltered, they succeeded in alienating many business elites who contributed to PAN's foundation along with other economic liberals under Gómez Morin's leadership.[9] Those same interests were alarmed by the administration's support of the creation of national confederations for the peasantry and organized workers, the Confederación Nacional Campesina (National Peasants' Confederation) and Confederación de Trabajadores de México (Confederaton of Mexican Workers).[10]

The party's Catholic social base suggests a certain conservatism in PAN, and its leaders' fondness for liberal economics definitely suggests placement of the party on the political right. An examination of PAN's doctrine allows us to even more confidently qualify the party as "right" on the basis of the conceptualization deployed in this book. PAN's first set of Principios were written and published in 1939, in the shadow of the Cárdenas government, and consist of fourteen articles, several of which address equality and inequality.[11] Article 3, "The State," is where the problem of social inequality first appears, with direct language regarding appropriate action for the state in light of inequality. The state should not be an actor in class struggle, which itself is deemed "false and inhuman." Rather, the role of the state is to maintain the common good, meaning protecting individuals, promoting justice and security, and defending collective interests. The state is thus a guarantor of social order, not an agent of change. Later, Article 7, "Work," describes the freedom all people have to work with dignity and the right to have opportunity for employment. While that may be true, Article 9, "Property," defends the private foundations of capitalism as the only way to support the nation, preserve the family, and guarantee individual human dignity. Article 10, "The Countryside," is perhaps the 1939 Principios' most direct comment on the party's understanding of social inequality. According to the text of this article, the countryside in the late 1930s was Mexico's gravest national problem. But the text of the article is also consistent with the party's desire to promote the common good and to undermine class-consciousness and conflict. It advocates "just and harmonious" relationships between landowners and peasants who work the land. Again, class conflict itself is undermined as a legitimate option.

These articles, taken together, advance a vision of PAN where inequality is recognized and tacitly accepted either through consistent focus on individual freedoms to work or through a steady eye on the common good. The implied society is organic in nature, depending on productive and peaceful relationships among its parts. Capitalism (through an emphasis on private ownership) is supported, an endorsement of the engine behind inequality. All told, these initial Principios sound like those of a right party with a tacit acceptance of social inequality as natural, as well as those generated by the social bases typically identified as influential at the party's foundation.[12]

During the extraordinary political isolation of the party during the 1940s and 1950s (when PAN rarely governed at the municipal level and typically garnered only about 10% in federal legislative elections), internal doctrinal debates grew especially fierce. It yielded in 1965 a revised set of Principios that reinforced several of the inequality-related provisions of the 1939 set but also, importantly, included a "Democracy" article (Article 5) staking out PAN's position as Mexico's pro-democratic opposition force. As the passage below demonstrates, democracy for PAN is based on preexisting equality of all human beings and has strongly liberal character. "Democracy" exists not to equalize members of society, but as a result of equality within society.[13]

> Democracy requires the effective participation of the people in the collective activities that shape their destiny. Because democracy as a system of life and government is founded on the essential equality of all human beings, it is the highest form of legitimation of political power and the optimal system for the respect of human dignity, which should be sustained materially by the economic satisfaction of all and spiritually by the possibility of access of all to the values of culture and in relation to human freedom, to respond to their conscience and to God's own destiny and that of their peers.

In addition to its often-noted religious and economic positions, PAN was stridently if peculiarly pro-democratic in its orientation from its foundation in 1939, and increasingly so after 1965.[14] But the politics of the PRI regime (in which PAN served as a loyal opposition with relatively little political influence) led PAN elites to turn inward in their practice of democracy, emphasizing clean, representative, and orderly internal contests for leadership and candidacy, and efforts by the party's devout membership to democratize Mexican society, one individual at a time.

The Transition Era: Ideological Stability and Ideological Layering

The idea of winning political office (or, more broadly construed, "political ambition") fostered stark internal divisions between pragmatic and doctrinaire factions that marked PAN's early history and conditioned the party's evolution during the transition era. So profound was the opposition to political ambition among doctrinaires to competing for office under PRI's authoritarian regime (which they believed dignified the regime by accepting its control of the political system) that they prevented the incorporation of winning office into the party's official goals until the 1970s. That position and many other elements of party life changed following inclusionary political openings, often engineered by the PRI regime, that incrementally introduced semicompetitive politics in Mexico. Each reform was accompanied by concomitant changes in PAN—taking a party that had been defined by its religious character and its devotion to economic liberalism and adding new layers of interests and objectives that within a generation obscured those Catholic and liberal commitments with avowed support for democratic alternation and effective public administration.[15]

The first two reforms occurred as a result of developments in electoral politics. In the presidential election of 1958, PAN and its candidate Luis H. Alvarez waged a polemical and damning campaign against PRI authoritarianism. PAN did not win, or even perform terribly well, but the frequency of fraud was quite high, signaling a concern by PRI elites about the party's performance and legitimacy.[16] A few years later, PRI passed the first significant opposition-friendly electoral reform, creating designated seats for the opposition in the lower chamber of the federal legislature. The absolute number of seats was modest, PRI's hegemony was never jeopardized, and parties that did not accept their seats (in protest, for example) placed their legal registries at risk; that is, sticks accompanied the carrots embedded in this reform. Still, it had the effect of bolstering the pragmatic faction inside PAN and intensifying party debates about participation in PRI's system, even if the party remained nationally weak, as the 1970 results shown in figure 9.1 demonstrate.[17]

A second reform had a more dramatic short-term effect on the party. Owing to the growing intensity of conflict between PAN's pragmatic and doctrinaire factions, the party failed to nominate a candidate for the presidential elections of 1976; no single candidate could reach the 80% convention vote share the party's statutes

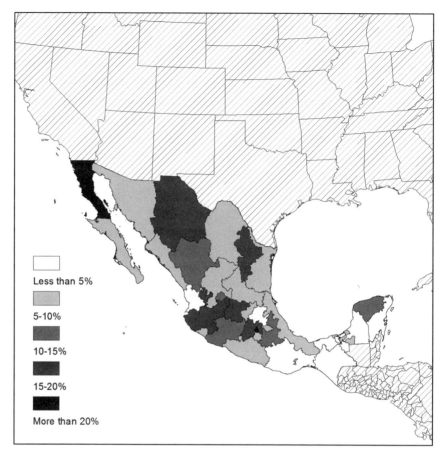

Less than 5%

5-10%

10-15%

15-20%

More than 20%

Figure 9.1. Percentage of the vote for the Partido Acción Nacional in the presidential election of 1970.

required at the time. The PRI candidate was thus left to run unopposed. While this was clearly a disappointment for PAN, the unchallenged nature of PRI's candidacy that year also exposed the regime's authoritarian politics, prompting an electoral reform in 1977 that added one hundred proportional-representation seats designated for the opposition to the Chamber of Deputies (which had been composed of only plurality, single-member district seats and the party deputies discussed above).[18] Existing pragmatic forces in PAN were again strengthened, but, more importantly, these developments repositioned PAN vis-à-vis segments of the electorate, most crucially a substantial segment of Mexico's business community that shortly thereafter recognized PAN as a potential electoral challenger to PRI. The arrival of these Neopanistas, after the PRI-led nationalization of the banking system in 1982, signaled a critical juncture in PAN's position as a right party.[19] Neopanista campaigns were not peaceably organized around the social Christian and economically liberal values and arguments of the party typical of earlier campaigns. Instead, while they were still clearly and perhaps more emphatically pro-business in orientation, these PAN candidates confronted PRI's authoritarian politics head on, and promised local democratic governance and good governance as an alternative.[20]

The late 1980s witnessed another political opening, led in part by the PRI regime, this time in response to a crisis of legitimacy stemming from the perceived mismanagement of the economy during the debt crisis and the failed response to a devastating earthquake that hit Mexico City in 1985. Facing increasing social protest and the prospects of a weak performance in the 1988 federal elections, PRI leaders sought to direct opposition into the formal political arena by creating another one hundred proportional representation seats in the Chamber of Deputies (as part of a more comprehensive electoral reform) in 1986. The election's outcome placed PRI in its politically weakest position since the 1930s in terms of seats and given the endemic fraud associated with the victory of PRI candidate Carlos Salinas de Gortari. Less than six months after the election, Cuauhtémoc Cárdenas, Salinas's main rival in 1988, led the formation of a new left party, the Party of the Democratic Revolution (Partido de la Revolución Democrática, or PRD).

Given a new competitor to its left, the by-then-neoliberal PRI regime was desperate for a political ally, and it turned to PAN. In exchange for PAN's cooperation on constitutional reforms in the legislature (which it could no longer pass on its own), PAN subnational victories were increasingly recognized (e.g., the first-ever election of an opposition governor in Baja California in 1989). For PAN, this juncture thus offered increased representation in the federal legislature and state governments and contributed to the image of PAN as an electorally and politically viable party, especially for entrepreneurs. The party's left-right positions remained distant from the average voter, but by this time the electorate was concerned less with distributive questions and more with democracy. Despite these more moderate, electoralist developments and the increasing pragmatism of PAN leadership during this time, the party retained sectarian rules that limited its ability to reach out to voters and become an effective electoral party.[21]

A final inclusionary reform (or, more accurately, cluster of reforms) occurred in the late 1990s as the opposition parties (PAN and PRD) were gaining strength both in the federal legislature and in subnational politics.[22] They leveraged that influence in 1996 to design a major electoral reform with four key components: (1) the provision of generous public finance for basic party operations and campaigns in federal election years; (2) the introduction of limits and audits of election season media coverage; (3) the fortification of the Federal Electoral Institute and the Federal Electoral Tribunal; and (4) the creation of proportional representation senators elected from a national list that were certain to amplify PAN and PRD influence in the upper chamber.[23] Together, this package of changes hemmed in many of PRI's informal prerogatives and offered new opportunities to the opposition. In contrast with earlier inclusionary reforms, however, by this time pragmatic forces in PAN were powerful enough to engineer changes to the party's internal institutional life that they believed would broaden the political appeal of the party toward the median voter. Its membership rules were adapted through the creation of an "adherent" layer of membership that required neither fees nor most of the other criteria for "active" membership. That adherent layer accounted for almost all of the party's growth in the late 1990s. Indeed, while active membership remained stable nationally at approximately 150,000 between 1995 and 1999, adherent membership grew from zero to about 300,000 members in the same period.[24] These adherent members often came from different demographic backgrounds and held contrasting political views to active members, realities that had little bearing under the PRI regime that would under democratic politics became more salient.

Over the twenty-five years of the transition period, PRI's authoritarian system and PAN evolved in a stepwise, interrelated fashion. PAN began the transition period as a niche party, a Catholic and liberal organization ideologically distant from Mexican voters and unable to attract office-seeking elites.[25] While scholars and pundits have pointed to heavy reliance of fraud by PRI to retain power, resource inequities among the parties and campaign effects were probably more important.[26] As democracy became more salient as an issue dimension (from 1976 on), and as those inclusionary reforms created greater opportunities for opposition representation, PAN's pro-democratic positions increasingly hid its right, conservative, and religious identities. That is, while PAN's official (i.e., statutory) ideals remained stable, its ideological placement in the eyes of voters shifted toward the center, introducing some internal contradictions within the organization. Still, by 2000, PAN was increasingly seen as viable challenger to PRI, an effective agent of governance at the state level, and had shed much of the public image associated with its earlier confessional and niche self.

Extrication and Consolidation

Mexico's protracted democratic transition ended in 2000 with the removal of PRI from the federal executive and its reduction to a minority party in Congress. That election left PAN with the presidency of Vicente Fox and, for a time, a plurality in the Chamber of Deputies. It thus solidified PAN's status as a mainstream electoralist party. But this moment of triumph for the party also revealed the internal contradictions it had developed during the transition period and the problematic positioning of the party relative to Mexico's electorate. PAN's ideological "transformation" of the transition period entailed no formal change in the ideals or doctrine of the party; its improved performance was not based on programmatic moderation. Instead, its electoral success grew from increasing identification of the party not as right, social Christian, economically liberal, or conservative, but rather as democratic.[27] According to Magaloni and Moreno, the politics of "democracy" enabled the party to be relatively opaque about its programmatic positions on "family values" issues like sexual freedom and abortion (both of which were opposed by ideologues in the party), and, to a certain extent, about the economy.[28] Rather than having a defined set of voters attracted to particular ideals advanced by the party, PAN voters in 2000 were "scattered all over the political spectrum along the economic and moral values dimensions."[29] Thus PAN was at the time advocating policy positions associated with a religious right and an economic right, but those positions were clouded by its pro-democratic credentials.[30] The outcome of 2000 was not a function of issue positions and left-right dynamics; instead, Fox won because of his (and PAN's) ability to achieve four tasks, all of which hinged on his ability to control the democracy issue dimension, not on left-right ideology: focus the campaign on democracy, counter PRI's reformist efforts, win pro-democracy voters from Cárdenas, and claim the political center.[31]

Despite its congressional plurality and an initial period of economic stability, Fox's government was by its first year's end facing criticism for its failure to make significant advances on public security and job creation, as well as on tax, energy, and labor reforms. That poor record did PAN no favors in the 2003 midterm elections: PRI took 224 of 500 seats in the Chamber of Deputies, while PAN's share shrunk to just 151. But although the 2003 midterm contest highlighted the challenges of governing in a multiparty democratic Mexico, the election (as in 2000) offered little in terms of the politics of left and right. That changed dramatically in 2006, when the regime-based axis of competition was clearly laid to rest, and Mexico's presidential candidates fought along clearly marked class lines. Panista Felipe Calderón Hinojosa and PRD-led coalition candidate Andrés Manuel López Obrador represented two diametrically opposed camps (both notably anti-PRI in nature): a right, market-based, economic agenda that supported the North American Free Trade Agreement paired with socially conservative values, with greater support among wealthy and middle-class voters, versus statist economic policies and a socially liberal agenda that found tremendous support among Mexico's poor. The campaign and election were novel in the Mexican context for their class and ideological content, but even in this case (which was marked by impressive social uprisings in the wake of the contested election) orthogonal issues presented to cloud the ideological nature of the contest. Specifically, voters appeared driven by concerns about economic stability. As Fox famously said, the election was a chance for voters to change the rider, not the horse, to maintain the modest economic growth and high oil prices that Mexico experienced late in his *sexenio*, and to avoid the dangers to that stability posed by the election of the populist left. These potential paths became dominant media representations of the showdown, dividing Mexico's population demographically and regionally and, after election day and the electoral court's ruling in favor of Calderón, producing a weak PAN president and a legislature even more fragmented than what Fox began with.[32]

Most Mexican voters associate the Calderón administration more with the drug war he launched upon assuming power in December 2006 than with any particular economic policy, though he did work to stabilize tortilla prices, create opportunities for first-time entrants to the labor market, and continue Fox's targeted social assistance program, Oportunidades.[33] The geographic extent of the drug-related violence and the rising death toll (estimated around 70,000) had dramatic effects in the 2009 midterm contests, where they reduced Calderón's delegation in the lower house to 143 seats, relative to PRI's 237 (in coalition with the Green Party) and PRD's 71. Those results suggest that, in the eyes of voters, Calderón's offensive against the cartels had placed PAN on the wrong side of public security, an additional orthogonal issue that has helped right parties elsewhere.[34] Mexico's voters in 2009 cast their ballots neither for democracy nor for socioeconomic equality. Instead, their vote for PRI represented a desire for civil stability and an escape from the violence that Calderón's offensive unleashed.[35] With that vote, Mexican citizens unfortunately also created a context of potential political intransigence—where the PAN president must negotiate important fiscal, judicial, police, and energy reforms with a PRI congress. According to the same electoral logic, PAN has also lost significant PAN states and municipalities (San Luís Potosí and Querétaro states and the cities of Guadalajara and Mérida), and in July 2011 underperformed in state elections in México, Nayarit, and Coahuila.

PAN struggled throughout the federal elections of 2012, hampered not just by the violence of the drug war but also by PRI's telegenic candidate Enrique Peña Nieto (the eventual winner) and the return of PRD candidate López Obrador. Its candidate, Josefina Vázquez Mota, ran a distant third throughout the campaign, and won just 25% of the popular vote. Analyses of the outcome suggest that while violence weighed on voters' minds, economic growth was more salient—and voters had more faith in PRI's ability to achieve it after relatively sluggish growth under Calderón. Paired with candidate quality and PRI's strategic and perhaps questionable use of television and the Internet during the campaign, Vázquez Mota thus faced serious challenges irrespective of her following's ideological composition (a theme to which I return below).

PAN as a Right Party

Table 9.1 shows the electoral growth of the party from 1970, as PRI hegemony was just beginning to show its cracks, through the most recent round of federal elections. Overall, the data document PAN's steady, incremental growth, and its eventual position as PRI's main competitor for national power (AMLO's 2006 performance notwithstanding). One might interpret this growth as a sign of right strength, but below I confound that interpretation on the basis of primary data and secondary analyses of PAN, its elites, and its supporters.[36]

Issue Positions

Public opinion polling on political issues did not get underway in Mexico until the 1980s, but between then and the present day, the polls have painted a fairly consistent picture of the Mexican electorate and Mexican party members. Mexican voters are centrist and relatively normally distributed.[37] It was true in 1990 as the transition was unfolding, in midtransition in 1996–97, and as Mexico democratized in 2000 (drawing in each case from the World Values Survey). Several other scholars drawing from several other polls confirm that general characterization. For example, Greene reached the same finding with 1998 Latinobarómetro data, and researchers at the Centro de Investigación y Docencia Económicas (CIDE) drew a similar conclusion while observing a slight rightward shift between 1990 and 2000.[38] They show that the average placement of the Mexican citizen on a left-right scale (scaled from 1 to 5) went from 3.14 to 3.45 between 1990 and 2000—a rightward shift but still remaining fairly centrist.[39]

As noted earlier, Mexico's 2006 election signaled a resurgence of left-right politics in Mexico and the clear passing of the democratic-authoritarian axis that had structured competition among the parties through 2000. In that election, four major issues structured the vote: (1) the privatization of electricity, (2) the legalization of abortion in cases of rape, (3) individual responsibility for one's welfare, and (4) strengthening the nature of trade ties with the United States.[40] While the average PAN and PRD voters had different preferences about electricity privatization, both were much more centrist than their parties. Likewise, when asked whether individuals should be responsible for their own welfare, the mean voters from PAN, PRI, and PRD showed relatively little difference of opinion (the mean responses in

TABLE 9.1.
Electoral performance of Mexican parties, 1970–2009

Year	Party	Presidential vote share (%)	Chamber of deputies vote share (%)
1970	PRI	87.8	83.53
	PAN	11.04	14.21
1976	PRI	92.75	85.17
	PAN	0	8.99
1982	PRI	71.63	69.29
	PAN	16.42	17.54
	Left	3.65	4.37
1988	PRI	51.22	50.37
	PAN	16.96	17.96
	Frente Democrático Nacional/Left	30.89	4.45
1991	PRI		58.47
	PAN		16.82
	PRD		7.91
1994	PRI	48.69	48.58
	PAN	25.92	24.98
	PRD	16.59	16.12
1997	PRI		39.11
	PAN		26.61
	PRD		25.71
2000	PRI	36.11	36.92
	PAN	42.52	38.24
	PRD	16.64	18.68
2003	PRI		23.14
	PAN		30.73
	PRD		17.61
2006	PRI	22.26	28.21
	PAN	35.89	33.39
	PRD	35.31	28.99
2009	PRI		36.75
	PAN		28.01
	PRD		12.20
2012	PRI	38.21	31.93
	PAN	25.41	25.89
	PRD	31.59	18.36

all three cases being a moderate "yes"). For all the profound differences between the leading candidates and the pitched ideological conflict among the parties, neither the campaign nor the candidates polarized the parties' voters. These findings should not come as a surprise, given that more than 25% of Mexican voters that year could not place themselves on a left-right scale.[41]

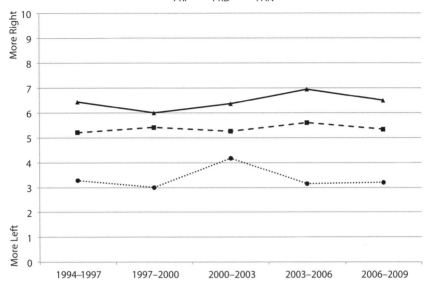

Figure 9.2. Left-right placement of Mexican political parties, 1994–2009.

PAN leaders' and activists' issue positions fall to the right of their PRI and PRD counterparts on three economy-related issues (the flow of foreign capital, individuals providing for their own welfare, and the centrality of private property to business).[42] PAN elites were also significantly to the right of PAN's own voters (as well as the median Mexican voter): PAN legislators placed themselves right of center (6.15 on a left-right scale of 0 to 10), and placed their party even further to the right (at 6.45), at least in the late 1990s.[43] Only when party elites began to significantly moderate in the late 1990s (or were perceived to, especially under the influence of Vicente Fox) did the party approach the self-placement of the median voter.[44] As figure 9.2 shows, by 2006, PAN leaders were again clearly right of center.[45] Its candidates for that election were pro-life, favored electricity privatization, expanded US commercial ties, and "believe[d] more in investment and individual responsibility to reduce poverty."[46] Taken together, these survey data suggest that PAN faces real limits in the ideological appeals it can successfully make to the electorate based on its underlying doctrine and its issue positions; indeed, a resurgence for PAN may depend on its positions on salient orthogonal issues in the future, something that has worked for the party in the past.

Voting

Klesner offers some insights into the municipal-level support bases of PAN in federal deputy elections between 1991 and 2003, highlighting positive and statistically significant effects of literacy, urbanization, manufacturing-based economies, the presence of Catholicism, and being in Mexico's north and center-west.[47] (Being in southern Mexico or the federal district had negative effects on PAN's electoral fortunes.) In terms of the presidential vote in 2000, relative to PRI (its main competitor that year), PAN had stronger support among more educated and younger voters, urban voters, those with salaries in the higher quintiles, and in Mexico's center-west and north. The inference is consistent and straightforward, confirming that the party draws consistent electorate support from segments of the voting population who (or municipalities with concentrations of voters that) are on the "winning side" of social inequality in Mexico—urban, literate, wealthy Mexicans.

Demographic distributions are not the only predictors of vote choice, of course. In the 2000 transitional presidential election, candidate qualities, issue positions, and campaign effects (including patronage) were important predictors of vote choice, and "Issue distance had a huge effect on the probability of supporting Fox," with both informed and uninformed voters showing a two-thirds likelihood of voting for Fox when they agreed with him on the issues (crime, privatization, and political reform).[48] That said, while the issues of the 2006 election differed dramatically from 2000, the social correlates of PAN support remained much the same.[49] PAN voters were reliably wealthier, more educated, more urban, and more likely nonunion than were voters for the other parties. Notably, additional significant differences were also evident in that contest—PAN voters were also more churchgoing, and were more likely to have family members in the United States. Regional divisions were also apparent in both executive and legislative voting, with PAN finding greater support in the north (where it competed with PRI) and in the Bajío states of central-western Mexico.

The 2012 presidential contest revealed several tendencies in the Mexican vote and specifically the PAN vote that confirm their complex ideological content. As noted earlier, PAN presidential candidate Vázquez Mota was a distant also-ran for the majority of the campaign season, but not because of her party's placement on the ideological right. In fact, despite PAN's program, she was favored in areas of the country with more marginal voters, high numbers of aid beneficiaries, and greater concentrations of informal sector workers—traditionally left party constituents. Díaz Cayeros et al. attribute this quizzical outcome to a policy legacy; namely, the success of twelve years of effective social policy administration through the Oportunidades program. López Obrador may have received the lion's share of support from formal sector workers and state employees, and Peña Nieto certainly maintained PRI's lock on rural and indigenous voters, but in this contest PAN showed an ability to appeal to a nontraditional electorate for the right.[50] Importantly, though, the affinity for the party appears to be predicated not on programmatic appeals (i.e., part of PAN's programs with reliable appeal to a segment of the electorate) but on the past provision of social benefits. It is thus unlikely that such an affinity would endure during a *sexenio* in the opposition for PAN.

Public Opinion and Party Identification in Mexico

The Latin American Public Opinion Project (LAPOP) surveys of Mexico offer more contemporary insight into the underpinnings of identification with PAN and its competitors.[51] The most recent LAPOP survey was conducted in 2010 and included several questions that bear directly on PAN's placement on the right of Mexican politics and on the right in the more global sense examined in this volume. On one level, the data confirm some findings noted above, that while political elites understand and appreciate PAN's position on the right, from the point of view of the Mexican voter or citizen, things are not as clear. Asked about the role of the Mexican state as an economic actor in its own right (i.e., relative to the private sector generally), for example, the data demonstrate that while PRD is ideologically distinct from PAN (as one might expect), differences between PAN and PRI are evident at the extremes but less so in the middle, more moderate positions (fig. 9.3).[52]

Asked about the Mexican state relative to individuals as the agents responsible for the well-being of the people, however, there is no statistically significant difference

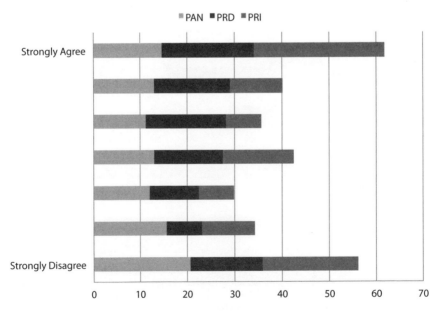

Figure 9.3. Support for the state as an economic actor (relative to the private sector), 2010.

among sympathizers of the Mexican parties. There was likewise no statistically significant difference among party sympathizers when asked about whether the Mexican state or private enterprise should be responsible for job creation.

The individual-level social correlates of Mexican party identification (or sympathy, as the LAPOP survey asks) are also relatively weak. The same survey revealed no statistically significant effect for gender, ethnicity, urban-rural differences, measures of political awareness, or income on partisan sympathies—a potential result of the catchall nature of PRI and the large share of the respondents that identified with the party (about 53%). Those skewed numbers are of course a function of prior institutional development, wherein PRI benefits from being the only party with an established national territorial organization and, as a result, strong party identifiers at the local level. While PAN and to a lesser degree PRD have worked to develop such a presence, they are unable to compete with the legacy of several decades of PRI rule.[53] Two social correlates were associated with differences in party sympathy: religiosity and education. But religiosity does not clearly engender sympathy for PAN, as suggested by figure 9.4.

Respondents' other group memberships offer additional contradictory evidence. For example, membership in community organizations and producer/commercial organizations was not associated with sympathy with a political party; the latter case is consistent with some of the secondary literature on business associations and parties in suggesting that business groups are strategic in their consideration of

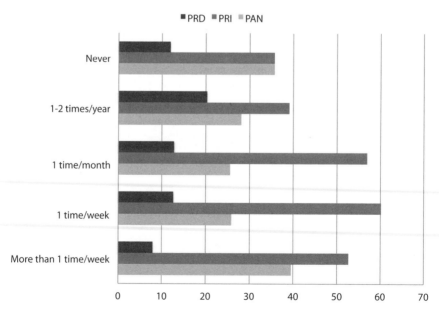

Figure 9.4. Religious service attendance and support for Mexican political parties, 2010.

partisan ties and are loath to form fixed relationships.[54] Although membership and attendance at religious organizations and political parties/movements held significant associations, increased religiosity of the respondents again favors PRI, not PAN.

The LAPOP data thus reveal some of the potential consequences of PAN's identification as a right party. While some cohorts of voters show some affinity for PAN, the underlying ideological character of PAN sympathizers is not clearly or strongly "right." Rather, in many ways, PAN supporters are not different from PRI and PRD supporters—suggesting (again) a disconnect between the party's doctrine, its elites' political commitments, and those of the citizens and voters who supported the party through the democratization process. While this interpretation of the LAPOP data is consistent with other data presented in this chapter, these particular findings may also be a function of a broader phenomenon in Mexican politics; namely, the turn away from political parties. Of the total Mexican sample for the 2010 wave of the LAPOP survey (1,537), only 28.5% sympathized with a party; of those sympathizers, as noted earlier, 53% sympathized with PRI. That is, while PAN may struggle to craft an ideological profile with electoral appeal, the Mexican system suffers from endemic weak partisanship that further complicates PAN's efforts.

Social Linkages

We can additionally assess the right character of the party through an analysis of its organized base—similar to what Gibson performed in Argentina but with particular attention paid toward the place of equality and inequality in the relationships between party organization and the organized citizenry.[55] As a Christian Democratic party, PAN has maintained a plural social base since its foundation. But different groups became the social base of the party under varied circumstances, as noted earlier: Catholic and religious associations provided PAN's social anchor in its first couple of decades, though selected leaders were drawn from business associations like the Confederation of Chambers of Commerce and the Mexican Employers' Confederation; they were later joined by Neopanistas from the 1980s. While the LAPOP data above suggest no significant relationship at the mass level between membership in producer organizations and sympathy for PAN, the composition of Mexico's legislature following the fiercely ideological 2006 election tells a different story. Of the deputies who were also listed as members of business associations, fully three-quarters were PAN members.[56]

The challenge from these data is that it is difficult to discern the weight of organized groups in the party's social presence or even its legislative delegation. Relative to 2003, the numbers in 2006 showed an increase, but does that mean greater power?[57] Are the represented interests changing too? Certainly those data are consistent with how PAN leaders perceive the party's core constituencies. They recognized several groups as especially important voting blocs for PAN: professionals, office employees, small business owners, students, and housewives.[58] Less important for PAN, unsurprisingly, were street vendors, labor (union and nonunion), peasants, public sector workers, and retirees.

Yet while PAN leaders are able to identify their core constituencies, and their legislative delegation includes a significant number of business association members, PAN has been reticent to establish formal linkages with those groups of voters. The party's 1965 Principios also included a blunt condemnation of PRI's corporatist system, and PAN leaders are always careful to specify that corporate membership in the party is not possible—only individuals need apply. That said, from the 1990s onward, and especially after disappointing midterm elections in 2003, PAN elites recognized a need to establish a stronger social base for the party to capture unattached voters and especially those who were detaching from PRI's corporatist system at the time.

Through a well-funded and new secretary for social linkage, the party reached out to organized voters through programs targeting the rural sector, the national teachers' union (the SNTE, or Sindicato Nacional de Trabajadores de la Educación), and urban popular movements, artists' groups, and business associations. That said, the party's reluctance to appear corporatist in the eyes of the electorate meant that the party has always been resistant to giving any particular group a quota of power in the party or sway over internal decisions.[59] The political payoff of these new initiatives and strategies remains unclear at best, though the staff devoted to this linkage work has increased substantially in recent years. In any case, because of the nonprogrammatic character of linkages between parliamentary elite and voters in Mexico, they seem unlikely to be a successful platform for PAN, barring a resort to patronage politics.[60]

Conclusion

There can be little debate about whether PAN qualifies as a party of the right. Inequality and equality are certainly present in its ideals, and the former is tacitly tolerated, as the party calls for limited intervention by the state in social matters and displays a serious aversion to class-based forms of politics. It is also clear that the segments of the voting public who may benefit from existing inequalities in society are more likely to support PAN. But PAN is a complex organization, in part because of its central role in Mexico's transition process, during which it began to approach a catchall party while somewhat contradictorily retaining its original ideological core: PAN sympathizers do not have markedly different ideological profiles than those of *other* parties, and they often have different profiles than that of their *own* party. There is likewise substantial evidence of ideological incoherence among PAN voters. PAN elites and the party's official positions demonstrate much greater consistency in their orientation, however, suggesting that while PAN members, sympathizers, and voters may not understand or appreciate the party's ideological placement on the right, its leaders do. Ironically enough, PAN's electoral fortunes have often depended on the obfuscation of that placement.

The ability of PAN to continue winning office on the basis of that ideological opacity is limited; more than a decade after the transition, its policy positions are now much more visible. The party now faces the challenge of integrating its ideological and electoral selves. PAN is a party of the right, and in the absence of dominant orthogonal issues its social policy and economic policy positions alienate the party from broad segments of the centrist Mexican electorate. That augurs poorly for the party in the context of left-right competition. PAN's prospects for returning to a position of political strength in federal-level politics may thus require the party to successfully incorporate other policy areas with broad political support into its appeals. In the short term, unfortunately, the party is on the losing side of the most salient issue: public safety and civil stability in light of Mexico's drug-related violence. Much of PAN's short-term potential thus depends on the actions of the PRI administration of Enrique Peña Nieto, and PAN's ability to identify new issues that it can incorporate alongside, or with which it can cloak, its underlying ideological profile.

NOTES

1. Luna and Rovira Kaltwasser, introduction, this volume.

2. Kathleen Bruhn and Kenneth F. Greene, "Elite Polarization Meets Mass Moderation in Mexico's 2006 Elections," *Political Science and Politics* 40 (2007): 33–38; Michael Coppedge, "A Classification of Latin American Political Parties" (working paper 244, Helen Kellogg Institute for International Studies, Notre Dame, IN, 1997).

3. Edward L. Gibson, *Class and Conservative Parties: Argentina in Comparative Perspective* (Baltimore: Johns Hopkins University Press, 1996).

4. Stathis N. Kalyvas notes similar patterns among European confessional parties. *The Rise of Christian Democracy in Europe* (Ithaca, NY: Cornell University Press), 1996.

5. Kenneth F. Johnson, "Ideological Correlations of Right Wing Alienation in Mexico," *American Political Science Review* 59 (1965): 656–64. On this early period, see also Donald J. Mabry, *Mexico's Acción Nacional: A Catholic Alternative to Revolution* (Syracuse, NY: Syracuse University Press, 1973).

6. Soledad Loaeza, *El Partido Acción Nacional: La larga marcha, 1939–1994. Oposición leal y partido de protesta* (Mexico City: Fondo de Cultura Económica, 1999); Yemile Mizrahi, *From Martyrdom to Power: The PAN in Mexico* (Notre Dame, IN: University of Notre Dame Press, 2003).

7. "Liberalism," because of its different economic and religious applications in this case, is avoided as a term for most of this chapter.

8. Michelle L. Dion, *Workers and Welfare: Comparative Institutional Change in Twentieth-Century Mexico* (Pittsburgh, PA: University of Pittsburgh Press, 2010), chap. 3.

9. Businessmen and bankers were a significant presence in PAN's founding of the National Executive Committee as well. See also Ben Ross Schneider, *Business Politics and the State in Twentieth-Century Latin America* (New York: Cambridge University Press, 2004), 73.

10. While these later became mechanisms of social and political control and vehicles for the distribution of patronage, from the vantage point of the 1930s, they were corporate institutions that empowered working classes. See Dion (2010); Kevin J. Middlebrook, *The Paradox of Revolution: Labor, the State, and Authoritarianism in Mexico* (Baltimore: Johns Hopkins University Press, 1995).

11. Partido Acción Nacional, *Principios de Doctrina* (Mexico City: Partido Acción Nacional, 1965 [1939]).

12. At the time of PAN's foundation, religious parties were explicitly banned in Mexico. It is thus no surprise that there is no explicit reference to the party's Catholic social base or the papal encyclicals from which its ideals draw.

13. As discussed in Evelyne Huber, Dietrich Rueschemeyer, and John D. Stephens, "The Paradoxes of Contemporary Democracy: Formal, Participatory and Social Dimensions," *Comparative Politics* 29 (1997): 323–42.

14. Steven T. Wuhs, *Savage Democracy: Institutional Change and Party Development in Mexico* (University Park: Pennsylvania State University Press, 2008).

15. These inclusionary reforms are elaborated in greater detail in Wuhs (2013), from which this section draws.

16. Alonso Lujambio, "Democratization through Federalism? The National Action Party Strategy, 1939–2000," in *Party Politics and the Struggle for Democracy in Mexico*, ed. Kevin J. Middlebrook (San Diego: Center for US-Mexican Studies, University of California, 2001), 54.

17. Map generated by author drawing from data presented in David A. Shirk, *Mexico's New Politics: The PAN and Democratic Change* (Boulder, CO: Lynne Rienner, 2005).

18. This reform also fixed, for the first time, the number of majority seats in the Chamber of Deputies at three hundred. Prior to this reform, districts were based on demographics, and as a result the size of the legislature varied. In 1976, just prior to the reform, there were 178 seats in the Chamber.

19. Yemile Mizrahi, "Rebels without a Cause: The Politics of Entrepreneurs in Chihuahua," *Journal of Latin American Studies* 6 (1994): 137–58.

20. While the Neopanistas were the public faces of the party in the 1980s, they were effectively excluded from the party's core leadership (the National Executive Committee) until the 1990s. See Steven T. Wuhs, "Barbarians, Bureaucrats and Bluebloods: Fractional Change in Mexico's National Action Party," in Middlebrook (2001, 150).

21. Mizrahi (2003).

22. PAN and PRD together ended the PRI majority in the Chamber of Deputies in 1997, the same year that PRD gained control of the Mexico City government in its first-ever direct election. Subnational politics opened in Mexico at the state level following the breakthrough election of PAN to the governorship of Baja California in 1989.

23. While funding levels were proportional to vote share in prior elections, the regulations dramatically increased the coffers of PAN and PRD, placed caps on PRI's budgets, and introduced strict auditing requirements for campaigns and operations expenses. Todd A. Eisenstadt, "Thinking outside the (Ballot) Box: Informal Electoral Institutions and Mexico's Political Opening," *Latin American Politics and Society* 45 (2003): 33–35.

24. Data provided by the Registro Nacional de Miembros, PAN.

25. Kenneth F. Greene, *Why Dominant Parties Lose: Mexico's Democratization in Comparative Perspective* (New York: Cambridge University Press, 2007); Bonnie M. Meguid, "Competition between Unequals: The Role of Mainstream Party Strategy in Niche Party Success," *American Political Science Review* 99 (2005): 347–59.

26. Greene (2007); Beatriz Magaloni, *Voting for Autocracy: Hegemonic Party Survival and Its Demise in Mexico* (New York: Cambridge University Press, 2006).

27. These are not mutually exclusive identities, of course, but the fact that PAN leaders sought to position themselves without regard to their Christian Democratic ideals is significant. The author thanks Mirjam Künkler for this observation.

28. Beatriz Magaloni and Alejandro Moreno, "Catching All Souls: The Partido Acción Nacional and the Politics of Religion in Mexico," in *Christian Democracy in Latin America: Electoral Competition and Regime Conflicts*, ed. Scott Mainwaring and Timothy R. Scully (Stanford, CA: Stanford University Press, 2003), 247–74.

29. Ibid., 261–65.

30. This even holds in the case of religiosity. Camp notes that PAN voters are in fact no more religious than PRI voters. Roderic Ai Camp, "Exercising Political Influence, Religion, Democracy, and the Mexican 2006 Presidential Race," *Journal of Church and State* 50 (2008): 101–22.

31. Greene (2007, 234–40). The success of 2000 also triggered several addition institutional changes through which the party opened itself to new segments of Mexico's voting public, leaving behind Mizrahi's "sectarian" rules for more inclusive selection processes for executive posts and the Senate to broader popular participation, and broadening its organizational presence across Mexico. See Wuhs (2008, chaps. 4 and 5).

32. With each major party holding more than 20% of the seats in the Chamber; see Eisenstadt (2003). PAN's relative resurgence between 2003 and 2006 (see table 9.1) likely reflects not Fox's performance but an overall improvement in economic growth due to rising oil prices. This allowed Fox and PAN not only to claim successful management of the economy, but also to (legally) use oil rents to benefit state and municipal governments, civic associations, agricultural communities, unions, schools, and other actors. See Alejandro Moreno, "The 2006 Mexican Presidential Election: The Economy, Oil Revenues, and Ideology," *PS: Political Science and Politics* 40 (2007): 15–19, citing Abel Barajas, "Dona PEMEX más en año electoral," *Reforma*, October 11, 2006, A1, 18.

33. Dion (2010).

34. See chapters 8 and 10, this volume.

35. Andrew Selee and Katie Putnam, "Mexico's 2009 Midterm Elections: Winners and Losers" (Mexico Institute, Woodrow Wilson International Center for Scholars, 2010). Ultimately, the micrologic of the voter is similar to that behind PAN's victory in 2006, when López Obrador's leftist positions were characterized as a threat to the stability of the Fox era.

In the 2009 case, though, when voters thought about stability, they harkened back to the pretransition era.

36. Data collected from Joseph L. Klesner and the Instituto Federal Electoral. While in recent elections the parties have often competed as alliances, for the sake of clarity, I continue to use the party names here, as the three main parties were the most powerful members of their respective alliances. Joseph L. Klesner, "Dissolving Hegemony: Electoral Competition and the Decline of Mexico's One-Party-Dominant Regime" (paper presented at the annual meeting of the American Political Science Association Washington, DC, August 1997).

37. Alejandro Moreno, "Changing Ideological Dimensions of Party Competition in Mexico, 1990–2006," in *The Global System, Democracy, and Values*, ed. Yilmaz Esmer and Thorleif Pettersson (Boulder, CO: Lynne Rienner, 2007), 16.

38. Greene (2007, 176); Fabrice Lehoucq et al., "Political Institutions, Policymaking Processes, and Policy Outcomes in Mexico" (working paper R-512, Inter-American Development Bank Research Network, 2005).

39. That consistency is appealing, though it underrepresents the complexity of the Mexican electorate by emphasizing only the economic-distributive dimension of political competition, when religious-secular dimensions and a crucial regime/anti-regime axis also structured voting behavior in the transition years. The redistributive dimension was powerful, and second only to Chile in its power in the 1990s. See Herbert Kitschelt, Kirk Hawkins, Juan Pablo Luna, Guillermo Rosas, and Elizabeth Zechmeister, *Latin American Party Systems* (New York: Cambridge University Press, 2010), 90. As Greene, Molinar Horcasitas, and others have shown, Mexico's party system was dominated from the 1980s through 2000 by that democratic-authoritarian axis. Greene (2007); Juan Molinar Horcasitas, *El tiempo de la legitimidad* (Mexico City: Cal y Arena, 1991).

40. Bruhn and Greene (2007, 36).

41. Ibid. Tomás Dosek reports a different finding, with only 13.53% of Mexicans unable or unwilling to respond regarding their ideological placement. "Do Left and Right Differentiate Citizens and Politicians in Latin America?" (Boletin 3, PNUD and Instituto de Iberoamérica March 2011), 3.

42. Some of the best empirical data available about their issue positions come from Greene's (2007, 144) analysis of a wave of party personnel surveys conducted in advance of the democratic transition of 2000. Along with PRD, it distinguishes itself from PRI in its advocacy of federalism and democracy and holds conservative positions on abortion as well.

43. Kitschelt et al. (2010, 101).

44. See Greene (2007, 216, fig. 7.2), who suggests that activists and members make a related shift toward the political center, as evident especially in his figure 6.1 (178).

45. Bruhn and Greene (2007, 36). Figure reconstructed by author from data presented by Jon D. Carlson, Mayra Chavez, Luis Miramontes, Abraham Olivares, and Llonel Onsurez, "Political Party Realignment in Mexico: Fragmentation, Consolidation, and Party Identification" (paper presented at the annual meeting of the Midwest Political Science Association, Chicago, IL, April 2009), 9.

46. Bruhn and Greene (2007, 36).

47. Joseph L. Klesner, "Electoral Competition and the New Party System in Mexico," *Latin American Politics and Society* 47 (2005): 112–14.

48. Greene (2007, 249).

49. Joseph L. Klesner, "The 2006 Mexican Elections: Manifestation of a Divided Society?," *Political Science and Politics* 40 (2007): 3.

50. Alberto Díaz Cayeros et al, "Mexico 2012 Election Report" (México Evalúa—Program on Poverty and Governance, Stanford University, and the Center for U.S.–Mexican Studies, University of California, San Diego, 2012).

51. These data were supplied by the LAPOP at Vanderbilt University, which takes no responsibility for any interpretation of the data.

52. This distribution is statistically significant: Pearson $X^2 = 59.2236$, $p < 0.041$.

53. Wuhs (2008, chaps. 5–6).

54. Schneider (2004); Steven T. Wuhs, "From the Boardroom to the Chamber: Business Interests and Party Politics in Mexico," *Journal of Politics in Latin America* 1 (2010): 107–30.

55. Gibson (1996).

56. Data are drawn from legislative biographies by the author and Michelle Dion. See Wuhs (2010).

57. Wuhs (2010).

58. Greene (2007, 181).

59. Wuhs (2008, chap. 6).

60. Per Bruhn and Greene (2007); Kitschelt et al. (2010, chap. 4).

CHAPTER TEN

Chile

The Right's Evolution from Democracy to Authoritarianism and Back Again

PETER M. SIAVELIS

Across Latin America, Chile stands out as one of only three countries where strong and durable right parties competed over relatively long periods of time while at the same time remaining, for the most part, democratically oriented.[1] Nonetheless, during the Augusto Pinochet dictatorship (1973–90), the parties of the right disbanded and unabashedly supported Pinochet. What is more, early in the democratic transition, the Chilean right's commitment to the democratic game was questionable. By 2010, however, with the victory of Sebastián Piñera of National Renewal (Renovación Nacional, or RN), the right had democratically assumed the reins of government for the first time in fifty-two years under the banner of the "new right." By most accounts, this new right is again electorally oriented and is a responsible player in the necessary alternation of government. What explains this trajectory of the right? Why did Chile's right seem to veer so suddenly from being a crucial player in Chile's notoriously high-quality democratic system to supporting a dictatorship that brought a violent end to democracy? What caused the right to be "rehabilitated"? Is Chile's new right really that new? What are the social bases of its various parties? What do the answers to these questions mean for contemporary Chilean democracy?

This chapter analyzes the development and evolution of rightwing parties in Chile. It begins with definitional issues, applying the insights provided by Luna and Rovira Kaltwasser in their introduction to this volume. It goes on to briefly analyze the historical and institutional trajectory of the right, underscoring key turning points in the development of its parties, offering an explanation for how the right went from being electorally oriented to authoritarian only to become once again electorally oriented in 2011. It suggests that three key variables explain whether the historic and contemporary right remains committed to the democratic game: (1) the existence of an underlying social pact on the limits of reform; (2) the ability of the right to protect its key interests; and (3) the extent to which the right is forced into a defensive and reactive, rather than proactive, position. In light of these arguments, this chapter explores the genesis of the contemporary right in Chile, arguing that it is really home to two rights, whose origins can be traced to divisions that first emerged during the military regime. This chapter analyzes their different origins, leadership, organizational structure, issue orientation, and ideological and electoral bases. It argues that the interaction between the two rights has been simultaneously constructive and problematic and demonstrates how this has been the case. This chapter then turns to the evolution of support for the right in recent elections, and evaluates how the Piñera campaign and government has helped to shape the construction of Chile's new right as a viable governing force.

In line with other chapters in this volume, the right here is conceptualized on the basis of its component parties' main beliefs about the sources of inequality. Parties of the right in Chile generally consider that "the main inequalities between the people are natural and outside the purview of the state." But party platforms and statements about the role of the state are often affected by the political moment and the context and climate of party competition. For example, the declaration of principles of both of Chile's undeniably rightwing parties—RN and the Independent Democratic Union (Unión Demócrata Independiente, or UDI)—state that "the essential purpose of the state is to promote the common good, understood as the set of social conditions that enables every person to realize spiritual and material fulfillment,"[2] which goes beyond what many rightist contemporary parties in the world would state or promote. In this sense, Luna and Rovira Kaltwasser's statement that programmatic standings may be "continuously evolving and relational" certainly apply to Chile.[3] What is more, the platform that brought the right to power in Chile in the most recent election was decidedly centrist. That said, notions concerning the right's attitude toward the sources and solutions of inequality provide the basic definition of the right for this chapter.

The Chilean Right as an Outlier

The pattern of division between liberal (laissez-faire, secular, and favoring a federalist/ decentralized state) and conservative (mercantilist, pro-Catholic, and favoring a strong/centralized state) parties was common in the rest of Latin America, and in general terms with the consolidation of real parties, Chile followed suit. The Chilean pattern of cleavages with social divisions spawning new parties begins with the most important initial cleavage in politics: the clerical/anticlerical divide, which led to the formal foundation of the liberal and conservative parties in 1836 and 1849, respectively.[4]

But the similarity of Chile's party system to others in Latin America ends there. First, following this initial divide, subsequent party development was unique in the region, and in many senses followed the European pattern, with the emergence of several generative cleavages and the development of parties along these cleavage lines.[5] In contrast to other Latin American countries, there was a stable nonpopulist party option for all political positions. In addition, Chilean suffrage expansion progressed, responding to and incorporating new groups. As suffrage gradually expanded, new leftist parties, including the socialist and communist parties, began to attract support from intellectuals and the working class beginning in the 1930s. This pattern of suffrage expansion occurred before the development of a powerful state bureaucracy, allowing parties to incorporate new groups and preventing the development of corporatist or authoritarian representation that emerged among parties of the right in many countries.[6]

Second, rather than a right based on personalities, populism, or fleeting political movements, the Chilean right demonstrates an evolutionary and constant lineage. For the concerns of this chapter, Chile, unlike other countries since independence, has always had a stable, well-supported right that, while evolutionary, has traceable elements of continuity from era to era.

Third, despite the late development of "real" party structures, Chilean conservatives, unlike other conservatives in Latin America, early on committed to the democratic order, supporting military subordination to democratic elites. While the military played an active role in the early years of the republic, after 1830 it was largely absent from any active political role. Elites used democratic procedures to protect their interests, which was key to the advancement of the democratic order and presages the argument made in this chapter concerning the reactionary and defensive attitudes of twentieth-century conservatives when they lost their ability to protect their interests under the rules of democracy during the Allende years.

Finally, a deeper social agreement underwrote Chilean politics, which reined in the right and the left and held Chilean politics together from the mid-1930s until the mid-1960s. Rather than any purposively negotiated settlement, it emerged primarily out of the recognition that no one social class had the ability to impose its will on the others, nor could the party representation of any social class achieve a majority in electoral politics. As a result, a de facto agreement of accommodation gradually developed.[7] Chilean party elites struck a bargain known as the *estado de compromiso*, which emerged as a consensus on the basic outlines of Chile's socioeconomic structure that included the protection of private property and business interests combined with state-led industrialization and a limited welfare state. The right remained in the game because it was assured that fundamental property interests would be protected. The left remained in the game because it was assured that social reform would continue apace with the expansion of the social welfare state.

The Authoritarian Right

In the 1960s both the *estado de compromiso* and the right's ability to defend its fundamental interests began to unravel, pushing the Chilean right into evermore authoritarian directions for three important reasons: the growth in leftist ideology, the decline in support for the parties of the right, and the rise of the Christian Democratic Party (Partido Demócrata Cristiano, or PDC).

In addition to a worldwide political shift to the left in the middle to late 1960s, changes in Chile's left also led to increasing support for this sector. After being outlawed between 1948 and 1958, the Chilean Communist Party returned to electoral politics and saw its support grow. What is more, the beginning of the 1960s saw tremendous unity on the left under the leadership of Salvador Allende.

The explosion of the electorate also diluted support for the right in relative terms. In 1932, only 15% of the voting age population participated in elections. By 1973, this figure was 69.1%.[8] This more inclusive electorate tended to support Chile's traditionally oligarchic parties less. In addition to an expanded electorate, massive migration from rural to urban areas undermined support for parties of the right. Between 1932 and 1971, Santiago went from comprising 25% to 40% of Chile's total population.[9] Not only was the right traditionally strong in rural Chile, but also the power of clientelism often induced even the rural poor to support the parties of their wealthy patrons. This ability gradually eroded, however; Figure 10.1 summarizes the evolution of support for the three ideological tendencies of the Chilean electorate. Though it rebounded moderately (mostly as a fearful reaction to the forceful resurgence of the left), support for the right bottomed out at 12% in 1965, sending the sector into a virtual panic.

The most important development of the 1960s was the rise of PDC, which transformed both the ideological bases of politics and the pattern of coalition formation at the heart of sustaining Chile's consensual democracy.[10] PDC grew quickly from its foundation, becoming Chile's majority party by 1965. This rapid rise took a toll mainly on conservative parties for a number of reasons. PDC's roots in the Catholic Church allowed it to cultivate the right's natural electoral base and to bring it into the center. As Valenzuela notes, "the Conservatives lost much more than just votes to the rise of Christian Democracy. They lost the essential element of their historical identity, namely, their connection to the Catholic church."[11] What is more, the Church also abandoned conservatives. As Smith argues, Catholicism shifted toward a more progressive role during the 1950s and 1960s.[12] Finally, the Radical Party's strong anticlericalism for many years forced many religious (though potentially more centrist) voters into the hands of the conservatives (and, after 1965, toward the National

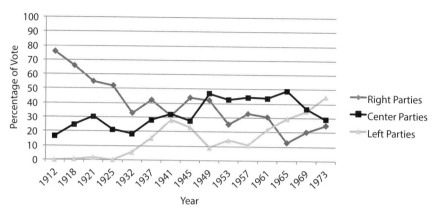

Figure 10.1. Electoral strength of the right, center, and left in Chile, 1912–73.
Source: Navia (2000)

Party). But PDC's embrace of the Church transformed the Christian Democrats into a new centrist party shed of the Radical Party's (PR) anticlerical baggage.

The election of Salvador Allende in a three-way race with neither a majority of the vote nor a majority in congress signified the end of the *estado de compromiso*. Allende challenged property relations with proposals for land reform and the nationalization of industries. Elements on the left including the Popular Unitary Action Movement (Movimiento de Acción Popular Unitario, or MAPU) and the Movement of the Revolutionary Left (Movimiento de Izquierda Revolucionaria, or MIR) became increasingly radicalized, and elements on the right also moved into more antidemocratic positions.[13]

The ability of the right to defend the *estado de compromiso* electorally and through participation in coalitions and in congress also broke down. As Garretón argues, the right lost its ability to defend its interests in congress (where historically rural voters had provided the right with an advantage) or through participation and partnership within government. This ability also disappeared because of the rise of PDC. This new centrist party was less willing to play the game of alliance formation than PR, and the system of coalition building structured around the ideological center broke down.[14]

As the right lost its ability to defend its interests, it became convinced that left would take Chile down the path of revolution, pushing the right into a defensive and reactive position. The National Party noted in its New Republic program that the "complicated crisis facing the country has multiple manifestations: demagoguery, lack of political authority, economic decline, social violence and cultural backwardness." The National Party opposed Allende on every front in congress, with the only exception being its support for a constitutional amendment nationalizing the copper industry. The traditional right, long priding itself on its democratic credentials, increasingly turned to antidemocratic rhetoric and activities. While opposition to Allende began among the wealthy, middle-class groups and military sectors increasingly joined. The right became strikingly nationalistic, and the traditional right joined smaller, radical groups like Patria y Libertad to oppose the Allende government.[15] Gradually, more elements of the right moved into the antidemocratic camp, and in the months leading up to the coup, the right's rhetoric became insurrectional. As Pollack notes, however, given Chile's long democratic tradition, the right had to be cautious in openly advocating the overthrow of Allende. It adopted the rhetoric of democracy, appealing for the "restoration" of Chilean democracy, and emphasized that it was the left that genuinely had antidemocratic values. Following the 1973 coup, the National Party called on all Chileans to support the new military government, signifying the right's "final and categorical rejection of the country's political and electoral system."[16]

Chile's "Two Rights"

With the return of democracy, fault lines on the right were increasingly visible, crystalizing in the formation of two separate parties. Both parties faced unique challenges in ensuring their survival and securing their electoral fortunes, but leaders also realized that the only chance for victory would lie in unity, given the realities of the electoral system, which make it difficult for a divided right to win any seats.[17] The result was a coalition that has contested all elections from 1989 to the present day. The coalition has changed name several times (Democracia y Progreso, 1989–92; Participación y Progreso, 1992–93; Unión por el Progreso, 1993–96; Unión por Chile, 1996–2000; Alianza por Chile, 2000–2009; Coalición por el Cambio, 2009 to present), but for convenience it is referred to here as simply the Alianza. In essence, the interaction between the two rights, to a great extent forced by the election system, was both beneficial and difficult for democracy and the parties. On the one hand, the alliance between UDI and RN helped position the alliance toward the center, with RN primarily pulling it away from an absolute identification with the dictatorship and enhancing its attractiveness to voters with different moral values and socioeconomic backgrounds. On the other hand, the alliance was a marriage of convenience, making for a coalition that did not always share the same programmatic ideals and electoral and political strategies. The best way to understand the genesis, perseverance, and the simultaneously constructive and problematic interaction of Chile's two rights is through a comparison of their origins, organizational structures, issue orientations, and electoral bases. Through such a comparison, these tensions and their constancy become quite clear.

Genesis

At the outset of the democratic transition, three groups whose influence had waxed and waned throughout the dictatorship comprised the right as a whole: the traditional right, the technocrats, and the military.[18] The military was concerned with a growing economic crisis during 1982–83 that had undermined Pinochet's confidence in the Chicago Boys (a group of young Chilean economists, most of whom trained with Milton Friedman and Arnold Harberger at the University of Chicago or at the affiliated economics department at the Catholic University of Chile) and thereby diluted the influence of technocrats. It also had spawned the first significant protests and activism because the dictatorship, unnerving the military, wanted stability and also to protect itself from potential trials or retribution by democratic authorities. The technocrats, however, sought to work through Pinochet to ensure that their economic policies and political framework for controlled democracy would be enshrined and protected by the constitution and the transitional framework. Finally, the traditional right's major goal was to position itself for electoral victory, walking a fine line between defending the legacy of the military regime while putting forward new and attractive policies.

Despite these divisions, some of which still exist, there were some unifying threads. Neoliberal transformation brought the rise of new technocratic cadres and economic groups as a result of privatization and reform. Whereas the right's core previously lay in the rural aristocracy, new technocratic and business elites tied to large economic conglomerates and the international economic system displaced the traditional right. These new groups share a common ideology that lionizes free market economics, technocratic solutions, and belief in management sciences.[19] This deeply held attitude translates into politics, where elites saw these basic tenets as antidotes to the older forms of clientelism and populism. This new economic elite had important ties to the Chicago Boys, with many serving in the government or made rich by their ties to it. What unified the right was essentially a common commitment to the new economic liberalism espoused by the Pinochet regime.

Beyond this commonality—and superimposed upon simmering divisions between traditional aristocrats, technocrats, and the military—Chile's partisan right has been consistently divided in two. This division was spawned with the rebirth of party politics and grew from different political traditions of the right's two parties, deep disagreements over the optimal strategy for confronting the democratic transition, and distinct strategies for building the partisan right electorally.

UDI originated with the Gremialista movement led by a group of young intellectuals who emerged from a student movement at the Catholic University of Chile. Its best-known leader, Jaime Guzmán, approaches messianic status among the party faithful. Essentially, Gremialista thought is based on organic notions of society and Catholic philosophical thinking. Though organic in its conception, it was also individualistic, holding up the concept of the individual as superior to collectivist notions of society.[20] It conceives that corporate functional groups better protect the rights of individuals than other political organizations, and do so much better than political parties. Guzmán conceived that even the traditional parties of the right in Chile had fallen victim to corruption and demagoguery, and a combination of trade unions, family organizations, and *gremios* (loosely defined as functional groups with a common purpose) would better protect the freedom of citizens. While initially influential, the potential threat that the organization of such groups could pose to the regime led Pinochet to abandon a commitment to any form of corporatist organization relatively early.

Guzmán served Pinochet as an advisor and is considered the most important brain behind the elaboration of Chile's 1980 constitution, where some of his ideas concerning social organization are reflected. His desire for a protected democracy is reflected in the constitution's strong checks on civilian authorities. Despite this commitment to corporatist social organization, the longer he served in the Pinochet government, the more his ideas began to evolve toward an embrace of Frederick von Hayek's ideas concerning freedom and the power of free market economics. One of the most renowned analysts of his thought contends that Guzmán was willing to embrace the neoliberal economic model despite its tension with communitarian Catholicism, because neoliberalism stressed the more important virtues of anti-statism and anti-Marxism.[21]

The party was also unwavering in its defense of Pinochet's institutional legacy and refused negotiations concerning any reform of the many undemocratic facets of the constitution. UDI remained staunchly Catholic, pro-Pinochet, and unyieldingly committed to the neoliberal economic model. It also sought to differentiate itself from the "traditional" right, which it painted as classist, oligarchic, and stuck in the past. As UDI consolidated its distinct programs, ideology, and campaigns, it would consistently seek to distance itself from the traditional right and cast itself as being "above" politics.

Following many years of fusion and division, both internally and in relations with UDI, RN eventually emerged as a more moderate option on the right. Unlike UDI, most of RN's initial membership had not been active participants in the military government and included remnants from the old National Party.[22] While UDI had core ideological commitments in the form of allegiance to Guzmán and the ideas of Gremialismo, RN lacked a unifying and uniform set of tenets and beliefs. RN's basic organizing principal was a commitment to ideological and philosophical pluralism in order to build a catchall party of the right.

The distinct strategic perspectives of the democratic transition accentuated differences between the "two rights." UDI initially favored an attempt to continue some form of Pinochetismo without Pinochet. In contrast to UDI's close ties to the regime, absolutist commitment against constitutional reform, and strategy of supporting Pinochet as a presidential candidate after the 1988 plebiscite, RN was convinced that such strategies would condemn the right to political marginalization with a return to democracy. Led by the young and charismatic Andrés Allamand, RN favored dialogue with the opposition and a distancing itself from Pinochet by confronting the regime's human rights abuses and political record. It was willing to accept constitutional reform in order to reach a negotiated return to democracy engaging the opposition, and favored presenting a candidate other than Pinochet as the right's electoral standard-bearer. RN essentially sought to position itself to best capture voters on the center-right with the eventual return of democracy.[23]

The parties also played different roles during the two first governments of the Concertación. Given their differing perspectives, during the transition RN developed a much more critical stance toward the authoritarian regime. While UDI was often absolutist in its commitment to Pinochet and his legacy, RN was more supportive of contributing to and participating in the *democracia de los acuerdos* that underwrote Chile's successful democratic transition. RN was consistently more willing to work with Concertación governments to reach agreements in and outside of congress.

The 1980 constitution was one of the legacies of the Pinochet government most fiercely defended by UDI. The constitution established a number of features that provided effective veto power for the right, tied largely to the ability to Pinochet and his supporter to name high-level authorities before leaving power.[24] During the first of the Concertación governments, while UDI ferociously opposed any type of constitutional reform, RN was willing to work with the center-left to amend the constitution. RN sought to present itself as a more moderate right in contrast to UDI, which was painted as an obstructionist, non-democratic opposition. Nonetheless, RN always cautiously approached the issue of constitutional reform to avoid alienating its more conservative constituency, agreeing to a series of constitutional reforms in the 1990s. Both parties of the right eventually supported the comprehensive constitutional reforms undertaken by President Lagos that eliminated the most authoritarian aspects of the constitution in 2005. Some have traced UDI's abandonment of its unyielding defense of Pinochet's constitution to a "forward looking" strategy.[25] But it is undeniable that the right's acceptance of reform also grew from the reality that these authorities' power of appointment increasingly fell to Concertación governments with the passage of time.

Finally, the two rights deeply differed on their essentialist views of what the right should be, what it should do, and how it should build an electoral party. In keeping with its foundational members and principles, RN brought a vision to the table that would reconstitute a right in the traditional mold. It would protect traditional conservative and landed classes and the new economic elite through competitive elections, within institutions inherited from the regime, and with some statist tendencies left over from the new right. UDI, channeling Guzmán, had a different perception of the new right that would endure after the period political domination by the military. In particular, the new capitalist business class would lead and dominate the party, but it would reach out to the poor though a combination of nationalism, clientelism, and a strategy to capture the votes of the poorest classes to build a truly majority party in Chile.[26]

Leadership and Organization

The differences between Chile's two rights are also reflected in the leadership and organizational structures that solidified as the democratic transition proceeded. Joignant and Navia underscore how, in contrast to RN, UDI's leadership and parliamentary contingents have been similarly socialized and are a homogenous group of young, technocratic, and neoliberally oriented elites.[27] In generational terms, UDI's leaders are similar in age and share backgrounds in Catholic universities, with a large number having served in provincial and municipal posts during the authoritarian regime. The party has strong lings with Opus Dei and other conservative Catholic organizations.

The leadership of RN is much less homogenous. While 73% of UDI deputies attended Catholic schools, only 46% of RN deputies had, with 39% attending public schools. The similar background and homogeneous value orientations of its members have provided UDI with unity and solidarity in terms of organization and policy. While UDI often directs its parliamentary contingents to vote a certain way, a high-level RN leader noted that "when it comes to values issues, we understand the importance of freedom of action."[28]

In terms of lower-level organization, UDI is cohesive, disciplined, and centralized. It set out from its strong electoral base in the capital to conquer new electoral districts throughout the country with the passage of every election.[29] Part of its ability to maintain and run such a disciplined organization lies in the intellectual and sociological homogeneity of its elite, which provides strong organizational glue. While UDI is unified and homogeneous, RN is a loose, heterogeneous, and decentralized party, lacking UDI's explicit conquering strategy. The party's territorial structure is much weaker, despite its rural origins. The foundational organization of RN was based on a diffuse and decentralized structure, creating tensions between regional and national leaders and often resulting in personalism and factional conflict.[30]

This is the case because RN is fundamentally an instrumental party to elect candidates, characterized by pragmatism and the lack of an established party culture.[31] The party was often divided, primarily in its earliest years when a hard-line, older Pinochetista faction led by Sergio Onofre Jarpa faced off against Andrés Allamand's younger, more liberal reformist faction.

Unlike RN, UDI has a centralized candidate selection process. Its electoral commission determines the districts where it has the best chance of winning and, even in nonelection years, identifies potential candidates and where they should run.[32] While some joked that UDI pulled candidates off the street to run for office in the first election, in subsequent elections it has done an excellent job of nominating visible and attractive candidates. UDI has used this selection process as a consistent strategy to pick up new seats both through expansion into the regions and to negotiate seats away from RN at the coalitional level.

While the vertically organized UDI makes most decisions at the top of the party elite and internal party politics and candidate selection are closed and elite affairs, RN has been criticized for being "excessively democratic" given the policies are openly discussed and debated.[33] The organizational weakness of RN is also reflected in candidate selection. Control over selection, though in the hands of the party, is decentralized. In addition, at the alliance level, because the party is a "loose association of leaders, elites are more than willing to give up other districts to the UDI if they can be guaranteed that they will not face strong competition from UDI candidates in their own districts."[34] RN also lacks the concerted strategy of candidate cultivation, a partial explanation for why it has consistently lost seats to UDI.

Issue Orientation and Ideological Placement

Three political dimensions differentiate Chile's two rights: ideological placement, campaigns and platforms, and messaging targeted toward particular constituencies. In terms of relative positioning, UDI has continually faced the awkward proposition of defending Pinochet's record and institutional legacy while attempting to build a new right with fresher ideas that move beyond a simple defense of the past. RN, in contrast, faced the uncomfortable position of attempting to maintain its core supporters (many of whom were sympathetic to the far right) yet reaching across to the center to attract more voters. In essence, the ideological placement of Chilean parties reflects these tensions.

Data from voters and from elites confirm that UDI is generally viewed as being further to the right than RN (on a scale of 1 to 10, with 1 as the left and 10 as the right, UDI scored 7.67 and RN 7.55). Interestingly, elites find both parties to be much further to the right than do the voters, and the distance between them to be greater than do voters, who were polled on the same question (on the same scale, placing RN at 7.24 and UDI at 9.60).[35]

With respect to campaigns and platforms, UDI has evolved from defending Pinochet to becoming a party focused on solving the problems of real people, often with technocratic solutions. Following Pinochet's 1988 plebiscite defeat, the right settled on Pinochet's former finance minister, Hernán Büchi, as its presidential candidate. Büchi was heralded as a young, technocratic problem solver. At the same time, however, he proved an unsatisfactory candidate on a number of counts. Despite efforts to portray him as bringing a new face of politics to the right, he remained associated with the policies of Pinochet and with an ambivalent attitude about human rights. His record of prudent economic management was undermined by rash and vague promises related to economic growth and job creation.[36] The campaign included broad promises to establish a free and open democracy, policies to permit everyone to flourish economically, an open educational system to prepare all for this new open economy, and an improvement in Chile's international standing. The only proactive policy involved the establishment of a new and open democracy, the credibility of which was as much undermined by the candidate's association with the previous regime as it was by the Concertación's more genuine claim as the real force for democracy. But all of the blame for Büchi's defeat cannot be laid at his feet. Part of the loss was due to the right's continued association with the Pinochet regime and its reactive and protective, rather than proactive, policy stance.

With the passage of time, UDI's message shifted from association with Pinochet to a stress on technocratic and "practical" solutions for real people. This message was reflected in the leadership of Joaquín Lavín, who served in a variety positions within UDI and eventually became the mayor of both Las Condes, a wealthy borough of Santiago (1992–99), and Santiago (2000–2004). Lavín expanded his hands-on approach as mayor to consistently (and sometimes flamboyantly) propose and implement technocratic and "apolitical" solutions to the problems of "everyday" people. Lavín is recognized to have forged a new way of doing politics in UDI. He contended (with an intentional broadside against the Concertación's politics of the *cuoteo*—or assigning positions based on party identification) that he would rely on the best people for the job rather than considering their partisan identification. This new form of rightwing populism would catapult him to the Alianza's presidency in 1993, though he was narrowly defeated in the second-round election. UDI continues to paint itself as the party of the people, even having taken on the moniker UDI Popular to stress its roots among average Chileans.

In terms of platforms, in contrast, at its birth, Renovación Nacional generally supported the economic policies of the outgoing regime but was less accepting of its political and human rights record. RN was consistently more amenable to dialogue between the military and the opposition to ease a transition to democracy. In terms of the ideological orientation and platform of RN, it is more varied among its members than UDI's given the much looser organization of the party. In general, however, RN is the more moderate party. In his study of party elites, Alcántara finds that RN is also more secular, with centrist views on abortion and divorce (even more centrist than PDC).[37] Its members were also more likely to see the military as a potential threat to democracy than members of UDI. Finally, in terms of health, education, and social welfare, RN was more likely than UDI to see some role for the state. These more moderate attitudes are also reflected in legislative voting patterns.[38] Toro's analysis of roll call votes shows impressive unity on the part of the governing coalition during the presidency of Ricardo Lagos. The opposition, however, showed much more differentiation, with RN oscillating between supporting the government and supporting the opposition.[39]

Renovación's decentralized nature and consistent divisions often made it appear to lack a coherent policy. With respect to human rights, the role of the military, and reform of the constitution (three of the most controversial political issues), the party has been divided between factions, though in general terms it has taken a softer line than UDI on all of these issues.[40]

Finally, in terms of targeting and messaging, the parties also followed different strategies. UDI was aware that it could not establish itself as a majority party by relying solely on its natural upper-class constituency. It has consistently followed a strategy of courting upper-class support by defending its interests and taking traditional conservative positions. At the same time, it has cultivated the support of popular classes through nationalistic appeals and clientelism. RN, in comparison, has focused its campaign rhetoric more on the virtues of individual candidates and pitched its message to capture the vote of upper and middle classes through the discussion of issues rather than interests.[41]

Electoral Bases

Following the transition to democracy, RN essentially built on the traditional electoral bases of Chile's right, relying on the rural middle classes who had been influenced by the rural aristocracy's long love affair with the traditional right.[42] It continues to compete well in rural areas and among the middle and upper middle classes. UDI has sought out a novel electoral strategy, assembling an unlikely alliance of new upper-class technocratic business elites along with popular sectors.[43] Figure 10.2 breaks down party identification by social class using education as a proxy, which is traditionally a better indication of class than income. It shows this general trend, with UDI having the lowest level of support from the highly educated of any major

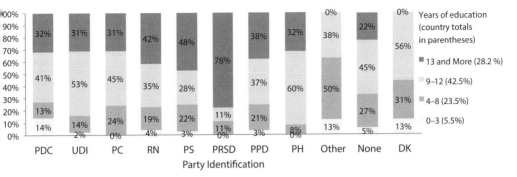

Figure 10.2. Party affiliation and level of education in Chile. *Source:* Adapted from data provided by the Centro de Estudios Públicos, CEP Chile, http://www.cepchile.cl

party (tied with the Communist Party), while RN has a more solid base in the middle class, with 11% more voters who have thirteen or more years of schooling than UDI.[44]

But recent data and arguments fail to capture the complexity of the transformation of support for the right with the emergence of UDI as Chile's predominant party. Writing in 1999, Pollack argued that UDI "continues to suffer from serious organizational weaknesses. Unlike RN, UDI is yet to become a national party with representation in most communes and regions of the country. It is still principally an urban party, most active in those areas where, through the *alcaldías*, it built up a network of supporters."[45] A more in-depth analysis shows that UDI's success has taken it beyond its core constituency since the outset of the transition. More subtle measures of party penetration based on nationalization measures show that UDI has expanded its reach throughout the country, presumably also to some rural areas. Figure 10.3 shows static nationalization figures (the territorial homogeneity of a party's vote distribution) since the return of democracy.[46] It demonstrates the dramatic inroads the party has made in penetrating the country, surpassing RN's nationalization levels in legislative elections.

The parties' relationships to their bases also differ along three additional dimensions: their relation to social groups, their cultivation of the popular sectors, and their use of clientelism. Garretón notes that while on the center and left parties tended to dominate civil society organizations in pre-Pinochet Chile, the opposite is true for the right.[47] In fact, powerful economic groups tended to be the most important social base of the right, and party organizations were simply their expressions, with rightist leaders having few connections to social groups, and certainly not mobilizational ones. The story of the transformation of Chile's right is partly told in a transformation of this dynamic, where UDI has built a constellation of support

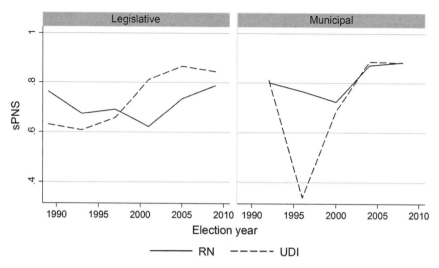

Figure 10.3. Static party nationalization in Chile in legislative and municipal elections, 1989–2009. *Source:* Scott Morgenstern, John Polga-Hecimovich, and Peter Siavelis, "Measuring Party System Nationalization: A Cautionary Tale from Chile" (paper presented at the Midwest Political Science Association annual meeting, Chicago, 2011)

among groups in civil society, perhaps given its corporatist roots. Further, given the duality of UDI's base, the groups with which it is connected are also dual in nature. At the popular level, UDI built on its historical connections in the localities during the authoritarian regime to build a series of local organizations, neighborhood *juntas, centros de madres,* and *directivas* in local *poblaciones* and working-class areas. In addition, while UDI was notorious for its effort to connect to cross-class organizations, RN is notable for its lack of connection. Pollack notes that "RN has to a large extent ignored developing what could be described as the more corporatist elements of party organization: those covering social sector activism."[48] While leadership in many forms of social organization has been the norm for UDI, with 48% of deputies having been members of some type of social group, only 28% of RN deputies have been leaders of *gremios,* federations, or other types of social associations, the lowest rate among any Chilean party.[49] UDI deputies are equally as likely to have performed these functions in the past as members of Chile's Socialist Party.[50]

The strategy of social mobilization was completely foreign to Chile's traditional right. Just as RN was the inheritor of the traditional right on many dimensions set out in this chapter, it also inherited this distaste for social mobilization. UDI, however, has embraced social mobilization. Unlike RN, UDI reached out actively to organize among Chile's poorest sectors, devising a concrete strategy with campaigns and party centers in *poblaciones* as early as the mid-1980s. It brought an antiparty message to this socioeconomic sector, simultaneously promoting an anti-Marxist message that stressed the importance of order, stability, and work.

But the UDI strategies described above have also allowed it to pick up centrist voters who previously voted for the Concertación, particularly PDC. UDI has been successful in gradually expanding its electoral base from the wealthiest and most conservative sectors of Chilean society, experiencing dramatic growth in support from the poorest sectors.[51] It has also made inroads among women who previously leaned toward conservative and confessional parties, particularly PDC. Nonetheless, there is convincing evidence that many poor female supporters of Lavín's 2000 presidential bid later shifted their support to Bachelet for the 2005 election.[52]

It was not only UDI's message that some sectors of the poor found appealing; it also much more actively developed and took advantage of clientelistic practices to cultivate support than RN. As James Loxton analyzes in chapter 5 in this volume, UDI exploited the position of its activists within the Pinochet government on the local level to distribute patronage and cultivate support. During the dictatorship, it promoted and diffused knowledge regarding how the poor could take advantage of state resources, particularly the minimal employment program and the occupational program for heads of households.[53] In advocating these programs, UDI simultaneously attempted to promote its image as a technocratic, problem-solving party rather than a "political" or "ideological" party.

There was an ingenious connection between the rich and poor, however. Luna underscores how UDI used its social bases within the Church (mainly Opus Dei) and business community to extract resources in a context of limited state financing for political campaigns. These resources were then used within the networks that UDI had established during the authoritarian government to establish nonprogrammatic linkages with potential supporters. He argues that the mostly upper-class and young party activists then reached out to these new (mostly working-class) groups, financed by the business community and socially conservative sectors. Essentially, the party used state resources to build clientelistic linkages and then switched to private money to buy off voters.[54] Through close connections with social groups, a mobilization strategy, and the creative use of clientelism, UDI has grown to be Chile's largest party, as summarized in figure 10.4, which shows dramatic growth its contingent in the chamber of deputies.

Return of the Electoral Right

During the height of Concertación governments, it appeared that the right was doomed to perpetual exile from government. As the years passed, the parties of the right became increasingly frustrated with their inability to win the presidency,

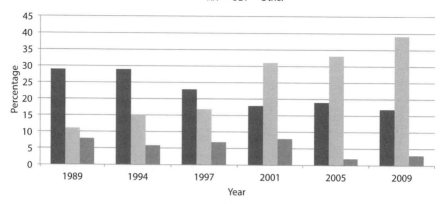

Figure 10.4. Evolution in support for parties of the Alianza in chamber of deputies elections, 1989–2009.

despite coming close and forcing elections to a second round in the 1999–2000 and 2005–6 election cycles.

During the early years of the transition this lack of electability really lay with the right's association with the Pinochet regime and its reactive and protective stance that contrasted sharply with the Concertación's proactive policies. The dynamic of each of these variables changed gradually, partly as result of public opinion regarding the exhaustion of the Concertación and the search for a new political alternative. But on a deeper level, Chilean democracy came to a crisis with the end of the *estado de compromiso* and the loss of the ability of the right to protect its key interests, forcing it into a defensive and reactive instead of proactive position. The right has again become an important and responsible player in the democratic system because the same historical incentives that once existed have returned.

First, elites in Chile have established a new *estado de compromiso*. Early in the democratic transition the unrepentant right was convinced that Concertación governments would fail. This sector of the right retained its old commitments as a way to hedge its bets against an eventual return to military rule. But, as it became clear that Concertación governments were not only going to remain in power but also that they were going to be successful, the right gradually realized it would need to work with the Concertación or it would be seen as a simple impediment to the establishment of full democracy. The Concertación also realized that it lacked the ability to completely impose its vision of economics and democracy and would have to strike a deal with potential veto players on the right. Therefore, across the political spectrum, actors eventually came to a new tacit agreement, including the acceptance of negotiated and gradual political reforms coupled with a market economy characterized by a process of limited reforms to blunt its sharpest edges.

The new *estado de compromiso* was also underwritten by deeper social transformations of Chilean elites during the Pinochet regime. The social bases of Chile's historic right were found among the Latifundista sector, large banks, and a limited number of owners of traditional industrial enterprises.[55] Chile's neoliberal transformation brought with it new private markets domestically and in the export sector along with a range of market opportunities created with the privatization of state enterprises, education, health, and social security. Ironically, despite some of the retrograde partisan political forces tied to Pinochet, his reforms helped to create a more diverse, modern, technocratic, internationally oriented, and less conservative set of business elites who held a more positive view of democracy and who eventually began to hold sway. The Pinochet government included part of this policy coalition, and its influence was felt during the transition and into Concertación governments.[56] Generational change, the growing acceptance of the indefensibility of the Pinochet's human rights record, and the realization that these new economic groups would continue to wield influence during Concertación governments reinforced the power of more liberal groups, at least with respect to their orientations toward democracy.[57]

The policy process reflected this new consensus. The Concertación consistently took the interests of the right into account when making policy. Concertación governments employed a strategy that has become known as *democracia de los acuerdos*, in which presidents consistently negotiated with both party actors and stakeholders on the right to agree on the details of legislation before legislating to assure passage.[58]

Second, the right has regained the ability to protect its fundamental interests within the bounds of institutions. This was the case both during the democratic transition (which helped underwrite its success) and in the posttransitional period. During the transition, many facets of the 1980 constitution—before its reform in 2005—gave the right the ability to influence the government and provided it veto power. The legislative electoral system significantly overrepresented the right throughout the transition period, and this overrepresentation was furthered by the existence of nine appointed senators drawn from institutions sympathetic to the right for much of the transition period. In addition, many of the institutions set down in the constitution—including the National Security Council, Constitutional Tribunal, and the courts—were packed with Pinochet appointees and civilian authority over the military was limited. While undemocratic, these institutions and rules provided the right guarantees of its fundamental interests, and Concertación governments took these interests into account in an effort to avoid destabilizing confrontations, especially early in the transition.[59]

But the right wielded this power in opposition to impede equity-enhancing reforms both at the economic and political levels. The military and the right's veto power imposed strict limits on the potential for political change under the Pinochet-imposed 1980 constitution. The right vehemently defended the binominal electoral system as an untouchable, stability-enhancing legacy of the Pinochet dictatorship. The political advantages afforded to the right by the system limited the scope of reform. Similarly powerful economic actors restricted the scope for significant economic and social policy reforms. Fairfield underscores how the influence and lobbying power of business and the partisan linkages of business actors on the right removed two of the most potentially equity-enhancing reforms from the agenda: corporate taxation and tax agency access to business information.[60] Similarly, powerful business lobbying associations and ties between business elites and the right limited the range of potential reforms, protecting the interests of the right and also preventing policies that would significantly affect steep levels of inequality.

With the return of full democracy following the 2005 constitutional reforms, the right has been able to return to its old pattern of using electoral politics and democratic institutions to advance its goals and protect is interests. The right's large legislative contingents (which were at first largely engineered) allowed it to block reforms it found unacceptable within the bounds of democratic institutions.

In this sense, during the time that the right enjoyed constitutional protections, it also underwent a learning process. Much has been said about the Chilean left as a prototypical example of political moderation and commitment to liberal democracy. But the Chilean right experienced a similar learning process in terms of accepting the democratic rules of the game. The right has internalized the idea that free and fair elections are fundamental and crucial aspects of democracy. It was not necessarily fast in coming, however. For much of the transition, many rightwing actors had a commitment to *democracia tutelada*, in which the unelected bodies noted here and an exclusionary electoral system prevented the establishment of full democracy. While a few actors on the right retain these views, most now view representative democracy as less threatening.

Finally, the right's abandonment of a defensive and reactive position has allowed it to gradually develop its own proactive policy options. At first, much of the right was bent on a maximalist defense of the Pinochet constitution as a result of perceived aggressiveness of the left to overturn it. Adding to the right's conundrum, in the policy realm, the right was denied the ability to make a proactive policy case because the Concertación stole its policy thunder, maintaining many of the most essential economic programs of the authoritarian government. But with the exhaustion of Concertación governments, the growth of corruption, and the demand for a new type of politics, a proactive policy space opened up for the right.

This discussion also raises some important points regarding democratic transition more generally. Much of the literature during the 1990s assumed that elite settlements of the Chilean type would have a positive impact on democracy.[61] As this discussion suggests, however, while such settlements may facilitate the installation and smooth functioning of democracy in the early years of a transitions, they may have negative effects later down the line with respect to the consolidation of democracy. By maintaining the broad outlines of the neoliberal economic model bequeathed by Pinochet and by accepting his political model in the form of the 1980 constitution, the Concertación arrived at an agreement with the right that kept powerful actors and veto players in the business community and on the right at bay, ultimately assuring its ability to govern and generate positive macroeconomic outcomes. In doing so, however, Concertación governments failed to address the remaining democratic deficits embedded in Chile's democratic institutions and the deep inequalities generated by the virtually unbridled acceptance of the economic model. Outside observers have puzzled at the rise of protest and discontent in what is supposed to be Latin America's success story. The seeds for this discontent were sowed in the elite settlement of the democratic transition.[62]

This phenomenon has deepened with the passage of time and with the consolidation of democracy. As Norris argues more generally, economic modernization and the institutionalization of electoral democracy around the world have led to the rise of "critical citizens" who are inclined to demand reforms to address democratic deficits.[63] In this light, both the Chilean right and the Concertación have promoted socioeconomic and political transformations that unintentionally spurred the rise of citizens who, while not completely disaffected, want a higher-quality democracy that addresses these deficits. They are asking more from democracy than they have gotten from the democratic transition.

Sebastián Piñera: The New Right in Power

The right's more proactive policy stance was reflected in Piñera's 2009–10 campaign promise to build what he termed a "new right," or *nueva derecha con una mayoria social*, both inserting an implicit criticism of the right as it had existed and suggesting that this new right would be attractive to many more Chileans. To do this, Piñera based his campaign on two themes and markedly moved key policy positions toward the center. The first theme was a negative one aimed at the Concertación.

Piñera had to be cautious. Outgoing President Bachelet left power with the highest rating of any modern president. Rather than attacking personalities or policies, Piñera focused his campaign on the idea that the Concertación was out of gas, had not fulfilled its campaign promises, and had failed. The attack focused on the growing sense that the Concertación had spent too many years in power and had become "corrupt" and exhausted (*agotada*). He criticized the politics of the *cuoteo*, or the growing sense that political power was distributed on the basis of political connections rather than talent. In terms of the more positive elements, he argued that Chile needed a new form of government based on efficiency and expertise and not on political connections. In this sense, he drew on the old right's technocratic appeals. There was also something new, however. It was not just a new model of government that Chile needed, but also a "second transition." Rather than lauding the military regime at all, Piñera's plan for government referred to a first "old transition" and that "we" (his use of the term being an effort to distance himself from the old right) needed to initiate a "second transition: the new, the young, belonging to the future and transforming Chile into a developed country without poverty."[64]

In addition, Piñera tacked remarkably toward the center in order to pick up centrist voters, particularly with respect to social issues. Because this was a three-way race, with dissident candidate Marco Enríquez Ominami competing on the left, Eduardo Frei, the Concertación candidate, had the most difficult position: attempting to attract voters from the left. This three-way race left the competition for centrist voters wide open for Piñera. He played up his family's Christian Democratic roots and the fact that he had voted against Pinochet in the 1988 plebiscite. Perhaps most importantly, with respect to economic policy, Piñera simply stole the Concertación's thunder, advocating much of the outline of the broad policy positions of the Concertación. Piñera's main economic policies were acceptable to the broadest ideological spectrum in Chile with a pledge to create a million jobs, to eliminate poverty, and to make Chile a developed country. The two alliances' similar campaigns in the 2009–10 elections underscore situational definition of the right with respect to policy platforms.

Piñera also took liberal stances on social issues. While stopping short of a full endorsement of gay marriage, in a controversial campaign advertisement, Piñera called upon Chileans to respect homosexual couples. Also, breaking with the Catholic Church, Piñera came out in favor of legalizing the morning-after contraceptive pill, as did the other candidates. The only deep policy difference related to legalizing abortion, with Piñera against, Ominami in favor, and Frei advocating for the legality of therapeutic abortion.

Conclusion

This volume has repeatedly recognized that a moderately powerful right is beneficial for the performance and maintenance of democracy. But by analyzing the long-
term evolution of the Chilean right, we can see that certain conditions provided the
right the kind of moderate power necessary to sustain and contribute to democracy
and governability. At the same time, two rights continue to exist in Chile, and their
interaction remains constructive and problematic. The interaction of the two rights
is constructive in assuring a more moderate, single competitive bloc that can provide
the type of responsible and competitive right this volume acknowledges as beneficial. But continuing division means that the right in Chile may not be a permanent
bloc and that voters are faced with a right characterized by sometimes-conflicting
ideals and programs.

What is more, despite the right's active participation in the new social pact that
exists in Chile, it is a mixed blessing that points to an irony that may ultimately
undermine democracy in the country in coming decades. While international observers and academics paint Chile as a democratic and economic success, massive
protests are spilling into the streets. There is widespread dissatisfaction with the
state of democracy, and the Piñera government's popularity evaporated at the end of
his term. Part of this dissatisfaction lies with the very social pact sustaining Chilean
democracy and the emergence of critical citizens.

In many ways the Chilean transition was Janus faced, on the one hand expanding the reach of democracy and on the other constraining its full development
by consistently privileging governability over representation and accountability. The
success of the Concertación (and, in turn, the democratic transition) was based on a
complex power-sharing arrangement, but it was one based on elite domination and
representation by quota, with little citizen participation. The sharing of electoral
spoils through negotiated legislative candidacies guaranteed peace between Chile's
parties but could only be undertaken through an elite selection process that precluded citizen participation. With respect to policy making, the model of *democracia de acuerdos* was built through party elites in concert with the president bypassing
congress to reach legislative deals with major social actors and veto players before
being considered by congress. The self-imposed limitations on reform set down by
the new social pact discussed here prevented reforms that could address Chile's
pressing inequalities. This pattern of politics was a stabilizing one, but one that
sidelined congress and the public and resulted in a pattern of piecemeal reform that
fell short of public demands for deeper transformations to the country's socioeconomic structure. This Janus-faced transition in large part explains Chileans growing

political alienation and dissatisfaction. A new social pact characterized by more equitable distribution of the fruits of Chile's economic success must be struck to underwrite more widespread satisfaction with democracy.

This analysis raises questions about the right more generally in Latin America. The right must have influence and the ability to protect its interests within the bounds of democratic institutions. But there is a fine line between guaranteeing the rights of all sectors and privileging the interests of the right and its allies, which can erode the long-term legitimacy of democracy over time. This is the fine line that must be redrawn in Chile.

NOTES

1. Kevin J. Middlebrook, "Introduction," in *Conservative Parties, the Right and Democracy in Latin America*, ed. K. J. Middlebrook (Baltimore: Johns Hopkins University Press, 2000), 4.

2. Renovación Nacional's home page, http://www.rn.cl/vi/; Unión Demócrata Independiente Popular's home page, http://www.udi.cl/website/home.php.

3. Luna and Rovira Kaltwasser, introduction, this volume.

4. Both parties existed earlier as inchoate political movements, though they were formally established in the years listed here. On the origins and history of the Chilean right, see Federico G. Gil, *The Political System of Chile* (Boston: Houghton Mifflin, 1966); Sofía Correa Sutil, *Con las riendas del poder: La derecha chilena en el siglo XX* (Santiago: Editorial Sudamericana, 2004).

5. Gil (1966); Timothy R. Scully, *Rethinking the Center: Party Politics in Nineteenth- and Twentieth-Century Chile* (Stanford, CA: Stanford University Press, 1992); J. Samuel Valenzuela, "Orígenes y transformaciones del sistema de partidos en Chile," *Estudios Públicos* 58 (1995): 5–80.

6. Arturo Valenzuela, "Chile: Origins and Consolidation of a Latin American Democracy," in *Democracy in Developing Countries: Latin America*, ed. L. Diamond, J. Hartlyn, J. J. Linz, and S. M. Lipset (Baltimore: Johns Hopkins University Press, 1999), 215.

7. Manuel Antonio Garretón, *The Chilena Political Process* (Boston: Unwin Hyman, 1989), 4.

8. Patricio Navia, "A Shrinking Electorate in Post-Pinochet Chile" (paper presented at the 2000 meeting of the Latin American Studies Association, Miami, FL, 2000), 18.

9. Ricardo Cruz-Coke, *Historia electoral de Chile: 1925–1973* (Santiago: Editorial Jurídica de Chile, 1984), 120.

10. Michael Fleet, *The Rise and Fall of Chilean Christian Democracy* (Princeton, NJ: Princeton University Press, 1985).

11. Valenzuela (1995, 48).

12. Brian Smith, *The Church and Politics in Chile: Challenges to Modern Catholicism* (Princeton, NJ: Princeton University Press, 1982).

13. Arturo Valenzuela, *The Breakdown of Democratic Regimes: Chile* (Baltimore: Johns Hopkins, 1978).

14. Manuel Antonio Garretón, "Atavism and Ambiguity in the Chilean Right," in Middlebrook (2000), 53–79.

15. Valenzuela (1978, 46).

16. Marcelo Pollack, *The New Right in Chile, 1973–1997* (New York: St. Martin's, 1999).

17. Patricio Navia, "Legislative Candidate Selection in Chile," in *Pathways to Power: Political Recruitment and Candidate Selection in Latin America*, ed. P. M. Siavelis and S. Morgenstern (University Park: Pennsylvania State University Press, 2009), 92–118.; Peter M. Siavelis, "The Hidden Logic of Candidate Selection for Chilean Parliamentary Elections," *Comparative Politics* 34, no. 4 (2002): 419–38.

18. Carlos Huneeus, *The Pinochet Regime* (Boulder, CO: Lynne Rienner, 2007).

19. Correa Sutil (2004).

20. For a complete overview of the thought of Jaime Guzmán, see Renato Cristi, *El pensamiento político de Jaime Guzmán* (Santiago: LOM Ediciones, 2000); Arturo Fontaine, "El miedo y otros escritos: El pensamiento de Jaime Guzmán," *Estudios Públicos* 42 (1991): 251–570.

21. Cristi (2000).

22. Pollack (1999).

23. Garretón (2000).

24. Peter M. Siavelis, *The President and Congress in Post-Authoritarian Chile: Institutional Constraints to Democratic Consolidation* (University Park: Pennsylvania State University Press, 2000).

25. Claudio Fuentes, "The Long Process of Democratizing Chile," in *Democratic Chile: The Politics and Policies of a Historic Coalition, 1990–2010*, ed. K. Sehnbruch and P. M. Siavelis (Boulder, CO: Lynne Rienner, 2014).

26. Correa Sutil (2004, 278–79).

27. Alfredo Joignant and Patricio Navia, "De la política de los individuos a los hombres del partido: Socialización, competencia política y penetración electoral de la UDI (1989–2001)," *Estudios Públicos* 89 (Summer 2003): 129–71.

28. Emmanuelle Barozet and Marcel Aubrey, "De las reformas internas a la candidatura presidencial autónoma: Los nuevos cambios institucionales de Renovación Nacional," *Política* 45 (Spring 2005): 187.

29. Garretón (2000, 63); Joignant and Navia (2003).

30. Barozet and Aubrey (2005).

31. Ibid.

32. Navia (2009).

33. Barozet and Aubrey (2005, 171).

34. Navia (2009, 111).

35. Peter M. Siavelis, "Elite-Mass Congruence, *Partidocracia* and the Quality of Chilean Democracy," *Journal of Politics in Latin America* 3 (2009): 3–32.

36. Alan Angell, *Democracy after Pinochet* (London: University of London Institute for the Study of the Americas, 2007), 43.

37. Manuel Alcántara Sáez, "La ideología de los partidos políticos chilenos, 1994–2002: Rasgos constantes y peculiaridades," *Revista de Ciencia Política* 22, no. 2 (2003): 68–87.

38. Ibid.

39. Sergio Toro, "Conducta legislativa ante las iniciativas del ejecutivo: Unidad de los bloques políticos en Chile," *Revista de Ciencia Política* 27, no. 1 (2007): 23–41.

40. Pollack (1999, 140–52).

41. Juan P. Luna and Cristóbal Rovira Kaltwasser, "Las derechas gobernantes en América Latina: Hacia una caracterización preliminar," *LASA Forum* 42, no. 3 (2011): 16–19.

42. Correa Sutil (2004).

43. Luna and Rovira Kaltwasser (2011).

44. Data on education and geographic support must be taken with a grain of salt, as most available surveys allow participants the option of choosing "none" for party identification. In both the most recent Latin American Public Opinion Project data and the Centro de Estudios Públicos data, a vast majority of respondents opted for this category, making the remaining sample of those who did identify entirely too small to make any definitive conclusions.

45. Pollack (1999, 129).

46. I borrow from Daniel Bochsler to generate the standardized party nationalization score using the Gini index to measure the spread of a party's district-level support and weighing that distribution by the number of districts and voters per district to generate a score between 0 and 1, where 0 indicates low static nationalization and 1 indicates high static nationalization. "Measuring Party Nationalization: A New Gini-Based Indicator That Corrects for the Number of Units," *Electoral Studies* 29 (2010): 155–68.

47. Garretón (2000, 55).

48. Pollack (1999, 130).

49. Barozet and Aubrey (2005, 187).

50. Joignant and Navia (2003, 167).

51. Juan Pablo Luna, "Segmented Party-Voter Linkages in Latin America: The Case of the UDI," *Journal of Latin American Studies* 42 (2010): 338.

52. Mauricio Morales, "La primera mujer presidenta de Chile," *Latin American Research Review* 43, no. 1 (2008): 7–32.

53. Marcus Klein, "The Unión Demócrata Independiente and the Poor (1983–1992): The Survival of Clientelistic Traditions in Chilean Politics," *Jahrbuch fur Geschichte Lateinamerikas* 41 (2004): 301–24.

54. Luna (2010).

55. Tomás Undurraga, "Rearticulación de grupos económicos y renovación ideológica del empresariado en Chile 1980–2010" (working paper, Instituto de Investigación en Ciencias Sociales–Universidad Diego Diego Portales, Santiago, 2011).

56. Eduardo Silva, *The State and Capital in Chile* (Boulder, CO: Westview Press, 1996).

57. This more liberal orientation does not necessarily extend into the social sphere, where there two rights continue to exist. While RN is much more liberal on social issues, some sectors of UDI maintain or have created stronger ties to conservative social groups (i.e., Opus Dei and the Legionarios de Cristo).

58. Claudio Fuentes, "Partidos y coaliciones en Chile de los 90: Entre pactos y proyectos," in *El modelo chileno: Democracia y desarrollo en los noventa*, ed. I. Jaksic and P. W. Drake (Santiago: LOM Ediciones, 1999), 191–221.

59. Siavelis (2000).

60. Tasha Fairfield, "Business Power and Tax Reform: Taxing Income and Profits in Chile and Argentina," *Latin American Politics and Society* 52, no. 2 (2010): 37–71.

61. John Higley and Richard Gunther, eds., *Elites and Democratic Consolidation in Latin America* (New York: Cambridge University Press).

62. Sehnbruch and Siavelis (2014) forcefully make this point.

63. Pippa Norris, *Democratic Deficit: Critical Citizens Revisited* (New York: Cambridge University Press, 2011).

64. Sebastián Piñera, *Programa de gobierno para el cambio, el futuro, y la esperanza: Chile 2010–2014* (Santiago: Coalición por el Cambio, 2009).

CHAPTER ELEVEN

El Salvador

Societal Cleavages, Strategic Elites, and the Success of the Right

RIITTA-ILONA KOIVUMAEKI

In the past decade, nearly all Latin American countries experienced a resurgence of leftist parties. Starting with the 1998 elections in Venezuela, country after country in the region chose a leftist president. Yet despite this region-wide trend, up until 2009 every postwar president of El Salvador came from the rightwing party Nationalist Republican Alliance (Alianza Republicana Nacionalista, or ARENA). ARENA also dominated the legislative assembly, either by itself or with its rightist allies.

After examining ARENA's historical trajectory and its contemporary electoral bases, in this chapter I explore the reasons for the party's long-lasting electoral success. I argue that ARENA's success was based on the electoral tool kit the party developed in order to attract voters. The tool kit consisted of three strategies: First, the party employed powerful media campaigns that enforced the preexisting wartime cleavage. Second, the party carefully studied the electorate and designed programmatic and valence-based issue appeals that were guaranteed to attract the masses. Third, it established an extensive territorial presence and clientelistic networks across the country. The effective implementation of these interconnected strategies allowed the party to attract voters election after election.

Understanding ARENA's trajectory and electoral strategies has important theoretical implications. As Luna and Rovira Kaltwasser note in their introduction to this volume, the existing literature on the Latin American right is notably thin. After the democratic transitions in the region, O'Donnell and Schmitter recognized the importance of the right's electoral success.[1] Yet few scholars have examined how the "resource-rich but vote-poor" right can capture votes among the "vote-rich but resource-poor" constituencies.[2] ARENA's trajectory can help us identify how an institutionalized rightist party can emerge as the principal vehicle for conservative policy demands. In particular, this chapter underlines the role of political actors. By adopting effective electoral strategies, elites can transform societal cleavages into political ones, thereby translating their resource advantage into electoral victories.

This chapter examines some policy outcomes of the ARENA governments, particularly in the economic realm. While the "resource-rich but vote-poor" party has often used economic issues in appealing to the "vote-rich but resource-poor" constituencies, the party has not been able to address some of the basic economic needs of the electorate. Latin Americanist scholarship frequently overlooks these types of policy outcomes,[3] partly because of broader trends in comparative politics: as the rational choice approach turned the field's attention to policy inputs, such as electoral systems and parties, policy outputs and results were often neglected.[4] To help us understand the variation in economic policies of different types of governments in Latin America and to complement the emerging literature on the left in the region, I analyze some results of ARENA's economic policies.

The first section of this chapter offers an overview of ARENA's development in the 1980s and early 1990s. The second section examines the party's electoral and societal bases and its ideology and party programs. The third section considers the reasons for ARENA's success, arguing that the party's effective media campaigns, high level of technocratic knowledge and research, and extensive territorial reach led it to electoral success. This combination of strategies—what I call ARENA's electoral tool kit—lost much of its strength in the presidential election of 2009 owing to the increased competition by the main opposition party Farabundo Martí National Liberation Front (Frente Farabundo Martí para la Liberación Nacional, or FMLN). The fourth and final section evaluates some of the policy outputs and outcomes of the ARENA governments, with a special focus on poverty and inequality.

Historical and Institutional Trajectory

The development of ARENA cannot be understood outside the context of the Salvadoran civil war (1980–92). In fact, the war and the cleavage it created were key parts of the foundation of ARENA in 1981. The party leader, former army officer Roberto D'Aubuisson, built much of the party organization on two existing organizations: Broad National Front (Frente Amplio Nacionalista, or FAN) and Nationalist Democratic Organization (Organización Democrática Nacionalista, or ORDEN).[5] The former was a short-lived civic organization with paramilitary tendencies, and the latter, established by military leaders in the 1960s and 1970s, was a well-established security network with paramilitary forces. While ARENA attracted support beyond FAN and ORDEN, much of its organizational foundations rested on these existing wartime networks.

The extreme polarization of Salvadoran society offered ARENA an opportunity to widen its support beyond paramilitary or semiparamilitary organizations. The official party, National Conciliation Party (Partido de Conciliación Nacional, or PCN), and its inability to govern in the economic and social turmoil of the 1970s, had disappointed most of the traditional oligarchy. After the coup of 1979, a new center-leftist junta threatened the elite's core interests by implementing an extensive agrarian reform and nationalizing the banks.[6] The failure of PCN and the junta's policies left the elite without political representation or access to the state. ARENA offered a promising venue for electoral competition. Moreover, D'Aubuisson's message appealed to masses tired of the conflict.[7] Consequently, the party made a phenomenal entrance to the political scene in the elections of 1982, 1984, and 1985.

ARENA was relatively quick to distance itself from the death squads, partly because ARENA's links to violent organizations led the United States to offer significant financial support to PCN in the early 1980s.[8] Much of the ARENA elite saw the lack of US support as a hindrance to further development. Consequently, in 1985, D'Aubuisson stepped down from the party leadership and gave room to businessman Alfredo Cristiani.[9] Successful upper-class businesspeople, many with ties to the traditional oligarchy, gained voice elsewhere in the party organization as well.[10]

ARENA continued to moderate its positions under the leadership of Cristiani.[11] From then on, the party defined the civil war as a fundamentally economic crisis.[12] The party program in turn shifted its focus to economic matters: policy proposals emphasized liberalization of foreign trade, reforms to the finance sector, and privatization of state property. This moderation continued into the early 1990s, after Cristiani won the presidency. By the next presidential election in 1994, the moderate elites had established themselves as ARENA's core. While anticommunism remained a key message for the party, the dominance of economic issues in the party program gave the party a new, more modern image.

Two institutions played an important role in ARENA's moderation. In 1983, the US Agency for International Development helped to found the neoliberal think tank Salvadoran Foundation for Economic and Social Development (Fundación Salvadoreña para el Desarrollo Económico y Social, or FUSADES). FUSADES was created as a nonsectoral and nonpartisan research organization with the goal of strengthening the Salvadoran private sector and national development. It quickly gained influence among many members of the Salvadoran elite. By offering technical and substantive training to business sectors and professionals, FUSADES shaped their views about privatization and deregulation of the economy and in this way had an important influence on ARENA's policy proposals during the party's development.[13]

Another institution that supported ARENA in policy development was the business peak association National Association of Private Business (Asociación Nacional de Empresa Privada, or ANEP). The antagonistic business-government relationship of the 1970s and 1980s transformed into more cooperative relations starting in 1989, when the business-friendly Cristiani government led many ANEP members to join ARENA. Although the government of Armando Calderón Sol (1994–99) had disagreements and conflicts with ANEP, the ANEP *técnicos* nonetheless continued to have direct influence on governmental policy making during the mid-1990s, most notably through the ministry of finance and the ministry of public works.[14] As the latter sections of this chapter will show, these two institutions were crucial in helping ARENA to develop its successful electoral tool kit.

ARENA's moderation and early electoral successes in the late 1980s and early 1990s had important implications. As William Stanley explains, ARENA's success in the late 1980s was crucial in distancing the Salvadoran elite from the military and adopting democratic vehicles of representation.[15] As I show below, however, many of ARENA's electoral tactics rested on the wartime cleavage and purposeful polarization of the society. In this sense, the conflict left a lasting legacy in party competition in El Salvador. The specific strategies through which the party enforced the cleavage are discussed below, after an examination of ARENA's electoral bases and programmatic and ideological linkages.

Bases and Party Platform

ARENA's ability to hold the presidential office for four consecutive terms makes it exceptionally successful. The presidential seat is particularly important in El Salvador, as the Salvadoran president holds significant informal powers in addition to the formal concentration of power in the chief executive.[16] In particular, many important posts in the country are distributed politically. A savvy president with a strong party backing can thus gain more power in the legislature through institutional tradeoffs—a tactic that ARENA presidents made much use of.

When it comes to ARENA's electoral results in presidential elections, the party has had decisive wins. In the first peacetime elections in 1994, ARENA candidate Calderón Sol faced a second-round challenger, FMLN coalition candidate Rubén Zamora. The second round went clearly to ARENA, with Calderón Sol winning with 68.3% of the vote against Rubén Zamora's 31.5%. In the following two elections, ARENA candidates won directly in the first round: In 1999, Francisco Flores of ARENA received 51.9% of the vote, and Facundo Guardado of FMLN received 29.0%. Five years later, ARENA's Tony Saca won against FMLN's Schafik Handal with a clear margin of 57.7% to 35.6% of the vote. Finally, in 2009, ARENA lost in an especially close election: ARENA candidate Rodrigo Avila received 48.68% of the vote, whereas FMLN candidate Mauricio Funes won with 51.34%. Table 11.1 summarizes the vote shares of ARENA's presidential candidates, and their main contestants, in the presidential elections between 1984 and 2009.[17]

In the legislature, ARENA had lost its majority to FMLN almost ten years before losing the presidential seat. Between 1994 and 1999, ARENA was the biggest

TABLE II.I.
ARENA's share of votes in presidential elections

Year	First round (%)	Second round (%)	ARENA candidate	Main candidate
1984	29.8	46.4	Roberto D'Aubuisson	José Napoleón Duarte (PDC)
1989	53.8	—	Alfredo Cristiani	Fidel Chávez Mena (PDC)
1994	49.1	68.3	Armando Calderón Sol	Rubén Zamora (FMLN and Democratic Change [Cambio Democrático, or CD])
1999	51.9	—	Francisco Flores	Facundo Guardado (FMLN-Social Democratic Unification [Unificación Cristiana Democrática, or UCD])
2004	57.7	—	Antonio Saca	Schafik Handal (FMLN)
2009	48.68	—	Rodrigo Ávila	Mauricio Funes (FMLN)

Sources: Data for 1984 from Artiga González (2001); data for 1989 from Zamora (1998); data for 1994, 1999, and 2004 from FUNDAUNGO (2009); data for 2009 from Resultados electorales (2009).

TABLE II.2.
Percentage of votes and number of seats for the main parties in legislative elections

Year	ARENA	PDC	PCN	FMLN
1985[a]	21.64 (25)[b]	(33)	(12)	—
1988[a]	50 (31)	(23)	(7)	—
1991[a]	44.23 (39)	27.96 (26)	8.99 (9)	—
1994	45 (39)	17.8 (18)	6.2 (4)	21.3 (21)
1997	35.4 (28)	8.3 (10)	8.7 (11)	33.0 (27)
2000	36 (29)	7.2 (5)	8.8 (14)	35.2 (31)
2003	31.9 (27)	7.8 (5)	12.9 (16)	33.9 (31)
2006	39.2 (34)	6.9 (6)	11.4 (10)	39.2 (32)
2009	38.5 (32)	6.9 (5)	8.8 (11)	42.6 (35)

Sources: Data for 1985–91 from Zamora (1998); data for 1994–2006 from FUNDAUNGO (2009); data for 2009 from the Political Database of the Americas (2009).
[a]There were sixty total seats in 1985, 1988, and 1991. For all other years listed here, there were eighty-four total seats.
[b]Values in parentheses represent the gained number of seats for each party.

party in the legislature with thirty-nine seats in 1994–97 and twenty-eight seats in 1997–2000, while FMLN held twenty-one seats in 1994–97 and twenty-seven seats in 1997–2000, as illustrated in table 11.2.[18] This changed in 2000, when FMLN received thirty-one seats in total and ARENA lost a few seats, settling for twenty-nine legislators. While ARENA lost a few more seats in 2003, the following three elections consolidated both ARENA and FMLN as the main legislative parties, with about thirty seats for each.

This section has shown that ARENA's victories in the presidential elections were oftentimes decisive, as the party won two of the three peacetime elections in the first round. In the legislative elections, ARENA's results were weaker, and the party lost its majority to FMLN as early as 2000. But the results in the legislative elections do not capture the political dynamics of lawmaking in El Salvador. In fact, ARENA maintained a working majority in the legislature throughout the 1990s and 2000s by allying with the smaller opposition parties Christian Democratic Party (Partido Demócrata Cristiano, or PDC) and PCN. In exchange for legislative support, PDC and PCN received offices in some of the most important political institutions of the country, such as Corte de Cuentas and Fiscalía General. While ARENA had not held the majority of legislative seats since the 1997 election, it was able to dominate in the legislature until the 2009 elections.

Societal Bases

Before proceeding to the reasons behind ARENA's success, it is important to examine the party's electoral bases. ARENA tends to draw stronger support from rural voters and voters with little or no formal education. Interestingly, the wartime cleavage seems to play less of a role in ARENA's electoral performance when compared to the main opposition party, FMLN. Moreover, as the parties compete for the same types of voters in the presidential race, party strategies seem to play at least an equally important role as any preexisting societal cleavages.

ARENA has traditionally drawn stronger electoral support from the countryside, whereas the support for FMLN has concentrated in the more populated central part of the country, especially the metropolitan area of San Salvador. Some of the geographical patterns of party support rest on the wartime cleavage. The municipalities most affected by the conflict, in the departments of Chalatenango and Morazán, have the highest electoral participation and remain most polarized between the two main parties. Moreover, FMLN has particularly strong roots in about a dozen municipalities, where the party wins with extremely high margins—a pattern not observed in the electoral bases of ARENA.[19]

The geographical cleavage is less clear when it comes to the presidential vote. Arevalo Quinteros finds that the level of urbanization and population are positively correlated with votes for both ARENA and FMLN.[20] In other words, voters in big, urban municipalities are more likely to support the two main parties than voters in smaller, more rural municipalities. Arevalo Quinteros concludes that this pattern owes to the importance of populous municipalities for the presidential vote, in turn suggesting that the wartime cleavage affects electoral results less than the campaign practices of the parties.

ARENA's rural base seems to be weakening. Table 11.3 presents the percentages that the two parties drew from the urban and rural voters in 2004 and 2009. While

TABLE 11.3.

Percentages of the urban and rural vote per party, 2004 and 2009

| | 2004 | | 2009 | |
	ARENA	FMLN	ARENA	FMLN
Rural	75.4	18.0	35.9	62.3
Urban	56.5	36.2	25.2	73.7

Sources: Data for 2004 from the 2008 Latin American Public Opinion Project (LAPOP) survey; data for 2009 from the 2010 LAPOP survey. See www.lapopsurveys.org.
   Note: Respondents were asked, "Which party did you vote for in the March 2004 presidential elections?" and "Which candidate did you vote for in the 2009 presidential elections?"

TABLE 11.4.

Percentages of the vote for ARENA and FMLN by education, 2004

Education level	ARENA	FMLN
No formal education	11.5	4.7
Primary (grades 1–6)	39.2	19.1
Secondary (grades 7–12)	38.3	50.4
Some university or technical education	11.1	25.8

Source: AmericasBarometer by LAPOP (2004). See www.lapopsurveys.org.
   Note: Respondents were asked, "Which party did you vote for in the past presidential elections in March 2004?"

75% of rural voters supported ARENA in 2004, the rural support for the party in the 2009 presidential elections fell to about 36%. As I argue below, this change indicates increased territorial competition from the part of FMLN rather than changes in any possible societal cleavage.

In terms of class support, more ARENA voters come from lower social classes when compared to the supporters of FMLN. According to municipal-level socioeconomic data, poorer municipalities are more likely to support ARENA. The relationship is the opposite for FMLN: municipalities with a higher level of economic development are more likely to vote for the left.[21] Individual-level survey data, presented in table 11.4, suggests a similar conclusion. In 2004, half (50.7%) of ARENA voters had either no formal education or some primary education. This societal group formed only a quarter (23.8%) of FMLN's voters. Conversely, ARENA drew 11.5% of its votes from people with higher than secondary education, whereas 25.8% of FMLN voters had higher than secondary education.

The class distinction between ARENA and FMLN supporters is even more evident when looking at the presidential election of 2009. As table 11.5 illustrates, 11.8% of ARENA supporters had some education at the highest education level, while 34.1% of FMLN supporters did. Voters with no formal education or only primary

TABLE II.5.

Percentages of the vote for ARENA and FMLN by education, 2009

Education level	ARENA	FMLN
No formal education	7.2	6.3
Primary (grades 1–6)	35.9	21.8
Secondary (grades 7–12)	45.1	37.9
Some university or technical education	11.8	34.1

Source: AmericasBarometer by LAPOP (2010). See www.lapopsurveys.org.
   Note: Respondents were asked, "What party did you vote for in the 2009 presidential election?"

education formed 43.1% of ARENA's support, whereas only 28.1% of FMLN's supporters came from this social class.

Finally, while rural and less-educated voters tend to support ARENA more than FMLN, ARENA clearly has a tight link to the highest sectors of society as well. In fact, profiles of party founders suggest that ARENA is a more class-based party than any other party in El Salvador.[22] The founders of ARENA are relatively homogenous when compared to founders of other Salvadoran parties. Specifically, ARENA founders come disproportionally from business classes.[23] The tight connection between the party and the highest socioeconomic classes has important consequences on party financing. Namely, ARENA's high-class support is the key cause of the resource asymmetry between the party and its competitors, which has allowed the party to develop its sophisticated electoral tool kit, as argued below.

ARENA draws much more support from poor voters and voters with little or no formal education than its main competitor. When it comes to the urban-rural divide, however, the picture is less clear. While ARENA used to draw much of its support from the rural parts of the country, this pattern seems to be changing. Part of the change might be explained by ARENA's loss of dominance in terms of territorial reach, to be evaluated later in the chapter. Finally, ARENA does attract support from the highest societal classes, too. In fact, ARENA founders come disproportionately from the highest classes of society, and the party's continuing resource abundance suggests that this relationship between the economic elite and the party has been long lasting. In fact, support from the wealthiest classes has helped the party to form credible linkages to rural and less-educated sectors of society.

Programmatic and Ideological Platform

In order to understand ARENA's success, it is necessary to examine the party's programmatic and ideological positions while at the same time keeping in mind the relative unimportance of party programs in El Salvador. Various analyses have pointed out that, because of the highly polarized competition, programmatic platforms play a marginal role in electoral campaigns.[24] As the analysis of the party strategy below suggests, the support of ARENA seems to owe less to its actual policy positions than to its effective campaign strategies. Before proceeding to these strategies, however, an analysis of ARENA's programs and ideology is in order.

Economic issues have played a major role in ARENA's platform ever since the election of Cristiani as the party head. Table 11.6 lists the key campaign issues of the peacetime ARENA candidates. While the first ARENA presidents, Cristiani and Calderón Sol, emphasized macroeconomic policies that aimed to restructure the Salvadoran economy, social issues gained importance in the party platform during the 1990s. This trend can be considered a response to demands from the lower classes. The Flores government especially drew heavy criticism for failing to address some of the pressing social issues in the country. Consequently, the Saca government implemented Plan Oportunidades, a combination of social programs that aimed to reduce poverty, particularly in rural areas.

Ideologically, ARENA's legislative representatives are in accord with the issue positions described above. In 1994, when legislators were asked to place their party on an ideological scale from 1 (left) to 10 (right), the average score for ARENA was 7.3.[25] Four years later, the average was even more to the right of center, at 8.6.[26] When asked to self-identify politically on the same scale, ARENA legislators in 1994 averaged 6.8 and 7.7 in 1998.[27] This slight movement toward the ideological right seems to have continued, as ARENA legislators for the 2006–9 period self-identified, on average, at 8.61.[28]

A description of ARENA's campaign platforms and a brief examination of the self-identification of the party's legislative representatives underline a few important points. First, ARENA has been programmatically consistent, emphasizing economic issues in all of the peacetime presidential elections. Second, the party seems to have "softened" its image over time by bringing more social issues to the platform. And, finally, the ideology of party members seems to correspond to the programmatic platform: the party's representatives in the legislative assembly self-identify as strongly rightist from year to year. In order to understand how a party with such a distinctive image succeeds electorally, we need to examine its electoral tool kit.

TABLE 11.6.
ARENA's presidential and vice presidential candidates, 1994–2009

Year	Presidential candidate	Profile	Vice presidential candidate	Profile	Main campaign themes
1994	Armando Calderón Sol	businessman and mayor of San Salvador, 1988–94	E. Borgo Bustamante	businessman	finalize the peace accords; increase crime penalties; finalize the economic restructuring started by Cristiani; pension reform
1999	Francisco Flores Pérez	university professor, deputy for ARENA, 1994–98; president of legislative assembly, 1997–98	C. Quintanilla Schmidt	lawyer	"Alianza por el trabajo, Alianza solidaria, Alianza por la seguridad": decentralize state services; stabilize the economy and especially the exchange rate of the colón
2004	Antonio Saca	sports journalist and businessman	A. V. de Escobar	economist	País Seguro; public security; respect for individual and social rights; progress with equality and integration to the world
2009	Rodrigo Ávila	director of Policía Nacional Civil, 1994–99 and 2006–8; deputy for ARENA 2000–2003	A. Zablah	businessman	"Somos gente de trabajo, somos gente de familia"

Sources: News reports in El Faro (www.elfaro.net), La Prensa Grafica (www.laprensagrafica.com), and El Diario de Hoy (www.elsalvador.com).

Factors of Success: Strategic Elites and the Electoral Tool Kit

Tool kits are a combination of specific but interacting electoral strategies. To understand ARENA's electoral success, it is crucial to take into account the particular tool kit that the party adopted during the 1990s and continued to develop during its rise to political prominence. In the case of ARENA, three strategies are particularly prevalent: media campaigning, research of the electorate, and territorial coverage. The first component allowed the party to spread its message effectively across the electorate, simultaneously reaching multiple segments of Salvadoran society. The second component ensured that the message was credible: while much of the media message rested on fear campaigning, the high-quality research the party conducted on the electorate allowed it to develop attractive program- and valence-based issue appeals. Finally, the message was disseminated through personalistic networks and clientelism, a strategy that seems to have targeted the lower social classes. Together these strategies formed an effective tool kit that ARENA used and reused, making changes when necessary.

The tool kit is rooted in the party's resource advantage, which in turn is based on ARENA's strong upper-class support. By constantly outspending its competitors in strategically smart ways, the party has been able to increase its electoral chances. Little information about party funding in El Salvador exists, given that the constitution does not require parties to disclose their finances. But some inferences about the resource asymmetry between ARENA and its main competitor can be drawn from party spending on advertisements, and different components of ARENA's tool kit have allowed the party to translate its resource advantage into electoral victories.

Media Campaigning

Over the course of the 1990s and 2000s, ARENA spent more on television, radio, and print advertisement than any of its competitors. As table 11.7 suggests, ARENA used about three times more funds on ads in the campaigns of 1994, 2004, and 2006 than the main opposition party, FMLN. While ARENA's resource advantage decreased in 2009, it still outspent FMLN by two to one. These numbers give a clear indication of ARENA's resource asymmetry in advertising. With the help of this powerful media campaigning, the party was able to reach more voters than its competitors.

ARENA's media campaigning has not been successful solely because of volume. The content has mattered as well. The party has employed a powerful fear campaign strategy based on wartime cleavage and aimed at reinforcing this cleavage. In fact, multiple sources suggest that war imagery has been a particularly important com-

TABLE II.7.
Advertisement expenditures of ARENA and FMLN

Year	ARENA	FMLN	ARENA:FMLN ratio
1994	₡12,094,884	₡4,040,671	3.0
2004	$5,051,461	$1,909,392	2.7
2006	$2,598,368	$740,912	3.5
2009	$10,965,460	$5,229,112	2.1

Sources: Data for 1994 from Obach (1994); data for 2004 and 2006 from FUNDE (2009); data for 2009 from Rodriguez et al. (2009).

ponent of ARENA's electoral strategy.[29] Some credit ARENA's victory in the first peacetime presidential and legislative elections of 1994 to the party's powerful fear campaigning in the media.[30] The party would continue to use this electoral strategy over the course of the following decades. Even as late as 2009, an important component of ARENA's media strategy was connecting FMLN to its violent past.[31]

Importantly, ARENA's ads ran at the same time the news media was reporting stories that were heavily biased against FMLN.[32] It did so because of the connections between ARENA and the Salvadoran media: media ownership is heavily concentrated among families close to the party and the country's economic elite.[33] Moreover, the media depend heavily on advertising money from the private and the public sector.[34] Together these factors have created an extremely asymmetric media environment. Both news reporting and advertising have favored ARENA at the cost of its main competitor. As the media strategy has led to ARENA's wholesale domination of the country's main news outlets, we can safely conclude that media campaigning has been a crucial component of ARENA's electoral tool kit.

Technocratic Knowledge

While much of ARENA's media strategy has been based on the wartime cleavage, the party has also appealed to voters with carefully designed program- and valence-based issue appeals. This strategy, in turn, is based on a high level of technocratic knowledge that the party has developed over the years. With a detailed study of the electorate, the party has been able to offer attractive policy proposals and to sell an image of high competence in various issue areas, such as the economy and public security.

When it comes to concrete policy proposals, the party has benefitted from the know-how of the think tank FUSADES and the business association ANEP. These institutions had tight links to the party, especially in the late 1980s and 1990s, but some of these ties persisted into the 2000s. For example, President Flores (1999–2004) established technical working groups that brought members of ANEP and business elites together with government officials. The participants produced concrete policy proposals that were included in governmental plans.[35] Similarly tight relations have been documented between the party and FUSADES.[36] With the help of these institutions, ARENA gained knowledge and technical skills needed for research of the electorate.

ARENA has not relied solely on external research institutions in crafting its electoral messages. Starting in the early 2000s, the party built three different institutions that aimed to enhance the technical and policy-making capabilities within the party. The strategic center ARENA Estratégica, founded in 2003, was created to plan party and campaign strategies, study the electorate, conduct surveys, maintain the membership list, and offer electoral training. The two other centers, Centro de Estudios Políticos Dr. José Antonio Rodríguez Porth (CEP) and Instituto de Formación Política Mayor Roberto D'Aubuisson, both founded in the early 2000s, focus on training municipal politicians. The latter offers lectures on party ideology, whereas the former provides more technical courses on policy solutions, municipal administration, and campaigning.

ARENA's high technical and professional capacity helps the party in program- and valence-based appeals, as the party's approach to the issue of public security illustrates. As Wolf documents, the so-called *mano dura* policies of the Flores government in 2003 were carefully designed to prevent ARENA from losing power.[37] Throughout 2003, polls had indicated that the governing party was suffering from the country's bleak economic situation. In October, however, insecurity arose as the most salient issue among the electorate. Consequently, ARENA and the media started an effective campaign to marginalize economic concerns and prioritize public security. After Flores's success with the first *mano dura* policies was evident, ARENA candidate Saca continued politicizing the issue. In this way, ARENA combined its capacity to study electoral preferences with its ability to position itself as the party with the most credible policy response. Together with the publicity machine, the party was able to politicize an issue in an electorally beneficial way.[38]

Territorial Reach and Clientelism

Finally, one of ARENA's key electoral strategies has been the establishment of a tight territorial net across the country. In 2006, ARENA was the only party that had participated in municipal elections in each of the 262 Salvadoran municipalities since 1994.[39] In the presidential elections, ARENA was considered a viable presidential candidate in 93% of Salvadoran territory in 2006, while FMLN's territorial reach had been increasing slowly by then.[40] These numbers suggest that ARENA has benefitted from its extensive presence across the country, especially when compared to the geographic reach of its main competitor. While FMLN increased its network before the 2009 election, ARENA had a better nationwide presence at the local level than any of its competitors during the 1990s and the 2000s.

ARENA's territorial reach is closely connected to the party's clientelistic practices. While little academic research exists on the topic, some scholars have highlighted ARENA's extensive clientelistic networks. Elisabeth Wood, for example, writes that ARENA's traditionally strong support in the countryside owes to the party's clientelistic networks.[41] The landlords in the coffee industry and rural paramilitary networks especially were able to draw support for the party through tight social control over their workers.[42] ARENA seems to have relied on social control in urban settings, as well, though clearly in less intense forms. In 2000, three surveys asked whether the respondent's boss had advised the respondent to vote for a certain party. In 2004, twice as many respondents had been advised to vote for ARENA than for FMLN.[43] Four years later, three times as many respondents had been advised to vote for ARENA.[44] Finally, in February 2009, just a month before the presidential elections, eight times as many respondents reported having been advised by their bosses to vote for ARENA.[45] These survey results suggest that ARENA's social control might extend beyond the clientelistic networks in the countryside.

ARENA's effective electoral tool kit has allowed the party to attract voters from election to election, with its main components including effective media campaigning, careful study of the electorate and design of program- and valence-based issue appeals, and a physical presence across the country. In the late 2000s, however, many components of the tool kit seemed to lose their effectiveness. ARENA lost the presidential seat in 2009, likely because increased electoral competition from FMLN weakened ARENA's previously successful strategies.

The Tool Kit Weakens: ARENA's Loss in 2009

Given ARENA's well-planned and effectively implemented electoral strategies, the party's loss in the presidential election of 2009 may seem surprising. But myriad factors made the 2009 contest difficult for ARENA. The party had occupied the presidential seat since 1989, and it consequently faced an electorate primed for change. Corruption had increased during the previous ARENA governments, and while President Saca had promised to combat corruption, no serious measures had been taken.[46] Finally, ARENA continued to face the ever-worsening situation of public security.

One of the key causes of ARENA's loss in 2009 was external to the party. Between the first peacetime elections in 1994 and 2009, the main opposition party,

FMLN, went through a moderation process that, while clearly still ongoing, cul-
minated in the nomination of journalist Mauricio Funes as the party's presidential
candidate in 2007.[47] FMLN's moderation made it increasingly hard for ARENA to
employ its traditional fear campaign strategies. Moreover, the organizational capabilities of Funes increased the territorial reach of FMLN, challenging another one of
ARENA's key strategies. In this way, the tool kit lost some of its effectiveness.

FMLN's moderation has been a gradual process. It was founded in 1980 to bring
together five different guerrilla organizations.[48] While there were always certain
tensions between the groups, a common enemy in the armed conflict provided powerful glue for FMLN, but this unified front changed after the peace of 1992. Soon
after the first peacetime elections, two of the five original groups left the party.[49]
Contrary to the expectations of some, the remaining three organizations failed to
achieve consensus. Instead, two conflicting groupings emerged: the orthodox and
the reformers. After the bad electoral performance of the reformers' candidate in the
1999 presidential elections, the orthodox strengthened their position. The unsuccessful presidential candidate Facundo Guardado was ousted from the party in a few
years' time, and the party took a step to the left in its policy proposals and rhetoric.

The moderates gained more power in 2006 after the death of Schafik Handal. As
an outcome of this new process of moderation, the party in 2007 nominated outsider
Mauricio Funes as their presidential candidate. Until Funes, the party had chosen
well-known guerrilla leaders, as table 11.8 illustrates. In fact, all of FMLN's previous
presidential and vice presidential candidates (with two exceptions) had held high
positions in the militant guerrilla factions: Facundo Guardado (vice presidential candidate in 1994 and presidential candidate in 1999), Nidia Díaz (vice presidential
candidate in 1999), and Schafik Handal (presidential candidate in 2004) were known
for their connections to the militant organizations. The more moderate public image
of coalition candidate Rubén Zamora (presidential candidate in 1994) and G. Mata
Bennett (vice presidential candidate in 2004) weighed little in their respective campaigns, thanks to ARENA's domination of the media.

Once FMLN nominated Funes, it was clear that ARENA was facing a new
opponent. Funes was a well-known television and radio news reporter who had been
critical of the government for years. The media, governing party, and many of the
previously vocal members of business groups could not connect the FMLN candidate
to the war. The fear campaign was fierce, yet, despite attempts to cast Funes as a
puppet of FMLN, the media was unable to cast Funes in a similarly negative light
as previous FMLN candidates.

Funes moderated the FMLN campaign programmatically as well. Unlike the
previous candidates, Funes emphasized the importance of economic growth and
good state-business relationships. Past FMLN candidates had often campaigned on

TABLE 11.8.
FMLN's presidential and vice presidential candidates, 1994–2009

Year	Presidential candidate	Profile	Vice presidential candidate	Profile	Main campaign themes
1994	Rubén Zamora	Frente Democrático Revolucionario	F. Guardado	Fuerzas Populares de Liberación Farabundo Martí (FPL), deputy for FMLN	finalize peace accords; reform the state; promote human rights and civil society
1999	Facundo Guardado	FPL, deputy for FMLN	Nidia Díaz	Partido Revolucionario de los Trabajadores Centroamericanos, deputy for FMLN, 1997–2000	more equal society; public security; democracy and citizen participation
2004	Schafik Handal	PC, deputy for FMLN, 1997–2006	G. Mata Bennett	doctor, activist, and leader in Colegio Medico	replace the neoliberal model of the state; prioritize social spending; fight poverty; revise the US free trade agreement; possibly reverse dollarization
2009	Mauricio Funes	journalist	S. Sánchez Cerén	FPL, deputy for FMLN, 2000–2009	enact wide social and economic reforms; retain the US free trade agreement and dollarization; focus on continuity in state-business relations

Sources: News reports in *El Faro* (www.elfaro.net), *La Prensa Gráfica* (www.laprensagrafica.com), and *El Diario de Hoy* (www.elsalvador.com).

extreme leftist positions, demanding the reversal of the neoliberal model or the dollarization, for example. In contrast, Funes focused on ensuring that the dollarization would not be reversed and that any policy risking foreign investment would not be implemented. This made ARENA's valence advantage disappear.

The nomination of Funes also had implications for FMLN's geographic reach. The intense grassroots campaign that Funes inspired decreased ARENA's territorial advantage, achieved through the civic organization Movimiento Amigos de Mauricio, founded at the end of 2007 by a group of businesspeople and other professionals. The goal of the organization was to support Funes with campaign funding and endorsements, but independently of FMLN. In addition to helping Funes to cast himself as a serious and experienced candidate, the movement increased the presence of the candidate across the country.[50] According to estimates provided by the organization, Amigos de Mauricio opened offices in 170 of the 262 municipalities of the country and brought the party 265,000 votes in the election.[51] While ARENA had enjoyed a clear territorial advantage in the previous elections, Amigos de Mauricio's strong grassroots-level campaigning reduced this advantage.[52] The electoral data discussed above support this point: the percentage of the rural population that voted for ARENA dropped from 75% to 35% between 2004 and 2009, suggesting a change in the dynamics of political competition in the rural areas.

ARENA's electoral tool kit lost effectiveness in 2007, thanks to the new characteristics of party competition. More specifically, the moderation and territorial extension of FMLN weakened many of ARENA's previously successful strategies; by nominating a moderate party outsider, FMLN made it increasingly difficult for ARENA to use its traditional strategies based on the wartime cleavage. Given Funes's personal image and policy proposals, ARENA was unable to cast him as an extremist guerrilla. And as Funes supporters built an extensive network of offices around the country, ARENA's geographical advantage was challenged. External changes and ARENA's inability to adapt to them lost them the presidential seat.

Policy Outcomes: Economic Policies, Poverty Reduction, and Inequality

So far, this chapter has focused on policy inputs and especially on ARENA's electoral strategies. An equally important question concerns policy outcomes, an understudied topic among contemporary Latin Americanists.[53] Given ARENA's long-lasting rule and its continuous emphasis on economic issues, we should evaluate the consequences that ARENA governments have had on Salvadoran society. Has the party managed to translate some of its key campaign issues into reality by improving the economic situation of the citizens? Below I discuss the importance of economic issues for ARENA and evaluate whether some economic indicators, such as the levels of inequality and poverty, indicate that the party has delivered to the electorate.

Ever since businessman Cristiani took over ARENA party leadership in 1985, the economy has been one of the party's main focuses. While macroeconomic restructuring policies started before Cristiani's presidency, these policies intensified dramatically after the peace accords.[54] During ARENA's rule, El Salvador liberalized trade, finance, and capital accounts; privatized and deregulated public companies; reformed pension and tax systems; entered into free trade agreements; and adopted the US dollar. According to McElhinny, ARENA's ability to comprehensively restructure the economy resulted from peace negotiations: FMLN traded access to economic policy making for access to electoral politics, whereas ARENA conceded political rights to the left in order to gain the ability to fundamentally reorganize the Salvadoran economy.[55] As ARENA allied with PDC and PCN in the legislature, FMLN was often unable to stop reforms that ARENA was committed to pushing through. Consequently, the economy is one of the issue areas in which ARENA's electoral victories have played the most significant role.

ARENA did not design the economic policies autonomously. On the contrary, many of the reforms resulted from tight cooperation between the government, economic elite, and institutions such as FUSADES and ANEP. Because the economic elite had direct access to the party and to the government, Alexander Segovia argues, the policy outputs reflected elite interests.[56] This connection lasted well beyond the restructuring during the first two ARENA governments. The speed of the adoption of the US dollar in 2001 and the Central America Free Trade Agreement in 2004 by the Salvadoran legislature indicate the continuing influence of the economic elite.[57]

The results of ARENA's restructuring policies in the 1990s are mixed at best. In general, in the first half of the 1990s, the macroeconomic restructuring was perceived to have been relatively successful. While there was still much room for improvement—in areas of transparency and education, for example—the country nonetheless attracted international investment, diversified exports with the introduction of the *maquilas*, and saw the economy grow at an average rate of 6% between 1992 and 1996.[58] Since the mid-1990s, however, the growth rates have declined sharply, and the per-capita output stagnated beginning in 2000.[59] The total factor of productivity growth turned negative after 1995.[60] In short, despite some early successes, the reforms implemented under ARENA did not foster sustainable growth.

Despite the unimpressive macroeconomic results, poverty in El Salvador has decreased. But sources disagree over scale: for the years between 1991 and 2002, estimates vary between a ten- and twenty-seven-point decline.[61] There is even more disagreement over poverty reduction in the 2000s. World Bank data suggest that the percentage of people living on under $2 per day dropped significantly in the second half of the 2000s, from about 25% in the late 1990s and early 2000s to 20.5% in 2005 and 15.2% in 2008.[62] These reports seem overly optimistic, however, given that the cost of food increased significantly in 2007 and the inflow of remittances declined sharply a year later.[63]

Figure 11.1 represents the percentage of the population living below the national poverty line, as reported by the World Bank and based on population-weighted sub-group estimates from household surveys. The biggest reduction took place during the 1990s, dropping from 59.7% in 1991 to 38.8% in 2000. The decline then slowed and reversed in 2007 and 2008.[64] According to FUSADES, however, poverty had already started to increase by 2001 in both urban and rural areas.[65] While disagreement exists over the development trends of the 2000s, various sources agree that poverty decreased in the 1990s.

The data regarding inequality are less conclusive. According to the World Bank, the income share of the highest quintile remained more or less steady at 55% until 2002, but it then dropped to 53% in 2003 and further to 52% in 2008.[66] The lowest quintile, on the other hand, held about 3.5% of the combined income in the late 1990s, and then decreased its share slightly below 3% in the early 2000s, but it seemed to increase its share again in 2003, 2005, and 2008.[67] But FUSADES reports that the income ratio between the richest and poorest quintiles increased in the 1990s, decreased steadily between 2002 and 2006, and began to increase again after 2006.[68] Given the food price hikes in 2007 and the recession in the United States in 2008, the numbers that the World Bank reports for 2008 seem overly optimistic. At the very least, these reports suggests that, while income inequality seems to have

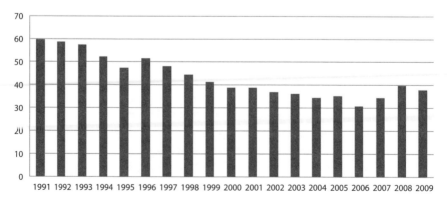

Figure 11.1. Percentage of the population living below national poverty line.
Source: World Bank Open Data, http://data.worldbank.org

decreased somewhat during the early 2000s, El Salvador remains a highly unequal society.

Remittances play an important role in explaining the patterns described above. The United Nations Development Programme (Programa de las Naciones Unidas para el Desarrollo, or PNUD) reports that 5.7% of the families that receive remittances live in a condition of extreme poverty.[69] Of the families that do not receive remittances, 14.5% live in extreme poverty. Were the recipient families to live without remittances, 37.3% of them would be living in extreme poverty. This is particularly true in rural areas, where discounting the remittances would increase the extreme poverty rate from 7.6% to 48.5%.[70] The importance of remittances has led some authors to conclude that the increase in remittances explains the observed reduction in poverty at least as much as economic growth or public policies.[71]

In February 2005, the government of Tony Saca implemented a set of new social programs called Oportunidades. One of the components, Red Solidaria, aimed at reducing extreme poverty with the help of conditional cash transfers and microcredits and improving state services. By the end of 2008, the program was working in seventy-seven of the poorest municipalities in the country. The initial reports of its effects have been positive, and President Funes continued the program with a new name, Programa Comunidades Solidarias Rurales.[72] While ARENA was unable to address inequality during the 1990s and 2000s, Saca's government deserves credit for designing and implementing a program that has the potential to alleviate poverty, especially in rural areas.

An evaluation of the outcomes of ARENA's economic policies does not give much reason for optimism. After the party left office in the end of the 2000s, El Salvador still faced high levels of poverty and inequality, and the intense macroeconomic restructuring of the 1990s had not led to sustainable economic growth. While the last ARENA government innovated in the area of social policy, the party's rule did not lead to significant advances in terms of the overall rates of poverty and inequality.

Conclusion

ARENA's electoral strategy led to impressive results in the presidential elections in the 1990s and early 2000s. With its unmatched resources, the party was able to develop an electoral tool kit that helped it connect with the masses. The tool kit consisted of three components—an effective media strategy, careful study of the electorate, and an extensive territorial network—and together these interconnected components reinforced each other. The powerful media strategy and territorial reach allowed the party elites to disseminate their policy appeals, which were based on detailed research of the electorate. The clientelistic networks, in contrast, helped the party to stay in touch with its bases, leading to more attractive electoral appeals and policy proposals.

The civil war–era societal cleavage was important for ARENA's trajectory. The war brought the founders of ARENA together, and, much like Roberts has argued, the organizational links between the founders were important in shaping the early party development.[73] After the peace accords, however, the cleavage did not depoliticize. In fact, ARENA's electoral tool kit was built on it. Using its financial resources and connections to the main news media, ARENA kept the cleavage alive by exploiting the biased media environment and casting its opponents as radicals who posed a serious threat to the future of the country.

The political climate shifted dramatically in 2007, when FMLN nominated party outsider Mauricio Funes as their presidential candidate. Since Funes could not be directly connected to the guerrilla's wartime actions, ARENA's fear campaigning lost much of its bite. Moreover, Funes's moderate policy positions and the support he drew from the business classes made him a more credible candidate than his predecessors. Finally, Funes's nomination led to the opposition's increased territorial reach. In other words, the different components of ARENA's electoral tool kit weakened after Funes's nomination, given the challenges that FMLN's new, moderate image and stronger territorial presence posed. These external changes were among the key factors that lost ARENA the presidential seat in 2009.

ARENA's loss ended the party's twenty-year rule. Even though the party has long prided itself on expertise in economic issues, an examination of some indicators from the 1990s and 2000s suggests that the results of the party's economic policies left much to hope for. As the country transitioned to peace and democracy, the economic growth rates did not stabilize. The poverty rates that had decreased during 1990 began to increase in the following decade, and inequality remained high throughout the 1990s and 2000s. Although the new social policies of the last ARENA government were promising, the party did not succeed in overcoming the country's longtime problems of poverty and inequality.

ACKNOWLEDGMENTS

The author thanks Edward Gibson, Kenneth Greene, Randy Sunwin Uang, Michael Wahman, Kurt Weyland, the participants of the conference at the Social Science Research Center Berlin, and especially Juan Pablo Luna and Cristóbal Rovira Kaltwasser for excellent comments. All remaining mistakes are of course the author's own. This chapter draws in part on research conducted for the author's MA thesis, "On the Right Track? Business, Economic Experts, and Conservative Party Building in Latin America: The Case of El Salvador" (University of Texas at Austin, 2009), which was supported by a Lozano Long Summer Field research grant from the University of Texas at Austin.

NOTES

1. Guillermo O'Donnell and Philippe C. Schmitter, *Transitions from Authoritarian Rule: Tentative Conclusions about Uncertain Democracies* (Baltimore: Johns Hopkins University Press, 1986).

2. For the resource-rich but vote-poor constituencies, see Herbert Kitschelt, "Linkages between Citizens and Politicians in Democratic Polities," *Comparative Political Studies* 33, no. 6–7 (2000): 845–79. For exceptions, see Edward Gibson, *Class and Conservative Parties: Argentina in Comparative Perspective* (Baltimore: Johns Hopkins University Press, 1996); Kitschelt (2000); and Juan Pablo Luna, "Segmented Party-Voter Linkages in Latin America: The Case of the UDI," *Journal of Latin American Studies*, 42, no. 2 (2010): 325–56.

3. For exceptions, see the recent studies on the economic policies of the Latin American left by Gustavo Flores-Macías, "Statist vs. Pro-Market: Explaining Leftist Governments' Economic Policies in Latin America," *Comparative Politics* 42, no. 4 (2010): 413–433; Kurt Weyland, Raúl Madrid, and Wendy Hunter, eds., *Leftist Governments in Latin America* (Cambridge: Cambridge University Press, 2010).

4. For this critique, see Brian Crisp and María Escobar-Lemmon, "Latin America's Reactive Assemblies and Proactive Presidents," *Latin American Research Review* 36, no. 2 (2001): 187; Kurt Weyland, "Limitations of Rational-Choice Institutionalism for the Study of Latin American Politics," *Studies in Comparative International Development* 37, no.1 (2002): 66; also Flores-Macías (2010, 414).

5. Ricardo Chacón, "Las campañas de los partidos," *ECA Estudios Centroamericanos* 39, no. 426–7 (1984): 229–50; Ignacio Martín Baró, "El llamado de la extrema derecha," *ECA Estudios Centroamericanos* 37, no. 403–4 (1982): 453–66, 457; William Stanley, *The Protection Racket State: Elite Politics, Military Extortion, and Civil War in El Salvador* (Philadelphia, PA: Temple University Press, 1996), 232.

6. Martín Baró (1982, 457–58).

7. Ibid., 464.

8. William Stanley, "El Salvador: State-Building before and after Democratisation, 1980–95," *Third World Quarterly* 27, no. 1 (2006): 101–14.

9. Luis Armando Gonzáles, "De la ideología al pragmatismo: Ensayo sobre las trayectorias ideológicas de ARENA y el FMLN," *ECA Estudios Centroamericanos* 58, no. 661–2 (2003): 1173–202, 1193; M. Dolores Albiac, "Los ricos más ricos de El Salvador," *ECA Estudios Centroamericanos* 54, no. 612 (1999), 841–64, 852–53.

10. Cristina Eguizábal Mendoza, *Partidos, programas y proyectos politicos en El Salvador* (San José: Universidad de Costa Rica, 1989).

11. The party was not unified internally during the process of moderation. For Calderón Sol's view of the conflict between the moderates and the radicals, see Gabriel Labrador and Efren Lemus, "Fuerza Aérea se le amotinó a Cristiani, según cables de la CIA," *El Faro*, January 23, 2012, http://www.elfaro.net/es/201201/noticias/7297/.

12. Eguizábal Mendoza (1989).

13. Kenneth L. Johnson, "Between Revolution and Democracy: Business Elites and the State in El Salvador during the 1980s" (PhD diss., Tulane University, 1993), 223–57.

14. Luis Mario Rodríguez, "La ANEP como grupo de presión en El Salvador" (MA thesis, Universidad Centroamericana José Simeón Cañas, 2005).

15. Stanley (2006, 109).

16. Danilo Alberto Miranda Baires, "La contribución de las alianzas a los poderes del presidente," *ECA Estudios Centroamericanos* 61, no. 696 (2006): 939–56.

17. Álvaro Artiga González, "El Salvador," in *Partidos políticos de América Latina: Centroamérica, México y República Dominicana,* ed. Manuel Alcántara Sáez and Flavia Freidenberg (Salamanca: Ediciones Universidad de Salamanca, 2001); Rubén Zamora, *El Salvador, heridas que no cierran: Los partidos políticos en la post-guerra* (San Salvador: FLACSO, 1998); FUNDAUNGO, *El Salvador: Monografía de los Partidos Politicos, 2009* (San Salvador: Friedrich Ebert Stiftung, 2009); Tribunal Supremo Electoral, "Resultados electorales 2009," 2009. http://www.tse.gob.sv/.

18. Zamora (1998); FUNDAUNGO (2009); Political Database of the Americas, "El Salvador" (Georgetown University and the Organization of American States, 2009). http://pdba.georgetown.edu/Elecdata/ElSal/elsal.html.

19. Nayelly Loya Marin, "Variables estructurales y distribución territorial del comportamiento electoral en elecciones de concejo municipal en El Salvador 1994–2004" (MA thesis, Universidad Centroamericana José Simeón Cañas, 2006).

20. Rogelia Varinia Arevalo Quinteros, "Variables estructurales y distribución territorial del comportamiento electoral en las elecciones presidenciales en El Salvador 1994–2004" (MA thesis, Universidad Centroamericana José Simeón Cañas, 2006).

21. Ibid., 101–03.

22. Zamora (1998, 48–50).

23. Ibid.

24. Centro de Información, Documentación y Apoyo a la Investigación, "Las plataformas de gobierno de ARENA y FMLN-USC," *ECA Estudios Centroamericanos* 54, no. 604–65 (1999): 217–32; Instituto de Derechos Humanos de la Universidad Centroamericana José Simeón Cañas, *Observatorio ciudadano de las elecciones presidenciales* (San Salvador: 2004).

25. Artiga González (2001, 135–78), based on Proyecto Élites Parlamentarias en América Latina (PELA), 1994–2004.

26. In the same surveys, FMLN legislators placed their party at 3.1 in 1994 and at 1.9 in 1998.

27. Artiga González (2001), based on PELA, 1994–2004. For FMLN legislators, the averages were 2.9 in 1994 and 1.9 in 1998.

28. For FMLN legislators, the average was 1.31. Instituto Interuniversitario de Iberoamérica, *Elites Parlamentarias Latinoamericanas: El Salvador (2006–2009)* (Salamanca: Universidad de Salamanca, 2008), 2.

29. Fundación Nacional para el Desarrollo (FUNDE), "Observatorio de castos de campaña publicitaria electoral: Primer Informe: Abril-Noviembre 2008," January 28, 2009, http://www.slideshare.net/Transparencia/transparencia-presentation-963580; Xavier Obach, "Patria o gente . . . ! Análisis de la campana televisiva de ARENA y de la Coalición," *ECA Estudios Centroamericanos* 49, no. 545–6 (1994): 213–56; R. B. G., "Los medios de comunicación en la campana electoral," *ECA Estudios Centroamericanos* 44, no. 545–6 (1994): 312–20; Nataly Guzman, "Las elecciones presidenciales de 2004: Un estudio desde la prensa escrita,"

ECA Estudios Centroamericanos 59, no. 667 (2004): 419–32; William Grigsby, "¿Perdió el FMLN o ganó el miedo?," *Revista Envio* (2004): http://www.envio.org.ni/articulo/2071; Marcos Rodríguez, Danilo Padilla, and Raúl Torres, *La propaganda electoral en El Salvador (2008–2009): Monitoreo y propuestas para transparencia* (San Salvador: FUNDE, 2009).

30. Leonard Wantchekon, "Strategic Voting in Conditions of Political Instability: The 1994 Elections in El Salvador," *Comparative Political Studies* 32, no. 7 (1999): 810–34. For a description, see George Vickers and Jack Spence, "Elections in El Salvador: The Right Consolidates Power," *NACLA Report of the Americas* 28, no. 1 (1994): 6–11.

31. For some examples, see Riitta-Ilona Koivumaeki, "On the Right Track? Business, Economic Experts, and Conservative Party Building in Latin America: The Case of El Salvador" (MA thesis, University of Texas at Austin, 2009).

32. Guzman (2004); Obach (1994).

33. Sonja Wolf, "Subverting Democracy: Elite Rule and the Limits to Political Participation in Post-War El Salvador," *Journal of Latin American Studies* 41 (2009): 440–41.

34. Ibid.

35. Rodríguez Rodríguez (2005).

36. See Johnson (1993).

37. Wolf (2009).

38. Ibid., 447–48.

39. Loya Marin (2006, 113).

40. Arevalo Quinteros (2006, 108).

41. Elisabeth Wood, "Civil War and the Transformation of Elite Representation in El Salvador," in *Conservative Parties, the Right, and Democracy in Latin America,* ed. Kevin Middlebrook (Baltimore: Johns Hopkins University Press, 2000), 223–54.

42. Ibid., 247–48.

43. Instituto Universitario de Opinión Pública, "Informe 103: Encuesta sobre el proceso electoral de 2004" (San Salvador, 2004), http://www.uca.edu.sv/publica/iudop/Web/2004/informe103.pdf.

44. Instituto Universitario de Opinión Pública, "Informe 118: Encuesta de evaluación del año 2008 y sobre el proceso electoral 2009" (San Salvador, 2009), http://www.uca.edu.sv/publica/iudop/Web/2009/informe118_e.pdf.

45. Instituto Universitario de Opinión Pública, "Informe 119: Encuesta de evaluación post-electoral de enero y sobre el proceso electoral de marzo" (San Salvador, 2009), http://www.uca.edu.sv/publica/iudop/Web/2009/informe119.pdf. All the differences are significant at the 95% level of confidence.

46. Gerardo Berthin, Yemile Mizrahi, Carlos Guerrero, and Antonio Cañas, *An Assessment of Corruption in El Salvador* (Alexandria: Casals and Associates, 2005), 24–25.

47. The conflictual relationship between President Funes and FMLN in the legislature after the 2009 elections suggests that the moderation of the left is easily exaggerated. In fact, Funes has never been particularly close to FMLN. The relationship between the two was warmest after Funes's nomination in late September 2007. Since then, and especially since the January 2009 legislative and municipal elections, Funes started to distance himself from the party. FUSADES, *Primer año del Presidente Funes: Apreciación general* (San Salvador: 2010), 9. Following the election, the relationship between the two has been openly conflicting, and the president has consequently built legislative support across party lines (ibid., 9–12). In

explaining ARENA's electoral loss, however, the nomination and campaign of Funes were enough to take the bite out of ARENA's traditional campaign strategies.

48. This account draws from Luis Armando Gonzáles's study of the development of FMLN's and ARENA's ideologies. "De la ideología al pragmatismo: Ensayo sobre las trayectorias ideológicas de ARENA y el FMLN," *ECA Estudios Centroamericanos* 58, no. 661–2 (2003): 1173–202, 1193.

49. Officially, the guerrilla organizations were dissolved after FMLN made the transition to democratic electoral politics.

50. Gonzáles (2003).

51. Daniel Caravantes Valencia, "Se fractura el movimiento Amigos de Mauricio Funes," *El Faro,* February 14, 2010, http://www.elfaro.net/es/201002/noticias/1161/.

52. Arevalo Quinteros (2006); Loya Marin (2006).

53. Crisp and Escobar-Lemmon (2001, 187); Weyland (2002, 66); see also Flores-Macías (2010, 414).

54. Vincent McElhinny, "Inequality and Empowerment: The Political Foundations of Post-War Decentralization and Development in El Salvador, 1992–2000" (PhD diss., University of Pittsburgh, 2006).

55. Ibid., 391–93.

56. Alexander Segovia, "La actuación y las políticas macroeconómicas a partir de 1989," in *Ajuste hacia la paz: La política económica y la reconstrucción de posguerra en El Salvador,* ed. James K. Boyce (Mexico City: Programa de las Naciones Unidas para el Desarrollo, 1999), 77–101. See also Alexander Segovia, *Transformación estructural y reforma económica en El Salvador: el funcionamiento económico de los noventa y sus efectos sobre el crecimiento, la pobreza y la distribución del ingreso* (Guatemala: Democracia y Desarrollo, Consultores; F&G Editores, 2002); *Integración real y grupos de poder económico en América Central: Implicaciones para el desarrollo y la democracia de la Región* (San Jose: Fundación Friedrich Ebert America Central, 2006).

57. For an analysis of the economic model in El Salvador, see Segovia (2002).

58. McElhinny (2006, 413).

59. M. Garza, C. Karacadag, C. Macario, and M. Papaioannou, "El Salvador, Background Notes on Selected Issues" (Country Report No. 05/270, International Monetary Fund, Washington, DC, 2005), 3.

60. Ibid.

61. McElhinny (2006, 412).

62. World Bank, "PovcalNet: The On-Line Tool for Poverty Measurement Developed by the Development Research Group of the World Bank," http://worldbank.org.

63. FUSADES, *¿Cómo está El Salvador?* (San Salvador: 2009), 142.

64. Nora Lustig's analysis based on Centro de Estudios Distributivos, Laborales y Sociales (Universidad Nacional de La Plata) and World Bank data concurs. According to her analysis, both extreme poverty and poverty decreased between 1990 and 2006. "Poverty, Inequality, and the New Left in Latin America," *Woodrow Wilson Center Update on the Americas: Democratic Governance and the "New Left"* 5 (2009): 1–27.

65. FUSADES (2009, 142).

66. World Bank Open Data, http://data.worldbank.org.

67. Ibid.

68. FUSADES (2009, 143–45).

69. Extreme poverty refers to a situation where the family income does not cover the price of the basic food basket.

70. PNUD, *Informe sobre Desarrollo Humano El Salvador 2005: Una mirada al nuevo nosotros. El impacto de las migraciones* (San Salvador: 2005), 67–68.

71. McElhinny (2006, 416).

72. FUSADES (2009, 168–69).

73. Kenneth M. Roberts, "Left, Right, and the Legacies of Neoliberal Critical Junctures" (paper presented at the annual meeting of the American Political Science Association, Philadelphia, Pennsylvania, August 30 to September 2, 2006).

CHAPTER TWELVE

Brazil

Explaining the Rise and Decline of the Conservatives

ALFRED P. MONTERO

Inequality in Brazil is a necessary condition for the establishment of sustainable clientele networks based on hierarchical relationships between powerful elites and poor clients. In this chapter I argue that the Brazilian right has historically depended upon such formulas of political domination at the subnational (state and municipal) level.[1] From this base, conservative elites gained the capacity to exert influence at a national level. The history of these models is long, evolving from *coronelismo* during the nineteenth and early twentieth centuries to more contemporary forms of political machine building under both authoritarian and democratic regimes. The other central claim of this chapter is that the subnational organization of conservative power produced an uneven geographic pattern for the quality of democracy, concentrating rightwing political domination especially where inequality is greatest in the poor states of the northeast. Zones of conservative rule in Brazil are marked by the continuation of these elites and their extended political families in power (*parentela*) and by voter attitudes that enable the continuity of political machines. The result is a pattern of political organization that can be best understood by analyzing how spatial logics link who Brazilian conservatives are, how they have organized, and who supports them.

The definition of the Brazilian right used here, which views the right's policy preferences and organizational choices as emerging from the structures of socioeconomic inequality, challenges several alternative conceptions of the right in Brazil. First, conservative rule has persisted through different regime types. While conservatives were closely associated with the bureaucratic-authoritarian regime (1964–85), making the most of their ties to the generals to enhance their influence, conservatives also adapted to nonauthoritarian contexts such as the populist party period of 1945–64 and the current democratic regime that began in 1985.[2] They survived the nonparty dictatorship of Getúlio Vargas (1930–37) and his corporatist Estado Novo (1937–45). Second, no single ideology, defined as a set of programmatic policy preferences, encompasses an understanding of the right in modern Brazil. Conservatives have embraced both statist and market-oriented forms of capitalist development. The right has also advocated a wide range of social welfare policies, provided that they did not threaten property rights.[3] While advocating for the poor during campaigns and distributing material rewards to poor clients are core tactics of conservatives, more systemic distribution of income and land is not an acceptable option. Third, the Brazilian right is evolutionary in that its base expanded from traditional rural-sector elites to encompass more urban, industrial interests. The latter is still "traditional" in the sense that the sources of power remain imbedded in clientele networks, but the right is also "modern" in that it broadened its class range as Brazil industrialized during the twentieth century.[4] Chief among its modernizing tendencies is the capacity of the right to maintain a closer and more pervasive interconnection between its social bases of power and the central role of the state in the economy. Although a segment of the right is "traditional" in the other sense, that it embraces conservative social mores, this aspect does not determine the composition of the right over time. The "traditional," the "conservative," and the "right" cohere as a single sociopolitical entity, and so these terms will be used interchangeably here. These terms refer to a historically defined political group in Brazil that differs from the more contemporary development of a center-right that is discussed below.

Two core premises undergird any understanding of the right in Brazil. The first is that inequality in Brazil, which is especially great in those regions of the country where conservatives have ruled the longest, is central to sustaining clientele networks. Poverty and material dependence on clientele networks can sustain political bosses in power.[5] In Brazil, conservatives created these networks but also embraced limited distributive policies that did not fundamentally challenge property rights. This balancing act allowed conservatives to weather the advent of populist politics and industrialization during the twentieth century, evolving the right from its nineteenth-century rural and exclusive regimes run by local bosses of landed elites (*os coronéis*; hence *coronelismo*).

The other core premise of any analysis of conservative rule is the primacy of subnational bases of power. Domination of governorships and state assemblies has been the main source of the right's political influence and continuity in contemporary Brazil. More than politicians of the center and the left, conservatives have been most consistent historically in scaling up their position in subnational bailiwicks to exert leverage at the federal level. The continuity of conservatives in power (*continuismo*) is a product of their ability to control state resources and extract political support from voters dependent upon the largesse of these elites. So an allied tendency in places dominated by conservatives is *governismo*—the tendency for voters to elect the incumbent repeatedly at higher rates. Conservatives' *continuismo* and the *governismo* that is acute in their states and municipalities reflect the capacity of these elites to consolidate political machines, differentiating them from the center-right and centrist politicians who practice clientelism but do not dominate their subnational base through extended political families.

Consistent with this view of the subnational bases of conservative rule, voters' attitudes toward politics vary spatially, mapping well between areas that have been held by conservatives versus the left or center-left. Voter attitudes concerning the importance of maintaining personal ties to politicians and the exchange of material rewards for political support are particularly strong in states long held by rightwing politicians, such as the nine states of the northeast.

Because of the right's dominance of its redoubts in the overrepresented northern and northeastern states, conservatives gained an upper hand in guaranteeing the stability and shaping the quality of Brazilian democracy after 1985. Much scholarship on the first two decades of Brazilian democracy emphasizes the continuous influence of traditional elites, and particularly those forming the right, in federal and subnational politics. For example, Frances Hagopian's seminal examination of traditional politics before and during Brazil's democratic period, known as the New Republic, is most interested in explaining "why [such elites] survive and continue to monopolize power."[6] Similarly, Timothy Power's essential studies of the right are most concerned with mapping out how the "durable political machines" undergirding conservatives contribute to their dominance in the post-1985 democracy.[7] Little consideration is given in these works to the possibility that the social bases of conservatives' political machines can change.

This chapter shows that assumptions that conservative rule will remain a loadstone around the neck of Brazilian democracy are obsolescing. Despite the pervasive influence that the right has had on democratic institutions and Brazilian governments, the erosion of its position at the subnational level, and especially in conservative redoubts in the states of the north and the northeast, has accompanied and made more sustained the decline of the right's influence in national politics. Analysis of the results of the 2006 and 2010 elections provide evidence that conservatives have failed to sufficiently protect their erstwhile sources of political power and will likely see a far more limited role as Brazilian democracy matures. I have explored the empirical causes of this decline elsewhere, so the analysis here will focus on the broader significance of this reversal of political fortune for conservatives.[8]

Defining the Brazilian Right

The Brazilian right has been a part of every governing coalition since independence in 1822 until the last decade. The definition of the right based on either ideological or historic-sociological terms must be able to encompass this long history. Ideological definitions do not travel well across time because the proclivities of conservatives in one period do not hold longitudinally. But an ideological-programmatic definition does lend itself well to operationalization of the right in terms of parties and governing programs during specific periods.[9] By contrast, a focus on the organization of clientele networks is broadly applicable throughout history but underspecifies the right in contemporary democracy where many parties and political persuasions, including some on the left, engage in clientelism. The approach taken by this study is to marry the two perspectives by emphasizing the socioeconomic bases for political clientelism used by conservatives and then to use the programmatic operationalization employed by Mainwaring et al. and Power in Brazil's post-1985 democracy.[10] The enduring link between the two approaches, I argue, is the subnational base for both the clientele networks and the parties of conservatives. To differentiate these further from contemporary centrists and some leftists, I emphasize the geographic focus of conservative rule in the nine states of the northeast and, less so, the five states of the north. To be sure, notable conservatives such as Paulo Maluf, the longtime friend of the military and stalwart of São Paulo politics, was a rightist, but he never consolidated his role in *paulista* and national politics the way that conservative political machines did in the northeast. My definition for the Brazilian right is imbedded in a conception of conservative rule that has as its core the dominance of subnational bailiwicks and the use of these bases to sustain the influence of conservatives in national politics.

Alternative definitions used for the right do less well in the Brazilian context. One might define the Brazilian right in terms of its core constituency from the upper classes and business, in terms of its position on the incorporation of labor into the political arena, or regarding its policy preference for market-oriented reform.[11] In contrast to Edward Gibson's definition, Brazil's rightists have primarily depended upon the support of low-income voters.[12] The Brazilian right may be the most friendly to business interests and the least congenial to labor, but these cleavages are insufficient to identify the right, because workers in the northeast plump for conservatives, and some business interests have abandoned them in the industrial south.[13] The same is true for the right's positions on market-oriented policies. It should be remembered that conservatives partnered with the armed forces during the authoritarian period to deepen the import-substitution model and to oppose trade liberalization, but they shifted to support neoliberal structural reforms during the 1990s and especially under the democratic administration of Fernando Henrique Cardoso.[14] Now that even leftists such as Lula da Silva (2003–10) and the Workers' Party (Partido dos Trabalhadores, or PT) support these reforms, these policy preferences are no longer useful indicators for defining the right.[15] The parameters of social welfare reform are perhaps the one exception in that conservatives are opposed to income distribution and land tenure reform that changes property rights. This is one of the reasons they

have been tolerant of conditional cash transfer programs and other poverty alleviation policies that avoid redrawing property rights regimes.[16]

One corollary of the support for market-oriented reforms is that conservative
parties in other Latin American countries have been partial to these reforms owing
to the influence of technocrats bound by fraternal and epistemic ties forged during
graduate training in the United States or the United Kingdom. Such cliques, which
proved so important to the embrace by establishment or conservative parties of neoliberal structural reforms in Chile and Mexico, are more diffusely organized within
the centrist, center-right, and conservative parties in Brazil. The Liberal Party
(Partido Liberal, or PL) once claimed the mantle of a bona fide "business party"
under the leadership of Guilherme Afif Domingos, who ran for president on the party's ticket in 1989, but the PL never developed into a coherent liberal party. Its leader
in 2002, José Alencar, even ran and served as Lula's vice president. The incoherence of
liberal ideology in the Brazilian parties may be less associated with the development
of these parties and considered to be more a product of the relative weakness of economic liberalism as a defining or unifying element of technocratic/bureaucratic development in Brazil. Unlike Mexico, Argentina, and Chile, Brazil maintained much
of its developmentalist economic bureaucracy and incorporated many of the policy
mechanisms of the import-substitution period in its structural reforms and trade
policies during the 1990s and 2000s.[17]

Below, I first consider the historical roots of clientelist forms in rural society and
particularly in the least industrialized states of the northeast. I then turn to the role
of control over public sector patronage at the subnational level and, finally, the use of
this base to exert influence at the federal level. This is a story that includes political
parties but is not driven by these organizations.

Traditional conservative elites in Brazil trace their roots back to the nineteenth
century, during which time political machines, landed families, and local strongmen
known as *os coronéis* "the colonels" ruled over peasants who depended upon these
figures for their livelihoods.[18] Conservative modernization of the countryside during the military regime accelerated the region's economic growth but left unchanged
erstwhile patron-client relations. In exchange for their abiding political support, the
generals transferred agricultural credit and subsidies to large landholders and channeled capital investment into once-defunct export enclaves in the sugar zone by
creating the sugar cane gasohol program, Proálcool. The expansion of agribusiness
crowded out subsistence agriculture, increased demand for imported staples, and
raised average food prices. All of these tendencies were "modernizing," but they
failed to raise citizens out of the erstwhile socioeconomic categories of dependency.

As is typical of the development of clientele networks elsewhere, those that were
forged on the basis of economic dependence and poverty in the northeast became

the lifeblood of conservative rule for decades, "modernizing" only in terms of tactics in the form of more elaborate and pervasive forms of vote buying, coercion, and machine building. What sustained the conservative, dominant class in these polities was their continued hegemonic control of the state apparatus, which they used to deprive nascent oppositions of the resources they needed to mount a challenge. In this way, traditional incumbents practiced what Gibson calls "boundary control" by undercutting the creation of possible alliances that could otherwise broaden political competition, limiting the elite to familiar networks rooted in kinship.[19] Since the parameters of political competition were narrowed to an "oligarchy of families that cross the blurred boundaries between state and society," only through "membership in or alliance with these families [was] . . . political advancement" assured.[20] These clans of friends and "extended family" (*parentela*) adapted to the modernization of the state and to democracy by becoming electoral families in subnational politics.[21]

The dominant elite's control over patronage at the subnational level required renewable sources of fiscal transfers from the federal government in return for political support to an array of different national leaders—authoritarian as well as democratic, military as well as civilian. Although the bureaucratic-authoritarian regime attempted to replace traditional elites with their handpicked "technical" governors, this effort failed and the generals would come to rely on conservatives.[22] The military's own political party, the National Renewal Alliance (Aliança Renovadora Nacional, ARENA), became a vehicle for these traditional elites.[23] From these bases, conservatives collaborated with the generals, representing their political interests in the federal congress through ARENA and its successor after 1979, the Democratic Social Party (Partido Democrático Social, PDS).[24]

Using the democratic-authoritarian cleavage as his standard, Power defines the political right as the cohort that affiliated with ARENA/PDS, but, as I have argued, this cohort is endogenous to the larger sociohistorical phenomenon of conservative rule in Brazil.[25] Power's framework, however, is useful in underscoring the high point of conservative rule under both the military and the subsequent democratic regime and in clarifying its modernizing tendencies. As his study demonstrates, the ARENA/PDS cohort retained its influence within the post-1985 democracy, choosing indirectly through an electoral college and accidentally through the death of the first civilian president, Tancredo Neves, on the eve of his inauguration, one of their own in José Sarney in 1985, the longtime boss of Maranhão state. Conservatives played a key role in solidifying the Centrão (literally, the "big center" alliance of rightwing politicians) that shaped the constitution of 1988, giving themselves the benefits of electoral malapportionment in the congress by overrepresenting the less populous states in the north and northeast that they dominated.[26] And while Sarney proved incapable of addressing the multiple crises of the developmentalist economy, the conservative elite was able to evolve in support of market-oriented policies, beginning with the ill-fated presidency of Fernando Collor (1990–92) and then most notably during the two terms of Fernando Henrique Cardoso (1995–2002).[27]

Unlike the experience of other Latin American countries, the Brazilian right's social base obviated the need to develop political parties to defend its interests. In all cases in which conservatives affiliated with a particular organization, regime insiders created these political parties—a distinctive aspect of rightwing parties in Brazil that differentiates them especially from leftwing parties, such as PT, that originated outside the state as the products of grassroots activism. Using a distinction first conceived by Martin Shefter, Mainwaring argues that conservative and center-right parties in Brazil were "internally created" by regime forces, while parties such as PT were "externally created," having been born during the opposition in the transition to democracy.[28] This makes Power's definition of the political right during the New Republic as the cohort that emanated from ARENA/PDS useful for identifying the individuals that fall into this group.[29] In addition, ARENA/PDS was, apart from the generals themselves, a vacuous organization without the involvement of the conservative governors and mayors that adopted the party label. As noted above, ARENA was initially divided by the *técnicos* appointed directly by the regime and the traditional (conservative) elite. The latter group regained control of state party machines during the political liberalization (*abertura*) process after 1973, effectively pushing out the *técnicos* from positions of power and restoring what these conservative elites had since the days of Vargas.[30] Continued recruitment into and career success within the Arenista cohort depended upon a politician's ties to the subnational political machines run by traditional elites. This group had been greatly strengthened during the late 1970s and early 1980s, when the generals cultivated their support in response to the official opposition, the Brazilian Democratic Movement's (Movimento Democrático Brasileiro, or MDB) electoral victories in state and national legislatures in 1974 and 1978.[31] Conservative elites remained strongest in the rural states of the north and northeast, and the regime fortified them by pouring resources into these regions in the form of development project money and fiscal transfers. The generals malapportioned the national congress to the benefit of these states in the 1978 electoral reform. Then, in the contest of 1982, when governors could be elected directly for the first time, the military provided them with great fiscal and policy-making autonomy. In lieu of creating a new, national political elite as a bulwark against MDB, the military scaled up the subnational networks of conservatives. These processes had lasting effects on conservatives themselves, even years later, as shown by Timothy Power's surveys of congressional elites between 1991 and 1997: conservative deputies are far more likely than others to identify with their region than their party.[32]

After the democratic transition in 1985, many of these politicians easily abandoned PDS to avoid the stigma associated with pro-military ties. Their preferred new party was the Liberal Front Party (Partido da Frente Liberal, or PFL), but also the catchall Party of the Brazilian Democratic Movement (Partido do Movimento Democrático Brasileiro, or PMDB), ironically the party of ARENA's rival during the period of restricted two-party competition (1966–78), MDB. During the constituent assembly (1987–88) that drafted the country's constitution, a fifth of PMDB representatives were former Arenistas.[33] Power's data for the 48th through 50th (1987–91, 1991–95, and 1995–99) congresses demonstrate that ARENA/PDS veterans also moved to other national parties such as the Party of Brazilian Social Democracy (Partido da Social Democracia Brasileira, or PSDB), where approximately 15% of the party's deputies during the first term of Fernando Henrique Cardoso's presidency were former Arenistas. ARENA/PDS veterans also migrated to smaller, regional parties such as PL, the Brazilian Labor Party (Partido Trabalhista Brasileiro, or PTB), and the various configurations of the merged organizations Progressive Party (Partido Progressista, or PP), Brazilian Progressive Party (Partido Progressista Brasileiro, or PPB), and Reformist Progressive Party (Partido Progressista Reformador, or PPR).[34] Based on the percentage of seats won in the chamber of deputies and the senate, the apogee of conservative influence during the post-1985 democracy occurred during the Cardoso administration. As table 12.1 shows, the rightwing parties averaged 43.8% of seats won in the chamber and 36.6% in the senate for the 1990–2002 period. PFL led all rightwing parties with an average of 17.8% of seats in the chamber and 21.5% in the senate. During the 2002–10 period, these averages fell to 33.1% for all rightwing parties in the chamber and 24% in the senate. PFL's gains were especially small (an average of 12.5% in the chamber and 14% in the senate) for the period.

These party labels remain useful as one indicator for identifying where the Brazilian right resides in the current democratic regime, as the organizations that were favored by the Arenista cohort remain the parties of choice for conservatives. If one employs a programmatic-ideological definition of the right, empirical evidence stemming from surveys of congressional leaders, analyses of legislative roll call voting, and the historical genealogy of who the members of the conservative right are, these parties continue to be associated with the right in Brazil.[35] Although their distinctive views may not travel well over broader periods of Brazilian history, the members of current conservative parties have similar programmatic preferences, including support for market-oriented policies, social conservatism (though varied across parties, it differs fundamentally from the positions identified with the left and center), and opposition to land reform.[36] Although centrist and populist politicians in major urban areas such as Rio de Janeiro and São Paulo have implemented hard-line (*mão dura*) approaches to maintaining law and order, such as invasions by military and

TABLE 12.1.
Percentage of total seats won in the chamber (C) and the senate (S) by conservative parties, 1982–2010

	1982		1986		1990		1994		1998		2002		2006		2010	
	C	S	C	S	C	S	C	S	C	S	C	S	C	S	C	S
Partido da Frente Liberal/Democratas			23.8	14.3	16.7	29.6	17.3	20.4	20.5	18.5	16.6	17.3	12.7	22.2	8.3	2.5
Partido Democrático Social[a]	49.1	60.0	6.6	4.1	8.3	7.4	10.1	3.7	11.7	7.4	9.4					
Partido Liberal/Partido da República			1.2		3.0		2.5	1.9	2.3		5.3	2.5	4.5	3.7	7.9	3.7
Partido Trabalhista Brasileiro	2.7		3.5		7.6	14.8	6.0	5.6	6.0		5.1	2.5	4.3	4.9	4.0	1.2
Partido Progressista[b]					0.4		7.0	7.4	0.2				8.2	1.2	7.9	3.7
Others[c]	0.0		1.2	2.0	15.2	7.4	2.4		1.6				1.2	4.0	4.0	2.5
Percentage of total seats	51.8	60.0	36.3	20.4	51.2	59.2	45.3	39.0	42.3	25.9	36.4	22.3	30.9	36.0	32.1	13.6

Sources: Mainwaring et al. (2000, tables 6.5 and 6.6); Tribunal Superior Eleitoral.

[a]Includes the seat shares of the Partido Democrata Cristão after 1993 as the Partido Progressista Reformador.

[b]Was previously the Partido Social Trabalhista and the Partido Trabalhista Renovador.

[c]Includes the seat shares of other parties not included in merged entities already listed here. For a list of other parties, see Mainwaring et al. (2000, 180–81).

paramilitary police squads to "pacify" *favelas*, rightwing parties are especially keen on these policies. In one study of nineteen states, Ahnen finds that rightwing governors tend to preside over states with higher-than-average incidents of homicides committed by police.[37] Though, even here, much depends on the relative dominance of conservative incumbents.[38]

The Geography of the Brazilian Right's Effects on Democracy

The right has been neither excessively strong nor exceedingly weak in terms of its effects on the quality of the post-1985 Brazilian democracy. Conservatives certainly played a stabilizing role by engaging the system ("staying in the game") and then supporting in the congress all of the presidents who were elected between 1985 and 2002.[39] But Brazilian democracy was institutionally weak when the generals relinquished power, which allowed conservatives to imprint their parochial interests on democratic procedures.[40] So "support" meant providing votes in return for patronage (pork barreling).[41] At the national level, the right was able to keep off the legislative table political reform and reversals of the fiscal transfer system that gave their bailiwicks access to federal resources without the need to extract taxes.[42] At the subnational level, conservatives' continued dominance of their states undermined the quality of democracy by weakening elite contestation, accountability, and government responsiveness. As I argue above, these two intergovernmental levels are linked, with conservatives' influence on national politics emanating from their dominance of their subnational polities.

As the political actor most loyal to the outgoing military leadership during the transition, securing the right's support for democracy guaranteed the stability of the regime but introduced a series of tradeoffs that hurt the quality of democracy. By far the most studied institutions in this regard are the Brazilian congress and the presidency. The Centrão, which the Arenistas dominated, embraced the above mentioned malapportionment of seats in the chamber of deputies, allowing overrepresentation of underpopulated states in the north and northeast and limiting the number of deputies from the more industrialized states of the south and southeast, the base for center-left and leftist opposition to the military.[43] The right also opposed provisions to increase the oversight powers of the congress and the courts, the transparency of the policy-making process, and a lower threshold for legislative quorums.[44] These positions all preserved conservatives' preferences for opaque, personal exchange–oriented forms of doing politics. And the right would continue to protect these preferences during the subsequent governments of Fernando Collor, Itamar Franco (1992–94), and especially Fernando Henrique Cardoso. Cardoso's PSDB decidedly shifted to the center-right during the 1994 campaign when it formed an alliance with PFL and then subsequently when Cardoso relied upon PFL chieftains such as Antônio Carlos Magalhães (Bahia) and his son, Luis Eduardo, to shepherd his legislative agenda in the congress. Despite Cardoso's previous attacks on what he called Fisiologismo (clientelist politics) and his long-held belief that PFL was at the core of the country's problems, the president recognized the practicalities of allying with conservatives who held more than 40% of the seats in the chamber of deputies.[45]

If the point of rightwing support for presidents such as Sarney, Collor, and Cardoso was the orientation of legislation and political careers around the reinforcement of subnational bailiwicks, it was the continuation of conservative dominance in these redoubts that provided the right its influence at the federal level. According to David Samuels, this meant that these elites played the game of gubernatorial politics well.[46] As his research shows, gubernatorial, not presidential, candidates have "coattails" in concurrent elections. Candidates for federal, state, and municipal office wish to associate with gubernatorial candidates, who have the mixture of name recognition, local connections (especially important for traditional elites), and campaign finance support. By using federal resources to reinforce their clientele networks at the subnational level, conservatives helped to undermine elite accountability and government responsiveness by limiting their rivals' access to power. To accomplish this, they employed erstwhile tactics for parochializing politics: using the state apparatus to dispense material incentives to poor voters and local political allies.

Parochialization limits electoral contestation de facto by allowing a few elites to mobilize citizen participation during electoral cycles. The best analysis of this phenomenon is found in Frances Hagopian's *Traditional Politics and Regime Change in Brazil*.[47] For Hagopian, traditional polities are authoritarian in the sense that the oligarchy controls representation, mobilizing citizens through vote and turnout buying and demobilizing them through turnout suppression. Voters can express their choices at the ballot box, but they are influenced *ex ante* by conservative elites through material incentives, realized or promised.[48] Consequently, political elites can compete for power, but a small, predictable few capture and hold it repeatedly. While the alternation, albeit seldom, of governments both within and outside the traditional elite in most Brazilian states would disqualify these polities as strictly authoritarian, de facto limitations on elite contestation weaken the pluralism of these systems.

The empirical indicators for the parochialization of democratic politics in the redoubts of conservative rule can be demonstrated through subnational electoral data and surveys of voters. The first set of indicators draws on an emerging literature that attempts to measure the quality of subnational democracy through the existence of excessively long mandates, large margins for incumbents, executive dominance over the legislature, and high reelection rates.[49] The second set of indicators measures the tendency of voters in states traditionally ruled by conservatives to engage in *governismo* and to evince political attitudes that embrace personalism and clientelist rule. These voters maintain fewer hopes of good government, but they expect the politicians they select to reward them personally and to improve their well-being.

Using electoral measures of limited contestation and *continuismo*, I construct an index to list the twenty-six Brazilian states from least competitive to most competitive. Drawing on work by Carlos Gervasoni and André Borges, the index is based on a single-factor score from a principal components analysis of four measures of contestation: the proportion of the valid vote won by the incumbent party in the first round of the gubernatorial elections, the proportion of the valid vote won by the incumbent partisan coalition in the first round of the gubernatorial elections, succession control (coded as 1, governorship is lost to opposition; 2, incumbent is succeeded by copartisan or similar political family; or 3, incumbent is reelected or returns to office in a nonconsecutive term if previously served),[50] and the percentage of seats in the state assembly won by the governor's party and party coalition.[51] The index pools data from four elections (1990, 1994, 1998, and 2002). It excludes the 1982 and 1986 contests owing to their different electoral rules, party systems, and the exclusion of new states. The index also omits the contest of 2006 because that election was relatively more competitive.[52] The analysis produced one significant factor (2.27 eigenvalue with a 1.504 difference over the second eigenvalue). The result is a baseline ranking of "electoral dominance."[53]

Table 12.2 places at the top of the list what scholars of Brazil routinely report as the least competitive polities. Most of these are located in the northeast region, the most notoriously clientelistic area of the country and also, as the last column of table 12.2 shows, the most unequal in terms of income distribution.[54] Not one state from the more populated and socioeconomically more developed and more equal southern or southeastern regions appears in the top fourteen entries. The first eleven slots on the list include the only four states to never have a second-round contest for governor (Alagoas, Amazonas, Mato Grosso, and Pernambuco). With the exception of Paraíba, these states all reelected governors at least once (five did twice; one, Amazonas, did so three times).[55] The dominant parties in these states tend to be the rightwing PFL and the center-right PMDB, commensurate with the conservative profile of these cases. The centrist social democratic PSDB, which is dominant in only the case of Ceará, elected a winning governor only five times (including one reelection) in the other states placed within the least competitive cohort. Notably, PT, the largest leftist party in Brazil, captured no governorships and found itself in only four partisan coalitions of successful candidates in this group prior to 2006. In virtually all cases, conservative candidates and rightwing parties retained control of the governorships of these states.

TABLE 12.2.

Electoral dominance and its components by state and region, 1990–2002

State	Region[a]	Mean electoral dominance index[b]	Mean winning gubernatorial vote share	Mean succession control	Mean winning party seat share	Mean winning coalition seat share	Average Gini coefficient 1994–2010
Ceará	NE	1.250 (0.635)	55.53	2.5	41.33	52.18	0.590
Tocantins	N	1.200 (0.676)	57.53	2	46.48	60.48	0.566
Bahia	NE	1.040 (0.574)	55.90	2.5	32.15	53.90	0.585
Paraíba	NE	0.926 (1.524)	53.68	2	38.20	51.43	0.612
Amazonas	N	0.801 (0.761)	55.85	2.75	16.70	59.43	0.551
Maranhão	NE	0.604 (0.597)	49.90	2.25	28.55	60.60	0.583
Pernambuco	NE	0.547 (0.347)	57.40	2.5	24.45	44.38	0.593
Goiás	CW	0.392 (0.771)	49.68	2.5	27.43	39.63	0.550
Mato Grosso	CW	0.343 (0.975)	60.70	1.5	24.98	41.70	0.550
Sergipe	NE	0.207 (1.238)	51.28	2	13.55	54.20	0.582
Alagoas	NE	0.186 (0.715)	63.30	2.25	16.65	31.45	0.577
Acre	N	0.059 (0.527)	49.18	2	23.95	37.48	0.589
Rio Grande do Norte	NE	−0.059 (1.174)	47.15	2	21.85	37.50	0.580
Roraima	N	−0.103 (0.690)	46.00	1.75	21.93	40.50	0.530
Paraná	S	−0.129 (0.887)	41.88	2.25	21.40	37.80	0.546
Santa Catarina	S	−0.238 (1.119)	43.35	1.75	21.25	38.75	0.488
Mato Grosso do Sul	CW	−0.340 (0.866)	48.55	2	16.68	30.23	0.544
Rio de Janeiro	SE	−0.405 (0.891)	49.10	1.75	17.85	28.93	0.559
Pará	N	−0.423 (0.838)	40.03	2.25	16.48	33.55	0.548
Piauí	NE	−0.467 (0.896)	44.75	1.25	24.18	30.83	0.592
São Paulo	SE	−0.608 (0.070)	34.08	2.25	20.53	27.75	0.531
Amapá	N	−0.696 (0.664)	42.33	1.75	13.98	29.43	0.557
Rio Grande do Sul	S	−0.814 (0.263)	43.10	1.25	20.00	23.18	0.539
Espírito Santo	SE	−0.874 (0.537)	51.43	1	10.83	22.48	0.567
Minas Gerais	SE	−0.954 (0.308)	43.30	1.5	11.05	25.68	0.555
Rondônia	N	−1.663 (0.570)	32.93	1	10.43	14.58	0.537

Source: Author's original data set, based on Tribunal Superior Eleitoral electoral data (www.tse.jus.br) and Gini coefficient data from the Instituto Brasileiro de Geografia e Estatística.

[a] CW, center-west; N, north; NE, northeast; S, south; SE, southeast.

[b] Values in parentheses represent the standard deviation.

The legislative profile of these elections follows the dynamics of the governor's races, with average seat shares for the winning coalition supporting the gubernatorial candidate standing at about half of each state assembly (49.9%). By contrast, the same figure for the bottom eleven entries in table 12.2 is just over half that amount (27.8%), which reflects the incentives even minor parties have for forging alliances to winning gubernatorial candidates, as it allows them to make claims on the governor's largesse, an essential factor in shaping political careers.[56] The northeastern states stand out for their high average concentration of gubernatorial bandwagoning.

As a group, conservative subnational governments have represented an appreciable number of all state governments. Data for the 1982–2006 period reveal that 28% of Brazil's state governments have belonged to this cohort.[57] Conservative subnational governments can be subdivided into the more traditional category of governments of the north and northeast led by parties favored by the Arenista cohort (thirty-eight cases, or 21% of the total number of governments). Conservative governors have served mostly in the northern and northeastern regions, where a full 77% of all such officials have run states in these regions. Relaxing the geographic parameter adds just twelve more cases. If all PMDB-led governments are coded as centrist,[58] then most subnational governments have been middle of the road (56.9%), albeit with a majority of these being center-right, judging from alliances between the catchall PMDB and the traditional conservative parties. Correlations among the presence of rightwing parties, the northeast region, and the electoral dominance index are strikingly consistent during the period of Brazilian democracy.[59]

Turning to voter attitudes as a second set of indicators for conservative rule, I attempt to develop longitudinally consistent indicators that identify the characteristics typical of a supporter of conservatives. This is difficult because, unlike political elites, most Brazilian voters have neither strong ideological tendencies nor acute partisan identities.[60] But conservative voters do consistently evince several characteristics. First, conservative voters are significantly less likely to identify with a party. In keeping with the interpersonal and informal dynamics of clientele networks, these voters tend to be more loyal to personalities than to organizations.[61] Second, since clientelism is based on a hierarchical relationship between elites and subjects, voters tend to take their cues from political bosses who exchange particular rewards for constituent support. Consequently, voting for incumbents (*governismo*) is higher in places ruled by clientele networks, and these have tended to be the redoubts of conservative rule in Brazil.[62] Third, as a function of personalism and *governismo*, conservative voters have less regard for how well their representatives follow the letter of the law than how well they provide particularistic rewards to their clients. To coin a phrase used to describe São Paulo politician Ademar de Barros, these voters accept the logic of the popular phrase "he steals but he gets things done" (*rouba mas faz*).

TABLE 12.3.
Dimensions of conservatism among Brazilian voters

Survey item	Voters in the northeast			Voters in the north and northeast			Urban versus rural voters			Self-identified conservatives			Average N
	2006	2008	2010	2006	2008	2010	2006	2008	2010	2006	2008	2010	N
Partisan identity													
VB10	0.154	1.080	0.041	0.211	0.483	5.572*	0.765	1.014	0.128	2.624	*7.471**	0.000	1485
B21	**10.160***	12.916*	1.131	2.866	25.326*	0.999	0.852	51.879*	0.049	*7.051**	*7.948**	*6.696**	1499
CLIEN1			3.916*			14.656*			31.761*			0.026	2031
CLIEN2			0.215			4.481*			10.068*			0.003	285
Governismo													
VB3	28.985*	27.517*	20.443*	30.360*	26.201*	25.005*	12.830*	9.235*	0.001	1.230	1.075	0.000	1212
VB60			7.374*			1.749			3.572			*4.279**	1396
VB20		62.991*	110.310*		62.282*	70.028*		8.701*	16.516*		1.468	*9.455**	1248
VB61			14.784*			2.170			0.976			3.217	1282
Rouba mas faz													
RM9	16.057*			19.892*			14.024*			21.189*			1107
RM10	22.779*			24.101*			13.359*			34.251*			1104
RM14	5.376*			5.478*			1.730			9.899*			1095
EXC18	11.235*	4.962*	4.739*	21.500*	12.413*	7.270*	0.400	4.778*	2.179	0.004	1.393	0.234	1450

Source: Author's own analysis based on LAPOP Brazil survey data for 2006, 2008, and 2010.

Notes: LAPOP survey items are as follows. (1) Partisan identity: does not declare a partisan identity (VB10); no confidence in political parties (B21); reports frequent offers of particular benefits from politicians (CLIEN1) that influenced their vote for candidates (CLIEN2). (2) *Governismo:* voted for presidential (VB3) or gubernatorial (VE60) incumbent in the first round of the 2006 election; intended to vote in the next election for the incumbent or candidate of incumbent for president (VB20) or governor (VB61). (3) *Rouba mas faz:* believes that a politician's efficacy is more important than if he steals (RM9); believes that a politician who does a lot of public works and steals a little is better than an honest politician who is less effective (RM10); believes that a politician who steals but does a lot of public works deserves the support of the people (RM14); believes in the necessity of sometimes paying bribes (EXC18). Values are Pearson chi-squares. Boldfaced numbers with asterisks are statistically significant. Italicized numbers with asterisks indicate significant results contrary to hypotheses. Asterisks denote significance at the 0.05 level.

In keeping with the geographic distribution of electoral dominance, these characteristics should cluster spatially. Using three separate waves of the Latin American Public Opinion Project (LAPOP) survey of Brazilian voters (2006, 2008, and 2010), table 12.3 compares the attitudes of northeastern and northern voters versus those in the developed south and southeast. It also compares urban and rural voters and self-identified conservatives versus those voters declaring a different ideological proclivity. The data demonstrate a geographic association for each of the three dimensions of conservatism, though *governismo* and *rouba mas faz* have stronger regional associations than the lack of partisan identity,[63] probably because the weakness of partisanship is more systemic and national than regional.[64] Given that several of the reported associations disconfirm the hypothesized direction, the results for partisanship are indeterminate. Respondents in the northeast and north are more consistent in reporting a tendency to vote for incumbents or their candidates and, most notably, support dishonest politicians provided that they are effective and initiate many public works. The associations between geography and *governismo* and *rouba mas faz* hold up more consistently than the rural placement of voters or whether they self-identify as conservatives.

The data show that the geographic distribution of conservative rule in Brazil has had a lasting effect on the quality of democracy at the subnational level in terms of electoral competition and at the level of individual voters. Social inequality coincides with these structures. As the history of clientelism in these polities underscores, inequality has formed an integral part of what has sustained conservative rule across different regimes, development models, and the modernization of Brazil. The main consequences of this history are that the Brazilian right is not the result of a national movement or the product of an ideational or transnational network. It is particularistic and specific to the subnational polities that sustain and enable it to engineer influence in Brazilian politics.

The Erosion of Conservative Rule: Elections of 2006 and 2010

More than thirty years ago, Brazilian political scientist Gláucio Soares argued on the basis of electoral data that conservatives in Brazil were in decline.[65] The continued influence of conservatives during the post-1985 democracy seemed to prove him wrong.[66] The maturation of Brazilian democracy, especially since 2006, suggests that his predictions were correct, but thirty years too early. As the data in table 12.1 demonstrate, rightwing parties suffered notable declines in congress after 1998. Rightwing parties in 1994 went from gaining almost half and one-third of seats in the chamber of deputies and the senate, respectively, when PFL allied with PSDB to support Cardoso's first administration to winning a third of the chamber's seats and a mere 14% of seats in the senate.

In Brazil's fragmented party system the right's seat shares still afford conservatives an appreciable influence at the national level, but given the erosion of their gubernatorial holdings, the right's continued decline seems assured. Table 12.4 shows a secular erosion in shares of votes going to conservatives in gubernatorial elections, which are central to the right's control of subnational bailiwicks, because holding the executive is crucial to the distribution of patronage.[67] Notably, the right's losses in their redoubts in the northeast are as substantial as their losses in more developed states, suggesting that their clientele networks are no longer sufficient to maintain their control over these polities. In the 2006 cycle in particular, conservatives lost control of most of their bailiwicks in the northeast, and these losses came notably at the hands of leftists, who are less likely to distribute patronage to conservatives in return for political support.[68] In 2010, leftists held onto these gubernatorial seats in all of these states except Maranhão and Rio Grande do Sul, both cases in which conservatives staged a comeback in part by retaining control of rural clientele networks.

These trends put in a different light Mainwaring et al.'s observation more than ten years ago that the gap of electoral fortunes for conservatives in the northeast and the more industrialized states of the south and southeast would narrow.[69] Conservatives' electoral performance has not been indicative of a relative interregional narrowing but a more systemic decline. And it is the erosion of their command over executive offices in their bailiwicks that spells their doom more than anything that has challenged the right since the advent of democracy in 1985.

One related question is whether traditional conservatives are simply being displaced by a stronger center-right that shares conservatives' policy views. PSDB is the most likely successor and leader of formerly rightwing politicians because it has competed against Lula and the PT and now Dilma Rousseff for the presidency in every election since 1994. In each case a variety of rightwing organizations and voters who tend to self-identify as conservative have supported the PSDB.[70] Although the PSDB shares with conservatives a defense of free markets and hard-line approaches to crime, its members do not embrace these issues with the same intensity as shown by ideological scoring done by Power and Zucco.[71] Nor can the PSDB claim to be a more progressive form of conservative party, because its use of clientelism is almost as extensive. More to the point, if conservatives have been displaced, particularly in their old redoubts in the northeast, it is not the center-right they can blame but the left, and particularly parties such as the PT and the PSB.[72]

Gláucio Soares's prediction about the decline of the right was incorrect because his focus was on national parties and not the subnational bases that would sustain conservatives during the bureaucratic-authoritarian period and the first two decades

TABLE I2.4.
Regional averages of conservative candidates' share of gubernatorial votes, 1990–2010

Region	1990	1994	1998	2002	2006	2010	1990–98	1998–2010	Average loss, 1990–98 and 1998–2010	Net loss, 1990–2010
Center-west	56	39	22	3	34	24	39	21	–18	–32
North	52	47	49	39	20	39	49	37	–13	–13
Northeast	56	37	37	41	26	33	43	34	–9	–23
North and northeast	54	42	43	40	23	36	46	36	–11	–18
Southeast	35	28	18	25	0.002	8	27	13	–14	–27
South	42	36	38	16	20	39	39	28	–10	–3
South and southeast	39	32	28	21	10	24	33	21	–12	–15
Brazil	48	37	34	26	19	29	40	27	–13	–19

Sources: Tribunal Superior Eleitoral (www.tse.jsu.br) and Jairo Nicolau, "Dados Eleitorais do Brasil, 1982–2006" (Instituto Universitário de Pesquisas do Rio de Janeiro, Rio de Janeiro).

of democracy after 1985.[73] The decline of conservatives in recent years suggests a deeper erosion of rightwing influence, given that it is occurring at both the national and the subnational levels. This decline may lead to a reconfiguration of the right into a broadened center-right, but there are few clues at present as to how that might occur, if it happens at all.

Conclusion

Inequality has provided a basis for conservative rule and thus a consistent foundation for the influence of the right in Brazil since independence. But contrary to the erstwhile figure of the traditional, landed "coronel," conservatives have adapted to a modernizing economy, an expanding state bureaucracy, and the changing mass politics of contemporary democracy. True to the nature of their unequal social base, conservatives have used nonprogrammatic ties with voters to effectively navigate modern, democratic politics, thereby lessening the ambivalence of the right toward democracy. During the bureaucratic-authoritarian period, rightists participated in the semiopen congress and were tapped by generals to head states and major cities. These experiences gave Brazilian conservatives a flexible hybridity not as evident in the right wing of other Latin American polities. Brazilian conservatives have prospered under different kinds of dominant economic agendas (developmentalism and neoliberalism) and regime types, and this has been true as much during as after the Cold War.

The evident decline of rightwing influence in national politics during the democratic period occurred late, almost twenty years after the regime transition of 1985. But here, too, the trajectory of conservative politics has differed from the rest of the region. Decline did not coincide with the erosion of market-oriented reforms but with their continuation during the PT presidencies of Lula and Dilma. One reason that conservatives failed to stage a comeback but survived the erosion of their national influence was because the leftist presidents presented little threat of overturning social structures and economic policies that preserved inequality—the base of conservative rule in the poor states. They did not respond to high levels of inequality with the imposition of sweeping redistributionist policies. Poverty alleviation programs such as Bolsa Família remained well within parameters acceptable to the Brazilian right. These tendencies attenuated any remaining ideological polarization and threats to democracy by the right, allowing for the decline of conservatives without the fear of extrajudicial backlash.

The basis for conservative power did not emanate from the typical sources underscored in other cases analyzed in this volume. The Brazilian right did not depend on the emergence of an entrenched neoliberal, technocratic elite in the state bureaucracy. Although supportive of market-oriented reforms, the right has not embraced these policies to the exclusion of developmentalist approaches, including industrial policy. Brazil's conservatives were latecomers to the Washington Consensus agenda, and then they never adopted it wholly. The PSDB-PFL alliance that characterized the Cardoso government and was supported by big business was as inclined to pursue a heterodox policy emphasizing price stability on the one hand but government subsidies and loans to industry to support exports and firm-level adjustments on the other.

Conservatives' power base has remained subnational. The right has proven resilient in Brazil only insofar as it has retained control of its subnational bases: governorships and state legislatures. Even in the waning years of the Cold War and as the past threat of redistribution of land and income faded, conservatives maintained their power base in the states of the northeast and north. This fact also explained why political parties remained secondary to the influence of the right, so long as localized clientelist networks maintained conservatives' influence in national politics.

The erosion of rightist influence was a direct consequence of a change in this bottom-up calculus, and it presented a fundamental challenge to the notion that conservatives and their clientelist machines enjoyed perpetual influence in Brazilian politics. Frances Hagopian's seminal examination of traditional politics before and during the post-1985 democracy offers no explanation for the possible decline of conservatives, as she is most interested in "why they survive and continue to monopolize power."[74] Similarly, Power is most concerned with mapping out how the "durable political machines" undergirding conservatives contribute to their dominance in Brazilian democracy.[75] Weyland attributes such lasting influence to traditional politics that he sees these actors as undermining the capacity of the Brazilian state itself.[76] All of these treatments of Brazilian politics emphasize the continuity of conservative rule.

The spatial argument of conservative rule and decline in Brazil also offers several theoretical implications for the study of the right in Latin America. First among these is that conservatives whose power base is subnational and can rely on federal structures that enhance the continuity of their rule can be sufficiently entrenched to withstand national political and policy shifts. Having survived military rule, a transition to democracy, the failure of two of their chosen presidents (Sarney and Collor), an alliance with another (Cardoso), and finally two popular leftist presidencies in Lula and Dilma, conservatives proved resilient. To follow on the factors underscored by Kenneth M. Roberts in chapter 1 in this volume, no sustained, widespread movement against neoliberal reforms emerged in Brazil, so it was not economic policy that undermined conservatives. No new forms of civic associationalism on behalf of expanded citizenship rights or enhanced democratic accountability weakened conservatives. Rather, it was the electoral erosion of conservative rule in their erstwhile redoubts in the northeastern states that undermined rightist influence. For similarly organized rightwing forces in other Latin American countries, future research ought to focus on the local bases of conservative power—clientelist networks and their evolution, especially in the context of poverty and inequality—to understand more fully the sources of resilience and the weaknesses of conservatives in the region.

Brazil's conservatives have avoided the deinstitutionalization of the partisan right seen in other countries such as Argentina, Bolivia, Ecuador, and Venezuela, in large part because their basis of power remains imbedded in the unequal socioeconomic structures that separate regions such as the poor northeast and the developed south and southeast. Any reconfiguration of Brazilian politics that seeks to bring conservatives back into the centers of power will need to conceive first policy and electoral strategies that involve the center-right and allow conservatives to reclaim control of the public sector apparatus in their old subnational redoubts.

NOTES

1. Although many politicians on the center-right, center, and even on the populist left also favor these tendencies, politicians of the right are overrepresented within the pool of those elites who sustain the localist-clientelist dimensions of Brazilian democracy. See Timothy J. Power, "Elites and Institutions in Conservative Transitions to Democracy: Ex-Authoritarians in the Brazilian National Congress," *Studies in Comparative International Development* 31, no. 3 (Fall 1996): 72n26.

2. Scott Mainwaring, Rachel Meneguello, and Timothy J. Power, "Conservative Parties, Democracy, and Economic Reform in Contemporary Brazil," in *Conservative Parties, the Right, and Democracy in Latin America*, ed. Kevin J. Middlebrook (Baltimore: Johns Hopkins University Press, 2000), 164–222.

3. Kurt Weyland, *Democracy without Equity: Failures of Reform in Brazil* (Pittsburgh, PA: University of Pittsburgh Press, 1996).

4. Paulo Fábio Dantas Neto, *Tradição, Autocracia e Carísma: A Política de Antonio Carlos Magalhães na Modernização da Bahia (1954–1974)* (Rio de Janeiro: IUPERJ, 2006a).

5. James Scott, "Corruption, Machine Politics, and Political Change," *American Political Science Review* 63 (December 1969): 1142–58; *Comparative Political Corruption* (Englewood Cliffs, NJ: Prentice Hall, 1972).

6. Frances Hagopian, *Traditional Politics and Regime Change in Brazil* (New York: Cambridge University Press, 1996), 20.

7. Power (1996); Timothy J. Power, *The Political Right in Postauthoritarian Brazil* (University Park: Pennsylvania State University Press, 2000).

8. Cf. Alfred P. Montero, "No Country for Leftists? Clientelist Continuity and the 2006 Vote in the Brazilian Northeast," *Journal of Politics in Latin America* 2, no. 2 (2010): 113–53; "A Reversal of Political Fortune: The Transitional Dynamics of Conservative Rule in the Brazilian Northeast," *Latin American Politics and Society* 54, no. 1 (2012): 1–36.

9. Mainwaring et al. (2000).

10. Mainwaring et al. (2000); Power (2000).

11. Ruth Berins Collier and David Collier, *Shaping the Political Arena: Critical Junctures, the Labor Movement, and Regime Analysis in Latin America* (Princeton, NJ: Princeton University Press, 1991); Edward Gibson, *Class and Conservative Parties: Argentina in Comparative Perspective* (Baltimore: John Hopkins University Press, 1996).

12. Gibson (1996); Mainwaring et al. (2000, 166).

13. Paulo Fábio Dantas Neto, "O Carlismo para além de ACM: Estratégias Adaptativas de uma Elite Política Estadual," in *Governo, Políticas Públicas e Elites Políticas nos Estados Brasileiros*, ed. Celina Souza and Paulo Fábio Dantas Neto (Rio de Janeiro: Editora Revan, 2006b), 247–86; Timothy J. Power, "Blairism Brazilian Style? Fenrnado Henrique Cardoso and the 'Third Way' in Brazil," *Political Research Quarterly* 116, no. 4 (2001): 621.

14. Timothy J. Power, "Brazilian Politicians and Neoliberalism: Mapping Support for the Cardoso Reforms, 1995–1997," *Journal of Interamerican Studies and World Affairs* 40 (Winter 1998): 51–72.

15. Wendy Hunter, *The Transformation of the Workers' Party in Brazil, 1989–2009* (New York: Cambridge University Press, 2010).

16. Marcus André Melo, "Unexpected Successes, Unanticipated Failures: Social Policy from Cardoso to Lula," in *Democratic Brazil Revisited*, ed. Peter R. Kingstone and Timothy J. Power (Pittsburgh, PA: University of Pittsburgh Press, 2008), 161–84.

17. Pedro da Motta Veiga, "Brazil Trade Policy: Moving Away from Old Paradigms?," in *Brazil as an Economic Superpower? Understanding Brazil's Changing Role in the Global Economy*, ed. Leonardo Martínez-Diáz and Lael Brainard (Washington, DC: Brookings Institution Press, 2009), 113–36.

18. Victor Nunes Leal, *Coronelismo, Enxada e Voto: O Município e o Regime Representativo no Brasil* (São Paulo: Editora Alfa-Omega, 1976); Marcos Vinicios Vilaça and Roberto Cavalcanti de Albuquerque, *Coronel, Coronéis*, 3rd ed. (Rio de Janeiro: Tempo Brasileiro/EDUUF, 1988).

19. Edward Gibson, "Boundary Control: Subnational Authoritarianism in Democratic Countries," *World Politics* 58 (October 2005): 101–32; *Boundary Control: Subnational Authoritarianism in Federal Democracies* (New York: Cambridge University Press, 2012).

20. Hagopian (1996, 16).

21. Linda Lewin, *Politics and Parentela in Paraíba: A Case Study of Family-Based Oligarchy in Brazil* (Princeton, NJ: Princeton University Press, 1987); Dantas Neto (2006a).

22. Hagopian (1996).

23. Dantas Neto (2006a).

24. Hagopian (1996); Power (1996).

25. Power (2000).

26. Richard Snyder and David J. Samuels, "Legislative Malapportionment in Latin America: Historical and Comparative Perspectives," in *Federalism and Democracy in Latin America*, ed. Edward L. Gibson (Baltimore: Johns Hopkins University Press, 2004), 131–72.

27. Mainwaring et al. (2000); Power (2000; 2001).

28. Scott P. Mainwaring, *Rethinking Party Systems in the Third Wave of Democratization: The Case of Brazil* (Stanford, CA: Stanford University Press, 1999), 165–66; Martin Shefter, *Political Parties and the State: The American Historical Experience* (Princeton, NJ: Princeton University Press, 1994), 30–31.

29. Power (1996; 2000).

30. Hagopian (1996); David Samuels and Fernando Luiz Abrúcio, "Federalism and Democratic Transitions: The 'New' Politics of the Governors in Brazil," *Publius: The Journal of Federalism* 30, no. 2 (Spring 2000): 51–52.

31. Power (1996, 62–63).

32. Mainwaring et al. (2000, 182); Power, (2000).

33. Power (2000, 77).

34. For a comprehensive view of the migrations of the ARENA/PDS cohort, see Power (2000, 75, table 4.1). A comprehensive list of all of Brazil's rightwing parties can be found in Mainwaring et al. (2000, 180–81, table 6.3). Since the list includes as many as eighteen parties, some which were merged in later years, I simplify the presentation by referring to the larger parties—PFL, PL, PTB, and the various mergers involving PDS (which merged with the Partido Democrata Cristão in 1993 to form PPR; PPR merged with PTB and PP to form PPB in 1995). PFL changed its name to Democratas in 2007.

35. Mainwaring et al. (2000); Power (2000); Timothy J. Power and Cesar Zucco, "Estimating Ideology of Brazilian Legislative Parties, 1990–2005: A Research Communication," *Latin American Research Review* 44, no. 1 (2009): 218–46.

36. For support for market-oriented policies, see Power (1998); for social conservatism and opposition to land reform, see Mainwaring et al. (2000).

37. Ronald Ahnen, "The Politics of Police Violence in Democratic Brazil," *Latin American Politics and Society* 49, no. 1 (Spring 2007): 141–64.

38. Using Ahnen's data, I retested his hypotheses and found that the police homicide effect is conditioned on whether conservatives are trying to get back into power after suffering earlier losses, not when they are in a dominant position. See Alfred P. Montero, "Trading Spaces: The Endogenous Dynamics of Subnational Authoritarianism in Brazil" (paper presented at the meeting of the Latin American Studies Association, Toronto, Canada, October 6–9, 2011).

39. Power (2000).

40. Power (1996).

41. Barry Ames, *The Deadlock of Democracy in Brazil* (Ann Arbor: University of Michigan Press, 2001); Mainwaring (1999); Weyland (1996); "The Brazilian State in the New Democracy," in *Democratic Brazil: Actors, Institutions, and Processes*, ed. Peter R. Kingstone and Timothy J. Power (Pittsburgh, PA: University of Pittsburgh Press, 2000), 36–57.

42. Alfred P. Montero, "Devolving Democracy? Political Decentralization and the New Brazilian Federalism," and David Samuels, "Reinventing Local Government? Municipalities and Intergovernmental Relations in Democratic Brazil," in Kingstone and Power (2000, 58–98, 77–98).

43. Snyder and Samuels (2004).

44. Power (1996).

45. Power (2001, 623–24).

46. David Samuels, *Ambition, Federalism, and Legislative Politics in Brazil* (New York: Cambridge University Press, 2003) 85–88.

47. Hagopian (1996).

48. On the different strategies used by clientele networks to shape the vote, see Simeon Nichter, "Vote Buying or Turnout Buying? Machine Politics and the Secret Ballot," *American Political Science Review* 102, no. 1 (February 2008): 19–31.

49. Cf. Carlos Gervasoni, "A Rentier Theory of Subnational Regimes: Fiscal Federalism, Democracy, and Authoritarianism in the Argentine Provinces," *World Politics* 62, no. 2 (April 2010): 315; Ellis Goldberg, Erik Wibbels, and Eric Mvukiyehe, "Lessons from Strange Cases: Democracy, Development, and the Resource Curse in the U.S. States," *Comparative Political Studies* 41, no. 4–5 (2008): 477–514.

50. Given generally weak parties and high personalism in Brazilian elections, it was easier to code the scores of 3 than the scores of 1 and 2. The scoring was done "by hand" through a comparison of party labels in winning and rival coalitions, candidate profiles, and ideological profile of parties at the time of the election.

51. André Borges, "Rethinking State Politics: The Withering of State Dominant Machines in Brazil," *Brazilian Political Science Review* 1, no. 2 (2007): 108–36; Gervasoni (2010).

52. Borges (2007, 113). Notably, inclusion of the 2006 contest only moves two states listed in the top twelve a couple of ranks, but it does not greatly alter the results presented here.

53. The term is Borges's, who conducts a factor analysis that produces a state ranking not very different from my own.

54. Ames (2001).

55. Although reelection for governor was not legalized until 1998, several governors returned for nonconsecutive second or more terms during the period prior to 1998.

56. Samuels (2003).

57. The data reported here are taken from the author's own data set of Brazilian states.

58. Mainwaring et al. (2000, 178) omit PMDB from the conservative cohort because its deputies evince notable distance on their views and voting records from the right wing. This is true despite the historical circulation of former Arenistas into the PMDB.

59. Cf. Montero (2011).

60. Andy Baker, Barry Ames, and Lucio R. Rennó, "Social Context and Campaign Volatility in New Democracies: Networks and Neighborhoods in Brazil's 2002 Elections," *American Journal of Political Science* 50, no. 2 (April 2006): 382–99; Alberto Carlos Almeida, "Ideologia e Comportamento Eleitoral: Evidências de que a Ideologia Não É Importante para Explicar o Voto" (paper presented at the 15th Annual Meeting of ANPOCS, Caxambu, 2001); *Por Que Lula? O Contexto e as Estratégias Políticas que Explicam a Eleição e a Crise* (Rio de Janeiro: Editora Record, 2006); Yan de Souza Carreirão, "Identificação Ideológica, Partidos e Voto na Eleição Presidencial de 2006," *Opinião Pública* 13, no. 2 (November 2007): 307–39; David Samuels, "Sources of Mass Partisanship in Brazil," *Latin American Politics and Society* 48, no. 2 (Summer 2006): 1–27.

61. Mainwaring et al. (2000, 196–97).

62. Cesar Zucco, "Poor Voters vs. Poor Places: Persisting Patterns and Recent Changes in Brazilian Electoral Patterns" (unpublished manuscript, Princeton University, March 9, 2010).

63. Pearson chi-squares (X^2) are reported in table 12.3, but directionality was assessed from independent-sample t tests. Respondents from the center-west (Goiás, Mato Grosso, and Mato Grosso do Sul) were excluded to facilitate the comparison between the poorest and richest states. Respondents reporting nonvoting or blank or spoiled ballots were not included on relevant items. Missing and nonresponsive answers were excluded for all items.

64. Samuels (2006).

65. Gláucio Ary Dillon Soares, *Sociedade e Política no Brasil* (São Paulo: Difusão Européia, 1973).

66. Hagopian (1996); Mainwaring et al. (2000, 222); Power (2000).

67. Fernando Abrúcio, *Os Barões da Federação: Os Governadores e a Redemocratização Brasileira* (São Paulo: USP/Hucitec, 1998), chap. 3; Power (1996, 72); Samuels (2003).

68. Montero (2010, 113–53).

69. Mainwaring et al. (2000, 165).

70. Carreirão (2007).

71. Power and Zucco (2009; 2012).

72. Montero (2011).

73. Soares (1973).

74. Hagopian (1996, 20).

75. Power (1996; 2000).

76. Weyland (1996).

CHAPTER THIRTEEN

Argentina

The Difficulties of the Partisan Right and the Case of Propuesta Republicana

SERGIO MORRESI AND GABRIEL VOMMARO

Although forces of the right have ruled Argentina for much of the last hundred years, conservative political parties have played only a minor role. Several factors explain their limited influence, including the fragmentation of the upper classes, the divorce between partisan and nonpartisan elites, the Argentine history of coups—in which rightist forces played a leading role—and the fragmented party system that followed each dictatorship. But the major reason for the weakness of the partisan right is its inability to cope successfully with populist forces, especially in their Peronist version. Since the new democratic period started in 1983, various rightwing parties have tried to exorcise the curse of their electoral failure using different strategies. So far, the most promising path appears to have been the subnational direction followed by Republican Proposal (Propuesta Republicana, or PRO).

PRO has governed the City of Buenos Aires (CBA, the Argentine federal capital) since 2007 and now appears to be a strong competitor for the 2015 presidential elections. Born around the leadership of Mauricio Macri, a businessman with neoliberal ideas, PRO not only incorporates elements of the partisan and nonpartisan classical right, but also recruits figures from the major national-popular Argentine parties and from the world of think tanks and nongovernmental organizations (NGOs). This chapter explains PRO's relative success. We begin with a brief review of Argentine rightwing history, and explain the weakness of its partisan expressions. We also present the context of the emergence of PRO, wherein we explore the post–2001 crisis scenario, the weight of subnational politics in Argentina, and some peculiarities of the CBA. Next, we go on to explain the political growth of the party through the examination of data on PRO electoral outcomes and the party's figures. Finally, we offer some remarks on PRO's place in Argentinian political space.

The Partisan Right's Paths to Power

McGee Deutsch and Dolkart claim that, for an important part of the public inside and outside Latin America, the expression "Argentine right" seems redundant. Argentina is usually regarded as a sort of "Nazi paradise" where Peronism imposed fascist practices and the military waged genocide against its own people.[1] Nevertheless, these perceptions fail to consider that Argentina received more emigrated Jews than any other Latin American country; that while Peronism flirted with fascism, this political movement never imposed it; and that a portion of the Argentinian population resisted the criminal actions of the last dictatorship. More importantly, these perceptions are not accurate because they seem to consider that the only kind of right that existed in Argentina was an "extreme right," a socially reactionary, culturally conservative, and economically retrograde force.[2] This type of right only occupied a marginal place in Argentine politics, however, generally as a minor and dispensable ally of traditional elites. In fact, what we might call the "center-right" has held the leading roles since the end of the nineteenth century.

While it is true that center-right (i.e., conservative, liberal, and—later on—neoliberal) alliances have ruled the country for almost all of its history, it is also true that, for much of the time, they accomplish this task without the help of political parties.[3] What is the origin of this peculiarity of the Argentine case? Several factors help to explain this uniqueness, but two causes deserve to be highlighted. First, the surge of populism produced a new political cleavage in Argentine politics that superseded the traditional division between left and right, making it difficult for the right to succeed in elections. Second, choices made by political actors throughout the past century resulted in a weak democracy and a poorly institutionalized party system, both factors that inclined rightist leaders to pursue nonelectoral paths to power. A brief historical summary offers a better understanding.

Direct Partisan Participation, 1880–1943

In the 1880s, the elitist National Autonomist Party (Partido Autonomista Nacional, or PAN) kept full control of the Argentine political landscape through informally restricted franchise. PAN administrations promoted church and state separation and laissez-faire policies but maintained oligarchic political practices such as the manipulation of elections, cronyism, and lack of press freedom.[4] By the 1910s, PAN had become a state party that served as umbrella for the alliance between liberal and conservative elites that mobilized the lower classes as a strategy aimed at maintaining an orderly society.[5] This "conservative order"[6] finished in 1912 with the enforcement of the Sáenz Peña Law (guaranteeing secret and compulsory ballots for adult males), which opened the door to an unstoppable advance of the Radical Civic Union (Unión Cívica Radical, or UCR), a modern-type party that organized the urban middle-class ranks.[7]

The conservative reformers had hoped that the advance of the opposition would be gradual, but UCR obtained the presidency in 1916. In order to undermine the rightwing sources of power, UCR decreed federal interventions in the conservative provinces and ignored legislative controls.[8] In this new scenario, the traditional elites were not able to fulfill their hopes of forming a modern rightwing party with genuine chances of curbing UCR.[9] Excluded from the executive branch in a strongly presidential country, the alliance of elites was forced to watch as its territorial strongholds were taken by UCR, and it eventually became a weaker alliance of exclusively local parties. These local parties reunited in 1930, however, when a military coup overthrew the UCR government. Between 1930 and 1943 (a period known as the "infamous decade"), Argentina was ruled by Concordancia (the agreement), a conservative electoral front that proclaimed attachment to liberal and republican values while practicing fraud and bribery.

Populist Defiance, 1943–55

In 1943, a nationalist coup overthrew the Concordancia government. It was in this context that the political figure of Juan Perón emerged, and he was eventually elected president in free and fair elections in 1946.[10] The rise of Peronism redefined Argentine political identities. On the one hand, Peronism seemed to share the goals of the nationalist right (such as the formation of a "Christian order" that fostered harmony between classes), but the regime did not abjure from liberal and republican principles, nor did it advance in the pursuit of an extremist path.[11] On the other hand, while some conservative forces were co-opted by Peronism, the main leaders of Concordancia became the backbone of a fierce opposition, to the point of allying themselves with UCR and even with communism in an attempt to defeat Perón. This high level of challenge had two sources: first, that Perón built his movement explicitly confronting liberal-conservative sectors, and, second, the kind of state-centralized popular mobilization led by Perón precluded any territorial political work by other parties.[12] The strange arrangement of Peronist and non-Peronist forces in the political scenario of midforties Argentina marks, as Pierre Ostiguy has noted, the rise of a new cleavage that surpassed the traditional left/right division and persists today.[13]

The high/low cleavage explains the ways of being and acting in politics, linked with cultural forms rather than with ideologies: "high and low have to do with ways of *relating* to people; as such, they go beyond 'discourses' as mere words, and they include issues of accents, level of language, body language, gestures, ways of dressing, etc."[14] According to Ostiguy, the Peronist pole is oriented toward a strong personal leadership and popular culture. In contrast, the non-Peronist pole is inclined to a legalist impersonal authority and to a polished "proper" social behavior. As each of the poles have their own right and left, one can conclude that, because the Peronists rise, "Argentina's politics and its party system are structured as a double political spectrum."[15]

Direct Nonpartisan Participation, 1955–83

Prior to 1943, the right ruled or sought to rule Argentina through its own partisan organizations, but after Perón's victories the electoral path to power appeared to be closed. Over the following decades, the partisan Argentine right would choose another strategy: direct access to power by inserting liberal and conservative political figures inside the military (or military-surveilled) governments that characterized the new period.[16] In this strategy, some factions were more successful than others.

After the coup that overthrew Perón in 1955, the traditional elites were divided into two fronts: the *federalistas* and the *liberales*.[17] The former was a heterogeneous network of parties with regional scope, led by strongmen of rightist orientation and linked to major fractions of local bourgeoisies.[18] The latter was formed by the liberal elites of Buenos Aires who were strongly linked to the interests of agro-exporters (and, later, to the financial economy and capital-intensive industries). Unlike the *federalistas*, the *liberales* parties never achieved electoral success.[19] That does not mean that *liberales* lacked relevance but that, as happened to other socioeconomic elites not linked with the partisan right, their political activity was channeled almost exclusively through personal contacts with the state, other political parties (such as UCR), and the military high commands.[20] The peculiarities of the *liberales* resulted in the formation of a political class oriented toward technocracy and thus more permeable to neoliberal ideas.[21]

The 1955 coup also gave rise a new political force on the right: the rightwing Peronist trade unions. During the ban of Peronism (1955–73), unions were mobilized from the right/low quadrant of the political spectrum, with a combination of authoritarianism and representation in strange but clear collusion with *liberales, federalistas*, and nationalists in order to stop the growth of a Peronist force on the left. Despite differences on many issues, the anti-leftist identity of these four groups allowed them to act together in bizarre combinations throughout this period.[22] The connection between these different forces on the right broke up with the 1976 coup, because this last dictatorship was aimed at "re-founding the republic" and destroying Peronism's populist legacy.[23]

Nondirect Partisan Participation, 1983–2001

The right-authoritarian project broke down after the Argentine invasion of the Malvinas/Falkland Islands. It was then that Álvaro Alsogaray, traditional leading figure of the *liberales*, founded the Union of the Democratic Center (Unión del Centro Democrático, or UCEDE).[24] The new party shared some leading cadres and political agenda with the moribund military regime, but also criticized it for being insufficiently liberal in economics.[25] In the 1983 elections, UCEDE was the only nation-based center-right party to obtain two seats in the national congress.[26] After 1983, the growing heterogeneity and political fragmentation of Argentina facilitated the neoliberal seduction of middle-class urban sectors,[27] and by 1987 UCEDE had consolidated its position as the third political force. This achievement allowed the Buenos Aires *liberales* to hegemonize the right of the political field.[28]

UCEDE's electoral success in the early 1980s can be tracked partially to the entrance of a growing number of young constituents that formed a powerful militant core. This new core occupied a lower position in the Argentine political spectrum and wanted to leave behind the *liberales'* tactic of reaching power through influencing other major players.[29] But the party's "historical" leaders (i.e., its founders and some allied *federalistas*) resisted the newcomers' rise and stood firm in their strategy of offering their cadres to a government that would accept them as allies.[30] Their opportunity came as a result of the neoliberal shift of the Peronist president Carlos Menem.[31]

The entry of UCEDE's leading figures into the Peronist government had mixed results: Menem's administration carried a neoliberal agenda, but its success produced the electoral decline of UCEDE, because its constituents started to see the Justicialist Party (Partido Justicialista, or PJ) as a viable option. By the midnineties, the Argentine right was, in one way or another, inside the Peronist government. This was something completely new, as one of the Argentine right's main features had been its rejection of Peronism. In 1997, however, Menem's former economy minister, Domingo Cavallo, founded his own party, Action for the Republic (Acción por la República, or AR). Cavallo defended the neoliberal agenda of Menem's government but accused him of being unable to carry it forward without corruption.[32] In partnership with other minor parties, AR quickly became the Argentine third party, allowing some liberal-conservative leaders to dream of a competitive right force that would not be "swallowed" by the major parties, as had happened with UCEDE.[33] Nevertheless, that dream was not fulfilled, largely because Cavallo joined the Alianza administration (the Alliance, an electoral front formed by UCR and the Front for a Country in Solidarity, also known as the Frente por un País Solidario, or FREPASO) that won the presidency in 1999. Because Cavallo and AR played major roles in the last months of the Alianza, they were blamed for the 2001 crisis. At the dawn of twenty-first century, rightist ideas were delegitimized for much of Argentine society.

Born from the Ashes: The Rise of PRO

In 2001, a few months before the collapse of the Alianza government, a group of political and social activists began to meet at the Creer y Crecer (To Believe and to Grow) Foundation in order to design political and policy projects. The foundation had been created by Francisco de Narváez, a Peronist entrepreneur who had ventured into politics, but was headed by businessman Mauricio Macri. Macri is the heir to one of the largest Argentine fortunes (his father was the head of SOCMA holding, an economic group that had grown exponentially in the 1970s and 1980s, mainly owing to state contracts), and in 2001 he was president of Boca Juniors (one of the two most popular soccer teams in Argentina). Macri had shown an interest in entering into politics in the midnineties but had delayed this decision until 2002, when he announced his candidacy for mayor of the CBA with an agenda that mixed neoliberal policies with moral issues and highlighted the newness, youth, and the technical background of his entourage. In the 2003 CBA elections, Macri won the first round but was defeated in the run-off election. Contradicting the expectations of the media, however, Macri and his people did not quit politics after this defeat, nor did they become a faction in a major party. On the contrary, they began to strive to strengthen the party.

The first years of the new century were a turbulent time in Argentina. Deep economic troubles and rising social mobilization framed a bleak landscape for political parties. So, why did Macri and his followers pick that moment to found a new party? Why did they prefer to focus on the CBA and reject campaigning nationwide? Why did they choose to strengthen their new political organization and not offer themselves as outsider leaders for other parties? To understand the reasons behind these foundational decisions, it is necessary to explain the context of PRO's rise and to describe in more detail its main characteristics.

Crisis and Opportunity

The depth of the 2001 Argentine crisis can be hardly exaggerated. The relative success of the institutional stabilization implemented by the acting government of Peronist president Eduardo Duhalde could not obliterate the consequences of the socioeconomic and political crisis that had been maturing in the 1990s and exploded in December 2001 when Argentinian citizens hit the streets, shouting, *¡Que se vayan todos!* "They must all go!"[34] In this chaotic context, Commitment to Change (Compromiso para el Cambio, or CPC) was founded. CPC (the original organization that would later become PRO)[35] was not a new label for an old party, nor was it a split of a traditional political movement. Unlike the case of Uribe in Colombia (analyzed by Laura Wills-Otero in chap. 8, this volume), Mauricio Macri was not the former leader of a traditional party who created his own electoral instrument. He was an outsider—coming from the corporate world—whose personal decision to enter politics seems to have been triggered by the 2001 crisis.[36]

The crisis situation must be considered in two ways. First, to be an outsider at a time when political parties and traditional leaders were seriously delegitimized was a clear competitive advantage. In fact, PRO widely emphasized this point, presenting itself as the only "really new" player in the field.[37] Second, founding a political party is a difficult task that requires the organizational support of a system of territorial, economic, and professional networks. The human resources necessary to staff these networks are not usually available for recruitment to a new political party. In the "critical juncture" of the 2001 crisis, however, some of these actors suddenly became available. Seeing themselves bereft of genuine electoral chances, and attracted by Macri's discourse and poll numbers, political figures from minor rightist parties, as well as militants and leaders from UCR and PJ, joined the new party.

The national context, together with some characteristics of the CBA (see below), thus allowed a moment of political experimentation, an auspicious "political opportunity structure."[38] Indeed, the context was, as a congressman interviewed in 2011 told us, "a unique occasion to create a completely brand new party."[39] To take advantage of this "unique occasion," and since the electoral timetable established the CBA elections in August 2003, Macri decided to dissolve the political alliance that linked him to De Narváez.[40] While the latter sought closer links with Peronism in order to enter national politics, the former chose to prioritize both the autonomy of the new party and the local contest in the CBA.

Subnational Strategy

In order to understand the local strategy adopted by PRO in 2003, it is necessary to focus both on the peculiarities of Argentine subnational politics in the last decade of the twentieth century and on the unique characteristics of the CBA. Argentina is shaped by a weak and unbalanced federal system: most of the provinces depend economically on the national government and, at the same time, the national government depends on the provinces to obtain political support.[41] As federalism provides each territory with its own constitution and authorities, Argentine subnational politics have always been important. In addition the neoliberal-oriented decentralization process undertaken by the military regime in the 1970s and continued by democratic governments in the 1990s was expected to increase the weight of subnational politics. But this did not happen for three reasons: first, the federal government did not provide the funds to support the new obligations of the provinces;

second, the sequence in which decentralization policies were adopted (starting with administrative reform, with fiscal and political transformations being implemented only years later and only partially) was not helpful; and, third, the devolution path was led by national administrations rather than by subnational coalitions.[42] As result of the failed decentralization, the balance of power between the national and provincial governments was not modified to a large extent,[43] but the process certainly helped to accelerate the federalization and fragmentation of the Argentine party system.[44] Thus the traditional power of the provincial bosses (*caudillos*) and the autonomy of municipal leaders were strengthened.[45] The course of reterritorialization was sinuous because it occurred simultaneously with a socioeconomic transformation and a political representation crisis with deeper roots and wider scope.[46] Nevertheless, some districts attained a remarkable autonomy during this time, as was the case with the CBA.

The CBA is located on the west coast of the River Plate estuary and has a size of 78 mi^2 (202 km^2). It is surrounded by Greater Buenos Aires (GBA), a 1,035 mi^2 (2,681 km^2) territory of the Province of Buenos Aires consisting of twenty-four counties thoroughly integrated with the CBA. With 2.9 million inhabitants (Argentina has 40 million, and GBA 13 million), the CBA is the most populated city in the country. Traditionally, the CBA's residents (*porteños*, in reference to the Buenos Aires port) possess a level of income and education far superior to the Argentine average and enjoy the best public services in the country, wider job opportunities (the CBA is the country's business center), and a variety of cultural and leisure activities.[47]

As the capital city of Argentina, the CBA was under the authority of the national government but had a municipal council elected by the people. The political forces that enjoyed majority status at the national level often were not favored by the *porteños*, who customarily supported opposition candidates, whether in democratic or undemocratic conditions. After 1946, the CBA thus became the most important anti-Peronist stronghold, and it has also been the focal point of almost all Argentine third parties (between 25% and 50% of the national vote for UCEDE and AR came from the CBA).[48]

In 1993, in order to gain UCR's institutional support to attempt his reelection, PJ's president, Carlos Menem, agreed to a wide constitutional reform agenda, including a special autonomy status for the CBA. At that time, the trends that would lead to the turn-of-the-century crisis were already developed, especially in the CBA.[49] The poor performance of Peronism in the CBA was customary, but it escalated in the mid-1990s, partly because of PJ's neoliberal conversion.[50] At the same time, UCR's accord with Menem's reelectoral ambition triggered a crisis in the main opposition party. In this context, a new center-left force emerged (the Broad Front, also known as the *Frente Grande*, that later integrated FREPASO) and became a major player in CBA's politics.[51]

Through the 1994 constitutional reform, the CBA became able to draft its own constitution; elect its mayor, who had previously been designated by the president; and establish its own electoral system and schedule.[52] In 1996, Fernando de la Rúa, a traditional and conservative UCR leader, won the first CBA mayoral elections. A few months later, UCR and FREPASO formed the Alianza that obtained a landslide victory in the 1997 legislative elections and won the presidency in 1999. As a campaign advertisement of that time said, the *porteños* helped their mayor to walk the hundred yards separating his office from the Casa Rosada (Argentine executive mansion). Nevertheless, the poor performance of President de la Rúa quickly led to Alianza's demise and to the deepening of the political representation crisis. It is true that the situation did not affect all actors in the same way, because, at the national level, the Peronist family (which occupied the "low" quadrants in Ostiguy conceptualization of Argentinian politics) was significantly less affected than the non-Peronist one (the high parties).[53] But the CBA's local Peronist crisis preceded the general one.[54] Also, as noted by Tomás Bril Mascarenhas, the party crisis had different intensities in different districts, and the CBA was most affected by far, as in the CBA an authentic "collapse of the party system" occurred.[55] The magnitude of the CBA's party system crisis, jointly with the national situation and the customary *porteño* support of the third parties, facilitated the political opportunity structure seized by PRO.

PRO's local strategy is not a completely new idea in Argentina. In the 1970s, the military dictators had already thought that the only way the center-right parties could defeat the traditional populist movements was to begin locally and slowly moving onto the national level.[56] The plan failed owing to the military regime collapse. The success of the strategy was not unthinkable in a new context, however, especially if some peculiarities of PRO are taken into account.

The Management Party

In 2003, after the center-left Peronist Néstor Kirchner was elected president for the Front for Victory (Frente para la Victoria, or FPV), Macri announced his candidacy for mayor of the CBA. His campaign was presented as part of a "new politics." PRO's novelty is a matter of controversy, because more than half of its leaders are experienced politicians with traditional backgrounds. But Macri's organization was born as a "new kind" of party, at least in a sense. As explained by Allan Sikk, "project of newness" parties (such as Berlusconi's Forza Italia in Italy) are neither purifiers of traditional ideologies nor prolocutors of a new and circumscribed demand;

they are new players who confidently step onto the territory of established parties to change the manner of doing politics rather than the contents of it.[57] In the case of PRO, the change of manner points to a managerial approach to politics that seems to have been successful at electoral level, and also to the construction of the party.

In order to agglutinate the heterogeneous elements available as a result of the political representation crisis (former UCR, PJ, and rightist incumbents that approached the new organization) and present itself at the same time as a new kind of party, PRO openly rejected the left/right traditional cleavage and proposed a neat management approach to public administration, combined with the promotion of some postmaterial values, which has allowed it to attempt a reframing of political debate. Through focusing on local administration and postmaterial values, PRO departed from the previous Argentine rightist parties experience and approached the so-called "new right."

The use of the term "new right" can be misleading.[58] But it could be useful to us because of the anomalous way in which PRO is a party of the right, at least in an Argentine historical perspective. PRO's uniqueness becomes clear when some political, social, and cultural values of its cadres are taken in account.[59] According to our 2011 survey, PRO leaders have consistently conservative positions on cultural issues (58% oppose even discussing a law legalizing abortion, and an astounding 77% support stricter regulation of foreign immigration in a country built by immigrants). Also, almost 60% of PRO cadres dislike the power of the unions and believe it must be reduced and 92% are in favor of controlling social protests, positions that traditionally belong to the Latin American right. At the same time, PRO leaders do not look so conservative regarding government intervention: a majority (77%) accepts that the reduction of income differences between social groups is a government's duty. This finding is compatible with the wide rejection (62%) of the idea that public health and education must be available only to people who cannot afford them through their own means. PRO leaders are also profoundly pro-democracy (90% think that it is the best political regime). Nevertheless, more than half of PRO leaders (58%) assert that the market is the better and more efficient mechanism of distribution. The ideology of PRO leaders seems to be culturally conservative, socially restrictive, and market oriented, but also democratic and open to government intervention in order to reduce socioeconomic differences.

At the time PRO was founded, the heterogeneity of its membership, mixed ideological positions of its cadres, and strong leadership of Macri misled some observers who had taken for granted that the newborn party was a sort of personal and temporary tool for Macri's political entrance. PRO was actually a party on a path of institutionalization, although this process was weak and had labile contours, as is the case in the vast majority of Argentine parties.[60]

How to Construct a Successful Right-of-Center Party in Contemporary Argentina

To explain the electoral success of PRO in the CBA, we first examine the different factions composing the PRO party and their ideology. Next, we offer some notes about diverse PRO political strategies and show that they are related not only with the widening of the electoral bases of the party, but also with its internal diversity.

Different Factions within the Party

PRO is made up of a combination of pieces of preexisting parties and different types of outsiders. This heterogeneity can be organized into five factions,[61] all of which dispute the leader's favor. The first one, which we call the "right faction," was formed by some minor *federalistas* parties (such as the Buenos Aires Partido Demócrata, or Democratic Party), some declining *liberales* parties (like AR), some minor conservative parties (such as the Partido Nacionalista Constitucional, or Nationalist Constitutionalist Party), as well as some former cadres of UCEDE and leaders of Buenos Aires liberalism that had played major roles in the last military dictatorship (such as Santiago de Estrada, who was secretary of social action in the de facto government). In 2003, this faction was doubly important: it not only had a relevant ideological role, but also made it possible for PRO to be present at elections.[62] It also provides some important actors, such as PRO's leader in the congress, Federico Pinedo, and some political economic cadres trained in neoliberal ideas. Thanks to this faction, PRO built specific political alliances at a national level with some provincial traditional conservative parties.

The second group was mostly composed of young professionals from think tanks and NGOs linked to research and promotion of public and social policies. We call this group the "NGO faction." In this faction, made up mainly of newcomers to politics, the weight of former members of the Grupo Sophia is especially important. This group was a think tank of neoliberal orientation created in the 1990s by Horacio Rodríguez Larreta, vice mayoral candidate in 2003. Most of the members of this faction were educated in Catholic high schools and studied social sciences degrees in private and confessional universities.

Leaders of the corporate world compose the third group, which we call the "business faction." It is a homogeneous faction, with solid business experience (mostly in technical and financial positions) and with close ties to Macri. The links between Macri and this group can hardly be exaggerated, since most of its members were former SOCMA senior employees who had already previously accompanied him when he was president of Boca Juniors.

The fourth group, which we call the "radical faction,"[63] is composed of individuals (or minor groups) coming from UCR, mainly of second rank in their own party who already worked in the CBA government and felt themselves displaced because, in 2003, Aníbal Ibarra, the Alianza's acting mayor, had oriented a more center-left Peronist coalition. Some of them had relevant grassroots organizations, however, and knew Macri from his time in the soccer business.

The fifth and last group, which we call the "Peronist faction," were PJ members from the CBA who faced a difficult situation in 2003: their own candidate in the district, Daniel Scioli, was chosen by Kirchner as running mate for the vice presidency. At the same time, for the CBA, President Kirchner favored a center-left alliance that relegated them. The offer to take major roles in the PRO campaign, when polls already showed that Macri could become Mayor, thus seemed advantageous to them. This group provided PRO with linkages to the popular electorate as well as to a grassroots organizations network mainly in the south, the poorest zone of the city.

The five factions do not work in the same way. Three of them (Peronists, radicals, and rightists) run like factions *stricto sensu*: as organizing groups in domestic competition. The other two (business and NGO factions) can be thought of in that way because of their internal cohesion in sociological and cultural terms, but they do not always work in a cooperative way. The business and NGO factions are much more alike. Both are formed by mostly inexperienced politicians; both have expertise-based incumbents and they are more deeply involved in the PRO party than radicals and Peronists (some of whom did not officially abandon their original parties). The heterogeneous conformation of the party also functions as a sort of division of labor. Each faction fills different roles. The experienced incumbents manage political areas in local government (mainly rightist), do legislative work (mostly radicals), develop grassroots political activism (mostly Peronist), and run electoral tasks when the elections come. The inexperienced incumbents work at social ministries (mostly NGO professionals) and manage the party and city finances (mostly businessmen).

The heterogeneity of the factions that compose PRO requires us to be careful when analyzing the ideology of this party. According to the results of our 2011 survey reported in table 13.1, the different factions have different ideas on many subjects. In cultural terms, the right, Peronist, and the business factions are closer to the rightist ideology as defined in Luna and Rovira Kaltwasser's introduction to this volume. Their incumbents are the ones who least agree with the intervention of the state to reduce the social differences, who agree in greater proportion with the idea that the market is the best and most effective mechanism of resource allocation, and who defend a kind of public policy of health and education oriented only to those people who cannot acquire those goods in the market.

TABLE 13.1.
The heterogeneous ideology of PRO incumbents

Issue	All (%)	Business (%)	NGOs (%)	Right (%)	Radical (%)	Peronist (%)
Immigration control	76.9	80	76.9	80	63.7	100
Leave behind the debates on human rights linked to the last dictatorship	61.5	77.7	33.3	80	57.1	72.8
Legalization of abortion	42.3	44.4	40	30	71.5	36.4
Support of state intervention to reduce inequalities	76.9	80	77	60	100	72.8
The market as the best mechanism of distribution	57.5	66.7	46.7	80	42.1	54.6
Public education and health support for the poor	38.5	22.2	33.3	60	28.6	45.4
Reduction of union power in society	59.6	77.8	73.3	60	42.9	36.4
Control of social protest	92.3	100	93.4	90	71.4	100
Self-consideration as right of the center	42.3	77.3	20	70	14.3	36.4
Rejection of left-right classification	13.5	0	26.7	0	28.6	9

The radical faction has positions nearer to the center and, in some cases, to the left: they agree with discussing a law legalizing abortion and have greater disagreement than the rest (except the NGO faction) that it is necessary to leave behind the debates on human rights linked to the last dictatorship, and to adopt stricter immigration measures. They agree entirely that the state must intervene in the economy to reduce inequalities, and they are less in favor than the others of defending the market as the best mechanism of resource allocation. At the same time, along with the Peronists, the radicals agree the least that the power of the unions in Argentinian politics must be reduced.

Finally, the NGO faction seems to set the tone in PRO ideology taken as a whole. The survey responses of their members place them, in almost all the subjects, nearer to the average of the total of the incumbents' responses. The proximity with Catholic ideas, especially with social Catholicism, makes the NGO faction a combination of conservative values in a cultural dimension (they are mostly against legalizing abortion); in some aspects of politics (they support the reduction of the power of the unions in politics); and some social-liberal ideas in other facets of politics (human rights) and the economy (state intervention).

This heterogeneity of political ideas of PRO incumbents has meant that, in the local house of representatives, PRO's vote was divided in the case of some laws connected with cultural and religious matters, such as same-sex marriage. This ideological diversity, as much between the factions as inside them, suggests that PRO oscillates between ideological pragmatism, especially when governing, and positions more directly linked with the traditional right (from liberal or conservative lineage). At the same time, because of PRO's attempts to build a political identity "beyond the left and the right," other political cleavages were proposed: "Citizens against politicians" and "federal district against national government" are some of the ways in which PRO tried to reframe political identities.

Electoral Results and Strategies

Since the beginning, the main factions of PRO aimed at gaining immediate access to municipal power to serve as a solid springboard to the national stage.[64] This goal to win elections quickly was probably the first uniting aspect among the different groups.

The 2003 campaign was framed in terms used by liberal-conservative forces, such as "efficiency" and "serious economy." Other topics that pointed to "moral questions," such as "zero corruption" and "political cost," were also used. Finally, the PRO campaign ventured into a new vein of social sensitivity, including in its discourse terms such as "universal social security" and "integration of lower strata" that were commonplace in postcrisis Argentina across the entire political spectrum. On the whole, PRO's political discourse was aimed at appealing not only to traditional right voters, but also to all middle-class *porteños*, especially to those that had become outraged at the political elites.[65]

The public presentation as an outsider was linked to Macri's disdain for "politicians" and the use of the political machine and the "taxpayers' money." Despite this strategy, the weight that groups associated with "old politics" still had in the new party, as well as the past of the leader linked to Menem's neoliberal government, resulted in a firm rejection of PRO by a good proportion of the electorate. Even though Macri said that he was "wrong to support the re-election of Menem," the identification of PRO with the right of the 1990s promoted by the opposition was successful and contributed to Macri's defeat among the progressive middle classes. Also, his choice of running mate, Horacio Rodríguez Larreta, a man of technocratic profile and patrician surname, seemed to confirm Macri's difficulties in breaking with the past. Despite having won more votes in the first round than the candidate of the center-left (37.55% against 33.54%), he was defeated in the *ballotage* (53.5% against 46.5%).[66] On the day of his defeat, Macri asserted, "we do not accept being confined to ideological labels that today are meaningless. We are a plural and open force." But this plurality was still under construction. Despite the defeat, PRO won eighteen seats in the city council (the CBA council has sixty seats), plus six for its unofficial allies from the Re-Create for Growth Party (Recrear para el Crecimiento, or RECREAR) and began a slow but systematic process to institutionalize the party and attract new members.

As shown in a study based on ecological regression, Macri's party inherited votes from UCEDE and AR.[67] But the same study shows that it also drew votes from the then-fragmented traditional parties (UCR and PJ). In fact, PRO, like AR before it and differently from traditional Argentine rightist parties, is not an anti-Peronist organization, and for that reason it was able to enjoy a larger potential electorate.[68] In the first round of elections in 2003, Macri reconstituted a social alliance that had already been successful in the 1990s (the one that had been built by Menem's Peronism). PRO subsequently managed to win at the same time in wealthier districts and in some poorer districts of CBA. In this election, however, Macri was defeated in middle-class neighborhoods, which are numerically crucial. In the second round, Macri managed to maintain control of the wealthy districts of the north, but he was defeated in the slums of the south (with the exception of La Boca, which is home to the football club of the same name, of which Macri was president).

To better understand PRO electoral growth, we focus briefly on the evolution of its performance in first round of elections for head of government and for national deputies from 2003 to 2011 in four communes (electoral districts into which the CBA was divided after the 2008 administrative reform). The communes we have chosen are socially and geographically divergent. Commune 2 is the most homogeneous wealthy district in the northern part of the CBA and the traditional electoral fortress of the right. Commune 13 is an upper middle-class area, traditionally identified with a non-Peronist vote and an important section of votes for progressive forces in the 1990s. Commune 5 is a typical middle-class, mostly non-Peronist area. Finally, commune 8, in the southern part of the city, includes the poorest CBA slums in which territorial and face-to-face politics play an important role in everyday residents' sociability.

Looking at the numbers included in figure 13.1, we can draw some conclusions. First, the main increase in the flow of votes to PRO occurs between the 2003 and 2007 elections. In the 2011 election, however, PRO manages to keep most of the votes captured four years earlier, especially among the middle and lower classes, but its power does not increase any further. Thus it is in the 2007 electoral strategy where the critical conjuncture of PRO electoral success should be found. Second, PRO manages to position itself early as the electoral choice in upper-class districts and among traditional voters for rightwing parties. Third, in 2007, PRO attracted a high proportion of the upper middle-class votes, which during the 1990s had mostly gone to progressive options. Fourth, the vote of the inhabitants of middle-class neighborhoods grew considerably between 2003 and 2007, but fell only slightly in 2011. Fifth, the percentage of the PRO vote in poor neighborhoods of the south was

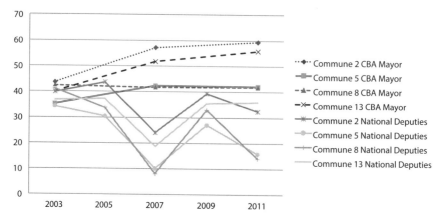

Figure 13.1. Evolution of PRO votes in four communes, 2003–7. Note that PRO was Compromiso para el Cambio in 2003. For Commune 2, section 19 was taken into account before 2008; for Commune 5, sections 8 and 9 were taken into account before 2008; for Commune 8, section 22 was taken into account before 2008; for Commune 13, section 16 was taken into account before 2008. *Source:* Electoral data from the Ministerio del Interior

the only one that did not grow throughout this cycle. Sixth, a striking difference can be observed between the vote for mayor of the CBA and that for national congressmen, which is perceptibly lower and changeable, probably owing to the lack of a PRO presidential candidate in 2007 and 2011. In summary, although PRO captured a heterogeneous electorate (through its ability to take sectors traditionally elusive for the right), it captured more electoral support in wealthier districts, and its vote was steady when local elections did not coincide with presidential campaigns, suggesting it might have some difficulties in becoming a national political force.

In 2005, Mauricio Macri presented his candidacy for national congress deputy for the CBA and forged an official alliance with RECREAR. The Republican Proposal Alliance (Alianza Propuesta Republicana), which later would become PRO, was born. In these elections, PRO won by 34% of votes, obtained six seats in the congress, and added thirteen more legislators in the city council, which it now dominated.

Between 2005 and 2007, Macri did not attend the national congress because he said it was a "boring and meaningless task." He used the time to flirt with the idea of a wide center-right alliance for the next presidential elections that included López Murphy (from RECREAR) and Jorge Sobisch, the Neuquén province governor for the Neuquén Popular Movement (Movimiento Popular Neuquino, or MPN), a traditional *federalista* party that converted to neoliberalism. But in April 2007, a teachers' union demonstration in Neuquén ended in excessive police repression and the murder of a union activist. The fresh memories of the police repressions of 2001 were revived, and Macri decided to break the alliance with MPN, not present a presidential candidacy, and rerun for the mayoralty of the federal district.

In 2007, even though Cristina Fernández de Kirchner, from the Peronist center-left FPV, won at the national level, PRO achieved a landslide victory in elections for mayor of the CBA and obtained a decent third place in the Province of Buenos Aires (where it was allied with the center-right Peronist de Narváez, the entrepreneur who had supported the Believe and Grow Foundation). Macri ran for the CBA office accompanied by Gabriela Michetti, a former leader of the Christian Democrats, a small party of Catholic social orientation, providing a semblance of social sensitivity and a progressive hue to the formula. PRO obtained 45% of vote in the first round and an astounding 61% on the second. After this victory, PRO grew in other electoral districts (including the provinces of Buenos Aires, Salta, and Santa Fe), and quickly consolidated in the federal district.

This victory was, at least partially, the result of a shift to the center of the political spectrum. Some traditional figures of the right were hidden during the campaign, and the political discourse lost some of its neoliberal flavor. PRO candidates followed the instructions of the campaign spin-doctor Jaime Durán Barba, who suggested fiercely to reject any ideological identification and to highlight the "newness" of the party. This rejection of ideological identification and the resistance of Macri to strongly endorsing RECREAR's López Murphy's candidacy for the senate produced some bitter arguments in the PRO alliance and, eventually, a breakup. The anti-populist campaign, headed by López Murphy, was the reason why Macri did not openly support him. After PRO's triumph, López Murphy's leadership in RECREAR was contested between those who wanted to maintain an independent party and those who wanted to merge with Macri's government; the latter faction won, and by 2009 the fusion was complete.

While in 2003 Macri showed some sympathy with Néstor Kirchner's new government, and in 2005 ambiguously characterized it, in 2007 the PRO leader took the place of opposition vacant in the city after the weakening of López Murphy. Against the candidacy of the minister of education of the national government, Daniel Filmus, Macri appeared to be the main opponent, and also a guarantee of the city's autonomy against a supposed colonization by the federal government. Moreover, the PRO campaign abandoned traditional partisan rallies, replacing them with personal visits by Macri to citizens. The advertising format acquired a systematic, strong identity. The party definitively adopted yellow as its color, and proposed television spots and posters on the streets with short slogans, associated with politics as management but also with the promotion of state intervention, which helped PRO to move away from its rightist profile. Positivity and the rejection of ideological confrontation were translated into "optimistic" slogans, such as *Va a estar bueno Buenos*

Aires "Buenos Aires will be cool." This strategy was combined with the already-classic attempt to build a discourse based on management: "For every assault [from national government], we offer a proposal" was another major campaign slogan. Unlike the elections of 2003, in 2007 PRO managed to win middle-class neighborhoods, thus attaining a heterogeneous electorate that combined social and ideological sectors: middle and upper classes, non-Peronist progressive votes, and traditionally right votes. The heterogeneity of this constituency corresponds to the heterogeneity of groups forming the party. That they had been able to present PRO as a new political force, detached from their identification with the neoliberal right and even more so from the traditional political parties, also corresponds to this heterogeneity of components that formed the new force.

As in the Uribe Vélez cabinet in Colombia described by Wills-Otero (chap. 8, this volume), PRO's first cabinet was a combination between experienced political leaders and newcomer technocrats linked to the private sector. As shown in table 13.2, some groups, such as NGO professionals and businessmen, are represented more than others. It is also clear that even if PRO rightist groups are not the most important quantitatively, they managed an important quota of values production and economic policies. It is also striking that there was only one minister from the radical

TABLE 13.2.
Macri's first cabinet

Minister	Area	Faction	Previous political experience?
Horacio Rodríguez Larreta	chief of cabinet	NGO	yes
Néstor Grindetti	finance	business	no
Guillermo Montenegro	security and justice	NGO	yes
Jorge Lemus	health	NGO	yes
Mariano Narodowsky[a]	education	NGO	yes
Daniel Chaín	urban development	business	no
Hernán Lombardi	culture and tourism	radical	yes
Esteban Bullrich[b]	social development	right	yes
Francisco Cabrera	economic development	right	no
Juan Pablo Piccardo[c]	environment and public space	business	no
Marcos Peña	general secretary	NGO	no

Sources: Argentinian newspapers *Clarín, La Nación,* and *Página/12,* as well as the CBA government website, available at http://www.buenosaires.gob.ar/.
[a]Replaced in 2009 by Esteban Bullrich from the right faction.
[b]Replaced in 2008 by María Eugenia Vidal from the professional faction.
[c]Replaced in 2009 by Diego Santilli from the Peronist faction.

faction. It is certain that PRO's first CBA cabinet privileged the people whom Macri trusted. The arrival of Diego Santilli to the government in 2009 meant the reinforcement of the Peronist faction, which was not previously represented in the cabinet. In the composition of Macri's cabinet, we can also see the debatable newness of PRO. The partisan actors all had political experience in public office, but the businessmen had no experience in state management. In the case of the professionals, the situation is more heterogeneous: most of them had experience in the area where they were designated.

The first two years of PRO's CBA government showed some of the limitations of the wide reform agenda proposed by the party. The city's strong employee unions, the bad relationship with President Fernández de Kirchner's office, the inexperience of PRO's cadres to deal with a heavy bureaucracy, and the fierce opposition by the left and center-left parties in the city council permitted only slow progress. Outraged, Macri complained in the media about "populism's obstruction machine" and began a strong confrontation with FPV. As part of this game plan of full opposition to national government, PRO allied again with de Narváez. The 2009 elections showed the mixed results of this strategy. On the one hand, de Narváez won a tight contest in Buenos Aires province, even though former president Néstor Kirchner was the main FPV nominee. On the other hand, PRO's CBA candidate for the national congress, the former vice mayor Michetti, won by a lower-than-expected margin. Partially because of this outcome, in the 2011 elections, Macri backed off and offered a nonconfrontational discourse. He was accompanied again by a woman, María Eugenia Vidal, former minister of social development, who seemed to occupy the same role played by Michetti in 2007: humanizing the leader. The bet paid off, and Macri was reelected as mayor of CBA by 65% in the second round (46% in the first round).

The 2007–11 period allowed PRO to progress in its reframing of political cleavages. To do this, as in the Peruvian case described by Carlos Meléndez in chapter 7 in this volume, PRO attempted to build new topics identified neither with the right nor with the left. During these years, PRO discourse focused not on redistributive issues but on the economic troubles caused by the national government's policies (such as the inflation allegedly originated by an overheated economy). The two main strategies to reframe the political debate were, first, to develop a public discourse on the rise of crime and insecurity and, second, to defend the idea of a new ecological public policy.

Carlos Meléndez considered (chap. 7, this volume) that a new type of rightist leadership based on law and security issues can gain preponderance in Latin American countries where a party system collapse has taken place. PRO was born in just these circumstances, and—in the middle of fierce discussions and public demonstrations on security matters—the party decided to focus on public safety policies in order to help its strategy of reframing traditional cleavages. In order to highlight its commitment to public safety, the PRO government in 2009 created a metropolitan police force. Although this proposal was an old demand of several parties, PRO justified it as a reaction to the lack of answers from the federal government.

Furthermore, PRO started two policies linked with the ecology: first, the construction of bicycle lanes and the implementation of promotional loans from the city bank for the purchase of bicycles; and second, campaigns to promote recycling of waste. Both policies seem to have achieved an identification of PRO with green values and practices. The idea of a "green city" intends to build some postmaterialist values that counteract the image of PRO as a conservative party.

Conclusion

How should Propuesta Republicana be placed in the Argentinian political space? In terms of Ostiguy's findings, what is the relationship that PRO establishes with the high and low? As Luna and Rovira Kaltwasser maintain in their introduction to this volume, the ideological classifications of the actors are relational: the actors place themselves in relation to their competitors, but they are also classified and labeled by them. In figure 13.2, we apply Ostiguy's framework to analyze the relative positioning of PRO in the Argentinian political space. PRO defines itself, in large measure, in opposition to the national government. In this sense, the resetting of Peronism accomplished by FPV, which manages to mobilize most of the Peronist factions, represents a challenge to PRO.[69]

Although in 2003 Néstor Kirchner represented, according to Ostiguy, the high left of Peronism, the abandonment of a strategy of transversality in pursuit of a rapprochement with classic Peronism (in a version linked to leftist Peronism positions) took FPV back to a place in the lower sector of politics. In this context, PRO inherited the electorate and discourse of rightist forces associated with non-Peronism, so occupying a higher area in Ostiguy's space. Because the CBA is the district with the greatest proportion in the high political sector, occupying this area seems to be enough to win elections. Because in 2007 PRO managed to appear as the main challenger to the Peronist national government inside the CBA, the main reason for the party success seems obvious. The construction of new issues—such as the environment—probably helps to go beyond left-right cleavage, but in the end it places PRO in the high sector.

Given the importance of the Peronist constituency (low hemisphere) in Argentina, the desire to become a powerful alternative at national level has led PRO to attempt to dispute a portion of the Peronist electorate. Doubtless, the existence of Peronist groups in PRO contributes to this objective: there exist some linkages with the popular electorate, as shown by the electoral results, as well as a capacity to

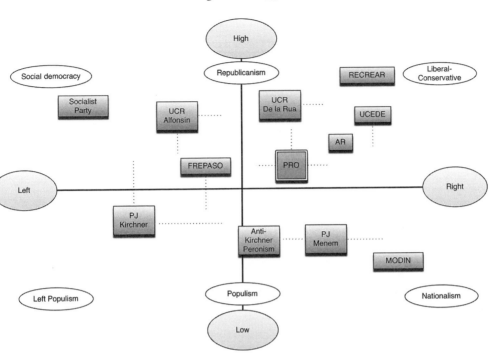

Figure 13.2. Argentina's double political spectrum. *Source:* Adapted from Ostiguy (2009)

attract the rightist Peronist constituency.[70] Nevertheless, the confrontation with the national government based on the defense of republican principles (recall that Propuesta Republicana means Republican Proposal) tends to distance the party from the low political area and bring it closer to institutionalist positions traditionally mobilized by the non-Peronist forces. To become a national majority force, PRO is trying to occupy more than one area in the political space. This is not an easy task to accomplish.

The support on issues not identifiable with the left-right cleavage seems compatible with PRO's heterogeneity. But it is not clear that these topics will obtain political support at the national level. In this regard, the more we move away from the municipal issues, the more relevant Ostiguy's high-low cleavage becomes. If PRO chooses to represent the high area of politics, its electoral chances will probably be reduced, because the party would lose the support of the low popular electorate.

PRO is playing a double game of political reframing by virtue of its aspirations to become a majority force. Macri's party appears to be aimed at going beyond left and right, but it also wants to supersede the high-low cleavage. So PRO tries to nourish itself from elements of three of the four quadrants of the Argentine political space at the same time. This attempt to go beyond both cleavages also endeavors to subordinate the different factions around a new political project. In this sense, the position of the leader is important: as a businessman trained in the neoliberal right, Mauricio Macri attracts the non-Peronist high constituency, but as former president of Boca Juniors, he conserves his ability to attract low sectors of the political spectrum.

A party that is both "beyond left and right" and "beyond Peronism and non-Peronism" appears to be in the process of establishing itself, but its future is uncertain. This uncertainty is due to the success of PRO in the CBA and lies mainly in two factors that do not seem to exist outside that district. First, the electorate in the CBA is peculiar: it is traditionally non-Peronist, identifies with the high hemisphere of politics, earns above the average national income, and has a cosmopolitan worldview and a relationship of proximity to—but not dependence on—public services and the state. This voter profile was not recently well represented by the other parties (especially not by UCR and progressivism). Second, the crisis of the main parties also opened an opportunity for the emergence of a political party that picks up "available" leaders, orphan militants, and disoriented electors. But the situation outside the CBA seems to be different, as Peronism remains strong in many districts and radicalism is socially rooted in others. In fact, the traditional parties even appear to have been reinforced after the crisis.

In 2011, President Cristina Fernández de Kirchner was reelected by 54% of Argentinians, strengthening the so-called Latin American "pink tide."[71] The same year, however, PRO obtained an astounding 64% in the runoff for the CBA's mayor's office. Also in 2011, PRO won the mayor's office of Vicente López (an important suburban area next to Buenos Aires) and came in a close second place in the gubernatorial elections in Santa Fe (the second most important province in Argentina) and Salta (a northern, traditional province).[72] Macri's strategy of not presenting his presidential candidacy that year, but rather keeping the government of the federal district and advancing the gradual national expansion of PRO, seems to have produced unequal results. While the first element was successful, the PRO nationalization continues to be unfinished business. Since then, the party and its leader have been actively visiting the provinces to establish new alliances and recruits. So far, however, only the traditional provincial conservative parties, some second-rank celebrities, and a few radical mayors have been recruited. The walk from the CBA's mayor's office to the Casa Rosada appears to be much longer for Macri than for the former president de la Rúa.

NOTES

1. Sandra McGee Deutsch and Ronald H. Dolkart, "Introduction," in *The Argentine Right: Its History and Intellectual Origins, 1910 to the Present*, ed. Sandra McGee Deutsch and Ronald H. Dolkart (Wilmington, DE: SR Books, 1993), i–xix.

2. Sandra McGee Deutsch, *Las derechas: La extrema derecha en la Argentina, Chile y Brasil 1890–1939*, transl. Noemí M. Girbal-Blacha and Julio C. Cortés (Bernal: UNQUI, 2005), 23–24.

3. Atilio A. Boron, "Ruling without a Party: Argentine Dominant Classes in the Twentieth Century," in *Conservative Parties, the Right, and Democracy in Latin America*, ed. Kevin J. Middlebrook (Baltimore: Johns Hopkins University Press, 2000), 140.

4. Hilda Sabato, *The Many and the Few: Political Participation in Republican Buenos Aires* (Stanford, CA: Stanford University Press, 2001).

5. Ezequiel Gallo and Roberto Cortés Conde, *La república conservadora* (Buenos Aires: Hyspamérica, 1986).

6. Natalio R. Botana, *El orden conservador: La política argentina entre 1880 y 1916* (Buenos Aires: Sudamericana, 1985).

7. David Rock, *El radicalismo argentino,* transl. L. Wolfson (Buenos Aires: Amorrortu, 1977).

8. Ana María Mustapic, "Conflictos institucionales durante el primer gobierno radical: 1916–1922," *Desarrollo Económico* 24, no. 93 (1984): 85–108.

9. The new Partido Demócrata Progresista (Progressive Democratic Party) was too liberal in the eyes of traditional elites, but the more conservative PAN was unable to win elections under conditions of universal suffrage. See Carlos Malamud, "El Partido Demócrata Progresista: Un intento fallido de construir un partido nacional liberal-conservador," *Desarrollo Económico* 35, no. 138 (1995): 715–42.

10. Robert A. Potash, *El ejército y la política en la Argentina*, transl. E. Tejedor (Buenos Aires: Hyspamérica, 1986).

11. Ricardo Sidicaro, *Los Tres Peronismos: Estado y poder económico 1946–55/1973–76/1989–99* (Buenos Aires: Siglo XXI, 2002). See also Loris Zanatta, *Perón y el mito de la nación católica: Iglesia y Ejército en los orígenes del Peronismo (1943–1946)* (Buenos Aires: Editorial Sudamericana, 1999).

12. Gerardo Aboy Carlés, *Las dos fronteras de la democracia argentina: La reformulación de las identidades políticas de Alfonsín a Menem* (Rosario: Ediciones Homo Sapiens, 2001).

13. Pierre Ostiguy, "The High and the Low in Politics: A Two-Dimensional Political Space for Comparative Analysis and Electoral Studies" (working paper 360, Helen Kellogg Institute for International Studies, Notre Dame, IN, July 2009a); "Argentina's Double Political Spectrum: Party System, Political Identities, and Strategies, 1994–97" (working paper 361, Helen Kellogg Institute for International Studies, Notre Dame, IN, October 2009b).

14. Ostiguy (2009a, 5).

15. Ostiguy (2009b, 3). The authors thank Pierre Ostiguy for his help and suggestions regarding figure 13.2.

16. Between 1955 and 1983, Argentina experienced four military coups (in 1955, 1962, 1966, and 1976) and only seven years of (not fully democratic) civil government.

17. Edward Gibson, *Class and Conservative Parties: Argentina in Comparative Perspective* (Baltimore: Johns Hopkins University Press, 1996), 66–68.

18. Such as the Partido Autonomista Liberal (Liberal-Autonomist Party) from Corrientes.

19. Such as the Partido Cívico Independiente (Independent Civic Party).

20. Gibson (1996); Raúl J. Romero, *Fuerzas Armadas: La alternativa de la derecha para el acceso al Poder, 1930–1976* (Buenos Aires: Centro de Estudios Unión para la Nueva Mayoría,

1998); Leonardo Senkman, "The Right and the Civilian Regimes, 1955–1976," in Deutsch and Dolkart (1993), 119–47.

21. Sergio D. Morresi, "Las raíces del neoliberalismo argentino (1930–1985)," in *Crisis y metamorfosis del Estado Argentino*, ed. Miguel A. Rossi and Andrea López (Buenos Aires: Luxemburg, 2011), 47–69.

22. Senkman (1993).

23. Vicente Palermo and Marcos Novaro, *La dictadura militar, 1976–1983: Del golpe de estado a la restauración democrática* (Buenos Aires: Paidós, 2003).

24. For a deeper analysis of UCEDE, see Gibson (1996, chaps. 5–6).

25. César L. Mansilla, *Las fuerzas de centro* (Buenos Aires: Centro Editor de América Latina, 1983).

26. Rosendo Fraga and Gabriela Malacrida, *El centro-derecha: De Alfonsín a Menem* (Buenos Aires: Centro de Estudios Unión para la Nueva Mayoría, 1990).

27. José Nun, Juan Carlos Portantiero, and Carlos Altamirano, *Ensayos sobre la transición democrática en la Argentina* (Buenos Aires: Puntosur Editores, 1987).

28. Gibson (1996).

29. Gibson (1996, 151–58). See also Fabián Doman and Martín Olivera, *Los Alsogaray: Secretos de una dinastía y su corte* (Buenos Aires: Clarín-Aguilar, 1989).

30. Alfredo Gutiérrez, *El derrumbe de la UCeDe: De Videla a Menem, la mutación liberal* (Buenos Aires: Ediciones Letra Buena, 1992).

31. Fraga and Malacrida (1990).

32. Domingo F. Cavallo, *El Peso de la verdad: Un impulso a la transparencia en la Argentina de los 90* (Buenos Aires: Planeta, 1997).

33. Sergio Daniel Morresi and Gabriel Vommaro, "El PRO en el contexto del espacio de centro-derecha argentino" (paper presented at the 10th Congreso de la Sociedad Argentina de Análisis Político, SAAP-Universidad Católica de Córdoba, Córdoba, July 27, 2011).

34. See, e.g., Inés Pousadela, *Que se vayan todos* (Buenos Aires: Capital Intelectual, 2006).

35. In order to simplify our description, we have decided to refer to Macri's party as PRO, its current name, even when at the beginning it was called CPC.

36. Gabriela Cerruti, *El pibe: Negocios, intrigas y secretos de Mauricio Macri, el hombre que quiere ser presidente* (Buenos Aires: Planeta, 2010).

37. Adriana Gallo, "El discurso político de la centroderecha argentina o la anulación de la alteridad izquierda-derecha," *Revista SAAP* 3, no. 2 (2008): 287–312.

38. Herbert P. Kitschelt, "Political Opportunity Structures and Political Protest: Anti-Nuclear Movements in Four Democracies," *British Journal of Political Science* 16, no. 1 (1986): 57–85.

39. For details about our study, see note 63 below.

40. Later, the roads of Macri and De Narváez reunited when transiently allied under the label "Unión PRO."

41. Nicolás Cherny and Gabriel Vommaro, "Territorios, Liderazgos, Partidos: La política Argentina a nivel subnacional," in *¿Qué cambió en la Política Argentina?*, ed. Isidoro Cheresky and Jean Michel Blanquer (Rosario: Homo Sapiens, 2004), 147–78. See Daniel Elazar, *Exploring Federalism* (Tuscaloosa: University of Alabama Press, 1987).

42. Tulia G. Falleti, *Decentralization and Subnational Politics in Latin America* (New York: Cambridge University Press, 2010).

43. Ibid., 76.

44. Edward Gibson and Julieta Suarez-Cao, "Federalized Party Systems and Subnational Party Competition: Theory and an Empirical Application to Argentina," *Comparative Politics* 43, no. 1 (2010): 21–40; Marcelo Leiras, *Todos los caballos del rey: La integración de los partidos políticos y el gobierno democrático de la Argentina, 1995–2003* (Buenos Aires: Prometeo, 2007).

45. Allyson L. Benton, "Presidentes Fuertes, Provincias Poderosas: La economía política de la construcción de partidos en el sistema federal argentino," *Política y Gobierno* 10, no. 1 (2003): 103–20; Mark P. Jones, Sebastián Saiegh, Pablo T. Spiller, and Mariano Tommasi, "Amateur Legislators—Professional Politicians: The Consequences of Party-Centered Electoral Rules in a Federal System," *American Journal of Political Science* 46, no. 3 (2002): 656–69.

46. Cherny and Vommaro (2004).

47. Marcelo Escolar and Pedro Pirez, "¿La cabeza de Goliat? Región metropolitana y organización federal en Argentina" (paper presented at the meeting of the Latin American Studies Association, Washington, DC, 2001); Perdo Pírez, "La Formación de la ciudad metropolitana de Buenos Aires: De la riqueza al deterioro," *EURE: Revista Latinoamericana de Estudios Urbano Regionales* 20, no. 61 (1994): 27–39.

48. Escolar and Pirez (2001); Miguel De Luca, Mark P. Jones, and María Inés Tula, "Buenos Aires: The Evolution of Local Governance," in *Capital City Politics in Latin America: Democratization and Empowerment*, ed. David J. Myers and Henry A. Dietz (Boulder, CO: Lynne Rienner, 2002), 65–94.

49. Juan Carlos Torre, "Los huérfanos de la política de partidos: Sobre los alcances y la naturaleza de la crisis de representación partidaria," *Desarrollo Económico* 42, no. 168 (2003): 647–65. See also Leiras (2007).

50. Steven Levitsky, *Transforming Labor-Based Parties in Latin America: Argentine Peronism in Comparative Perspective* (Cambridge: Cambridge University Press, 2003).

51. Juan M. Abal Medina, "The Rise and Fall of the Argentine Centre-Left: The Crisis of Frente Grande," *Party Politics* 15, no. 3 (2009): 357–75.

52. However, law number 24588 (known as the Cafiero Law) delayed the transfer of much of the national administration power to the city.

53. Steven Levitsky and Maria Victoria Murillo, "Argentina Weathers the Storm," *Journal of Democracy* 14, no. 4 (2003): 152–66; Torre (2003).

54. Levitsky (2003).

55. Tomas Bril Mascarenhas, "El colapso del sistema partidario de la ciudad de Buenos Aires: Una herencia de la crisis argentina de 2001–2002," *Desarrollo Económico* 47, no. 187 (2007): 367–400. See also Leiras (2007, 104–7).

56. Richard L. Harris, "Centralization and Decentralization in Latin America," in *Decentralization and Development*, ed. G. Shabbir Cheema and Dennis A. Rondenelli (Beverly Hills, CA: Sage), 183–202. Benjamin Goldfrank advances a similar idea for leftist parties' cases. *Deepening Local Democracy in Latin America: Participation, Decentralization, and the Left* (University Park: Pennsylvania State University Press, 2011).

57. Allan Sikk, "Newness as a Winning Formula for New Political Parties," *Party Politics* 18, no. 4 (2011): 465–86.

58. Piero Ignazi, *Extreme Right Parties in Western Europe* (Oxford: Oxford University Press, 2006), 28–29.

59. These data come from a survey (hereafter referred to as the 2011 survey) by questionnaire to PRO "leading cadres" with executive or legislative positions in the CBA. The questionnaire included closed-ended questions, half-closed-ended questions, and half-open-ended questions that covered city legislators, district representatives, and officials of the CBA (from ministers to undersecretaries) between May 1 and December 10, 2011. Of the total identified cases ($U=76$), fifty-two were surveyed ($N=52$), meaning 68.4% of the universe. To avoid the overrepresentation of certain posts, the presence of at least two cases in each ministerial unit was guaranteed, and at least 60% of each of the types of posts was covered. Six ministers (out of nine), three secretaries (out of five), twenty-two undersecretaries (out of thirty-one), four national representatives (out of seven), and seventeen legislators of the city (out of twenty-four) comprised the sample. In terms of areas of responsibility, 44.2% of the sample belongs to the political area, 28.8% to the area of social and human rights policies, 11.1% to economic and human resources areas, and 7.7% to infrastructure area, which is the same percentage as security and justice. Together with the survey, eighteen in-depth interviews were conducted in selected cases.

60. See Steven Levitsky and María Victoria Murillo, "Theorizing about Weak Institutions: Lessons from the Argentine Case," in *Argentine Democracy: The Politics of Institutional Weakness,* ed. Steven Levitsky and María Victoria Murillo (University Park: Pennsylvania State University Press, 2005), 269–90.

61. We define factions as partisan groups that dispute the control of the party and the selection of the candidatures. See Scott Morgenstern, "Organized factions and Disorganized Parties: Electoral Incentives in Uruguay," *Party Politics* 7, no. 2 (2001): 235–56; Giovanni Sartori, *Parties and Party Systems: A Framework for Analysis* (New York: Cambridge University Press, 1976).

62. Without institutional support of prior legally constituted parties, PRO would have not been able to submit all its nominations at that moment.

63. We use the term *radical* in Spanish to denote UCR's affiliation, not an extremist ideology.

64. In one of the in-depth interviews we conducted, a congressman said, "this is not the UCEDE. We are not here because of ideology but to offer an alternative to power."

65. Gallo (2008).

66. Sebastián Mauro, "La campaña electoral por la Jefatura de Gobierno de Buenos Aires: Estrategias políticas e inteligibilidad de la agenda," *Revista Argentina de Sociología,* no. 4 (2005): 78–98.

67. Martín Alessandro, "Clivajes sociales, estrategias de los actores y sistema de partidos: La competencia política en la Ciudad de Buenos Aires (1995–2005)," *Revista SAAP* 3, no. 4 (2009): 581–614.

68. Regarding relations between Argentina's rightist parties and anti-populism, see Ostiguy (2009b). Also, one of our interviewees from the "right faction" said that, at first, the CPC founders even considered competing from inside Peronism.

69. In the presidential elections of 2003, in the federal district, FPV would have attracted votes as much by virtue of its identification with the Peronism as with the center-left. These identifications settled an alternative for the voters of both sectors of the high-low axis and left-right axis. See Alessandro (2009).

70. In the legislative elections of 2005 in the CBA, PRO was the main recipient (but with a number outside the parameters) of the high right-of-center vote (UCEDE in 1995). As

we expect because of the "popular" style of Macri's candidacy, however, it also takes a significant proportion from the PJ vote of 1995, a territory forbidden for other rightist candidates, such as Lopez Murphy. See Alessandro (2009, 602–3). Thus we do not consider, as Alessandro (2009) does, that PRO structures its candidacies according to the left-right axis. The fact is (and it is even more true in 2005) that when PRO had still not finished incorporating postmaterialist issues, like the emphasis on management and the ecology, the party gained the traditional votes of the right and of the high side of the political space (the non-Peronist right). But this does not mean that it was a strategy looked for by the actors. On the contrary, we maintain that PRO tried (and still tries) to extend that "natural" niche of voters.

71. Originally raised by the media, the expression "pink tide" was quickly adopted by the academic community to refer to the leftward shift in several Latin American countries, including Argentina.

72. In January 2013, PRO leader Mauricio Macri announced that he would present his candidacy for the presidency of Argentina in 2015.

Right (and Left) Politics in Contemporary Latin America

JUAN PABLO LUNA AND CRISTÓBAL ROVIRA KALTWASSER

Against the backdrop of a region that in recent years has "turned left," this volume analyzes rightist politics in contemporary Latin America.[1] As Kenneth M. Roberts argues in chapter 1, the political right is on the defensive in much of the region owing to a particular historical juncture that is marked by three factors: the end of the Cold War, the institutionalization of democratic politics, and the birth of a postneoliberal adjustment era. Although this is not the first time that the right has experienced a difficult context in Latin America (e.g., in the 1960s), new constraints have emerged for both electoral and nonelectoral rightist action.

On the one hand, regarding electoral competition, the "economic model" around which rightist programmatic platform was crafted during the 1980s and 1990s has been put on the defensive. Instead of celebrating neoliberal ideas, the Latin American electorate seems to be interested in supporting a stronger state, particularly when it comes to managing natural resources and advancing social policies. Moreover, the Catholic Church, one traditional "programmatic" ally for the promotion of socially conservative values, has also weakened because of secularization and the advance of evangelical groups that seek political influence in a more decentralized and pragmatic way.[2] On the other hand, the emerging context also poses significant challenges to rightist nonprogrammatic electoral tactics. The decline of traditional patron-client relations (especially in the countryside) has weakened the electoral performance of rightist parties in numerous countries. A paradigmatic example of this challenging situation for the right can be found in Alfred P. Montero's contribution on the decline of the conservatives in Brazil (chap. 12). In addition, the most prominent mechanism for conservative interests to seek power and interest representation in the region (i.e., "running to the military barracks") is no longer conceived of (with only minor exceptions) as a legitimate alternative.[3]

Both electoral and nonelectoral traditional vehicles for rightist interests to seek political influence in Latin America became less effective and less legitimate in recent years, which in part also helps explain the left turn. And at least partially, the perceived "collapse" of the right might justify the lack of academic attention to rightist politics in the region. Yet the central message we articulate in this book is that to assume that the right has become irrelevant in the region is simply naive. In our view, the recent and growing academic interest on the left might substantiate the false impression that conservative forces have almost no influence in contemporary Latin America.

Even in countries where rightwing parties are almost nonexistent and left-of-center governments are in power, the right has the capacity to shape the political agenda and policy outcomes. As argued in our introduction to this volume, the political economy of inequality, social policy, and tax reform constitute a perspective through which one could assess the relative influence of rightist interest in critical policy arenas. To better understand this perspective, one must consider that such influence can be structured on the basis of different types of "vehicles," depending on the strategic situation that rightist groups confront in each country of the region.

We return to our original typology of three main vehicles for rightist political action in Latin America on the basis of the different contributions to this volume. We then seek to identify the factors that explain the use of those different vehicles across time and space. Finally, we close by deriving the broader implications of our analysis and outlining a research agenda on rightist politics in Latin America.

Reassessing the Three Vehicles for Rightist Political Action

In our introduction to this volume we identified three vehicles through which rightwing forces can seek power and policy influence: nonelectoral mechanisms, nonpartisan electoral strategies, and party building in order to pursue elective office. In this section we draw on the contributions to this volume to provide a comparative analysis on the relative prevalence and specific characteristics of each vehicle in post-1990s Latin America. We begin by differentiating between nonelectoral and electoral strategies, and then differentiating between nonpartisan electoral strategies from party building.

The Nonelectoral Right

Rightist forces do have several options when it comes to acquiring political influence through nonelectoral strategies. Historically, one of the favored alternatives has been the intervention of the armed forces.[4] But today's hemispheric and global circumstances severely constrain this option, particularly because of the institutionalization of democratic politics across the region. In light of this welcome development, it is not surprising that the right has turned to alternative nonelectoral strategies to promote its ideas and defend its interests.

According to Kent Eaton's analysis in chapter 3, rightist interests in the region have recently used three approaches. The first approach is targeted at state institutions and involves seeking political influence through technocrats and epistemic communities with access to the policy-making process. The second approach is more broadly targeted at civil society and entails efforts at shaping public opinion and processes of social preference formation through control of the media and the funding of research centers and foundations. Finally, a third approach entails engaging in processes of identity formation (e.g., anchored around territorial, cultural, or functional divides). The first type of approach might be the more universal of the three, in part owing to the operation of transnational epistemic communities that "push" state agents (either through agenda setting or by conditioning funding) to enact a given set of policy reforms. The reliance on the second and third types of nonelectoral vehicle seems to vary more widely across time and space.

In settings in which the electoral right is weak, and rightwing forces are not well organized (e.g., contemporary Argentina and Venezuela), the most feasible option is to engage in strategies targeted at civil society (e.g., media campaigns, funding of think tanks and foundations). By contrast, where there is no viable electoral right, but rightwing forces are able to organize around a stronger social coalition, they engage in nonelectoral collective action. As argued by both Kent Eaton and James D. Bowen in chapters 3 and 4, rightist elites could either engage in corporatist strategies (e.g., Ecuador) or exploit regional cleavages to foster social mobilization against the left (e.g., Bolivia). According to Bowen, the economic dependence of the Ecuadorian state on business elites has facilitated elites' capacity to cooperate with and extract concessions from the leftist government led by Rafael Correa. Instead, in Bolivia, where decentralizing and market reforms provided the national elite a great deal of autonomy from the central government, oppositional and autonomic movements have emerged in the so-called *medialuna* (Santa Cruz, the richest region of the country). Not by coincidence, this movement advances an agenda against the taxation policies implemented by the leftist government headed by Evo Morales.[5]

In chapter 5, James Loxton develops a novel argument regarding the nonelectoral and authoritarian roots of rightwing parties that turned out to be electorally successful after democratization. Loxton's argument shows how nonelectoral strategies can eventually pay off in terms of developing electoral (party-building) strategies. His contribution reveals that in El Salvador and Chile, the incumbent authoritarian government and its base of support had the ability to form new and successful political parties, drawing on resources inherited from the authoritarian regime (e.g., organizational infrastructure, a patron-client network, etc.). This argument resonates well with those analyzing the electoral success in Europe of new rightwing parties (e.g., the populist radical right in Western Europe) and leftwing parties (e.g., postcommunist forces in Eastern Europe), who found these parties to be connected to the availability of preexisting resources useful for party building.[6] In sum, this approach suggests that nonelectoral strategies could eventually lead to efforts at party building. The Bolivian case, in which the Santa Cruz movement has led to the emergence of new parties (the most prominent of which is Los Verdes), illustrates this possibility in contemporary Latin America.[7] In such a case, a process of territorial identity formation can eventually lay the foundations for the more recent development of an electoral vehicle with a partisan nature.

The Nonpartisan Electoral Right

Within electoral vehicles for rightist political action, we distinguish between partisan and nonpartisan subtypes. Whereas the former entails persistent efforts over time to develop a political party, the latter is usually characterized by the reliance on leadership-based appeals, which might rapidly emerge around a charismatic personality frequently with an antipolitical approach. When is the right better able to succeed electorally by substituting party building for a nonpartisan strategy?

Chapter 6, by Cristóbal Rovira Kaltwasser, provides initial hints at an answer. Rovira Kaltwasser explores the rise and fall of neoliberal populist presidents during the 1990s. According to his argument, the electoral triumphs of Collor de Mello in Brazil, Fujimori in Peru, and Menem in Argentina are related to the economic debacle experienced by those three countries by the end of the 1980s. Against this backdrop, a populist ideology and electoral appeal turned out to be effective methods for not only attacking "the elite" and mobilizing "the people," but also arguing in favor of radical solutions to the problems considered salient by the electorate. While the political opportunity structure of the 1990s favored the emergence of rightist populist actors who endorsed neoliberalism, the current political opportunity structure facilitates the rise of leftist populist leaders who seek to expand the capacity of the state to intervene in the economy. Yet under propitious circumstances (e.g., growing dissatisfaction with the established political parties and the emergence of issues in which the right has a strong policy reputation), rightist leaders can claim power electorally without engaging in party building.

Carlos Meléndez, in chapter 7, develops two important and interrelated arguments regarding nonpartisan vehicles. On the one hand, he argues that nonpartisan political forces have recently prospered in the region by downplaying the role of distributive issues and by emphasizing the salience of crime and insecurity. The strong electoral showing of Keiko Fujimori in the 2011 Peruvian presidential elections relates to her ability to center the campaign on issues of law and order while downplaying economic proposals. Meléndez's argument regarding Keiko Fujimori is backed by the comparative evidence presented in Nina Wiesehomeier and David Doyle's essay (chap. 2), in which they found that Latin American rightwing voters are more likely to worry about issues such as crime and insecurity. On this basis, Meléndez (as well as Wills-Otero for the case of Colombia; see chap. 8) claims that this type of rightist leadership can also gain preponderance in other Latin American countries where a collapse of the party system has taken place, and the issue of crime and security is electorally salient. On the other hand, in a parallel argument to that of Loxton, Meléndez claims that Fujimorismo has evolved into a proto–political party, characterizing it as Peru's most institutionalized electoral vehicle. He likewise claims that the Fujimorista identity crafted under Alberto Fujimori's tenure in office has provided a solid foundation from which to relaunch its electoral movement. In sum, this argument suggests the possibility that nonpartisan vehicles could initially evolve into partisan ones.

In chapter 8, Laura Wills-Otero explores a second case in which Álvaro Uribe in Colombia successfully crafted a personalistic electoral vehicle, also on the basis of rallying support through a programmatic platform centered on anti-insurgency and anticrime measures. Uribe's rise to power, as well as the high approval ratings he obtained during his two-term tenure, was associated with the pursuit of an antipartisan discourse. The Colombian case is of particular interest because of the historic strength of the partisan right in that country.[8] Yet in the wake of the "representation crisis" that took place in the Andean region during the 1990s, and that made traditional parties increasingly illegitimate in the eyes of citizens, Uribe broke with the Liberal Party to create a new and personalistic electoral vehicle.[9] This new approach allowed Uribe to present himself as a political outsider, and to bank on that condition in order to advertise his capacity to solve the country's most pressing problems. Although functionally equivalent to the career paths of leftist outsiders that rose to power in other Andean regions, according to Wills-Otero, specific institutional variables and the sociopolitical context in which Uribe's candidacy emerged (e.g., the high salience of the security agenda vis-à-vis that of distributive issues) explain why in Colombia the crisis of democratic representation did not lead to a left turn, but rather to the continuity of rightist strength (though now in a nonpartisan fashion).

The Partisan Right

The second electoral vehicle for rightist political action entails the pursuit of party building. Five chapters of this volume analyze and compare rightist party-building efforts in the region, selecting those cases in which a partisan right has developed at least relatively successful partisan vehicles. The first lesson we draw from a comparative analysis of those cases is that, whereas party building takes sustained overtime effort and expense, it can also end in somewhat rapid demise. Both the cases of the Brazilian and Colombian traditional right substantiate that latter claim. If party building is a relatively protracted process, and the construction of viable electoral parties takes sustained effort over a relatively long period of time, each organization's historical trajectory in a party system is important to analyze in addition to more recent developments. But not every past period counts equally. The contributions in this volume clearly suggest that the authoritarian period is a critical moment to study in order to explain postauthoritarian rightist success in Latin America.

While Loxton's essay (chap. 5) develops this theoretical argument in detail, chapters 10 and 11, by Peter M. Siavelis on Chile and Riitta-Ilona Koivumaeki on El Salvador, respectively, provide in-depth case studies that lend empirical support to such an argument. Both the Nationalist Republican Alliance (Alianza Republicana Nacionalista, or ARENA) and the Independent Democratic Union (Unión Demócrata Independiente, or UDI) owe a great part of their success to the inheritance of valuable resources from the previous authoritarian government. These parties have been strong defenders of the previous regime and only recently have made a more clear commitment to democratic politics—although they maintain a narrow understanding of democracy. At the same time, the formation and consolidation of these parties are related to the confrontation with strong leftist projects (i.e., the Frente Farabundo Martí para la Liberación Nacional in El Salvador and the Unidad Popular government in Chile) that, by significantly threatening rightist interests, catalyzed the emergence of a strong rightist identity and a social constituency that these parties could eventually mobilize electorally after democratization.[10]

As chapter 9, by Steven T. Wuhs, on the Mexican National Action Party (Partido Acción Nacional, or PAN) indicates, the cleavage emerging around the confrontation between pro-authoritarian and pro-democratic forces can enable the electoral success of a rightwing party. To better understand this mechanism, PAN should be considered both an old and a new rightist political party. On the one hand, PAN had a long history of promoting socially conservative values along with a pro-business economic position, in which the state should restrain from distorting market relations or social inequality. On the other hand, during Mexico's protracted transition to democracy, PAN reinvented itself, transitioning between a niche party that represented a relatively small elite and a more moderate party that focused its platform on the enactment of democratic reforms. Not by coincidence, PAN won the presidential elections in 2000 and 2006 by drawing on a moderate political discourse (downplaying the role of more radical conservative values) and the primacy of its pro-democratic stance.

Although party building takes time, party demise can be rapid and quite unexpected. Three chapters on the partisan right illuminate process of conservative party decline. Siavelis's contribution on Chile (chap. 10) portrays the relative decay of Renovación Nacional, the heir of the traditional Partido Nacional of the pre-1973 period. Although the party has not permanently declined (President Piñera was elected in 2009 as a Renovación Nacional leader), it has progressively lost ground to UDI. But examples of more drastic declines can be seen in the case of traditional rightist parties in Brazil and Colombia. Montero (chap. 12) and Wills-Otero (chap. 8) analyze why traditional rightwing parties have experienced electoral decay. Whereas, according to Montero, in the case of Brazil, the expansion of targeted social policies promoted by the left has undermined the electoral supremacy of the right at the subnational level in poor and rural areas, in the case of Colombia, according to Wills-Otero, the "crisis of representation" has created an antisystemic mood that proved increasingly difficult to deal with for both traditional parties. Decentralization, as well as the constitutional reform of 1991, also contributed to the traditional party crisis in Colombia.

In addition, chapter 13, by Sergio Morresi and Gabriel Vommaro, on the Propuesta Republicana party in Argentina, reveals that rightwing parties can emerge at the subnational level in contemporary Latin America. While having an electoral stronghold at the subnational level is certainly an important asset for rightist parties, conquering power at the national level seems to be a daunting task. This is particularly true in a country like Argentina, where the Peronist party is dominant and has been able to adopt various economic policies over time. PRO has therefore tried to confront Peronism by recruiting some of its members and developing an alliance with different political factions. But, as Morresi and Vommaro argue, PRO also has a nonpartisan nature, as it is controlled by a successful businessman—Mauricio Macri—who appears to be a strong competitor for the 2015 presidential elections.

The comparative analysis of different case studies suggests that while history matters for successful party building, relatively new rightist parties (usually emerging within recent authoritarian regimes) have proven more able to adapt and compete electorally than traditional conservative parties. Within the latter group, only those that could adapt by advancing a new programmatic platform could still prosper in post-1990s Latin America. At the same time, the rise of a new rightwing party at the subnational level seems to be another way of competing against the left. Yet electoral success at the local level is not easily translated into the formation of a strong rightwing party at the national level.

Some Comparative Notes

There are some additional comparisons to make. First, the three vehicles for rightist action we have identified in this book are and could also be used by leftist forces. In this guise, the turn to the left in Latin America is related only in some places to its capacity to build strong political parties (e.g., Brazil and Uruguay). Nonelectoral and nonpartisan strategies have also been crucial for both the breakthrough and electoral persistence of left-of-center governments in several countries of the region. By way of illustration, while transnational advocacy networks have certainly played an important role in terms of promoting and supporting a leftist agenda in countries like Bolivia and Ecuador, personalitistic leadership strategies are key in the cases of Hugo Chávez in Venezuela, Cristina Fernández de Kirchner in Argentina, and Rafael Correa in Ecuador. As in the case of the right, leftist forces seem to favor some of these vehicles over the alternatives, on the basis of relevant contextual conditions.

Second, although we expect a given vehicle to predominate over others in each case and time period, the use of one vehicle at a given time could eventually facilitate the emergence of new ones in a subsequent period. The case of Bolivia, for instance, is one in which social movements have been transformed into partisan electoral forces, both by the left (Movimiento al Socialismo) and the right (Los Verdes). In Peru, Fujimorismo might be undergoing a transition from a personalistic electoral vehicle to a partisan one. As the research on the rise of ethnic politics in contemporary Latin America suggests, under certain circumstances, established social movement organizations create partisan vehicles to defend their ideas and interests.[11] Nothing precludes this transition from a movement to a party from being employed by the right in some countries of the region.

Third, previous research on the right in Latin America has stressed the importance of path-dependent developments, which means that the institutionalization of conservative forces is related to past political conflicts and settlements, which feed back into contemporary politics. For instance, Kevin Middlebrook has argued that, despite considerable variations among national experiences, there are good reasons to think "there is a significant association between conservative political forces' prior strength or weakness and conservative parties' electoral performance following the instauration or restoration of democratic politics in Latin America in the 1980s and 1990s."[12] Whereas we continue to observe relatively stronger conservative forces in traditional rightist strongholds in Latin America (e.g., Chile, Colombia, Mexico), our findings also suggest an important amendment to the conventional path-dependent explanation. In general, even if developing in countries where the right has been historically strong, our "success" stories are instead new parties (e.g., UDI in Chile and ARENA in El Salvador) or personalistic electoral vehicles that in practice have shown little interest in developing broader political organizations (e.g., Partido de la U in Colombia). Meanwhile, traditional parties of the right—such as the Conservative Party in Colombia, the Brazilian right, or Renovación Nacional in Chile—have electorally declined because they have not been able to adapt to a new historical scenario, which is marked not only by the concentration of the electorate in urban areas and the increasing secularization of society, but also the institutionalization of free and fair elections as the only legitimate method to win office. The consolidation of electoral competition across the region, as well as significant sociostructural changes observed in many Latin American societies, have evidently turned unsustainable the traditional strategies that rightwing parties have pursued in the past.

Fourth, according to the argument developed in this volume by both Loxton (chap. 5) and Meléndez (chap. 7), previous authoritarian regimes have helped germinate new and electorally successful parties. This was particularly the case in Chile, El Salvador, and Peru. In the absence of a highly institutionalized party system, or in context of economic or public security crises, powerful rightist leaders have emerged (e.g., Uribe in Colombia, as well as the populist actors of the 1990s analyzed by Rovira Kaltwasser in chap. 7). Whereas in the 1990s those leaderships could succeed by not giving too much information about their economic policies and implementing radical reforms in favor of the free market once in power, contemporary rightist leaders seem to have fared better when competing on noneconomic issues and avoiding the adoption of deep structural reforms associated with the neoliberal model once power.

Fifth, valence- and candidate-centered appeals around topics such as public security, efficient administration, and job creation seem to be promising alternatives. In consequence, the evidence compiled in this volume suggests that in spite of the arguably increasing constraints that rightwing forces are experiencing in contemporary Latin America, rightist actors and parties, when facing a favorable opportunity structure, can obtain a competitive edge by engaging in innovative mobilization strategies. Those strategies could entail: (1) establishing an electoral platform centered on valence issues (especially, but not restricted to, public security); (2) engaging in innovative leadership development by drawing on popular discontent with political insiders or unpopular incumbents; or (3) mobilizing lower classes through nonprogrammatic appeals. Overall, these three strategies have also been advantageous to successful leftist forces in the region, and, consequently, it is again possible to identify important similarities between left and right politics in contemporary Latin America, particularly when it comes to developing successful electoral campaigns and maintaining high approval ratings in office.

To close this comparative overview, figure C.1 summarizes our classification of each case. We first distinguish between nonelectoral and electoral (partisan and nonpartisan) vehicles and then identify relevant subtypes. Within the partisan right, we further distinguish between new parties (e.g., ARENA in El Salvador, UDI in Chile) and old parties (the Brazilian and Colombian right). Further distinctions could be drawn within this category between parties that compete predominantly on the basis of programmatic appeals (e.g., PAN in Mexico) and parties that compete predominantly on the basis of nonprogrammatic appeals (ARENA in El Salvador,

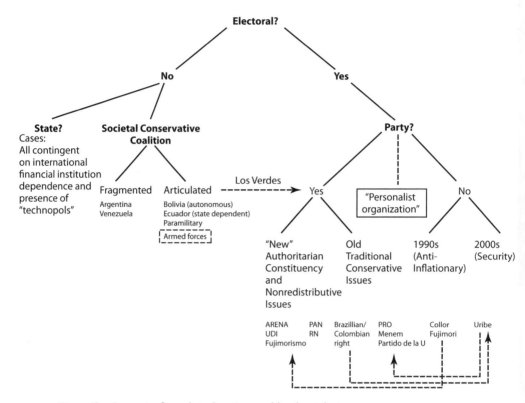

Figure C.1. Strategies for political action used by the right in contemporary
Latin America.

traditional rightist parties in Brazil). The Chilean right, as well as PRO, constitute
intermediate cases in this regard. For the sake of clarity, these distinctions are not
directly reflected in figure C.1. Further distinctions are also possible regarding the
type of programmatic platform (which issues are primed and deflected) in each party's
(programmatic) strategy. The cases of Collor in Brazil, Uribe in Colombia, and
Fujimori in Peru clearly belong to the nonpartisan electoral right. The case of
Menem in Argentina is a more ambiguous one, given the influence of the Partido
Justicialista on Menem's electoral campaign and government.

The left side of figure C.1 displays nonelectoral rightist vehicles. Among them,
we distinguish two subtypes. The first subtype entails indirect political actions, as
described in chapters 1, 3, and 4, by Roberts, Eaton, and Bowen, respectively. Those
actions range from participating in epistemic communities, engaging in party and
campaign financing, and pursuing interest group politics and lobbying. The second
subtype entails more direct forms of political action that range from the organization of paramilitary groups, the development of conservative social movements, and

the reliance on the armed forces to stage a coup d'état. While the latter has become less frequent in Latin America, the other two have recently become particularly prevalent in the Andean region. Finally, figure C.1 also identifies (with dotted lines) several possible overtime trajectories regarding shifts from one type of vehicle to others. For example, successful nonpartisan leaders can eventually engage in party-building efforts (the Partido de la U in Colombia and Fujimorismo in Peru exemplify that type of trajectory), and social movements or paramilitary groups could also give birth to nonpartisan electoral candidacies or party-building efforts.

A New Anti-Incumbent Cycle?

Latin America's enduring left turn might suggest that a rightist electoral comeback is unlikely. But political shifts do not last forever, and alternation in office is something intrinsic to democratic politics.[13] As Kenneth M. Roberts has recently argued, the "left turn" might provide a foundation for the reconfiguration of party systems around a programmatic cleavage, contributing to crystallize each of the poles of the left-right continuum around strong electoral currents.[14] But even if this does not occur in the near future, a new anti-incumbent cycle could take place in various countries of the region for at least two reasons.

First, rightist leaders and parties can benefit from the internal confrontation that leftist forces might face in office. Left-of-center governments usually need to strike a difficult compromise between programmatic moderation (usually driven by party officials and economically orthodox cadres) and more audacious policy proposals (normally demanded by specific constituencies and more radical leaders in the leftist coalition).[15] The tension between different leftist factions and groups is particularly evident in the case of moderate left governments, which have preferred to eschew mass mobilization and take a more technocratic approach to policy making.

The electoral victory of the right in the Chilean presidential elections of 2010 exemplifies that type of scenario. Piñera's victory is to a great extent related to the growing difficulties of the left-of-center alliance that governed the country between 1990 and 2010. Part of the problem that the leftist coalition faced was parties' increasing detachment from their social bases and from civil society in general.[16] Under these circumstances, the right developed an astute electoral campaign centered on the figure of Sebastián Piñera, who made salient a series of well-identified campaign issues.[17] On the one hand, he promised to maintain the social agenda of the previous governments and even promoted a liberal stance regarding moral issues. On the other hand, Piñera pledged to fight crime and foster economic growth with the aim of generating new jobs. Finally, he also promised to bring to Chile a "new governing style," which he explicitly contrasted to the leftist coalition's ("inefficient and corrupt") "old ways."

Second, if the left cannot properly address problems that are relevant for the electorate, the right has the opportunity to improve its electoral chance by criticizing leftist failures and by developing a programmatic discourse centered on a series of valence or nondistributive campaign issues. The fact that high levels of inequality and poverty characterize Latin American societies does not always translate into a majority of the electorate identifying economic redistribution as the main problem facing the country. Equally important are issues of law and order, which can lead to the support of iron fist policies that circumscribe civil rights and underpin a particular understanding of democracy. This is a relevant point that scholars dealing with the state of Latin American democracies sometimes forget, or analyze as institutional failures rather than as something intrinsic to the way in which political order is being constructed across the region.[18] Because high levels of violence affect the day-to-day lives of many Latin American citizens, it is not surprising that law and order is an extremely salient issue for the electorate.

As Nina Wiesehomeier and David Doyle argue in chapter 2, a significant fraction of Latin American voters, irrespective of their left and right political identifications, consider crime to be one of the most serious problems that their countries face today. This certainly seems to be a major challenge for current left-of-center governments, which have been neither fast nor successful in coping with citizen security issues.[19] Even so, campaigning on the fight against crime is not necessarily the key to the electoral success of the right everywhere, since growing support for human rights issues across the region might pose a daunting scenario to political actors and parties campaigning on iron fist "solutions" to insecurity.[20] Instead of taking for granted that the Latin American electorate is inclined to advance class-related demands for redistribution or public security demands for iron fist policies, scholars should try to put more attention not only on voters' preferences, but also on whether voters' preferences change over time owing to transformations occurring in the societies in which they live.

Beyond the question of whether the left will remain in power in most Latin American countries in the coming years, future governments will not have absolute liberty when it comes to managing and reforming social policies.[21] If it is true that Latin America's turn to left is the product of an exhaustion of the conservative modernization project that the region experienced in the 1980s and 1990s, and that we are witnessing a variety of answers to a second incorporation crisis, then it is difficult to imagine that forthcoming rightist governments will be able to reverse the antipoverty and equity-enhancing reforms implemented by the left.[22] In Mexico, one of the flagship conditional cash transfer programs in the region (the Oportunidades program) has been maintained, expanded, and improved under the rightist governments of PAN.

At the same time, these programs are potentially attractive to the right. Although popular, they do not involve massive redistribution from the wealthy to the poor and are relatively inexpensive in comparison with classical social policy programs such as pensions or publicly provided health insurance. Moreover, given that the reforms implemented by left-of-center governments benefit specific constituencies, they can provide interesting and unintended opportunities for marginal groups to defend their ideas and interests. These new programs can strengthen existing, or support the formation of new, "latent coalitions for egalitarianism." David Brady has coined this concept, alluding to diffuse and often accidental groups of diverse citizens who come together to support redistributive policies and who become especially visible when political actors try to implement reforms that are at odds with normative expectations about alleviating poverty and establishing social equality.[23]

Future Research Agenda

As argued in our introduction to this volume, research on the right in contemporary Latin America is scarce. That being said, we hope that the theoretical and empirical arguments introduced in this book contribute to a more balanced debate on the influence of the right as well as the comparative analysis of rightist and leftist forces in contemporary Latin America. With this aim in mind, we explore here a few avenues for further research on both the right as a particular political project and on comparative analyses of leftist and rightist politics in Latin America.

First is the identification of successful electoral strategies by both leftist and rightist forces. To what extent do these forces employ similar or different tactics for winning elections? While it is true that a host of chapters in this volume explore hypotheses on election strategies, a fundamental set of aspects remains unexplored. Benjamin Goldfrank has argued that Latin America's turn to the left started in certain countries at the subnational level, when leftist leaders and parties realized the importance of obtaining power at the local level in order to promote alternative policies while publicizing their capacity to provide more effective governance.[24]

It is important to examine whether certain rightist actors and parties are developing a similar strategy to conquer power at the local level—chapter 13 by Morresi and Vommaro reveals that this is occurring to a certain extent in Argentina, while Wuhs's analysis in chapter 9 on the rise of PAN in Mexico also contributes insights in this regard. At the same time, the employment of a nonpartisan strategy (and usually antiestablishment rhetoric) has been an effective pathway for leftwing (e.g., Correa in Ecuador) and rightwing (e.g., Uribe in Colombia) leaders to win elections. Nevertheless, the use of nonpartisan strategies for winning elections does not rule out the possibility that successful leaders invest resources in developing a partisan structure after winning office. It is worth studying under which circumstances a transition from nonpartisan to partisan approaches seems to be more likely.

A second topic alluded to in several chapters of this book, though not addressed in detail, is the policy impact of rightwing governments. In fact, many scholars are delving into the question of the performance of left-of-center governments in Latin America. Kurt Weyland, Raúl Madrid, and Wendy Hunter, for example, maintain that the "moderate left" (e.g., Lula da Silva in Brazil) has been much more successful than the "contestatory left" (e.g., Hugo Chávez in Venezuela) in terms of fostering economic and democratic development.[25] It would be interesting to compare the policy output of rightwing and leftwing governments either within the context of a single case in which alternation has been observed (e.g., Chile, El Salvador) or between countries sharing similar structural conditions but governed by parties or leaders of the left and the right at different points in time (e.g., Brazil vs. Mexico; Colombia vs. Venezuela; El Salvador vs. Nicaragua). One of the crucial questions to ask is whether the left or the right has been better able to deal with some of the most pressing problems that Latin American societies face (e.g., social inequality, public security, and economic sustainability). A final argument concerning this possible line of inquiry relates to the role of both rightist and leftist forces in the opposition, since nonpartisan and nonelectoral strategies can produce tangible effects on policy making and the quality of democratic regimes. Future research might seek to more clearly identify the mechanisms that produce such effects across cases with different political and structural configurations.

This edited volume has also addressed to some degree (and it is worth exploring in more detail) the influence of international and transnational networks on the Latin American right. Several chapters in this book reveal that the conservative modernization project advocated by the Latin American right during the 1980s and 1990s counted on the support of technocrats trained in the United States, whose academic and political networks were crucial for obtaining assistance from abroad and for legitimizing the reforms at the national level. But the resurgence of the Latin American left is also related, to a certain extent, to the influence of transnational advocacy networks. These networks have provided significant economic and ideological resources for promoting alternative policy proposals,[26] which implies that the projects defended by both leftist and rightist forces in Latin America should not be seen in isolation, but rather in the context of global debates and strategies about how to foster economic and political development.[27] Seen in this light, future studies could examine the relationship between political actors and parties and foreign agencies, international think tanks, transnational nongovernmental organizations, and global institutions.[28]

The Latin American right has historically supported conservative values and has been close to traditional religious orders. The chapters in this book demonstrate that this continues to be the case today. Yet the contributions to this volume also suggest that many rightwing forces have moderated their agenda in relation to moral issues. Accordingly, a fourth research topic that may be important to investigate is the relevance of conservative values for society in general and for rightwing leaders, parties, and voters in particular. Not only does the old battle line of secular versus religious seem to be less relevant in contemporary Latin American societies, but also the Catholic hegemony has eroded in the region. As Frances Hagopian has indicated, "Across Latin America the days of formal and informal concordats between church and state are over, divorce is legal, and social life is no longer effectively demarcated by religious denomination. Self-identified Protestants now comprise roughly one-fifth of the population, about one in ten Latin Americans identify with no religion at all, and only about 70 percent of the population is nominally Roman Catholic."[29] Does this imply that the religious cleavage has little salience in contemporary Latin America? To answer this question, it would be relevant to map the attitudes of voters with different religious backgrounds across the region and to study the role that moral issues play in the manifestos and electoral campaigns of political parties and leaders.

Finally, one of the core themes of this book is the capacity of the right to advance its political agenda, which usually implies the defense of ideas and interests that are at odds with the promotion of equity-enhancing reforms. In contrast to recent scholarship that underlines the inevitability of redistributive politics in contexts marked by high levels of socioeconomic inequality, this book reveals that the Latin American right can hinder the realization of equity-enhancing reforms either by employing nonelectoral strategies, or by using nonpartisan and partisan strategies that are effective for winning elections, and thus obtaining governmental power. The recent history of Latin America demonstrates that unequal democracies can survive despite their low institutional quality. After all, even though democracy is based on the idea of "one person, one vote," there are many barriers to political equality, and a high level of income inequality is certainly a key aspect.[30] In the words of Adam Przeworski, "When unequal individuals are treated equally, their influence over collective decisions is still unequal . . . The rules of the game treat everyone equally, but this only means that the outcome of the game depends on the resources participants bring to it."[31]

As we indicated in our introduction to this volume, rather than studying the impact of rightist (and leftist) forces on the stability of the democratic regime, much more emphasis should be placed on the ways in which the right (and the left) hinder the realization of reforms aiming at countering socioeconomic inequality. Although it is outside the scope of this conclusion to elaborate this argument in detail, we conclude by pointing out that existing research shows valuable lines of inquiry. For instance, some scholars have analyzed the mechanisms the right employs in some Latin American countries to impede a more progressive taxation system.[32] At the same time, Larry Bartels argues that electoral majorities in the United States regularly appear to vote against their own economic interests owing to the capacity of the Republican Party to obtain campaign funds from the rich and also promote a business cycle that generates economic growth the year preceding a presidential election, thus playing in favor of retrospective voting behavior.[33] In the context of Latin America, Stephen Kaplan[34] and Daniela Campello[35] have recently argued that the structural shift in the global financial architecture from cross-border bank loans to global bond issues and the hyperinflation crises suffered by many countries of the region have diminished the capacity of governments of any political color to experiment with unorthodox economic policies.

In conclusion, one of the key arguments of this book is that it is simply wrong to take for granted that the median voter in Latin America favors socioeconomic redistribution or opposes the policies of the Washington Consensus as a whole.[36] Scholars should think more thoroughly about "the social psychology of individual actors and the way this is shaped by larger political and social environments in which they are embedded."[37] As Andy Baker has argued,[38] the neoliberal reforms of the 1980s and 1990s have transformed Latin America's social fabric in the sense that the liberalization of the economy has facilitated the emergence of consumption-based interests across socioeconomic classes: regardless of income group, most citizens are enthusiastic about having low inflation and access to imported goods, but they are also inclined to be at odds with the privatization of public enterprises and strategic sectors of the economy. To what extent voters also call for more socioeconomic redistribution is not self-evident, but rather related to the capacity of social actors to politicize the existing levels of inequality and mobilize the electorate around this topic. Instead of assuming that Latin American voters demand redistribution and thus are inclined to support the left, future studies should analyze which factors favor or hinder the framing of inequality and redistribution (relative to other alternative issues) as a central cleavage for political debate and policy making.

NOTES

1. See, e.g., Maxwell A. Cameron and Eric Hershberg, eds., *Latin America's Left Turn: Politics, Policies, and Trajectories of Change* (Boulder, CO: Lynne Rienner 2010); Steven Levitsky and Kenneth Roberts, eds., *The Resurgence of the Latin American Left* (Baltimore: Johns Hopkins University Press, 2011); Francisco Panizza, *Contemporary Latin America: Development*

and Democracy beyond the Washington Consensus (London: Zed Books, 2009); Eduardo Silva, *Challenging Neoliberalism in Latin America* (New York: Cambridge University Press, 2009); Kurt Weyland, Wendy Hunter, and Raúl L. Madrid, eds., *Leftist Governments in Latin America: Successes and Shortcomings* (Cambridge: Cambridge University Press, 2010).

2. Paul Freston, *Evangelical Christianity and Democracy in Latin America* (Oxford: Oxford University Press, 2008); David Stoll, *Is Latin America Turning Protestant? The Politics of Evangelical Growth* (Berkeley: University of California Press, 1991).

3. Kevin Middlebrook, "Conclusion: Conservative Politics, the Right, and Democracy in Latin America," in *Conservative Parties, the Right, and Democracy in Latin America*, ed. Kevin Middlebrook (Baltimore: Johns Hopkins University Press, 2000), 287. While it is true that this mechanism came to the fore in the 2002 coup against Chávez in Venezuela and in the 2009 coup against Zelaya in Honduras, both cases represent the exception rather than the rule in contemporary Latin America.

4. Brian Loveman, *For la Patria: Politics and the Armed Forced in Latin America* (Wilmington, DE: Scholarly Resources, 1999).

5. Kent Eaton, "Conservative Autonomy Movements: Territorial Dimensions of Ideological Conflict in Bolivia and Ecuador," *Comparative Politics* 43, no. 3 (2011): 291–310.

6. David Art, *Inside the Radical Right: The Development of Anti-Immigrant Parties in Western Europe* (Cambridge: Cambridge University Press, 2011); Anna M. Grzymala-Busse, *Redeeming the Communist Past: The Regeneration of Communist Parties in East Central Europe* (New York: Cambridge University Press, 2002).

7. Los Verdes is a new party that emerged from the mobilization of the Cruceño identity (the color green is a symbol of Santa Cruz) against La Paz and the national government headed by Morales. Their platform combines a demand for the deepening of regional autonomy, as well as the promotion of a pro-business position.

8. Kevin Middlebrook, "Conclusion: Conservative Politics, the Right, and Democracy in Latin America," in Middlebrook (2000, 285–92).

9. For an account of the Andean representation crisis, see Scott P. Mainwaring, Ana María Bejarano, and Eduardo Pizarro, eds., *The Crisis of Democratic Representation in the Andes* (Stanford, CA: Stanford University Press 2006).

10. Kenneth Roberts, "Latin America's Conservative Party Deficit" (paper presented at the meeting of the Latin American Studies Association, San Juan, Puerto Rico, 2006).

11. See, among others, Raul L. Madrid, *The Rise of Ethnic Politics in Latin America* (New York: Cambridge University Press, 2012); Roberta Rice, *The New Politics of Protest: Indigenous Mobilization in Latin America's Neoliberal Era* (Tucson: University of Arizona Press, 2012); Donna Lee Van Cott, *From Movements to Parties in Latin America* (New York: Cambridge University Press, 2005).

12. Kevin Middlebrook, "Introduction: Conservative Parties, Elite Representation, and Democracy in Latin America," in Middlebrook (2000, 50).

13. Adam Przeworski, *Democracy and the Limits of Self-Government* (New York: Cambridge University Press, 2010), 164.

14. Kenneth Roberts, "Market Reform, Programmatic (De)Alignment, and Party System Stability in Latin America," *Comparative Political Studies* 46, no. 11 (2013): 1422–52.

15. For an internal tension between governing and maintaining grassroots linkages, see Steven Levitsky and Kenneth Roberts, "Conclusion: Democracy, Development, and the

Left," in Levitsky and Roberts (2011, 399–427). See also Hernán Gómez Bruera, *Lula, the Workers' Party and the Governability Dilemma in Brazil* (London: Routledge, 2013).

16. Sofia Donoso, "Dynamics of Change in Chile: Explaining the Emergence of the 2006 Pingüino Movement," *Journal of Latin American Studies* 45, no. 1 (2013): 1–29; Juan Pablo Luna and Rodrigo Mardones, "Chile: Are the Parties Over?," *Journal of Democracy* 21, no. 3 (2010): 107–21.

17. Cristóbal Rovira Kaltwasser, "Rechtsruck in Chile: Beginn einer neuen politischen Ära?," *GIGA Focus* (2010): 2.

18. Enrique Desmond Arias and Daniel M. Goldstein, eds., *Violent Democracies in Latin America* (Durham, NC: Duke University Press, 2010).

19. Deborah Yashar, "The Left and Citizenship Rights," in Levitsky and Roberts (2011, 184–210).

20. Alisha Holland, "Right on Crime? Conservative Party Politics and Mano Dura Policies in El Salvador," *Latin American Research Review* 48, no. 1 (2013): 44–67; Randy Sunwin Uang, "Campaigning on Public Security in Latin America: Obstacles to Success," *Latin American Politics and Society* 55, no. 2 (2013): 26–51.

21. Kenneth Roberts, "The Politics of Inequality and Redistribution in Latin America's Post-Adjustment Era" (working paper 8, United Nations University–World Institute for Development Economics Research, 2012), 16.

22. On the impact of contemporary left-of-center governments on socioeconomic inequality, see, among others, Evelyn Huber and John D. Stephens, *Democracy and the Left: Social Policy and Inequality in Latin America* (Chicago: Chicago University Press, 2012); Nora Lustig, Carola Pessino, and John Scott, "The Impact of Taxes and Social Spending on Inequality and Poverty in Argentina, Bolivia, Brazil, Mexico, Peru, and Uruguay: An Overview" (working paper 13, Commitment to Equity, Working Paper Series, Tulane University, April 2013).

23. David Brady, *Rich Democracies, Poor People: How Politics Explain Poverty* (Oxford: Oxford University Press, 2009).

24. Benjamin Goldfrank, "The Left and Participatory Democracy: Brazil, Uruguay, and Venezuela," in Levitsky and Roberts (2011, 162–83). See also Eleonora Passotti, *Political Branding in Cities: The Decline of Machine Politics in Bogotá, Naples, and Chicago* (New York: Cambridge University Press, 2010).

25. Weyland et al. (2010). See also Gustavo Flores-Macías, *After Neoliberalism? The Left and Economic Reforms in Latin America* (Oxford: Oxford University Press, 2012); Jennifer Pribble, *Welfare and Party Politics in Latin America* (New York: Cambridge University Press, 2013).

26. Kenneth Roberts, "The Mobilization of Opposition to Economic Liberalization," *Annual Review of Political Science* 11, no. 1 (2008): 340–41.

27. Ives Dezalay and Bryant G. Garth, *The Internationalization of Palace Wars: Lawyers, Economists, and the Contest to Transform Latin American States* (Chicago: Chicago University Press, 2002).

28. See, e.g., Clifford Bob, *The Global Right Wing and the Clash of World Politics* (New York, Cambridge University Press, 2012); Martin Durhman and Margaret Power, eds., *New Perspectives on the Transnational Right* (New York: Palgrave Macmillan, 2010).

29. Frances Hagopian, "Introduction: The New Landscape," in *Religious Pluralism, Democracy and the Catholic Church in Latin America*, ed. Frances Hagopian (Notre Dame, IN: Notre Dame University Press, 2009), 1–64.

30. Robert Dahl, *On Political Equality* (New Haven, CT: Yale University Press, 2006); Dietrich Rueschemeyer, "Addressing Inequality," *Journal of Democracy* 15, no. 4 (2004): 76–90.

31. Przeworksi (2010, 92).

32. See, among others, Daniela Campello, "The Politics of Redistribution in Less Developed Democracies: Evidence from Brazil, Ecuador, and Venezuela," in *The Great Gap: Inequality and the Politics of Redistribution in Latin America*, ed. Merike Blofield (University Park: Pennsylvania State University, 2011), 185–216; Tasha Fairfeld, "Business Power and Tax Reform: Taxing Income and Profits in Chile and Argentina," *Latin American Politics and Society* 52, no. 2 (2010): 37–71.

33. Larry Bartels, *Unequal Democracy: The Political Economy of the New Gilded Age* (Princeton, NJ: Princeton University Press and Russell Sage Foundation, 2008).

34. Stephan Kaplan, *Globalization and Austerity Politics in Latin America* (New York: Cambridge University Press, 2013).

35. Campello (2011).

36. Andy Baker, *The Market and the Masses in Latin America: Policy Reform and Consumption in Liberalizing Economies* (New York: Cambridge University Press, 2009).

37. Robert F. Kaufman, "The Political Effects of Inequality in Latin America: Some Inconvenient Facts," *Comparative Politics* 41, no. 3 (2009): 373.

38. Baker (2009).

JAMES D. BOWEN is an assistant professor of political science at Saint Louis University. His current research focuses on how economic and political elites navigate political instability in Latin America, particularly Ecuador, and the political economy of sustainable development.

DAVID DOYLE is a university lecturer in the Department of Politics and International Relations at the University of Oxford, and a fellow of St. Hugh's College. He is also a member of the Latin American Centre. His current research is concerned with the political economy of partisanship across Latin America. His work has appeared in such journals as *Comparative Political Studies, Political Research Quarterly, Political Science Research and Methods, Journal of Public Policy,* and *Journal of Politics in Latin America,* among others.

KENT EATON is a professor in the Department of Politics at the University of California, Santa Cruz. His recent articles on subnational politics in Latin America have appeared in *Comparative Politics, Comparative Political Studies,* the *Journal of Development Studies,* and the *Journal of Latin American Studies.*

RIITTA-ILONA KOIVUMAEKI is a PhD candidate in the Department of Government at the University of Texas at Austin. Her dissertation examines the recent oil and gas nationalizations in Bolivia and Venezuela. Her other research interests include international institutions, multinational corporations, and ideology in Latin America.

JAMES LOXTON is a PhD candidate in government at Harvard University. His research focuses on conservative party building in Latin America, as well as on new parties' inheritance of resources from defunct authoritarian regimes.

JUAN PABLO LUNA is an associate professor at the Instituto de Ciencia Política of the Pontificia Universidad Católica de Chile. His research interests include political parties, the state, and the political economy of Latin America.

CARLOS MELÉNDEZ is a PhD candidate in political science at the University of Notre Dame, where he received a Kellogg Institute fellowship. His research interests include electoral behavior, political parties, and party change in Latin America. He is coeditor with Alberto Vergara of *La Iniciación de la Política: El Perú político en perspectiva comparada* (Fondo Editorial de la Pontificia Universidad Católica del Perú, 2010).

ALFRED P. MONTERO is the Frank B. Kellogg Chair of International Relations and chair of the Political Science Department at Carleton College. He is the author of *Brazil: Reversal of Fortune* (Polity Press, 2014); *Brazilian Politics: Reforming a Democratic State in a Changing World* (Polity Press, 2006); and *Shifting States in Global Markets: Subnational Industrial Policy in Contemporary Brazil and Spain* (Pennsylvania State University Press, 2002). Montero is coeditor with David J. Samuels of *Decentralization and Democracy in Latin America* (University of Notre Dame Press, 2004).

SERGIO MORRESI is an associate professor in the Politics Department of the University of General Sarmiento and an assistant researcher at the Argentinian National Research Council. His work focuses on political theory, especially neoliberal and conservative political thinkers, and contemporary Latin American history. He is author of *La nueva derecha Argentina y la democracia sin política* (Biblioteca Nacional, 2008) and coeditor with Gabriel Vommaro of *Saber lo que se hace: Política y expertise en la Argentina contemporánea* (Universidad Nacional de General Sarmiento, 2011), and he has published various articles in academic journals and contributions to edited books.

KENNETH M. ROBERTS is a professor of government at Cornell University. His research explores the transformation of party systems and political representation in Latin America's neoliberal era. He is the coeditor with Steven Levitsky of *The Resurgence of the Latin American Left* (Johns Hopkins University Press, 2011).

CRISTÓBAL ROVIRA KALTWASSER is an associate professor at the School of Political Science at Diego Portales University in Chile. His research is focused on democracy, political parties, and populism in a comparative fashion. He is coeditor with Cas Mudde of *Populism in Europe and the Americas: Threat or Corrective for Democracy?* (Cambridge University Press, 2012), and his research has been published in the journals *Democratization, Government and Opposition,* and *Political Studies.*

PETER M. SIAVELIS is a professor of political science and the director of the Latin American and Latino Studies Program at Wake Forest University. His research interests include electoral, legislative, and presidential politics in Latin America and political recruitment and candidate selection. He is coeditor with Scott Morgenstern of *Pathways to Power: Political Recruitment and Candidate Selection in Latin America* (Pennsylvania State University Press, 2008).

GABRIEL VOMMARO is an associate professor in the Politics Department of the University of General Sarmiento and an assistant researcher at the Argentinian National Research Council. He is author of *Lo que quiere la gente: Los sondeos de opinión y el espacio de la comunicación política en Argentina (1983–1999)* (Prometeo, 2008); editor of *La carte rouge de l'Amérique latine* (Éditions du Croquant, 2008); and coeditor with Eduardo Rinesi and Gabriel Nardacchione of *Los lentes de Víctor Hugo: Transformaciones de la política y desafíos para la teoría* (Prometeo, 2007).

NINA WIESEHOMEIER is a lecturer in politics at the University of Swansea in the United Kingdom. Her research interests are comparative political institutions, political parties, and representation. She has published in the *Journal of Politics*, *Political Science and Research Methods*, and the *Journal of Peace Research*.

LAURA WILLS-OTERO holds a PhD from the University of Pittsburgh and is an assistant professor in the Department of Political Science at the Universidad de los Andes in Bogotá, Colombia. Her research focuses on political institutions, political processes, electoral systems, and political parties. She is editor of the journal *Colombia Internacional* and chair of the program Congreso Visible. Her recent research has been published in edited volumes and in the *Journal of Latin American Politics and Society*, the *Journal of Politics in Latin America*, and *Revista de Ciencia Política*.

STEVEN T. WUHS is a professor of political science at the University of Redlands. He is the author of the book *Savage Democracy: Institutional Change and Party Development in Mexico* (Pennsylvania State University Press, 2008) and articles in *Party Politics*, the *Journal of Politics*, and others. His current work focuses on the geography of party organization in Germany and Mexico, for which he was an Alexander von Humboldt Fellow in Germany from 2011 to 2014.